Developmental Guidance and Counseling:
A Practical Approach

by

Robert D. Myrick, Ph.D.

i

Dedicated to:

Kaylen Casey Myrick
and her "buddies"
Clint Geer
Lindsey Geer
Chad Easterly
Justin Myrick

Library of Congress Catalog Card No. 86-083095

ISBN 0-0932796-20-6

Printing (Last Digit)

9 8 7 6 5

Publisher—

Educational Media Corporation®
P.O. Box 21311
Minneapolis, MN 55421

Production editor—

Don L. Sorenson

Graphic design—

Earl Sorenson

Table of Contents

v

List of Figures

Preface

Almost everyone has had the experience of purchasing something that needed to be assembled at home. If you are like a lot of people, you first try to recall how the model looked in the store or catalog and say, "Hey, this shouldn't be so difficult." Then you start. After reaching a point of frustration and uncertainty of what to do next, you finally grab the "How to Assemble Manual" and look for instructions.

It seems, however, that many "how to" manuals are written in technical language that only an engineer could understand. Plodding ahead, you read the "easy-to-follow steps and procedures," studying the figures and diagrams and hoping you have all the parts and tools. The adventure continues until eventually you have a finished product.

Counseling can be a little like that. First, there are some general theories which describe how we might go about the process of helping people. However, theories, at times, seem to be only fully understood by a few professors and human engineers. After attempting to apply some counseling theories in the schools, you too may begin looking for some simple diagrams and illustrations. You may want more specific steps or procedures.

Counseling is such a complex process that it seems almost impossible to chart a course or diagram a plan of action. Putting together a developmental guidance program, and related counseling strategies, might seem similar to times when you assembled one of those "gadgets." You recognize some familiar pieces and have a general idea of what you are trying to accomplish. But, it would be easier if you had a simple and practical "how-to-manual" beside you.

This book is designed to be a counselor's manual—a resource guide which can help make your job easier. If you are already a counselor, this book will help you identify ways in which you can improve your skills and be even more effective than you already are. If you are a student or a beginning counselor, it will give you confidence and start you in a productive direction. It may help you avoid some unexpected pitfalls. Or, if you are a teacher, administrator, school psychologist, social worker, or someone in education who is interested in knowing more about school counseling and guidance, then this book will help you gain a picture of how counselors and others can work together to help students to learn more about themselves and others and to create a better learning

vii

environment. Even though this book is written from the point of view of a school counselor, it can provide a framework and reference for counselors in other settings who want to know more about the developmental approach.

The book is based on many of the professional dialogues and experiences I have had over the years. Fortunately, I have known many outstanding school counselors, teachers, and administrators who have contributed to my work. It is impossible to acknowledge all of them here, including those who have worked closely with me on research and staff development projects. In addition, there have been many people who have attended my workshops and classes, who have stimulated my thinking, clarified ideas, provided me with examples, and—most important—tested theories and concepts by putting them into practice. It has been a rewarding search and adventure for many of us.

In particular, however, I wish to acknowledge the support of my colleagues in the Department of Counselor Education, University of Florida, Gainesville, Florida, especially that of Joe Wittmer, who shares with me a belief in the Facilitative Model. John Lucas and Sue Mihalik of the Texas Education Agency, Laura Swanson of the North Carolina Department of Education, and Billie Jackson of the Florida Department of Education have kept me focused on the practical issues facing school counselors. I am also indebted to many guidance coordinators and administrators of school districts for their interest. They made it possible to test these ideas in their schools, including: Harriette Merhill (Orange County Schools, Orlando, Florida); Bill Highland (Sarasota County Schools, Sarasota, Florida); and Dr. Charles Blair (LaPorte Community School Corporation, LaPorte, Indiana). In addition, I am thankful for the efforts of several of my former students, who are now counselor educators, and their students who have confirmed many of the approaches and strategies in this book.

Don Sorenson deserves a lot of credit for his consistent encouragement and production expertise. My wife, Linda, has been a reliable source of personal and professional support. She also provided thoughtful insights and critiques, as we talked and worked together on projects related to *Developmental Guidance and Counseling: A Practical Approach.*

Chapter 1

The Emergence of Developmental Guidance and Counseling

What do you remember about the days when you went to school? You may remember when you had lots of fun and perhaps reminisce about some "glory days." But do you also recall the personal concerns and conflicts that you and your classmates experienced as part of growing up? Do any of the following sound familiar?

"I wish I had more friends."
"My grades aren't what they should be."
"My parents don't trust me."
"I'm not sure what I want to do after graduation."
"I need someone who will listen to me."
"Sometimes my friends pressure me to do things I don't want to do."
"School is so boring."
"I like somebody very special, but...."
"My parents are always nagging me."
"Nobody seems to understand me."

As you look back, you might be amused by some of your past worries and difficult situations. But, at the time, they were serious encounters and it may have seemed that your very survival hinged on them.

There are approximately 45,000,000 elementary and secondary school students in the United States. All of them have special needs and interests which influence the way they learn. And, they all have problems. While some problems and concerns are a sign of the times—unique to a new generation and a new society—there are many familiar ones which are associated with the developmental stages of life.

Some student problems, more than others, are disruptive of the learning process in the schools. In addition, the intensity of an experience or the significance of a particular problem is relative from one person to another. For example, adults may dismiss a broken relationship between a young boy and girl as only a matter of puppy-love and of no real consequence, especially compared with other problems. However, some teen-age suicides testify otherwise. Young people who are severely depressed and feeling at a loss can do irrational things. No matter the problem, growing up is serious business.

To help young people cope with the issues and problems of growing up, organized guidance and counseling programs have become an integral part of the educational process in the nation's schools. These programs are designed to enhance personal, social, vocational, and academic growth. The primary goal is to help students learn more effectively and efficiently. These programs can help make school life more satisfying and rewarding.

Surprisingly, in many respects, comprehensive developmental guidance and counseling programs have been relatively slow to make their appearance in school systems. Developmental guidance attempts to meet the needs of all students, addressing the typical concerns, questions, and choices facing young people. They learn about interpersonal skills and relationships. They learn how to take an active part in school, to set goals, to develop study skills, to make responsible decisions, and to solve problems. To be systematic and effective, a comprehensive developmental guidance and counseling program requires the understanding and cooperative efforts of counselors, teachers, administrators, parents, and students. All must know their respective roles and support one another.

This book is an attempt to advance these programs by recommending a basic working model for school counselors that is relevant to public and private schools (K-12). However, many of the concepts presented can be applied in other settings.

School Guidance and Counseling Defined

Although most people agree that students need guidance and would benefit from counseling, only a few people seem to have a clear understanding of the programs and processes that are involved. Even the terms "guidance" and "counseling" can be elusive. Let's take a closer look at these concepts.

Guidance

The term "guidance" has always presented a confusing picture because of its imprecise meaning and usage (Aubrey, 1977). It is a term in education that has been flip-flopped with the word "counseling" for more than 50 years.

Guidance has been considered a pervasive force within the school curriculum or instructional process which aims at the maximum development of individual potentialities. In this sense, guidance is a general educational philosophy or an educator's state of mind in which individual uniqueness is valued. When it permeates the school environment, good teaching is considered good guidance.

More traditionally, guidance is an "umbrella" term which encompasses a constellation of services aimed at personal and career development and school adjustment. These services are commonly delivered by professional educators, such as teachers or counselors, although other support personnel may be involved.

Most schools have guidance programs. They are outlined by a set of objectives and certain related services. There is a formal, or at least implied, curriculum. Some programs, more than others, are clearly defined and distinct. They are better organized and the roles of personnel are more explicit. Services are more systematic and accountable. Guidance, when used to describe an overall school program, is a term that implies personal assistance to students, teachers, parents, and administrators.

In addition to describing a program, guidance has been used, on occasion, to describe a helping process. Vocational guidance, for example, might be defined as a process of assisting an individual to choose, enter, and progress in an occupation. Guidance also can be described as an instructional process in which a student is given information and told how to move progressively toward a personal goal. For example, students might receive guidance in choosing or registering for courses. They might be given suggestions regarding how to apply to a university or how to interview for a job. Finally, guidance has also been used to identify structured learning activities or group lessons which guide or lead students to reach better understandings of themselves and others.

Thus, we have such terms as *guidance* program, *guidance* service, *guidance* activity, *guidance* lesson, *guidance* personnel, *guidance* counselor, and *guidance* materials. The matter becomes more confusing when people interchange the terms "guidance" and "counseling."

Counseling

Counseling has been perceived as a process in which someone who has a problem receives personal assistance, usually through a private discussion. The term is not used exclusively by school counselors. Lawyers, social workers, ministers, and teachers claim that they "counsel" people. How are their jobs, and what they do, any different from the work done by a school counselor? And, if teachers and others in a school can provide counseling, why is a certified specialist needed in the guidance office?

The term "counseling" is used by people in the counseling profession to describe a special type of helping process. There is a trust relationship in which the focus is on personal meaning of events and experiences. Rather than rely on general interpretations of information or behaviors, counseling focuses more on personal awareness, interests, attitudes, and goals. It has a philosophical and theoretical base which conceptualizes learning, human behavior, and interpersonal relationships. Counseling is considered a professional endeavor by a professionally trained and certified person.

Let us suppose that some high school students want to know more about career planning. They might meet with a counselor in the school guidance office. As a part of guidance, they could be given some information or they could be directed to places where more career resources might be found. They could talk about the characteristics of job fields or they might examine how their own goals are related to certain job areas. They could take part in group guidance activities with other students who have similar interests.

If the same students were frustrated and worried about their choices or if they were experiencing excessive anxiety which hindered their decision-making, then a more personal and intense intervention, such as counseling, might be appropriate. The students might still meet in a group; but in counseling, the discussion is likely to be more personally intense and problem-centered. The counselor might pose questions and use special procedures which encourage students to explore their feelings and values in greater depth, such as helping them to identify the major forces which influence their vocational plans.

In this case, counseling is both a job function and a helping process. It identifies the work or service of the counselor and the way in which the counselor helped the students.

When counseling and guidance are both used to refer to a helping process, there is a tendency to view counseling as more specific and more personal than guidance. However, that depends upon one's perceptions and the meaning that the experience has for the person. Intensity and personal meaning are often related to readiness and can be a product of the experiential moment, more than what is planned by counselors or teachers.

Other Helping Processes

To further complicate matters, just as the terms "guidance" and "counseling" have been used interchangeably, "counseling" and "psychotherapy" have been used synonymously. The most common distinction between counseling and psychotherapy (or therapy) is that counseling is for students or clients who are within the normal range of functioning. While the problems in counseling may be as serious and complex as those one might find in psychotherapy, counseling dwells more on current situations and related feelings and behaviors. There is not as much effort to explore hidden meanings, deep-rooted sources of conflict, or long-standing psychological problems.

Counseling usually takes place with clients in a non-medical or non-correctional setting. Psychotherapy, on the other hand, tends to happen in medical or clinical settings with dysfunctioning clients or patients who have more severe or chronic problems. Psychotherapy is typically more intense, longer in duration, and there are more attempts to gain insights through detailed explorations of the past.

In reality, counseling and psychotherapy can share many of the same interpersonal dynamics, helping skills, process variables, and behavioral goals. School counselors may provide guidance or counseling services to students who are also seeing psychotherapists in private practice. The setting, the job title of the helper, theoretical assumptions, and the approach could be different, but the desired outcomes may be the same.

Even if school counselors are trained as psychotherapists and use some sophisticated therapeutic techniques with students, the intervention is still called counseling when it happens in the schools. Behavior or personality changes resulting from counseling may go far beyond school settings, but school counselors are concerned first with helping students develop their positive differences and to be better learners.

The general public prefers that academic learning and school adjustment be the focus of a school counselor's work. Although there are young people who need therapy, most taxpayers want school counselors to assist these students when their problems are related to the school environment. Counselors are encouraged to refer deeply troubled students to community agencies, such as mental health centers or counseling psychologists in private practice. School counselors, limited by both job training and job setting, must be realistic and practical in the services that they provide.

What about the term "teaching?" Guidance, counseling, and teaching are related educational processes. They help students learn. If there is a difference, guidance and counseling concentrate more on personal interests, problems, meanings, experiences, behaviors, and goals. Because classroom teachers are charged by school boards to "teach" an academic curriculum, classroom teaching tends to be more subject-oriented and product-centered. It is often more instructional and directive than exploratory and facilitative of personal interests and goals. Classroom teaching is typically aimed at the majority of students and is more judgmental and evaluative than guidance or counseling.

However, effective counselors use teaching, coaching, directing, tutoring, training, and instructing to help students. Counselors, like teachers and other school personnel, are primarily concerned that students get the most out of school and in doing so, realize their potential as responsible and productive citizens.

Some Working Definitions

For our purposes, the term "school guidance" will refer to a generic set of personal development services offered to students. Counseling is one of those services. These services are provided through an organized guidance program with specific objectives which focus on the academic, personal, social, and career development of students. The term "guidance" will also be used as a modifier (adjective) to identify a helping process which focuses on general developmental needs, interests, concerns, and behaviors of students who are within the normal range of functioning.

The term "counseling" will be used to identify a personal relationship and interaction in which students confidentially explore their feelings, ideas, and behaviors with a professionally trained counselor. School counseling has an educational base and is limited in scope and duration. The process may have far reaching personal effects on students, but it is not intended to be a form of psychotherapy. Counseling may be provided to an individual student or to a group of students.

Although attempts have been made to sharpen the definition of guidance and counseling by differentiating them from other helping processes, the distinctions are arbitrary and sometimes difficult to defend in practice. They may not even be necessary.

The Formative Years

The history of school guidance and counseling can be traced to several trends and events which happened in the United States during the latter half of the eighteenth century. The introduction of more humane care of "mentally disturbed" patients and the application of scientific methods in studying human behavior were especially influential. By the turn of the century, there was a greater awareness of how people learned and the influence that one's environment had on the development of a person. Noted philosophers and educators, such as John Dewey, emphasized the importance of the student in the educational process.

While educators were revising their concepts about child development and how students learn best, other developments were happening in psychology which would lay the groundwork for counseling. For instance, Sigmund Freud and his colleagues, such as Alfred Adler and Karl Jung, made significant contributions to the development of modern psychology and the need to understand human behavior. When Freud gave a series of lectures at Clark University in 1923, he introduced several new dimensions to therapy and general psychology. Among these was the concept that childhood experiences are determinants of adult behavior and that personality development is shaped by authority figures in a young person's life.

About the same time, J.B. Watson was formulating many of the concepts that would lay the foundation of behaviorism and social learning theory. His studies led to a broader understanding of how human beings learn and behave.

G. Stanley Hall is given credit for encouraging the child study movement. He emphasized that each child has unique characteristics and that systematic observation was necessary to identify and meet the special needs of children. Subsequently, additional attention was directed toward dysfunctioning children and how they coped with their environments.

The Foundation Begins

While more humanistic approaches to child psychology and education were being developed, early pioneers in vocational guidance were introducing guidance programs in the schools. Frank Parsons (1909) organized the Vocational Bureau of Boston. Eli Weaver laid vocational guidance foundations in the New York public schools. Jesse B. Davis worked in the schools of Grand Rapids, Michigan and helped form the first professional guidance association (National Vocational Guidance Association) in 1913. These men were primarily concerned with matching young people to jobs and preparing them for the world of work. They have consistently been identified as the founders of school guidance (Aubrey, 1982).

Providing occupational information, vocational assessment, and job placement came to be seen as legitimate guidance functions. School guidance went beyond teaching students "readin', writin', and 'rithmetic," as schools were seen as places to encourage young people to plan for jobs and participation in society.

The testing movement of the 1920s stressed the measurement of personality traits. Test results were used in schools, industry, and the military. When the "great depression" hit the nation, even more emphasis was placed upon individual assessment and ways of making the best use of worker skills and aptitudes (Williamson, 1950). It was about this time that state guidance directors were appointed to develop and coordinate testing programs.

During World War II, as had been the case in World War I, tests were needed to screen and place draftees. The use of tests, personality inventories, and psychological counseling received a boost. As these processes became a routine part of the military, they soon found their place in high school guidance programs.

It was during the 1950s when the term "mental health" was first used. An affluent and rapidly changing society created a need for more psychological services. Crime and divorce rates were increasing, traditional values were being challenged, the population was becoming more mobile, and urbanization created more personal stress, as well as opportunities. Mental and correctional institutions were becoming overcrowded and there was a demand for more psychological services and trained professionals. Both the American Personnel and Guidance Association (APGA), now the American Association for Counseling and Development (AACD), and the American Psychological Association (APA) were formed during this decade.

The Sputnik Spark

However, it was the spectacular launching of Sputnik in 1957 by the U.S.S.R. that sparked the rapid development of school guidance and counseling services. That event stunned the nation. It dramatized the scientific and technological achievements of the Soviet Union. Congress immediately responded by passing a landmark piece of legislation—the National Defense Education Act of 1958. This bill is perhaps the single most important event in the history of the school counseling profession. First, it recognized the value of guidance and counseling, and more important, it provided funds for the preparation of school counselors. It gave credibility to the idea that a specialist in guidance and counseling was needed in the schools.

Counselor education departments in universities and colleges across the nation began to develop graduate programs to train counselors. During this time, most counselor preparation was directed toward high schools. A counselor's job was perceived primarily as identifying and encouraging talented youth to attend college, particularly those who showed interest and aptitude in math and science.

While the intent was clear and the effort a noble one, preparation of school counselors was inadequate. Nobody was sure what counselors should do. In most states, classroom teaching experience was necessary before counselor certification could be granted. This requirement restricted entry into the profession to school teachers. In addition, early university programs were limited in scope and entrance requirements were minimal. It was common for teachers to take four or five graduate courses and then be able to apply for state certification as school counselors. The course work, frequently taken during the summer, usually consisted of 1) counseling theories; 2) tests and measurements; 3) occupational information; and 4) general introduction to guidance services. Only a few graduate school programs required a supervised field or practicum experience.

Although there were many outstanding people who became school counselors, and who were eager to help young people, training and entry requirements enabled thousands of minimally qualified people to hold school counselor jobs. They did not know much about the nature of counseling, related job skills and services, nor did they have a clear idea of the role of a guidance specialist in the schools.

Without adequate preparation and well-defined guidance programs, many school counselors drifted into quasi-administrative positions. They became schedule changers, test coordinators, record keepers, and administrative assistants. Some were seen as resident substitute teachers, clerical aides, or disciplinarians. Many counselors saw the position as a step toward becoming a building principal and opted to work in an administrative role when given the opportunity.

Despite a shaky start, school counseling was emerging as a profession. The American School Counselor Association was formed in 1958 as a division of APGA (now AACD). With more leadership came a vision of what school counseling could be for students at all grade levels.

The Counselor in a Changing World

APGA appointed Dr. C. Gilbert Wrenn to chair The Commission on Guidance in the American Schools. This commission studied the role and function of school counselors, as well as their preparation, and made strong recommendations which resulted in a significant report written by Wrenn in 1962. It was entitled *The Counselor in a Changing World*. This work solidified the goals of the school counseling profession.

The report recommended that counselors should provide individual and group counseling to students, as well as consultation to parents and teachers. There was considerable emphasis upon counselors being well-informed about student developmental needs. While the traditional work of psychological appraisal and assistance in making educational-vocational plans was advocated, counselors were encouraged to take an active part in curriculum development.

It was evident that the commission envisioned the counselor as providing services to maximize student potential by emphasizing personal growth, self-determination, and self-responsibility. Even though Wrenn (1973) later said it was probably too conservative, the report provided a needed and valuable reference for counselor educators and school leaders.

The federal government continued to influence the development of school guidance and counseling during the 1960s through legislative acts and funds. For example, the 1965 extension of the NDEA Act provided the impetus for the growth and development of elementary school counseling. It provided funds for the training of elementary school counselors through special institutes and graduate stipends. Later, the Elementary and Secondary Education Act of 1965 (Titles I and III) provided more support for elementary school guidance. The federal government also continued its influence through such programs as the Manpower Development and Training Act, Job Corps, Youth Opportunity Centers, and Employment Services.

Thus, as characterized by Mitchell and Gysbers (1980), the first few years of school guidance might be viewed as a time when occupational selection and placement was emphasized (1900-1920), followed by school adjustment (1930-60), and then personal development (1960 to present).

Four Approaches to Guidance and Counseling

Four general approaches to guidance and counseling can be identified. These are: 1) Crisis; 2) Remedial; 3) Preventive; and 4) Developmental. It may sometimes appear that these four approaches overlap one another and it is certainly possible to incorporate all of them into a developmental approach. However, each approach has a salient theme which influences program direction, the type of services provided to students, and how professional personnel spend their time.

The Crisis Approach

Everyone has problems. The crisis approach to counseling and guidance is to wait and react to critical situations. When people reach a point where their welfare, or the welfare of others, is threatened or when a decisive action must be taken, a crisis intervention may be provided by a counselor.

Crisis interventions are an inevitable part of a school counselor's work. A teacher and student, for example, may exchange angry words. Suddenly, there is an awkward and uncomfortable confrontation which needs attention. Or, maybe a boy reports to school and unexpectedly bursts into tears, as thoughts of his parents' pending divorce sadden him. A crisis moment has occurred and a counselor may help. A girl may refuse to attend a class because a classmate is threatening her. A student may be caught with illegal drugs. In each of these cases, a turning point is at hand and the crisis might receive attention by a counselor.

Counselors, by nature of their training and job assignments, are likely to be involved when students lose self-control and need quick attention. Counselors sometimes act as mediators. At other times, they help negotiate or assist people to talk with one another. Frequently, counselors listen and talk calmly with people in crisis, helping them find a reasonable and responsible next step.

Sometimes a crisis can be avoided and at other times it cannot. For instance, a counselor or teacher might suspect that a student is under a lot of stress and pressure, but the moment of crisis cannot be predicted. It might appear that a student is behaving in a responsible way, given a difficult situation. Then, suddenly, there is an unpredictable change of events which results in an outburst and the counselor reacts with a crisis intervention.

Not all problems are of a crisis nature, but they may have that potential if ignored or allowed to build up unnecessarily. For example, a boy may be the butt of jokes by his classmates. As the jokes continue, the conflict might increase and a verbal exchange could erupt into a physical fight. The crisis, in this case, had a history. Other interventions may have been possible earlier. There may have been some critical moments which preceded the crisis which were less intense, but it was the fight that abruptly brought the problem to everyone's attention and called for a strong and immediate response. Unfortunately, too many people wait until a crisis is at hand before recognizing the seriousness of a situation and asking for counselor assistance.

Personal and social problems frequently spill over into the classroom. Teachers do what they can. If some annoying problems persist, then students are often sent to guidance specialists, such as school counselors, for "counseling." The expectation is that a counselor will do something to make matters better, if not for the students, at least for the teachers.

From the beginning, when counselors were first employed, they have been in the "fix-it-up business." If students were squabbling over something, a counselor was supposed to "patch things up." If students had poor attitudes about school, a counselor was to "set them straight" or "put them back on course." It was as though the counselor had some magic solution or inspiring speech which, when administered to disruptive students, would make them more cooperative.

The crisis approach to guidance and counseling is an inevitable part of every school environment, but it fails to address the real issues. It forces teachers and counselors to attend to the immediacy of an incident. The circumstances for working out solutions are usually not the best, as the persons involved are frequently too tense, emotional, and defensive. In far too many schools, the operational mode is to wait and react to crises.

It appears to be human nature to put things off. Sometimes problems are postponed until they become explosive and difficult to manage. For instance, a teacher may notice that a boy is unhappy with school and sulks when his work is criticized. But, nothing is done. The problem is ignored. Then, one day he "flies off the handle" and stomps out of class after insulting a classmate. The boy is suspended for his behavior and told to see the counselor before returning to class.

The number of students who are having conflicts in school is increasing. Yet, the sources of the conflicts generally remain the same. They are found in the personal relationships that happen at home and in school. While counselors complain that they do not have time to see all the students who need their help, there is always time to react to a crisis.

The pressure to "hurry up and fix it up" is a primary cause of burnout among counselors. One crisis seems to lead to another and the same students keep showing up for more counseling as they continue to get into trouble.

On occasion, if it forces some needed changes, a crisis can be helpful. A critical situation might produce enough personal discomfort to make a person take some positive action or try a new start. It might be the precipitating event which encourages a person to seek out a counselor or someone who can provide some assistance.

But, the crisis approach is too expensive, inefficient, and time consuming to be the only one used in a guidance program. In addition, there are not enough helpers available to attend to all the critical issues and problems that occur. Consequently, many problems that are on the verge of becoming crises are often ignored or quickly dismissed in the hope that "things will get better in time." Counselor time is premium time and it can be quickly consumed by responding to crisis after crisis.

The Remedial Approach

The remedial approach focuses on identifiable deficiencies. A remedy is suggested or applied in the hope that a student will be able to make normal progress and avoid a crisis situation.

Some students do not, for different reasons, learn various basic skills as they pass through the grade levels. They may miss important developmental experiences or tasks. These students can benefit from a learning or re-learning approach which helps them make up their academic or social deficits. Through student assessments, and then special counseling and guidance interventions, they can catch up before their lack of preparation creates problems.

Suppose that a student from a socio-economically disadvantaged family has trouble relating to students and teachers. Perhaps social courtesies were missed or interpersonal skills were unexplained. This student might participate in counselor-led group activities where interpersonal skills could be discussed and practiced. As the student makes up the social deficit, relationships with teachers and other students might improve.

The Preventive Approach

One popular approach to guidance and counseling is to think about preventing problems. For instance, instead of waiting until a girl gets pregnant, it would be better if young people knew something about birth control, so that an unwanted pregnancy could be prevented. Instead of waiting until a boy physically hits a teacher, it would be better to teach the boy some communication skills, so that differences could be discussed instead of acted out.

The preventive approach tries to anticipate problems and then stop them from happening. Think of all the things that society is trying to prevent young people from experiencing.

Sexual promiscuity
Unwanted pregnancies
Drug abuse
Excessive absenteeism
Poor study habits
Juvenile delinquency
Smoking
Over-eating
Laziness
Indifferent voting

Reckless driving
Abuse of property rights
Unemployment

And, that is not all. The list seems endless. The problem of this approach is that we must know what it is that we want to prevent. Teaching or counseling strategies are then developed for each one.

If we want to prevent children from catching polio, then we administer a polio vaccine. Or, if we want to prevent students from writing a disorganized letter, then we teach them about grammar, punctuation, and paragraphing. If we want them to keep from being disruptive in a classroom, then we teach them appropriate classroom behaviors and ways to cope with their teachers' needs and styles. The potential problem is identified and a plan to prevent it is designed.

While the term "prevention" attempts to capture the spirit of education and the goodness of helping, it is too limited. It requires drafting a list of things to prevent or to be avoided, which is likely to become long and confusing. The list can change, depending upon who is setting the priorities or drafting the list. Another problem is that it concentrates on what we do not want, instead of what we do want to happen. By nature of its perspective, it is a negative way of looking at things and it sometimes forces us to think about obedience more than achievement.

The Developmental Approach

The developmental approach is an attempt to identify certain skills and experiences that students need to have as part of their going to school and being successful. Learning behaviors and tasks are identified and clarified for students. Then, a guidance curriculum is planned which complements the academic curriculum. In addition, life skills are identified and these are emphasized as part of preparing students for adulthood.

In the developmental approach, students have an opportunity to learn more about themselves and others in advance of problem moments in their lives. They learn interpersonal skills before they have an interpersonal crisis. If a crisis situation does happen, they can draw upon their skills to work themselves out of the problem.

Students are usually more open to learning when they are not on the defensive. As students learn how to be positive and interact effectively with others through developmental guidance, they take a more active part in learning. They help create positive school environments.

Skill building in the developmental approach is related directly to developmental stages, tasks, and learning conditions. Sometimes it may appear there is less personal energy or student involvement because hypothetical situations are frequently used to explore ideas, feelings, and behaviors. It may appear to be too indirect to arouse student interest. But, skilled teachers and counselors prefer to motivate students in the developmental approach instead of relying on the excitement and fragmented energy of a crisis situation.

When the developmental approach is used, it incorporates the preventive, remedial, and crisis approaches. The developmental approach looks at teaching, coaching, tutoring, instructing, informing, and counseling as part of the helping process. It is a flexible approach that draws upon whatever is appropriate to meet student needs.

The developmental approach to guidance emphasizes the importance of the learning environment. It also recognizes that students and teachers, as well as personnel in a school building, work in concert to form the learning climate. Therefore, interpersonal relationships are an essential part of this approach and everyone in the school is considered a facilitator of personal, social, and academic growth.

The four general approaches to school guidance and the work of school counselors can probably be found to some extent in all schools. However, history suggests that one approach or another has dominated different grade levels and subsequently, determined the current status of guidance and counseling in our nation's schools.

Guidance and Counseling in a Changing World

Born out of the desire to help students with vocational information and planning, school guidance first found its place in the nation's high schools. Vocational guidance was an observable need of adolescents, one which was especially acute during the war years and the times of depression. It is still a viable concept which deserves a special place in a guidance program.

As the years passed and society changed, the needs of adolescents also changed. Young people are now confronted by a host of opportunities, decisions, and conflicts that past generations have never known. While many problems apparently remain the same from one decade to another (e.g. conflicts with teachers, parents and peers), contemporary youth are growing up in a different world, a different society, and one in which there is a need for different helpers.

A Changing Society

Within the past decade we have witnessed the appearance of digital watches, video tape recorders, electronic games, video arcades, inexpensive calculators, and personal computers. Life styles have been influenced by physical fitness centers and running gear stores. Popular songs, movies, clothes, and people have changed. But, only when we take a closer look do we see significant changes that have affected families and children.

There has been, for example, more than a 600% increase in the use of convenience foods within the past decade. Eating habits have changed. The family dinner, once a rallying point for family members, is not a nightly scene as much as it once was, as more people are eating out in restaurants or before their television sets.

Family life is changing in many ways. There is a rising number of working parents, which has meant that more children are spending their after-school hours alone and unsupervised. Although there is a concern about elementary school children, people are forgetting about the young adolescents (12-15 years of age). Many of them drift aimlessly. At a stage in their lives when they are full of energy and needing to further develop the skills learned in school, they often lack a secure place to go—somewhere besides shopping malls—to meet their friends and to interact with adults.

Approximately three out of ten high school students "shoplifted" within the last year. A study by the California Department of Education showed that three-fourths of the high school students surveyed admitted to cheating on tests. The students said that most of their classmates accept cheating as a general practice. In a similar vein, 88% of the nation's ninth graders reported lying to their parents once or more during a year.

In 1982, approximately 22% of all children under 18 years of age were living in single parent families. This amounted to an increase of more than 50% for 10- to 17-year-olds between 1970 and 1980. Of course, these same children were most likely to have a working parent who was unable to supervise them after school or in the evenings. A record 19.5 million women with children under six were working or looking for work in 1984. Thus, about 61% of the women with preschool or school-age children were in the labor force.

Lack of supervision often leads to other problems. Approximately one half of all the serious crimes in the nation are committed by young people. Juvenile crime has risen twice as fast as that of adults since 1960, and more girls are committing violent crimes.

There are more opportunities to become involved in the use of drugs and alcohol. It is estimated that 20 to 30% of eighth graders drink excessively and that heavy drinkers among older adolescents report that they took their first drink at age 12 or younger. Four out of 10 high school seniors in 1984 reported getting drunk once or more during a two week period and 28% reported participating in 40 or more alcohol-use events in a one year period. In addition, a survey of 8,000 fifth through ninth grade students showed that one out of ten fifth and sixth graders reported being drunk one or more times during a year.

Similarly, there has been increased use of illegal drugs among young people. Drug abuse has reached into every community in the United States. It is estimated that 81% of high school students have tried some form of illicit drug (marijuana, cocaine, heroin, and hallucinogens) and the use of drugs is dropping rapidly into the elementary schools.

Another sad fact of a changing society is the increasing number of teen-agers who are getting pregnant. About one million teen-age girls in the United States become pregnant each year. Of these, approximately six out of 10 result in live births, three in abortion, and one in a miscarriage. It is estimated that 40% of current 14-year-old girls will become pregnant at least once before they are 20. In addition, it is estimated that teen-age pregnancies will cost the nation six billion dollars in welfare benefits for the next two decades.

The dropout rate of high school students is also higher than what might be expected for a nation that is moving from an age of industry to one of high technology. In the next decade, 80% of the nation's jobs will require a high school education as more emphasis is given to automation and electronics.

Reknown commission reports and task forces blame teachers and schools for a lack of academic excellence. Yet, the nation invariably turns to educators and the schools for more help with society's serious social problems. While the public continues to demand that schools expect high academic performances from students, it also asks that these same students learn to be responsible citizens who can live socially productive lives.

There are no simple solutions to the dilemmas that face educators. However, schools and educators themselves must change, as well as school guidance programs.

Guidance in the High Schools

Before the 1960s most books about school guidance were directed to teachers in elementary and secondary schools (e.g. Gordon, 1956; Arbuckle, 1950). There were few counseling specialists and most of them were found in the large urban school districts.

The first wave of high school counselors after Sputnik concentrated most of their time on testing programs and college placement, but it was not long before they were asked to exceed the vocational needs of adolescents and to help young people with their personal problems. Many teachers were at a loss of what to do with a new generation of students who were growing up in a different world than they had known. Administrators were worried that school discipline was breaking down and that students needed more help in adjusting to school. Parents pleaded for help and the schools began to take on more responsibilities.

The number of high school counselors increased because of national security interests. Beating the Russians in the race to the moon and the conquest of outer space was an exciting adventure that captured the imagination of politicians, scientists, and educators. However, the race paled in terms of the everyday problems that young people faced at home and in the schools. There was a need for more counseling services in the schools and a need for counselors to re-examine their roles and functions.

Carl Rogers' book, *On Becoming a Person* (1961), and his earlier book, *Client-Centered Therapy* (1951), helped change the role of school counselors forever. First, the personal counseling theory was clear and the methodology was deceptively simple, compared to other counseling theories. It appeared that the basic concepts could be learned easily and adapted quickly to the work of school counselors.

Rogers' theory appealed to many counselors because it placed responsibility on the client. It was the client who accepted the burden of problem-solving and decision-making as the counselor assumed the role of an attentive listener. It appeared that the theory could be implemented without extensive training or knowledge of therapy. Consequently, it was possible to provide school counselors with a model that could be used with students.

The door was opened for personal counseling and other theories and methodologies. According to Aubrey (1982), "...The area of school guidance became open game for numerous advocates of counseling, ranging from such diverse fields as psychiatry, clinical psychology, psychoanalysis, learning theory, and pastoral counseling. Collectively, the advocates of these approaches offered to school counselors a bonanza of tools and techniques (p. 199)." There was more acceptance of the idea that school counselors could and should be involved with students who were having personal adjustment problems.

Nevertheless, many counseling ideas were not openly welcomed in the high schools. Counselors felt inadequately prepared to provide personal counseling services or to draw upon accepted therapeutic techniques. Moreover, the theories and techniques seemed out of context. Skepticism regarding their efficacy started to spread. After a few years of experimenting, the large majority of counselors concluded that the published and popular counseling theories and techniques of the time were not applicable to school settings. And, they were right.

The result, however, was that a new image of a helper had been created—that of a counselor, not just a guidance worker who gave tests and passed out information. Unfortunately, this image became tarnished as only a few counselors were willing or able to counsel and work with troubled students. Most counselors said that other duties and responsibilities did not allow them enough time to provide "counseling" to students, even if they had the skill (Wells and Ritter, 1979).

By the 1970s, high school counselors were receiving public criticism. One counselor, in defense of the profession, said, "We are always ready to help, to listen to students, to understand, and to sincerely care about them." But in light of the studies of the national student-to-counselor ratios which showed an average of 450 to 1, this seemed like an unrealistic statement. In some metropolitan areas, ratios soared as high as 1,000 to 1. It was difficult, if not impossible, for counselors to meet and talk with their assigned counselees on an individual basis for much time. Individual counseling for all students seemed almost out of the question.

Group procedures were suggested to compensate for the high counselor-student ratios. But, group counseling methods were suspect, especially since they were an outgrowth of the flamboyant and deeply introspective group movement of the late 1960s and early 1970s. The idea of leading an encounter group was a frightening thought for many high school counselors. The public, too, was skeptical. People worried that "sensitivity groups" would incite more rebellion than cooperation and more psychic trauma than psychological support. There was also the charge that such groups were a form of brainwashing.

Group counseling, at the time, was synonymous with encounter and therapy. Counselors feared that they would do more damage to students than good. Only a few counselors had training in group work. The horror stories about people "breaking down" in groups and needing therapy after experiencing an incompetent group leader were enough to discourage all except the most confident and adventuresome counselors.

Group procedures, for the most part, were dismissed as inappropriate for high schools, although group counseling was more efficient, and perhaps more effective, than individual counseling. The few counselors who applied the newest group skills and methods frequently lacked support from colleagues, teachers, and parents. Groups were considered a less personal approach and a passing fad.

High school counselors were failing to provide a systematic and carefully organized response to the problems of adolescents. Many had not won the trust of students and too often fell into the trap of lecturing, clarifying rules and regulations, or disciplining students who had problems. Consequently, many students kept their distance.

The result was shouted in a banner headline of the *National Observer* (Gribbin, 1973), which described high school counselors as "No-Help Helpers." Public criticism mounted. Pine (1976) described it as relentless. Parents saw very little guidance being offered. They were critical of the traditional helping role of the high school counselor and only 20% saw counselors helping their students with career guidance (Gallup, 1979). Opinions had not changed by 1983 (Gallup, 1983).

While high school counselors defended themselves on the basis that preparing students for college took much of their time, a national study of 1,100 high schools found that college counseling, too, was inadequate (Tugend, 1984). Although colleges were sending out more information than ever before, it was not reaching students. The study also found that a typical high school junior or senior received only 20 minutes of a counselor's time as a basis which to begin the complex process of planning an education and career. This same study also found counselors defensive. More than 99% of the counselors rated their college-guidance programs as effective. Yet, less than 25% of the counselors had asked their students and parents for any type of feedback or evaluation.

It is alarming that close to a million school-aged youths annually drop out of school. Yet, according to Wells (1983), over 50% of the dropouts have no record of disciplinary infractions and only 17% are failing. In more than 40% of the cases, the reason for leaving school was because of unfavorable teacher-student relationships. Some dropouts used terms such as "they put you down," "they put you aside," or "they give you a hard time" to describe their relationships with teachers.

Convinced there are no adults in the school to whom they could turn, it is not surprising that 72% of the dropouts in a national survey reported that they did not consult with any school personnel before leaving. And, more than 70% said they might have stayed if school had been different, particularly "if teachers paid more attention to students," "if we were treated as students not as inmates," and "if teachers made it fun to learn" (Wells, 1983).

We know there are many students who believe that their counselors were helpful and some may credit their counselors for having been the single most important difference in their getting through school. But, this has been the exception and it is getting to be more so.

Where does this leave the counselor? Unfortunately, there is not much evidence that high school counselors make a positive difference in their work. Accountability studies at the high school level are limited. Some high school counselor positions have been eliminated or cuts have been threatened (Atkinson, Skipworth and Stevens, 1983; Leviton, 1977; Orlando, 1981) and ironically, this is coming at a time when societal changes are putting increased demands on school counselors and emphasizing a need for their services (Macnow, 1982).

Counselors in one Texas independent school district, for example, were confronted by their superintendent and school board. They were unhappy with the work of the counselors and told them to change their roles and image or their jobs would be eliminated. After some initial anger, disappointment, and feelings of being unappreciated—after all, they saw themselves as busy and working long hours—the counselors grouped together to examine their job functions, priorities, and counseling skills. Consultants were brought into the district to help counselors and district personnel clarify roles and the direction in which they wanted their programs to move. Counselors participated in workshops where they learned some new counseling strategies and revised some old ones. Accountability studies were planned as district projects. Consequently, four years after adopting a developmental guidance approach, the school board was more satisfied and the counselor positions were secured. Most important, the counselors liked their new image, felt more positive about their work, and enjoyed being in more control of their roles and responsibilities.

Drury (1984) said school counselors were an endangered species and claimed, "The tragedy is that they have been and are still participating in their own destruction." Counselors have problems in role definition. They create and poorly manage piecemeal programs which depend upon the particular interests of counselors themselves, and they ignore the public relations aspect of their jobs. She concluded, "Counselors must stop contributing to their own extinction and take a proactive role in ensuring the survival and growth of the profession."

Is high school guidance in trouble? Peer (1985), based on his survey of state guidance directors, said that "It is—unless and until secondary counselors assume the initiative...to revitalize their guidance programs." He saw the status of guidance programs eroding and felt a sense of urgency in challenging counselors and their supporters to give a greater commitment to change and development.

High school guidance programs can no longer remain the same as they once were (Peters, 1980). Times are different and counselor roles and functions are being carefully examined and evaluated. The obvious conclusion: There is a need for a developmental approach to guidance and counseling in the high schools. In addition, responsibility for the program cannot rest alone with counselors and other specialists. Classroom teachers must become more systematically involved in helping meet the demand for guidance and counseling services.

Guidance in the Junior/Middle Schools

Junior high schools came into existence about the turn of the century when educators agreed there was a need for an intermediate school between elementary and high school to meet student needs. Since that time there have been several organizational schemes, with the highest percentage of school systems adopting the 6-3-3 plan. This puts grades 7, 8, and 9 in the same junior high school. The 6-2-4 has been the next most popular, where grades 7 and 8 attend the junior high. To a much lesser extent are the 5-3-4 and 4-4-4 plans.

Because of the different plans that have been tried over the years, it has been difficult to evaluate the effectiveness of the junior highs. While some are outstanding, others appear less than satisfactory in meeting the needs of students.

One problem that has continued to plague junior high schools is that few teachers have been specifically prepared for teaching early adolescents. Many junior high school teachers were certified as high school teachers and their preparation focused primarily on a departmentalized curriculum that was subject-matter oriented. Another criticism of junior high schools is that they are too often an imitation of high schools. Thus, they fail to ease the transition of students from elementary to high school.

In response to providing a better school for students with unique developmental needs, the middle school movement gathered strength during the 1960s. Although there are different kinds of organizational schemes, the middle school is preferably based on the 5-3-4 plan. This age grouping is a logical outcome of studying the social, physical, mental, and emotional characteristics of children from kindergarten through grade 12.

A combination of other factors—such as social change, more rapid maturation rates, increased pressure for the ninth grade to be part of a college-preparatory group, and the social activities of older adolescents—have also contributed to school reform. Currently, the national trend is to replace junior high schools with middle schools, although many of the curriculum objectives remain the same. The 6-3-3 plan appears to be on its way out. This reorganization of schools and the renewed emphasis upon early adolescence has opened new doors for developmental guidance and counseling programs.

Middle schools are based on an accepted body of knowledge about the developmental needs of students in the age bracket of ten to fourteen. These ages are marked by dramatic body changes and growth. Puberty and sex-role identification, changes in self-concept, and the search for personal values are joined with the desire for peer approval and autonomy, unpredictable emotional fluctuations, and the need to be recognized as a competent and unique being. Although contemporary youth are probably more sophisticated than in years past, the growth patterns are much the same and the socialization process is just as vital. It has simply taken time for the middle school concept to be accepted.

If you were to visit a junior high school and then visit a middle school, you would probably be able to identify the differences in guidance programs. Junior high schools tend to have traditional programs that look like those in the high schools. Career planning and school adjustment are given highest priority. There is, primarily, a crisis approach to counseling; whereas, middle schools tend to have a developmental focus.

In addition, junior high guidance programs rely on school counselors to provide most of the guidance and counseling services to students. The guidance program frequently centers around orientation to school, career exploration, and crisis-interventions. Large group or classroom guidance activities are almost absent. Most important, junior high school teachers are rarely involved in the guidance process, unless it is with troubled students.

Middle schools, on the other hand, emphasize that teachers are an integral part of guidance and sometimes there is no distinction between a guidance teacher and a classroom teacher. While a certified and well-prepared counselor is needed, the core of the guidance program is centered in the total curriculum and teaching faculty.

Most middle schools incorporate organized guidance periods into the school schedule. Students are usually assigned or given the opportunity to choose a teacher who will be their advisor and referral base. Teachers as advisors meet with all their advisees during regularly scheduled homeroom or homebase periods. The homeroom is the foundation for a group approach to guidance. In many middle schools, one or more homeroom periods a week are scheduled for group guidance activities. Students can raise questions, identify problems, and talk about their feelings, behaviors, and goals.

Some of the issues discussed in homeroom are related to personal matters, such as peer relationships, getting along with parents and teachers, and finding out more about one's self. Other discussions might evolve from school issues, such as homework, study skills, time-management, and meeting teacher expectations. The homeroom group can be divided into sub-groups for special group activities and learning experiences.

For the most part, the homeroom is not a place to take care of routine administrative details and procedures. For example, it is not a place to take attendance and compile absentee lists for the office, to make daily announcements, or to report briefly before going to class. It is not just a study hall, or where students gather to socialize "before school really begins." To the contrary, homeroom is a core class period, no matter the time of day that it is scheduled, and it has a developmental guidance curriculum.

Calling a school a middle school is no guarantee that developmental guidance will happen. For instance, a recent survey of 141 junior high/middle schools indicated that student apathy was a problem and that ninth graders in the junior high felt little intellectual challenge. Most important, the survey reported few counseling programs for ninth grade students and no group counseling activities. Counseling was viewed by the counselors in the survey as a remedial activity in which they corrected problems instead of a developmental process to help prevent them (Lounsbury, 1984).

The most important consideration for any guidance program is personnel. The reputation of a school frequently depends more upon the personnel who are employed and their skills than the physical plant or classroom lesson plans. It is somewhat surprising, therefore, that most middle school teachers have not had much preparation in guidance. Their instruction in how teacher-advisors work with advisees in a homeroom period and the fundamentals of a developmental guidance program is often limited.

Inservice training of teachers is a pre-requisite for a successful guidance program. Teachers need to know how to facilitate students in guidance activities and how to apply some brief counseling skills with their advisees. It is also important that teachers understand the role and function of school counselors and how counselors and teachers can work together to implement a total guidance program for all students.

Guidance in the Elementary Schools

Elementary schools are typically organized into classrooms where one grade level teacher is responsible for 25 to 30 students. A few schools may have more than one grade level of students placed in the same room with a teacher or team of teachers. Other schools may be organized into grade level teams and teachers work together to meet the needs of the students assigned to them. Within a team, however, each teacher is usually assigned to a few students who receive their special attention for guidance.

Every school has students who have problems and some are very serious. The elementary school is no exception. However, it has been recognized for many years that developmental guidance is the best approach for elementary school students.

Elementary school teachers work with fewer numbers of students than do junior/middle and high school teachers. In the elementary school, there is more opportunity to observe children's behavior patterns and to take note of any changes that may happen. It is easier to identify students who have special needs and who are not realizing their potential. The school environment is more controlled, and the teacher with an understanding of guidance is in a position to intervene when children are most amenable. The elementary school teacher works with children during some of the most formative years of their lives.

"Guidance in the elementary school is an integral part of the learning process. The teacher should not accept the premise that guidance concerns itself primarily with problems or serious maladjustment. With the possible exception of the child's parent, no single person has a greater influence on personality development than the classroom teacher" (Wiley, 1960, p. 1).

Historically, the teachers in self-contained classrooms have been responsible for guidance activities. It has only been within the past twenty years that guidance specialists, such as school counselors, have been employed to assist them.

Elementary school counselors were employed in the schools as early as the 1920s. However, they were few in number and only in large urban cities. Their role was close to that of a social worker and was influenced by high school guidance. The counselor worked with cumulative folders, administered tests, analyzed student data, consulted with teachers, and provided individual counseling to students with adjustment problems. The number of elementary school counselor positions grew insignificantly through the next three decades.

Again, events in the 1960s changed counseling in the elementary schools. Developmental guidance and counseling was described in more detail (Blocher, 1974; Meeks, 1968). Guidance activities were organized and presented in a more systematic way. Prevention was highlighted and the learning climate received particular attention since it affected all children (Chase, 1975; Stanford, 1972).

One of the most influential writers of the time was Don Dinkmeyer Sr., who was the first to advocate a comprehensive developmental approach to guidance (e.g. Dinkmeyer and Caldwell, 1970). He was the first editor of *Elementary School Guidance and Counseling*, an AACD (American Association of Counseling and Development) publication which went to press for the first time in 1965. This journal provided a vehicle through which counselor educators, teachers, counselors, and others could communicate their ideas about elementary guidance. It helped establish the counselor in the elementary schools.

In the beginning, it was not economically feasible to talk about counselor-student ratios. To have a reasonable ratio would have required too many counselors to be employed at one time. Therefore, to help establish the counselor in the elementary schools, emphasis was placed upon the counselor's consultation role and counselors were viewed more in terms of their ratio to teachers.

Verne Faust's classic book for elementary school counselors was titled the *Counselor-Consultant in the Elementary School*. He listed a hierarchy of roles, and consultation with teachers was first. Group counseling came next and individual counseling was last. Emphasis was determined by efficient use of the counselor's time as much as anything else (Faust, 1968).

Eckerson and Smith (1966) used the term "child development consultant." They reported that elementary principals most wanted their guidance specialists (the counselors) to consult with parents, teachers, and children, and in that order. It was easier to sell budget-minded school boards and the public on the idea that a counselor-consultant would be of great assistance to teachers and administrators than it was to request counselors based on counselor-student ratios. When teacher-counselor ratios were the first consideration, the conclusion was that most elementary schools in the nation needed a full-time counselor.

Some school districts started formalized guidance and counseling programs in their elementary schools by assigning one counselor to more than one school. Funds were limited and it was not considered politically wise by many administrators to float a bond issue for additional school personnel, especially for such an unknown position as an elementary school counselor. In addition, other professional personnel were building a case for employment (e.g. social workers, media specialists, exceptional education teachers, and health-related staff).

It was during the 1970s and 1980s that developmental guidance services and programs, and the roles of school counselors, were further clarified (Muro and Dinkmeyer, 1977; Myrick, 1980). There was less concern about "why" counselors should be employed. More questions were asked about "how" counselors really functioned in their jobs and accomplished their goals. More specifically, counselors were starting to be seen as a part of an elementary school guidance team. Less emphasis was given to testing, educational planning and individual counseling. Rather, consultation and group approaches were advocated.

Elementary school counselors provided classroom guidance units and peer facilitator training, and they coordinated other guidance procedures such as testing, parent conferences, child study teams, and exceptional student placement. In addition, these counselors accepted the challenge of accountability, knowing that their jobs depended upon it. Consequently, there is more published professional literature on the effectiveness of elementary school counselors than at any other school level.

A new type of school counselor was coming to the front. These counselors found it practical and feasible to move their work into places outside of the guidance offices—classrooms, playgrounds, cafeterias, and hallways—to have access to students and teachers. Because these counselors used a developmental approach instead of waiting to react to crises, the need for privacy seemed less of a concern. Students often saw other students meeting and talking with a counselor in different places within the school. Elementary school counselors had high visibility because they did not remain in their offices.

Elementary school counselors were among the first to use published classroom guidance activities. Kits such as *DUSO* (Dinkmeyer, 1970), and workbooks such as *Magic Circle* (Human Development Institute, 1970) helped teachers and counselors provide classroom guidance. Glasser's "classroom meetings" (1969) became an accepted activity to encourage students to learn more about themselves. The value of psychological education (Mosher and Sprinthall, 1971; Sprinthall, 1971) in the classroom has continued to gain support.

Although the basic concept of classroom guidance was not new, the curriculum materials and group methods were. Guidance sessions were sequentially organized around developmental guidance objectives and lesson plans, with activities and discussion questions. Because of their convenience, these kits and materials helped teachers provide more classroom guidance activities to students than ever before.

It is surprising, in many respects, that formalized guidance programs and services were first instituted in high schools. If the problems that older students experience are to be prevented, then more attention must be given to the early school years where the foundation for learning is laid.

Developmental Guidance for all Schools

Guidance and counseling in the schools has a significant history, although a short one. At this point in time, the developmental approach has become the most accepted approach for all school levels. It is an approach that has influenced the work of counselors in other settings too.

Developmental guidance and counseling programs are an evolutionary product of what has already taken place in the schools and what is demanded for the future. With new variations and new methodology, a comprehensive guidance program can meet the growing needs of students and the adults who work with them.

Chapter 2

Developmental Guidance: A Comprehensive Approach

In order to build a comprehensive developmental guidance and counseling program in your school, it is important to know the basic assumptions and principles behind such an approach. Moreover, it is helpful to understand how school personnel work together to implement the program. Then, attention can be given to the skills and strategies that make a counselor's job unique and rewarding.

Basic Assumptions and Needs

Developmental guidance and counseling assumes that human nature moves individuals sequentially and positively toward self-enhancement. It recognizes there is a force within each of us that makes us believe that we are special and there is nobody like us. It also assumes that our individual potentials are valuable assets to society and the future of humanity.

But, this innate drive for personal expression and uniqueness that each of us possesses oftentimes necessitates compromise with environmental forces. These come from other individuals, who are striving for their own special destinies. They also come from society, which represents a collection of attitudes, values, and laws that are designed to help people live together. Sometimes these inner and outer forces clash and conflict results. Sometimes personal growth and development suffer.

The developmental approach considers the nature of human development, including the general stages and tasks that most individuals experience as they mature from childhood to adulthood. It centers on positive self-concepts and acknowledges that one's self-concept is formed and reformed through experience and education. It further recognizes that feelings, ideas, and behaviors are closely linked together and that they are learned. Therefore, the most desired conditions for learning and re-learning are important considerations for development. The ultimate objective is to help students learn more effectively and efficiently.

A developmental program requires the help of all school personnel in order to accomplish its goals, which are organized around a guidance curriculum. Counselors and teachers, in particular, must work closely together to provide appropriate guidance and counseling services to students in school. There is a need, therefore, to identify the roles of school personnel in comprehensive guidance and counseling programs and to recognize how they complement one another. Further, there is a need to specifically define the job functions and basic interventions of school counselors, who are the guardians of the program.

Times have changed and there is a need for comprehensive developmental guidance and counseling programs that extend from elementary through high school. In addition, there is a need to reorganize guidance curricula, to retrain school counselors and teachers for new guidance and counseling roles, and to be more accountable in meeting the developmental needs of young people. It does not involve a revolution in education, but it does advance the evolution of guidance and counseling in the schools.

The Theory of Developmental Guidance

In order to build a developmental guidance and counseling program, there are a few concepts about human development to acknowledge. It is true that you could act professionally and competently in your relationships with others and not have any knowledge of psychology, human development, or counseling skills. We do not stray too far beyond common sense when we work with people. However, increased effectiveness and efficiency in our work often takes us beyond intuition, imitation, and habit. Rather, success depends more upon a thoughtful reflection of such concepts as why and what we are trying to do and the directions we want to go.

Since the term "developmental" is so prominent in counseling and guidance, what else can be said about it? First, human development is a life-long set of physiological, psychological, and social processes that begins at birth and continues until death. Second, this development involves an interaction between what a person is given genetically at birth and the different environments in which that person lives and grows. Human development is a journey from birth to death in which the personality unfolds, changes, and changes again.

In addition, development is a term that we commonly use when talking about orderly changes or ones that appear to have some kind of direction. Of course, this order and direction can be disrupted if certain factors are introduced which thwart natural inclinations. In addition, the nature of social institutions and cultural dimensions influence life's process and stages.

Developmental Stages and Tasks

During the 1960s, increased attention was given to child study. The developmental needs of children were being recognized. In particular, the growth needs of children were highlighted in the works of such people as Benjamin Bloom (1964), Robert Gesell, Frances Ilg and Louise Ames (1946 and 1956), Robert Havighurst (1953), and Jerome Kagan (1962). They emphasized how heredity and environment together shaped a child's personality. They suggested that achievement of developmental tasks at one stage of life influenced success with tasks in later stages. It was further assumed that individuals who failed to learn developmental tasks at particular periods of life were almost certain to have difficulty with later tasks, to experience disapproval and rejection from society, and to be frustrated and unhappy.

The work of Jean Piaget (1970) emphasized the cognitive development of children. He and his colleagues concluded that intellectual development appeared to take place in stages and, therefore, no stage could be eliminated, since each one was dependent on the preceding one. The four stages identified were: Sensorimotor (0-2 years); Preoperational (2-7 years); Concrete operations (7-12 years); and 4) Formal operations (12 years and older).

For example, according to Piaget's theory, children starting school are entering a stage when symbols are used to carry out mental activities. Children are learning that properties can change in appearance but some factors remain the same, that objects can be quantified, and that reasoning can result from examining the

Figure 2.1
Developmental Stages/Tasks

Infancy and Early Childhood (Ages 0-5)

1. Learning to walk
2. Learning to take solid foods
3. Learning to talk
4. Learning to control elimination of body wastes
5. Learning sex differences and sexual modesty
6. Forming concepts and learning language to describe social and physical reality
7. Learning to relate emotionally to parents and siblings; identifying relationships
8. Getting ready to read
9. Learning to distinguish right and wrong and beginning to develop a conscience

Midddle Childhood (Ages 6-11)

1. Learning physical skills necessary for ordinary games
2. Building wholesome attitudes toward oneself and a sense of self-concept
3. Learning to get along with age mates—moving from the family circle to groups outside the home
4. Learning the skills of tolerance and patience
5. Learning appropriate masculine or feminine social roles
6. Developing fundamental skills in reading, writing, and calculating
7. Developing concepts necessary for everyday living
8. Developing conscience, morality, and a scale of values
9. Achieving personal independence
10. Developing attitudes toward social groups and institutions, through experiences and imitation

Adolescents (Ages 12 to 18)

1. Achieving new and more mature relations with age mates of both sexes
2. Learning socially approved feminine and masculine roles and behaviors
3. Accepting one's physique and learning to use the body effectively
4. Achieving emotional independence of parents and other adults

Developmental Guidance and Counseling

5. Setting vocational goals for economic independence
6. Selecting and preparing for an occupation, relating interests to abilities to choices
7. Preparing for marriage and family life
8. Developing skills and concepts for civic competence
9. Desiring and achieving socially responsible behaviors, taking account values of society
10. Acquiring a set of values and an ethical system as a guide to behavior
11. Setting realistic goals and making plans for reaching these goals

Early Adulthood (Ages 19-30)

1. Selecting a mate—developing intimate relationships
2. Learning to live with a marriage partner
3. Starting a family
4. Bearing children
5. Managing a home
6. Getting started in an occupation, sometimes neglecting other tasks during this period
7. Taking on civic responsibility
8. Finding a congenial social group

Middle Age

1. Achieving adult civic and social responsibility
2. Establishing and maintaining an economic standard of living
3. Assisting teen-age children to become responsible happy adults
4. Developing adult leisure-time activities
5. Relating oneself to one's spouse as a person
6. Accepting and adjusting to the physiological changes of middle age
7. Adjusting to aging parents

Later Maturity

1. Adjusting to decreasing physical strength and health
2. Adjusting to retirement and reduced income
3. Adjusting to death of spouse
4. Establishing an explicit affiliation with one's age group
5. Meeting social and civic obligations

(Drawn from Havighurst, 1972).

---

whole and parts of an object. Problem-solving improves by the middle school years because thoughts can be more deductive and can focus on the future.

Robert Havighurst, as early as 1948, presented a theory of human development which focused on developmental tasks. "A developmental task arises at or about a certain period in the life of the individual, successful achievement of which leads to his happiness and to success with later tasks, while failure leads to unhappiness in the individual, disapproval of society, and difficulty with later tasks" (Havighurst, 1972, p.2). Stages of development were outlined and developmental tasks within these stages were identified. (e.g. see Figure 2.1).

Erik Erickson (1963), in his classic book, emphasized that everyone experiences crises or conflicts in development and that adjustments to conflicts play an important part in the development of an individual's personality. Most important, the resolution of conflicts tends to be cumulative in that a person's manner of coping and adjusting to conflicts at one stage in life influences the ways of handling the next conflict. All of us, through our everyday experiences, with some experiences being more critical than others, develop a set of complex behaviors which influence our actions throughout our life.

From Erickson's viewpoint, there are eight stages of human or psychosocial development. Each stage presents critical learning experiences that exerts influence over one's remaining life span. For example, autonomy needs are especially important to toddlers (the "me do it" syndrome), but throughout life, people must continue to test the degree of autonomy that they can express in each new relationship and stage in life. Erickson's work on emotional development has proven to be a valuable reference point for many people, as they attempt to conceptualize developmental stages and tasks. Generally, his eight stages of development included:

Stage 1: Trust (birth to 2 years of age)
Stage 2: Autonomy (2 to 4 years)
Stage 3: Initiative (4 to 6 years)
Stage 4: Industry (6-12 years)
Stage 5: Identity (12-18 years)
Stage 6: Intimacy (18-25 years)
Stage 7: Generativity (25-50 years)
Stage 8: Integrity (50 years and older)

Although times and values change and the marvels of the medical world have extended the average life span, Erickson's "ages of man" still seem to be relevant. He further suggested that if the tasks at different ages are not achieved, then at each stage emotional consequences occur: 1) mistrust; 2) doubt and shame; 3) guilt; 4) inferiority; 5) confusion; 6) isolation; 7) stagnation; and 8) despair.

For example, when an adolescent starts middle school, there is more need for self-exploration and peer relationships. Discovering one's identity or sense of uniqueness from others becomes a significant emotional task. An individual's level of awareness in this search varies, depending upon personal history, achievement in preceding stages, anticipation of the future, and the interpersonal skills that have been learned.

In over 20 years of research of moral development, Lawrence Kohlberg (1971) developed a three-level, six-stage approach to moral development which has also helped counselors and teachers gain insight to personal development. Kohlberg's theory attempted to show how there is a moral element in behavior. In each stage the orientation and thinking process might be:

Preconventional: Based on meeting personal needs.
Stage 1: Punishment and obedience "I'll do it, so I don't get punished."
Stage 2: Instrumental-relativist "I'll do it, if you do something for me."

Conventional: Based on meeting group norms
Stage 3: Good boy or girl orientation "I'll do it to please you."
Stage 4: Law and order "I'll do it because it's my duty."

Postconventional: Based on moral principle
Stage 5: Social-contract "I'll do it because it's best for the majority."
Stage 6: Universal ethics "I'll do it because my conscience tells me it's right."

Kohlberg suggested that people generally reason more than half the time at any one level, with the rest of the reasoning at other levels. People do not generally regress, but remain where they are or move slowly toward the next higher level. In addition, conflicts often result when individuals do not understand the reasoning process, especially when they are made up of lower and higher level arguments. Finally, it is evident that moral development in this case is dependent upon intellectual or cognitive development.

Don Super (1970), of career guidance fame, based his work on five developmental stages. They are: a) Organizational (birth to about age fourteen); b) Exploration (age fifteen to thirty); c) Realization (thirty to about fifty); d) Stabilization (fifty to sixty-five); and e) Examination (after sixty-five). While the age limits are generally descriptive, they are only approximations and can vary from one individual to another. In addition, these ages may be influenced by new developments in society, such as a longer life-span and career as a consequence of advances in modern medicine. We also know that young people are maturing faster now than they were fifty years ago and these maturational changes can effect development in terms of life stages.

One inevitable conclusion is that if students are taught to master certain tasks and skills that coincide with the different stages, perhaps learning life-long skills and attitudes, then they are more likely to feel a sense of control and success in their lives. The result is a more positive experience of life.

Human development is complex and has been discussed in much greater detail elsewhere. In summary, most theorists see it as a rather patterned, orderly, and distinct process. They agree that it is affected by cultural forces and the events that take place in a person's life. Also, human development, while following some general expectations at certain stages of life, must take into account individual uniqueness.

The Concept of Self

Self-concept has been recognized as an important variable in human development and learning. Both self-concept and self-esteem are considered products of how people talk and interact with one another. As the self-concept develops, various attitudes and personal styles take shape, which in turn become part of the learning process. It appears that significant attitudes about self, others, school, and society, which affect how a person learns and later functions as a mature adult, are formed while young people are growing up in their families and attending school. Student achievement in school has been directly related to self-concept (Purkey, 1970).

Therefore, to consider developmental tasks and stages, without giving attention to self-concept, might be considered folly. In addition, it seems clear that one's self-picture is shaped by interpersonal relationships and that these relationships are part of the conditions in which people learn.

Developmental Conditions for Learning

It was during the 1960s that interpersonal relationships were closely examined. It was an era that might have been called the "Search for Intimacy." There was a drive to learn more about human relationships and how people relate to each other. It was a time when close encounters took place and the human relations movement was born. Sensitivity groups of all kinds sprung up around the nation.

It was partly from these growth groups, as well as from research about interpersonal skills, that a renewed interest was taken in studying the interactions between teachers and students. After all the studies were reviewed, it was easy to conclude that the quality of a teacher-student relationship affects learning outcomes and that students learn best in an environment where people interact positively with one another.

Interpersonal relationships can be for better or for worse. Carl Rogers (1957) and others (e.g. Carkhuff and Berenson, 1967) drew attention to the desired conditions in a helping relationship, especially for counseling and therapy. These same conditions also held true for teaching and parenting (Purkey, 1970). Included in a list of such helping conditions are caring, understanding, acceptance, respect, and trustworthiness. Other conditions sometimes cited include genuineness, warmth, and concreteness. All these are in contrast to such conditions as cold, distant, sarcastic, judgmental, superior, inflexible, and unconcerned.

Some writers have focused upon the "affective" and "cognitive" domains (e.g. Bloom's Taxonomy, 1956) in an attempt to describe the learning process. But, it is impossible to learn anything of meaning or value without personal involvement and emotion. Likewise, it is impossible to make any sense of what one is feeling and experiencing without using cognitive ideas to conceptualize them. To focus on one domain at the exclusion of the other is something that might be done as an academic exercise, but it does not work that way in practice. Learning happens best when both domains are given attention, whether you are in a classroom or a counseling office.

Developmental Guidance
Curriculum and Goals

There is an organized curriculum within the developmental approach to guidance. Based upon developmental stages, tasks, skills, and learning conditions, the guidance curriculum is a planned effort to provide each student with a set of skills and experiences that helps enhance all learning. Such an approach embraces all the goals of education.

More specifically, the goals and objectives of a developmental guidance program are related to facilitating the instructional process (Aubrey, 1979). Some people may see personal development objectives as supplemental to academic ones, but they are an integrated part of the total education program. While the objectives appear to focus primarily on personal growth, the outcomes might be considered desirable for any educational program.

There are many guides which have been published by school systems which attempt to describe program goals and objectives. Some are more extended and detailed than others. Titles, phrases, choices of words, and a particular emphasis may be a little different from one system to another, but a thorough review would show that there are several common themes.

There are eight goals which characterize almost all developmental guidance and counseling programs. For the most part, regardless of school or school system, general and specific objectives can be organized around them. They are:

Goal 1: Understanding the School Environment
Goal 2: Understanding Self and Others
Goal 3: Understanding Attitudes and Behavior
Goal 4: Decision-making and Problem-solving
Goal 5: Interpersonal and Communication Skills
Goal 6: School Success Skills
Goal 7: Career Awareness and Educational Planning
Goal 8: Community Pride and Involvement

Each goal is further delineated by a set of general objectives, which in turn can be described more specifically through expected observable outcomes. In addition, each of the eight general goals are true for all schools (K-12). Particular attention and emphasis to various objectives are usually grade level related, considering developmental stages and tasks appropriate for each age group.

Goal 1: Understanding the School Environment enables students in whatever school they are attending to become more familiar with facilities, procedures, and programs. It includes helping students to learn more about guidance services and the roles of school counselors and teacher-advisors.

Goal 2: Understanding Self and Others focuses on such matters as helping students learn more about their abilities, interests, and personal characteristics. Students learn to identify their strengths and areas in which they want to improve. They also think about and develop skills related to their relationships with peers, teachers and other adults. This goal includes self-assessment, self-acceptance, and the development of self-confidence. It values positive differences and uniqueness among people.

Goal 3: Understanding Attitudes and Behavior continues with an emphasis on understanding of self and others, but gives particular attention to how habits, attitudes, and perceptions can affect behavior. Also examined are how feelings and behaviors are related to goals and consequences, and how behavior can be changed, if desired.

Goal 4: Decision-making and Problem-solving attends to setting goals and making responsible decisions. It involves an increased awareness of factors that influence change and decision-making, as well as helpful procedures for problem-solving. There is an emphasis on responsibility and individual choice.

Goal 5: Interpersonal and Communication Skills emphasizes the value of developing positive interpersonal relationships and how communication skills affect the way in which people interact with one another. Interpersonal and communication skills are related to friendships and working relationships with students, teachers, and family.

Goal 6: School Success Skills is designed to help students be more successful in school. This includes study skills, learning behaviors, time management, conflict resolution with peers and teachers, and developing positive attitudes and habits which enable one to get the most out of school.

Goal 7: Career Awareness and Educational Planning is aimed at one of the most traditional aspects of school guidance and counseling. There have been many attempts to integrate or assimilate career information and guidance within academic curricula. This goal, however, helps students to understand more about the world of work, to increase their career awareness, and to do some in-depth career exploration related to personal skills, interests, and abilities. In addition, attention is given to making educational plans, including selecting courses, preparing for graduation and future education, developing employability skills, and learning how to search for a job.

Goal 8: Community Pride and Involvement stresses community involvement. It emphasizes how students can be responsible and productive people in their communities. It also focuses on community resources.

Some school systems have not only identified the general goals of a guidance program, but have proceeded to specify objectives, related counselor interventions and services, possible counseling and guidance activities, expected observable outcomes or indicators of success, and methods for measuring results. Handbooks, outlining and cross referencing activities from popular publications, have also been assembled in almost every school system. These books may provide a rationale and description of the guidance program. They might describe various guidance roles of teachers, counselors, and administrators.

Principles of Developmental Guidance

In addition to program objectives, there are seven principles of developmental guidance programs. (See Figure 2.2.) These assumptions provide some direction as to how a program can be implemented and evaluated. They include the following:

Figure 2.2

Principles of Developmental Guidance Programs

Developmental guidance is for all students.
Developmental guidance has an organized and planned curriculum.
Developmental guidance is sequential and flexible.
Developmental guidance is an integrated part of the total educational process.
Developmental guidance involves all school personnel.
Developmental guidance helps students learn more effectively and efficiently.
Developmental guidance includes counselors who provide specialized counseling services and interventions.

Developmental guidance is for all students. Although some young people have more problems or are more troublesome than others, and while some need special attention because of their particular needs or circumstances, developmental guidance is directed to *all* students. There will be times, of course, when disruptive incidents happen or when a crisis-type intervention may be an appropriate response. However, an effective guidance curriculum provides continuous assistance, support, and meaningful growth experiences to all students.

Developmental guidance has an organized and planned curriculum. Within this curriculum, there are general and specific objectives to assist students in their development. The curriculum is built upon helping students with their cognitive, affective, and physical growth, giving special attention to individual appraisal, potential, motivation, and achievement. It concentrates on learning conditions and emphasizes the human aspect of the educational process.

The guidance curriculum is concerned with behavior as much as self-concept. It encourages responsible decision-making and individual uniqueness. It also acknowledges society and community expectations, as well as the rights and self-worth of individuals. The curriculum is designed to help students to be sensitive to others, to cope and adjust, and to be personally assertive, self-confident, and self-directed.

The curriculum goals and objectives are usually organized into guidance units. Each unit, with its general and specific objectives, is further organized into guidance sessions which are presented to students. For example, if the general objective of a unit is to "develop a positive attitude about school," then a more specific objective—perhaps addressed in a particular session—might be "to be able to compliment another person." In this case, it is assumed that positive attitudes are related to positive relationships with others and that the skill of recognizing and complimenting others is a valued part of interpersonal relationships.

Developmental guidance is sequential and flexible. Experience with students at different age levels provides some idea about when particular guidance units are best presented and studied. In this sense, there is an attempt to provide some continuity to the program. It is assumed, for example, that all students need to be oriented to the school building and general procedures during the first part of the year. It is also assumed that shortly after orientation, students will want to assess their goals and examine their classroom behaviors. It is not enough to wait until students have problems in their classes or have misunderstandings with their teachers before they receive some guidance. Rather, students can benefit by identifying the kinds of classroom behaviors that are related to achievement and then rating themselves or comparing ratings with teacher ratings. Next, students might identify those behaviors upon which they want to improve. This unit may then be followed by a "study skills unit" in which students learn to manage their time and concentrate on study habits.

The program must be flexible so that guidance units or sessions can be moved around to accommodate student and teacher readiness. In addition, sometimes new units must be developed and inserted into the scheduled curriculum to address a particular need or a growing concern.

Although each guidance unit might be carefully planned and presented at what is considered to be an optimal time of the school year, it is also possible that some guidance units need to be repeated, others need to be modified, and still others introduced at other times than when first scheduled.

In addition, teachers and counselors must be flexible enough to seize upon moments when "timely teaching" is appropriate. There are special times when students are ready to learn. Sometimes something out of the ordinary has happened and this might provide extra motivation or student interest. Ideally, it always best to present a guidance activity when there is an obvious eagerness to learn. Counselors and teachers can take advantage of those times when guidance lessons are particularly appropriate or have special meaning.

Developmental guidance is an integrated part of the total educational process. Although there is an identified curriculum that appears to be separate from the academic curriculum, developmental guidance permeates the school environment. Timely teaching is part of an effective developmental guidance program. Likewise, counselors may create a personalized guidance lesson which draws upon and applies something that has been learned in an academic class. For example, students learning to write letters in an English class can also apply those skills to writing for more information about careers or perhaps applying for a summer job.

Developmental guidance involves all school personnel. Teachers, counselors, administrators, and all support personnel are responsible for guidance services in the school. Some guidance units might best be delivered by teachers through their assigned classes or maybe during a special guidance period when they are working as advisors to students. Other guidance units might best be delivered by guidance specialists, such as counselors, school psychologists, resource teachers, or outside consultants or resource people.

Although school counselors have been identified as those who will take the lead in organizing and planning a developmental guidance program, the program cannot be implemented without the full support and assistance of teachers and administrators. The guidance program is not something that can be shuffled off to specialists alone. It requires cooperation among all the adults who are working with students.

Developmental guidance helps students learn more effectively and efficiently. While guidance and counseling emphasize personal growth and individual potential, it does not do so at the expense of academic achievement. In fact, everything in the guidance program is eventually directed at helping students learn more effectively and efficiently. All guidance objectives have an educational base and all services are related to helping students get the most out of school.

Developmental guidance includes school counselors who provide specialized counseling services and interventions. While many guidance objectives can be met within the general framework of the instructional program and guidance curriculum, there are occasions when more specialized services, such as brief counseling, are needed by students. Counseling is provided by certified school counselors who are knowledgeable about counseling theories and skills.

School counselors are viewed as human behavior and relationship specialists within a school. They have training in individual and group counseling skills. They also have more flexible time than teachers. Subsequently, they can give extra attention to some students and provide them counseling experiences when appropriate.

Counseling services are not considered therapy. The guidance program is not designed to provide psychotherapy for the psychologically deviant. However, many students who have serious personal problems still attend regular school. They have to cope with the limitations of the school setting and to adjust to classroom conditions. They often need help in establishing working relationships with teachers and classmates.

Some students with serious personal problems respond well to guidance units or brief counseling by school personnel. Many teachers and counselors recognize the importance of establishing positive relationships with troubled students and do so effectively. Regardless of what they do and their effectiveness, the helping process is not labeled therapy. Assisting troubled students to adjust to school not only improves their learning and well-being, but it improves the learning environment for others. If a student is having problems with a teacher, that student is not learning and is probably distracting others' learning as well.

School counseling is based upon brief-counseling theory and draws upon counselor interventions that can be delivered within six to eight counseling sessions. In a developmental guidance program, counseling is focused. General "rap sessions" in which students talk with counselors in unstructured meetings are not as common as they once were. High student-counselor ratios and limited counselor time make unorganized or meandering kinds of discussions impractical, although they may be interesting, productive, and desirable on occasion.

In addition to individual and small group counseling and classroom guidance, counselors provide other services, such as consulting, training peer facilitators, testing, and coordinating other guidance activities. These job functions of the school counselor will be discussed in the remaining chapters of this book.

Roles of School Personnel in Guidance

It is a mistake to think that guidance and counseling services are the function of specialists alone. This could only lead to a crisis-type approach, as there are not enough specialists employed in schools to meet the needs of students.

Good guidance permeates the school environment. Where specific guidance and counseling programs are present, there is also better school morale among students and teachers. There is a positiveness that can be experienced throughout the school. But, effective programs take the cooperation and active participation of all school personnel.

Schools across the nation are organized differently. Job titles and assignments vary from one school to another and some schools have more personnel and resources than others. Regardless, a comprehensive developmental guidance program is built primarily on the work of: 1) administrators; 2) teachers; 3) counselors; and 4) other support personnel. Listed below are some of their basic job functions in a guidance program.

Principal

To provide leadership for the guidance program.

To provide personnel to the school's Guidance Committee. (This committee will probably consist of representatives from each teaching team and be co-chaired by a school counselor and a teacher.)

To provide administrative support and encouragement.

To participate actively in defining and clarifying the guidance assignments and roles.

To provide adequate time, space, facilities, and materials needed to implement the program.

To consult with the Guidance Committee regarding the organization, monitoring, and evaluation of the guidance program.

To see that guidance services are implemented and evaluated.

To help identify guidance needs in the school and to recommend possible guidance units or interventions. And, on occasion, to co-lead a guidance activity with a teacher or counselor.

To establish supportive and cooperative working relationships among administrators, counselors, teachers, and other student service specialists.

To assist in the establishment of a comprehensive guidance plan and structure, including a teacher-advisor program that can be implemented within the school's schedule.

To communicate the philosophy and structure of the program to parents and the general public.

To consult with the Guidance Committee regarding special issues, concerns, or problems that develop among students and school personnel.

School Counselors

To assume leadership in organizing and developing a comprehensive developmental guidance and counseling program.

To provide individual counseling services to students.

To provide small group counseling services to students.

To organize and lead large group guidance units, sessions, and activities.

To train and coordinate peer facilitators.

To consult with parents, teachers, and administrators regarding special concerns and needs of students.

To consult with teachers and administrators about guidance and counseling interventions for students.

To develop guidance units that evolve from student needs.

To help develop and coordinate a teachers as advisors program (TAP).

To co-lead, on occasion, a guidance unit or session with a teacher, perhaps during TAP.

To serve as a professional resource to teacher-advisors about brief counseling and behavior change.

To help identify students who have special needs or problems and to help find alternative education or guidance services for them.

To coordinate faculty and staff development programs related to guidance.

To coordinate other guidance related services (student assessment, advisement, community resources, special education, and placement).

Teachers

To help develop and implement a comprehensive developmental guidance program within the school.

To help identify students who need special attention in learning more effectively and efficiently.

To work as a teacher-advisor with approximately 20 to 25 students, meeting them individually and in a group during TAP time.

To attempt to know personally each student who is in the TAP group.

To follow up with advisees regarding academic progress, grade reports, discipline referrals, special concerns, and general information.

To know their advisees' parents/guardians and work as a liaison between home and school, facilitating communication.

To build a group cohesiveness among an assigned TAP group of students so that they might be resources to one another.

To seek assistance for advisees whose needs are beyond the limits of TAP or classroom guidance.

To identify student needs and to make recommendations to the Guidance Committee.

To consult with counselors, and other school personnel, regarding the guidance needs of the advisees.

To participate in staff-development programs that will help in providing guidance activities and "brief counseling" experiences for students.

Occupation Specialists or Career Counselors

To develop and organize a comprehensive Career Resource Center.

To collect and disseminate national, state, and local publications; materials; and other career resources.

To provide career development guidance units that can be used during TAP time.

To co-lead TAP advisory groups with teachers on occasion and when appropriate.

To consult with teachers regarding career interests skills and aptitudes of student advisees.

To help identify the vocational interests and needs of students.

To work with students and parents in terms of career and educational planning.

School Psychologist

To diagnose and study individual students.

To evaluate various aspects of a student's home and school experiences and to make recommendations for guidance services and educational placement.

To provide intensive individual and group counseling or remediation experiences for disturbed students.

To work as a liaison between school and community psychological resources.

To help design educational and therapeutic strategies for students who need special assistance.

To consult with teachers, counselors, and others in a school regarding the limitations, strengths, and special needs of students.

To organize, lead, and take an active role in child study teams, particularly those staffings regarding exceptional children and their educational placement (i.e. P.L. 94-142).

School Social Worker

To work with needy families and coordinate guidance interventions between school and home.

To serve as a liaison between the school and public health and rehabilitation agencies.

To study individual students and their family situations, providing case information that is relevant to school guidance and counseling interventions.

To consult with school and district personnel regarding the needs of families and implications for educating children in schools.

Other Administrators and Support Staff

Other support staff and administrators might include: attendance officers, Deans or Assistant principals, activities directors and coordinators, placement specialists, speech therapists, special education teachers and aids, and paraprofessionals. Their roles and functions related to developmental guidance might consist of:

To work with a TAP group when appropriate to reduce the number of students assigned to teachers.

To help identify student needs and interests.

To co-lead, on occasion, guidance units or sessions.

To help teachers follow up with specific advisees.

To lead a guidance unit that has been specifically designed for special needs of some students.

To lead a special group of advisees who have been identified as needing special attention, such as those who have not been able to adjust to TAP group.

To assume responsibility for duties that need attention during TAP time so that teachers and others may make the most use of TAP.

Summary

These roles are meant to give school personnel some responsibility and direction. They revolve around traditional roles and expectations, but they highlight job functions as related to a developmental guidance program.

There are probably other job assignments, duties, and responsibilities. The lists are not meant to be all inclusive. However, if these roles are ignored or neglected, then the guidance program will probably suffer and personnel will struggle.

Chapter 3
The Teacher as Student Advisor

After 13 years of steady decline, elementary and secondary school enrollments began to show an increase in the fall of 1985. A new era of education was starting, as the "baby boom" of the late 1970s reached school age. Consequently, more attention is likely to be directed toward this new generation of students, including their guidance needs.

Our schools have accommodated the public for many years, adjusting successfully to a host of demands. More students from different racial, cultural, and social backgrounds are being served in our schools. More handicapped students, who were previously ignored or pushed out, are being included in the mainstream of school experiences. Experimental and alternative education programs of many kinds have been introduced, as the schools try to be a cure for all of the nation's social ills. Yet, there has been an erosion of public confidence in the nation's schools.

There is a concern, almost a post-Sputnik echo, that our nation is at risk because of neglecting its educational system. National and state commissions have issued reports which urge higher academic standards and a push for educational excellence (e.g. Boyer, 1983; Gardner, 1983; Goodlad, 1983).

Some people say there is a "tide of mediocrity" in the schools, as indicated by declining achievement scores on national tests, although it appears that this trend is reversing itself. "Our students need to be more competitive with students from other nations, whose performance scores in math and science are higher than ours," is a statement that has become a genuine concern among critics. In response, almost every state legislature has passed laws requiring students to attend school for longer hours, to take more academic classes, and to pass more subjects.

Surprisingly, very little attention, if any, was given to school guidance in the recent state and national reports. It is as though guidance is a fringe benefit instead of being directly linked with student learning. None of the reports mentioned a guidance curriculum or the need for more guidance and counseling services. Rather, the emphasis for change has been primarily on proficiency in the core curriculum areas of English, math, science, and social studies (Aubrey, 1984; Taber, 1984).

Yet, we know that learning is a consequence of the environment, for better or for worse. Teachers and students working together create a learning climate, which plays a critical role in educational excellence. If students are to learn more effectively and efficiently, to achieve more academically, and to be productive and responsible citizens, then developmental guidance must be a part of the total school experience.

Teacher Concerns

Expenditures for education in the nation reaches into the billions of dollars, as there are about 44.5 million students in public and private schools. About 2.5 million elementary and secondary school teachers are trying to help educate them (National Center for Education Statistics, 1985). These teachers have many concerns about students.

Teachers have consistently expressed their concerns about students who are disruptive, who are disrespectful of teachers, who use obscene language, who are tardy or frequently absent, or who lie, cheat, or deface school property. Many teachers are unsure of what to do with students who are unmotivated, depressed, withdrawn, resentful, discouraged, and who are having conflicts with peers or parents. Teachers worry about students who do not follow classroom or school procedures, who are unresponsive to suggestions, and who appear unwilling to change. They are concerned about school discipline. Student-teacher relationships appear to be the central issue of these concerns.

Teachers need help. They need help in understanding students. They need more classroom management skills or new ways of building positive working relationships with students. They also need to re-examine the type of guidance services that are available to students in their schools and to clarify teacher roles in a guidance program.

The second annual Metropolitan Life Poll of the American Teacher by Lou Harris (September,1985) showed that many teachers are considering leaving teaching and entering another occupation. While 51% of all teachers said that they have considered leaving the teaching profession at some point in their careers, 27% said that they are likely to do so within the next five years. The percentage was higher for urban areas (36%). More secondary than elementary school teachers expressed disenchantment with education and appeared more likely to leave.

Ironically, fully three-fourths of those who considered leaving but stayed did so because of the satisfaction that they derive from their relationships with students! These teachers have many of the same complaints as the other teachers who left—inadequate compensation, limited resources, lack of professionalism, and increasing student needs and problems—but they like teaching young people and the personal rewards that it brings.

In a developmental guidance program, teachers are encouraged to work personally with students. More time is made available for teachers and students to become better acquainted, and there are more opportunities to build close working relationships, which benefit both students and teachers.

The Teacher and School Guidance

The first books about school guidance were directed exclusively to classroom teachers. For many years there were so few counselors or other support personnel that the only way students received personal guidance was through their classroom teachers. Good teaching was considered good guidance.

Since the 1960s, studies have shown that the way teachers interact with students can make a difference in how well students learn (e.g. Amidon and Flanders, 1967; Flanders, 1965; Purkey, 1970; Wittmer and Myrick, 1980). If students see their teachers as caring

ing and interested in them, then they are more likely to be inspired and to enjoy going to school. They feel encouraged and try harder.

Interestingly enough, effective teachers have the same characteristics as effective guidance and counseling specialists. Among these are the willingness and ability to:

See the student's point of view.
Personalize the education experience.
Facilitate a class discussion where students listen and share ideas.
Develop a helping relationship with students and parents.
Organize personal learning experiences.
Be flexible.
Be open to trying new ideas.
Model interpersonal and communication skills.
Foster a positive learning environment.

It appears that good guidance and good teaching are closely related in terms of a helping relationship.

When students have problems, they turn to those who they think can be of most help. Surveys repeatedly show that elementary students first turn to their parents and then to their teachers. Adolescents turn first to peers and then to relatives and teachers. Generally, the first line of helpers are among those people who students see almost every day, especially if they have positive relationships with them.

It may come as a surprise to some people that school counselors and other support personnel, who are professionally trained in helping people with personal problems, are usually not the students' first choice of a helper. There are some good reasons. First, counselors often lack the visibility of teachers or student peers. Second, their image is often too aligned with authority, discipline, and administrative procedures. In fact, it is not uncommon to see professional counselors near the bottom of a student's list of potential helpers because of the image that they have among students. One group of high school students, for example, portrayed their counselors in a school skit as being large computer-like boxes that kept repeating impersonally, "Sorry, but that's the policy... but that's the policy... but that's the policy."

School teachers have a long history of helping students who have personal problems. Some teachers continue to be a source of guidance to their students long after they have finished their studies at the school. This is especially true when the teacher-student relationship has been a personal and meaningful one to both parties.

To build such a relationship, of course, takes some time and a special set of experiences or circumstances.

It also appears that the most popular and assertive students are usually the ones who are able to establish endearing and helpful relationships with their teachers. There are many students who need adult guidance and a mature relationship that they can draw upon. Yet, some of them are too shy or withdrawn to reach out to teachers for help. Some students assume they are not liked well enough to compete with popular students for teacher attention. Still others are aware that their attitudes and behaviors in school are not what is expected and assume that teachers are not interested or concerned about them.

Teachers are busy people and they often feel burdened with their responsibilities. Their time is limited and they cannot build close personal relationships with all their students, especially at the secondary level. The reality of schedules and class arrangements in school frequently forces teachers to be selective and to take a greater interest in some students than in others. The favored students receive teacher support and personal guidance while the others must turn elsewhere.

Elementary school teachers have traditionally accepted their roles as guidance teachers and recognized the value of classroom guidance. They work closely with their students in self-contained classrooms and the situation enables teachers to be keenly aware of student needs and interests. Because they work with the same students for most of a school day, elementary school teachers have more opportunities to build close relationships with their students and to provide them timely guidance lessons and activities.

Secondary school teachers, on the other hand, work with a larger number of students and spend a limited amount of time with them. For example, it is common for many of the core curriculum teachers in junior and high schools to have six classes, with as many as 30 or more students in each class. A high school teacher may meet with more than 180 students a day, seeing each of them for less than an hour in a class where academic skills are emphasized. It is no wonder that so few secondary school teachers understand the needs, interests, and problems of their students (Powell, 1985).

Teachers as Student Advisors

There is a need for teachers to be directly involved in developmental guidance. The single most innovative approach to meeting this need has been through programs where teachers are designated as student advisors and they are assigned a group of students who are their advisees. This is often called an advisor-advisee program or a teacher as advisor program (TAP). It is designed to provide continuous adult guidance within a school (Jenkins, 1977).

The need for more advisement by teachers and counselors was supported by a Missouri needs survey. It showed that about 48% of the students had not spoken with a school counselor regarding future educational and vocational plans and that only 52% believed that the schools had provided opportunities for parents to discuss their child's educational plans. Moreover, 41% of the students felt that they did not know one teacher well enough to whom they might talk if they had a problem (Johnson and Salmon, 1979).

The teacher advisor-advisee concept was highlighted when it was introduced into the middle schools (Daresh and Pautsch, 1981). Middle schools, following the lead of elementary schools, place an emphasis on developmental guidance. Students are no longer in self-contained classes with one teacher as they were in the elementary schools. Instead, they generally work with a team of teachers and they are also assigned to a homeroom or homebase group where they meet regularly with teacher-advisors (Alexander and George, 1981; Michael, 1986).

Teachers have regular academic assignments based on their interests and training, but each teacher also has a group of about 20 students or advisees. There may be less or more advisees, depending upon the number of students who attend a school and the number of faculty and staff who are available to be student advisors. The best ratio is about 1 to 15 students, but in practice it has been lower in a few cases and it has been as high as 1 to 30 when space and personnel were limited.

It is assumed that each student needs a friendly adult in the school who knows and cares about the student in a personal way. The advisors are responsible for helping their advisees to deal with the problems of growing up and getting the most out of school. It is the advisor-advisee relationship that is the core of guidance in a school.

A teacher-advisor is usually responsible for an advisee's cumulative folder, work folders, teacher-student conferences, parent conferences, group guidance experiences, and follow-up on academic progress reports. Advisors also consult with other teachers, school counselors, and support personnel about their advisees.

Teacher-advisors meet with their advisees regularly through a homeroom or homebase group. The "homebase" or "homeroom" period is a home within the school for most students. It is here that they have a supportive group of peers with whom they can explore their personal interests, goals, and concerns. It is here that issues which get in the way of effective academic learning can be addressed.

These homebase periods are about 25-30 minutes in length and preferably happen at the beginning of each school day. At least two days of the week are scheduled for developmental guidance activities. The other three days are more flexible and might be used for supervised study, silent writing, silent reading, exploration of music and the arts, or for more guidance activities.

Some schools have other arrangements for scheduling homebase meetings. The five scheduled meetings described above seem ideal. Regardless, it appears that the homebase period should be no less than 25 minutes if a guidance curriculum is to be delivered with any degree of effectiveness. It simply takes that amount of time to guide students through most structured guidance activities. Less time leads to rushing and impatience. Time must be managed very carefully and there is a need to be task-oriented. Some guidance activities cannot be used if there is not enough time to experience them or discuss their meaning.

Guidance in the middle schools embraces the developmental guidance concepts. The guidance curriculum, which for the most part is delivered in homebase meetings, is based on the assumption there are certain guidance experiences which will help students personally, socially, and academically (Clark and Frith, 1983). The curriculum can be organized into guidance units, each with guidance sessions. There are guidance objectives and guidance activities. When there is a scheduled time to help meet the guidance needs of students, classroom time in academic studies can be more productive.

A guidance unit focuses on a particular topic. Some representative units by topic and general objectives are listed in Figure 3.1. These are representative of those used in the Orange County Schools, Orlando, Florida. The list is not meant to be all incusive and, as occasions call for it, other guidance units can be developed in light of special student needs or interests.

Figure 3.1

Developmental Guidance Units—TAP

UNIT 1: GETTING ACQUAINTED

To help advisor group members to know each other.
To build facilitative relationships within the group.
To lay the foundation for advisor-advisee group meetings.
To help advisees learn how to participate in a group.
To help advisees make positive transitions in school.
To review school handbook and school procedures.

UNIT 2: STUDY SKILLS AND HABITS

To evaluate one's study skills and habits.
To develop effective time-management plans.
To learn and practice classroom listening skills.
To identify various tests and test-taking situations.
To learn ways to cope with test-anxiety.
To understand grade point average (GPA) and report cards.
To discuss school success skills.

UNIT 3: SELF-ASSESSMENT

To identify classroom behaviors related to achievement.
To identify one's strengths in classroom behaviors.
To identify classroom behaviors that need to be improved.
To assess teacher-student relationships.
To assess attitudes about school, self, and others.
To set goals and learn to monitor progress.
To develop an appreciation of individual differences.
To identify one's interests, abilities, and uniqueness.

UNIT 4: COMMUNICATION SKILLS

To identify and practice interpersonal kills related to the
    facilitative conditions and facilitative model.
To learn how to be sensitive and "tune in" to others.
To learn how to be a careful listener.
To learn how to clarify and explore ideas.
To learn how to ask and to respond to thoughtful questions.
To learn ways to compliment and to confront others.
To identify behaviors which block effective communication.
To learn how to be an effective group participant.
To learn how one's behavior has an effect on others.

UNIT 5: DECISION-MAKING AND PROBLEM-SOLVING

To learn models for decision-making and problem-solving.
To learn how to identify alternatives and consequences.
To identify common teen-age dilemmas and factors which
    influence decision-making and problem-solving.
To show how decision-making and problem-solving skills can be
    used at home and school.
To examine the consequences of not meeting school and family
    obligations and responsibilities.

UNIT 6: PEER RELATIONSHIPS

To examine sex roles and sex stereotypes in society.
To develop positive ways of interacting with peers.
To recognize the power of peer influence.
To assess one's self and peer relationships.
To learn how to develop friendships.
To learn ways to resist undesirable peer pressure.
To increase awareness of how personal needs and interests affect
    relationships.

UNIT 7: MOTIVATION

To become more aware of one's interests, needs, and desires.
To recognize how one's self-esteem and attitudes are related to the
    way in which a goal is approached.
To recognize the value of setting personal goals.
To differentiate between intrinsic and extrinsic rewards.
To identify motivational techniques, such as goal setting,
    monitoring, self-talk, action steps, and positive thinking.
To show how skills and practice are related to success.

UNIT 8: CONFLICT/RESOLUTION

To identify the nature of conflict, how and when it can occur.
To learn constructive ways of dealing with conflict.
To identify conflicts related to developmental stages of life.
To practice applying communication skills to conflict moments.
To identify how conflict/resolution skills can be applied with
    teachers, parents, or peers.

UNIT 9: WELLNESS

To identify common health problems in our society.
To identify positive aspects of living a healthy live.
To discuss how exercise, nutrition, positive attitudes, and personal
    living habits can affect one's life.

To be aware of the characteristics of "high risk" people, such as: alcohol and drug abuse, suicide, and potential dropout.
To examine the value of wellness and prevention strategies.
To examine the long-range consequences of abusive behaviors.
To develop and practice effective ways of coping with stress.

UNIT 10: CAREER DEVELOPMENT

To examine the affect of changing times on the world of work.
To recognize job opportunities and their value to society.
To identify how jobs, occupations, and careers are related to one's interests, needs, skills, and opportunities.
To identify tentative job goals.
To become aware of the factors that influence job choice.
To recognize how job goals are related success in school.
To identify how job tasks relate to skills learned in school.

UNIT 11: EDUCATIONAL PLANNING

To recognize options that are available for planning.
To illustrate the need to plan ahead.
To learn a language of educational planning (common terms).
To learn the sequence of academic courses.
To identify academic requirements and electives.
To develop an educational plan for middle or high school.
To register for next year's courses.

UNIT 12: COMMUNITY INVOLVEMENT

To develop pride in the community.
To identify responsibilities of citizens in the community.
To see the value of volunteering for community service.
To identify ways in which young people can help make the community and neighborhoods better places to live.

The units are organized sequentially according to a school's guidance calendar and the major events of a school year. For instance, an orientation unit might be presented in the homebase periods during the first three weeks of school. It can help students become more familiar (or review) school facilities, procedures, policies, and resources. This unit is typically followed by a unit about study skills, which could assist advisees to develop better study habits and to think about how they manage their time. A third unit on self-assessment might then follow. In this unit, students think about their classroom behaviors and what must be done if they are to succeed. They also identify areas of personal strengths and those areas upon which they want to improve.

Each guidance unit might be organized around the general scheme of six sessions (5 + 1). That is, students take part in guidance activities for five sessions and then one session is used to help evaluate the unit. This enables teacher-advisors to complete a unit with their advisees in three weeks, if they are meeting twice a week. If the evaluation in the sixth session showed that the unit's objectives were not met or that more time was needed for some skills, then additional guidance sessions could be scheduled.

Some sessions are more structured than others. Some are designed to build group cohesiveness and a sense of belonging among the advisees in their homebase period. Other sessions attempt to anticipate the developmental needs of students, while still other sessions depend upon what students want to talk about and the particular needs and interests that emerge.

One teacher-advisor argued that students did not like or benefit from a study skills unit which had been delivered during homeroom guidance. However, further examination showed that the teacher was depending exclusively upon printed materials which told students how to study. The materials were distributed for study during homebase and students answered questions related to them. This teacher missed the point of how homebase time can be used and the value of a teacher-advisor program.

It was suggested that the teacher put aside the materials for the time being and that students be encouraged to talk about study habits from their own experiences. It was a time to find out how they approached their homework. What seemed to work for them and what did not? In addition, advisees could develop their own plans based upon information that came out of the group's discussion. This type of approach made the topic personally meaningful and led to the use of the printed materials later when there was student readiness to examine them.

TAP: An Essential Guidance Program

If the teachers are to be part of a school's guidance program, then they must have time to meet with students. Homeroom or homebase periods can provide time regularly. The teachers as advisors concept makes a guidance program more manageable and enables more students to benefit from guidance and counseling services.

The same concepts that have proven their value in the middle school also make sense for high schools (Sprinthall and Erickson, 1974). In fact, we can use the term TAP (Teachers as Advisors Program) to refer to either a middle or high school guidance program which involves a teacher working with a group of students as an advisor.

Although developmental stages and tasks are different for older adolescents, the need to provide developmental learning conditions and developmental guidance remains the same. There is still a need to assist students in their intellectual, social, and personal growth. There may even be a more pronounced need to personalize and humanize education.

The Ferguson-Florissant School District, Ferguson, Missouri, started a high school advisement program that was part of a project funded by the Kettering Foundation. The program was later revised and expanded under ESEA Title IV-C funds and subsequently, became a validated model program for many other school districts. The program provided more guidance services to students. Other high school programs, particularly in such states as Maryland, New Jersey, and Georgia, have helped demonstrate the value of TAP. Special funds from outside sources can stimulate school districts to develop such programs.

In January, 1985, the Florida Legislature appropriated two million dollars for 39 high schools in the state to pilot a "teachers as advisors program (TAP)." Each school was given the opportunity to develop an organizational scheme. Each school employed a TAP coordinator and an aide, who helped develop guidance units and materials. Funds were also made available for teacher workshops and seminars for program and skill development.

Many high school teachers have never had a guidance course and many are unsure of how to lead a group discussion with adolescents when there is no academic lesson to be taught. It is difficult for them to put aside old teacher modes and habits and to become better listeners and facilitators. Many are uncertain as to how to use TAP time, and far too many do not understand the basic principles of developmental guidance. Yet, considerable progress has been made within a short time. For instance, most of the Florida schools, after only five months of experience with TAP, moved in the direction of providing more time for teachers to meet with advisees. Students in most schools liked TAP and wanted more time for the program.

Administrators at Pasco High School, Dade City, Florida, credited their TAP program, which was one of the pilot schools in the state, for improving school attendance. The program was limited since only marginal students who seemed to need help were scheduled to meet with teacher-advisors and organized meetings happened only once every two weeks. However, because of the initial success of the program, more time was scheduled for TAP in its second year and additional training was given to teachers.

The Counselor's Role in TAP

One critic voiced the opinion that TAP was simply a device where teachers did the job that counselors were supposed to be doing. And, teachers were not prepared to be counselors. Within the same school, at least one counselor was concerned that TAP would take away counselor jobs, since teachers were to be student advisors.

To answer part of the criticisms and fears of counselors and teachers, it is important to identify the roles that each plays in a TAP program. First, teachers are not asked to be counselors or to take on the responsibility of meeting all the counseling and guidance needs of students (Pilkington and Jarmin, 1977; Trump, 1977). Some students will need to be referred to counselors or other specialists. Second, counselors will continue their own programs and activities throughout the school day, but during TAP period they will probably pay particular attention to the following roles.

1. Counselors will help co-lead some guidance units and sessions with teachers. Some teachers will invite counselors to work with them on occasion, including teachers who are very successful. Then, at other times, counselors will work with teachers who are having trouble managing their groups. Counselors might model some group guidance skills or serve as a consultant to these teachers.

2. Counselors will develop some special guidance units based on particular needs of a student group or student population. For example, in one school, older students were bullying younger students. The counselors prepared a four-session guidance unit which they presented to some homebase groups. In another school, some racial slurs increased the potential for student violence and the issue was addressed through a special guidance unit. In a sense, these counselors developed a "road show" which they took to the TAP groups.

3. Counselors will meet with small groups of students for small group counseling during some of the TAP periods. Because of these TAP time meetings, counselors disrupt academic classes less during a school day to meet with students and have fewer scheduling problems.

4. Counselors will pull students who are disruptive or who are having trouble adjusting from their homebase groups during TAP time and target them for special attention. These students might receive some small or large group guidance and counseling experiences which focus on their problems. In another situation, some students might need to obtain and discuss information or guidance materials which particularly affect them more than other students. For example, financial aid or college applications might be topics for groups who meet with counselors during TAP time, especially on those days when the teacher-advisor is not presenting a guidance activity.

5. Counselors will meet with some students for individual counseling. However, individual counseling is usually reserved for other times during the day, since it is easier to draw individuals than groups of students from academic classes. Therefore, the counselor's work emphasis during TAP is on small and large groups, either with a teacher-advisor group or with a counseling group organized from several teacher-advisor groups.

6. Counselors will serve as consultants and resources to teachers. If a full or part-time TAP coordinator is not employed in a school, it is common for a school counselor to assume leadership and coordinate TAP. This is usually done with a teacher as a co-leader or through a committee. However, it is the flexible time of counselors and the fact that TAP is the central part of developmental guidance that tends to involve school counselors as leaders and coordinators.

7. Counselors will avoid any routine duties during TAP time which take them away from working with teachers or students. Teachers want counselors to be a part of TAP and to be both available and visible during that time. It is important that counselors be accountable for their time during TAP. The counselor's role and job functions are given attention in Chapter 4 and it will be easy to see how these roles and functions are related to TAP.

Building Support for TAP

Despite the apparent value of TAP, there are some middle/junior and high school teachers who are reluctant to adopt it. In general, about 20% of most secondary school faculties will quickly embrace the program. These teachers like the idea of developmental guidance and they have the skills and personality to put the program in practice without much preparation. They can make it work with a minimum of support, as they thoroughly enjoy the opportunity to form closer helping relationships with students.

There is another 20% of a school faculty, generally, who are clearly skeptical and resistant. They argue against it and see only an extra preparation for themselves. To them TAP is a waste of time. They try to discourage others, erroneously believing that guidance should be left to specialists, such as counselors and school psychologists. This disinclined group needs special assistance or inservice training, if they are ever to be supportive and become involved in building a program. Unfortunately, of this 20% probably half of them do not have the personality, skills, interests, or energy to make TAP work and they may need to be assigned other duties.

The middle 60% of the faculty can make the critical difference. If this group is for TAP, then the program will make a positive contribution in the school. If the majority of this middle group is against it, then the program will have trouble surviving. It will be sabotaged. There will be a tremendous waste of time and energy. Student needs will not be met and, being disappointed with TAP, students will "add fuel to the fire" by their criticism and lack of interest.

What makes the difference whether or not the middle 60% moves toward supporting TAP and developmental guidance? The result seems to depend upon the following:

Teachers need to understand the philosophy behind TAP and how it is related to developmental guidance. This includes an understanding of student needs and awareness of student problems. It also includes a recognition of how guidance is directly related to helping students learn more effectively and efficiently in their academic work, including helping them grow socially and personally.

One group of high school teachers, who did not support TAP, were asked how they would describe the program. Given a three-minute limitation, all struggled to talk about it. None could clearly define TAP or cite essential concepts. None of their statements were student-centered.

The time commitment for TAP needs to be adequate. Time management or the organizational scheme of TAP is a critical factor. Sometimes, TAP programs suffer because there is not enough time for advisors to meet with their advisees. For example, in one school, teachers met with their advisees for about 30 minutes once every two weeks. In another school, they met for one hour once a month. There is very little chance that valuable helping relationships between teachers and their advisees will develop in such little time. Commitment is not there. When meeting times are scheduled far apart, there is not much opportunity for continuity and consistency. TAP works best when it is scheduled every school day. This gives advisors an opportunity to know their advisees and to talk with them individually and in groups. During supervised study time, teachers can work with student folders and make plans to follow up with other teachers.

Scheduling TAP two days a week seems to be a minimum. Otherwise, there is a tendency for a teaching faculty to view TAP as an unimportant adjunct program instead of an integral one within an organized curriculum. It is difficult to feel committed to a program that is not a part of the regular weekly schedule. When it just seems to pop up on occasion, teachers tend to think less about it and to rely on whatever spontaneously happens. As one teacher said, "I just wing it and hope for the best." Without a weekly commitment, teachers are less concerned about how they can best use the TAP period with students, since that time is such a little part of their assignment. This type of situation inevitably sows seeds of discontent among teachers and students.

TAP must have a developmental guidance curriculum, with supporting materials and activities. Teachers are accustomed to having curriculum guides and they often depend on learning activities that stimulate student thinking and participation. Therefore, teachers like to have organized guidance handbooks which contain various activities that they might use in TAP.

Some schools have developed comprehensive sets of materials, including guidance units and suggestions when they might best be used during TAP. Teacher-advisors have the liberty of discarding any suggested activity that seems unsuited for them or their group, perhaps modifying an activity or substituting another one.

However, the evaluation of the unit should remain consistent across all TAP groups. Thus, the guidance objectives are more important than any activity and it is an advisor's professional judgment which determines how best to meet those objectives.

Teachers need preparation in guidance and interpersonal skills. Since most teachers have not had a course in guidance, many do not understand how a guidance program is developed to meet student needs and how some guidance interventions can be used to help students. Some teachers have limited interpersonal skills and many have not had much preparation in how to manage groups. More specifically, far too many teachers rely on one group arrangement—all students facing the front of the room—and need more training in how to get students working cooperatively in small groups.

Most teachers talk too much at students. Only a few have learned to facilitate class discussion with group discussion skills. They need help in knowing more about group dynamics and how to facilitate a group (e.g. Myrick, Highland, and Highland, 1986). Also, many of them need assistance in learning how to help a student think about a personal problem and to take some steps in solving that problem. This does not mean that the advisor is a problem-solver. Rather, the advisor helps students explore situations, alternatives and consequences, and possible plans of action.

The basic facilitator skills discussed in Chapter 4 of this book are considered essential for teachers as advisors. With the use of the facilitative model, teachers and students find TAP more productive and rewarding.

TAP needs administrative support. Most administrators try to accommodate their teachers and to make teaching an enjoyable endeavor. They are fully aware of how difficult teaching can be and how some students—and teachers as well—can dampen the spirit of a school. Some students and teachers make everyone's work more difficult and the school environment unappealing.

Administrators set the tone of a school. Their personal style and commitment is the glue that holds the program together. If they are supportive, then teachers will try harder. If they are indifferent, then teachers find other places to invest their time and energy. Therefore, they must not only speak favorably about TAP, but they must take time to understand how TAP works and to find ways to show their support.

Administrators can increase their visibility in the schools by visiting TAP groups and talking with students when discipline is not an issue. They can talk with TAP coordinators about guidance units and, on occasion, they might lead or co-lead a discussion in one of the TAP homerooms.

TAP needs to be evaluated. In order for TAP to be an accountable program, it must be monitored and evaluated. Evaluations provide data upon which to make decisions and to decide what new directions, if any, might be taken. Student and teacher evaluations of TAP are essential if it is to develop progressively into an effective program.

Very few schools are able to immediately implement TAP, especially the way they visualize how it could be. It takes time to develop an excellent program. There are adjustments to be made, new things to be added and others deleted. Priorities must be set and people must learn to work together. With feedback from students and teachers, it is possible to keep TAP moving in a desired direction.

Teachers: Key to Developmental Guidance

There are not enough school counselors and other specialists to implement a developmental program, if they have the sole responsibility for guidance. Only with teacher involvement and commitment, at all grade levels, is developmental guidance possible.

Teachers are the heart of a school's guidance program. They work directly with students in their classes and student-teacher relationships influence the school atmosphere. They work as student-advisors and they collaborate with other specialists to assist students.

Counselors support teachers in their work. They work for and with teachers. Counselors also need teacher assistance if they are to fully understand a student's world. Teacher cooperation is needed if counselors are to have access to students for counseling interventions. In order for counselors to excel in their work, school faculties must understand the nature of a counselor's job and how counselor job functions are related to the work of teachers and other specialists.

Teachers, when working as student advisors, can draw upon the skills and resources of guidance specialists such as school counselors. Sometimes counselors may help lead a guidance unit or a session with a teacher-advisor. On other occasions, counselors may develop a guidance unit and lead a homebase group through a unit or through some sessions. Teacher-advisors, recognizing their own limits in time and skill, can identify students who need attention from a counselor or other specialist.

Working together, counselors and teachers can define their roles in guidance and differentiate their responsibilities. In a comprehensive developmental guidance and counseling program, they work together as a team.

Counselor-Teacher Relationships

Some counselors have been criticized by teachers who are unsupportive and uncooperative. These teachers believe that counselors have very little impact on student behavior. Some of these teachers prefer that counselors not work with students from their classes. They dislike sending students to the guidance office and sometimes refuse to do so. They argue that counselors do not help and missing class time only penalizes students by putting them farther behind in classwork.

There are also some teachers who are suspicious of counselors and they do not want counselors observing students in their classes. These teachers worry that their teaching methods are being evaluated. Some even think that counselors are the "eyes and ears" of the administration and unfavorable comments are passed to building principals.

Still other teachers believe that counselors always align themselves with students at the expense of teachers. One teacher said, "Counselors are simply crying towels for students. They believe everything that the kids tell them, when half of it is not true. They sit in judgment of teachers and always take the kid's side. They never listen to what we teachers have to say."

Another teacher complained, "Kids go to the counselors and talk about us. That does not do any good. If a kid has a problem with me, he should talk to me first. Then, if that does not work out, he could go to a counselor. The kids should be sent back to talk with their teachers instead of gossiping about them with counselors."

Obviously, there is not much trust or understanding between these teachers and school counselors. Students probably would not go to counselors and complain about teachers if they thought that they could go to the teachers. Many students are intimidated by teachers who become defensive when their classroom procedures are challenged. Students respond with, "Teachers never listen to us, so why talk with them."

The counselor is caught in the middle. There is apparently a fine line between supporting teachers and listening nonjudgmentally to students. When teachers, however, know more about how counselors work with students who complain about teachers, they have less to fear and they are more supportive.

The real challenge is for counselors and teachers to find ways to communicate what they believe about developmental guidance and to discover how they can work together to make their jobs easier. As counselors and teachers talk about their differences and mutual interests, they can arrive at some common agreements about guidance and the role that each plays in the total guidance program.

For too many years, counselors—often out of a misunderstanding about confidentiality and the privacy of the counseling relationship—failed to work closely with teachers. Counselors frequently appeared to be distant and uncommunicative about students. They worked in mysterious ways, cloaked in the privacy of their offices where they became the confidantes of students. They were the child-advocates and in charge of the affective domain, or so some said. Teachers took note that such claims seemed to exclude them. They also resented the implied accusation that teachers were insensitive, unfeeling, and too busy to help students. In too many cases, counselors and teachers developed uncooperative relationships.

Counselor-teacher teamwork is critical in a developmental guidance program. An open and supportive relationship makes the work of teachers and counselors easier and faster. There is a mutual respect that goes beyond the roles that each has agreed upon. The roles are complementary and there is a team spirit. One is not superior to the other, nor does one assume to be the most important helper or most skilled professional. Helping students through guidance is a shared experience.

School Guidance Committees

One practical way that counselors and teachers can improve their working relationships and build a team framework is through a school guidance committee. This committee is usually co-chaired by a counselor and a teacher, and it has representatives from the teaching faculty and support services.

Every school needs a guidance committee. The committee helps identify student needs and recommends different kinds of guidance programs and activities. It serves as a funnel through which information can be processed by both counselors and teachers. It searches for ways that all school personnel can work together better.

There are certain procedures and general practices that are part of operations in a school. Sometimes it is necessary to elicit support from faculty before some guidance and counseling procedures can be initiated. The guidance committee of a school is an excellent place to start.

School guidance committees listen to school counselors' ideas and the different counseling interventions they have in mind. If an intervention involves teachers, then the teachers on the committees can be polled for their opinions. They try to anticipate what other teachers might think or how they might react. Committees can be an initial sounding board for new ideas and programs that are being considered.

A guidance committee, regardless of school level, might: 1) review guidance materials and activities; 2) recommend guidance strategies and interventions; 3) identify students who need special assistance; 4) examine student data to identify target populations that need guidance and counseling services; 5) help evaluate the guidance program; 6) discuss ideas before they are presented to the total faculty; and 7) serve as a resource group to the counselors.

Almost every elementary school counselor has formed a guidance committee, composed of the counselor and about four or five teachers. Ironically, such a committee is found much less in the secondary schools where there are more communication problems because of larger faculties.

Although counselors are often perceived as those who are responsible for school guidance, in reality the guidance program is a joint effort by administrators, teachers, counselors, and other support personnel. The counselor does not work alone. But, there are specific counselor functions and responsibilities which can influence the direction of a guidance program. The management of these functions and responsibilities ultimately determines a counselor's image and effectiveness.

Advantages, Limitations, and Conclusion

Advantages of Teachers as Advisors

1. High counselor-student ratios make it impossible for school counselors to know all students personally. TAP is based on one teacher per 20 students, a ratio that enables all students to personally know an adult in the school who cares about them and who can assist them with some guidance.

2. TAP is the only way that a comprehensive guidance and counseling program can be fully implemented in a school because it involves all school personnel.

3. TAP helps create positive learning environments in a school.

4. Differentiated staffing makes the most use of school personnel.

5. More students receive more guidance services because there is a guidance curriculum which is presented in a regularly scheduled time period.

Limitations of Teachers as Advisors

1. Not all teachers can work effectively as teacher-advisors to students. Some need more preparation and others lack interest or commitment.

2. The success of TAP depends upon administrator and teacher knowledge and support. Currently, TAP is misunderstood in many places and is dismissed as a passing fad, an old homeroom program, or an infringement on academic time.

Conclusion

A school's learning climate can be positively affected when teachers, counselors, administrators, and students work together to personalize education. All students have developmental guidance needs that require attention if they are to be effective and efficient learners. When adult to student ratios in a school are low enough, each student feels there is an adult in school who cares and who can be of assistance. TAP puts teachers in an advisory role with a limited number of students. As advisors, they provide their advisees with guidance units and services. When TAP is given a scheduled time within a school week and teachers are given the responsibility of delivering guidance units to students in TAP meetings, then developmental guidance becomes a reality for all students.

Chapter 4

The Counselor: A Developmental Guidance Specialist

School counselors are developmental guidance specialists who assist students with their educational, personal, and social development. Counselors understand the developmental nature of people and how they progress toward educational and career goals. Counselors are human behavior and relationship specialists who provide counseling and guidance services to both students and adults.

In 1984, the American Personnel and Guidance Association (APGA) changed its name to the American Association for Counseling and Development (AACD). This historic event was a sign of changing times, when counseling and personal development were recognized as the major thrusts of the organization.

The American School Counselor Association (ASCA), a division of AACD for school counselors, was founded in 1953. In 1979, the ASCA Governing Board attempted to define developmental guidance:

> "Developmental guidance is that component of all guidance efforts which fosters planned interventions within educational and other human services programs at all points in the human life cycle to vigorously stimulate and actively facilitate the total development of individuals in all areas, i.e. personal, social, emotional, career, moral-ethical, cognitive, and aesthetic; and to promote the integration of the several components into an individual's life style."

Yet, the statement does not mention counselors by name or give any hints about what they will do in their jobs. What does a counselor do? How does a counselor function in a developmental guidance and counseling program?

During the formative years of the school counseling profession, there were very few guidelines regarding how counselors might spend their time on the job (Boy, 1962 and 1972; Kehas, 1980). Even today, school counselors appear to be many things to many people, depending upon the schools in which they are employed and how they usually spend their time. School counselors have been viewed as administrative assistants, school psychologists, social workers, mental health personnel, educational placement officers, academic advisors, and friendly disciplinarians—or any combination of these roles.

Now, during these challenging years in the school counseling profession, counselors are defining or re-defining their roles and functions to obtain a clear professional identity (e.g. Bonnebrake and Borgers, 1984). If school counseling is to survive as a profession, counselors must be able to describe their unique roles, specify their job functions, and show how their work is related to helping students learn better. School counselors of the future will need a sharper role definition and they will need some new theories and strategies.

Counseling Theories Revisited

Counseling theories help us think about the counseling process. They provide us a systematic way of observing common phenomena and they give us a working framework. We use theories in counseling to describe behaviors, illuminate relationships, and develop interventions. They also provide us a common language so that we can share ideas and communicate more about our observations and methodology.

It has become customary to refer to counseling theories as counseling models, maybe because people are eager to see practical applications of theoretical constructs. Most of us want a comfortable structure, or a set of guidelines, from which to work.

Good theories are like good maps. They tell us what to look for, what to expect, and where we might go. They are explicit and precise, avoiding poetic statements that are inspiring but which fail to give us direction. Good theories are also comprehensive, applicable in many situations, and yet, specific enough to be feasible in a particular situation.

The school counselor's basic role as a helper is found in several counseling theories, which are studied by almost every graduate student in counselor education. These theories, conceptualized by some prominent psychotherapists and educators, are an outgrowth of attempts to assist people with their personal problems.

Some classic theories seem to have stood the test of time. Since they are usually presented in most counseling theory courses, they will not be discussed in detail here. Instead, a few are reviewed briefly to emphasize their importance to developmental guidance and counseling. To keep things simple, there are four theories of counseling which you will find particularly helpful. Let's look at those first.

Client-centered Counseling

Client-centered therapy and counseling are almost synonymous. If you have studied counseling theories, then you knew this theory would be listed here. Carl Rogers' book, *Client-centered Therapy* (1951), introduced an important term and focus to counselors and therapists. It started a wave of humanistically oriented therapists, the effects of which have been felt in counseling, therapy, and other areas such as teaching, social services, pastoral training, and human relations skills programs (Prout and Brown, 1983).

Client-centered therapy or the person-centered approach emphasizes that "fully functioning" individuals are open to experiences in life and trust themselves to do those things that "feel right." Generally, client-centered counseling is based on the following premises:

1. A human being functions as a total organism and any change to one part may produce changes in other parts (e.g. physical, psychological, behavioral).

2. Individuals have their own perceptual fields, which is their reality. People interact with their environments from their perceptual fields and this leads to the development of a person's self-concept.

3. The self-concept is a learned sense of self. It is dependent upon the positive regard and respect that one has experienced from outside the self, usually from significant others who impose or create personal relationships.

4. Any experience that is not consistent with the self-concept is perceived as a threat, although one can learn to be flexible and accepting of the environmental realities that come with daily living.

5. Conflicts arise when self-concepts and external events are incongruous. Tension increases and reactions to the realities of the environment may be for better or for worse, depending upon one's ability to accept, to cope, to adjust, and to integrate.

These five principles are the heart of the theory. It is assumed that people have the capacity to discover for themselves the necessary resources for their growth. If certain helping conditions are present in a client's life, then the person will become more "self-actualizing" and naturally move toward more positive and self-enhancing behaviors.

Therefore, counselors do whatever they can to provide counselees with a genuine caring experience that fosters feelings of personal respect, regard, warmth, understanding, and self-worth. According to client-centered theory, a genuine caring relationship is more important than techniques.

When Virginia Axline wrote her famous book, *Play Therapy* (1947), it was based on client-centered therapy. Axline's approach is still considered relevant today because the premises cannot be improved upon. She suggested that counselors enter the child's world by following the lead of the child. She created the helping conditions and set the stage for a child to change and grow in a positive direction. It is hypothesized that the absence of the helping conditions created the need for therapy in the first place. Children, like adults, have the capacity to take responsibility for resolving conflicts in their lives and will grow positively if given the opportunity.

In years past, client-centered therapy was the first and only counseling theory taught to school counselors while they were in training. It is considered a simple and practical model founded on a democratic and humanistic philosophy about life (e.g. Boy and Pine, 1963). It does not require a knowledge of complex psychological principles or special diagnostic skills. It requires very few, if any, techniques. It is deceptively simple because it appears that the clients, or students, do all the work, as the counselors follow their leads. The primary focus is on what a person is experiencing, assuming self-disclosing talk produces the necessary insight for change.

The theory can easily be applied to developmental guidance. It emphasizes that the counselor be a listener and encourage the client to talk. Therefore, with limited time for preparation, the first counselors in the schools, especially after Sputnik, may have left graduate school thinking that this was the only theory of counseling.

Since the early years of school counseling and Carl Roger's early work, there have been many extensions of this classic counseling theory. There are many practitioners and other theorists who have embraced most of Rogers' ideas, although advocating specific skills to help create therapeutic relationships (e.g. Carkhuff, 1969; Gazda, 1977; Gordon, 1970 and 1974; Hart and Tomlinson, 1970; Truax and Carkhuff, 1967).

Client-centered or person-centered counselors are concerned about the atmosphere in which counseling happens. They want to help students feel cared about and safe and to experience empathy, respect, and genuineness from the counselor. Such an approach requires patience and relies on students to assume responsibility for their own direction.

Rational Emotive Therapy

Albert Ellis (e.g. 1973) is given credit for devising an ABC model for behavior: A is the activating event; B is the belief system; and C is the emotional consequence. According to Ellis, most people have problems because their belief systems have gone astray. It is assumed that we talk to ourselves—thinking in words, phrases, and sentences—and this talk determines how we behave. People who become dysfunctioning or emotionally disturbed are really telling themselves a chain of false statements which are irrational and personally destructive.

Rational Emotive Therapy (R.E.T.) recognizes there are many illogical ideas which permeate our lives that we have learned through our parents, teachers, peers, and society generally. Our life experiences influence our self-talk, which can be for better or for worse. If it is the source of our problems, then self-talk needs to be re-evaluated, sometimes eliminated, and positive self-talk put its place.

This theory, and some variations (e.g. Roush, 1984), fits easily into a developmental guidance and counseling program. As in the client-centered approach, you first establish a close working relationship by attending to student problems. You are alert to illogical ideas and confront them. As ideas are challenged, resistance is anticipated and worked through as part of the counseling process.

In contrast to the client-centered model, after forming a therapeutic alliance, the counselor plays a more active role in analysis (using the ABC method) and teaching. R.E.T. theorists believe that the expression of feelings and a nurturing relationship is not enough to get to the root of irrational thinking and client problems.

Common irrational thoughts about self and behavior can be addressed through developmental guidance units, maybe before such thoughts become ingrained in a students' self-perceptions. For instance, some typical irrational beliefs that can be confronted as part of developmental guidance or as part of a problem-solving situation are:

1. "I must be loved by everyone to be happy." Such a belief means that you would have to be self-sacrificing most of the time to please everyone and you cannot be loved and approved by everyone because there are so many people in your life who have their own needs and interests.

2. "I must be perfect and beyond reproach." It is impossible to be totally competent in everything and not experience failures. To be unwilling to receive criticism dooms you to safeguarding yourself until you do not enjoy the spirit of living.

3. "People who make mistakes are worthless and should be punished." Everyone makes mistakes and to err is human. Punishment is not very effective when it comes to changing behavior.

4. "Others are responsible for making me unhappy, like my parents, teachers and classmates." Unless you are physically abused or deprived, happiness is a function of perceptions not people or events, and perceptions can be controlled.

5. "You cannot overcome your past." The past cannot be denied. It is real and cannot be changed. But, the past does not have to determine future needs, interests, attitudes, or behaviors. You can change present and future behavior independent of what has happened in the past.

6. "There is always a correct and best answer to every problem." Maybe this could be so, but it is a frustrating and, often times, futile activity to search for the perfect solution to

things. Believing there is only one best answer or approach to something results in discouragement and dissatisfaction with life.

Teachers and counselors might use these and other illogical beliefs as topics in a guidance unit, looking for fun and creative ways to present them. Some guidance activities can facilitate student thinking about self-talk and how it is related to learning in school and getting along with others. Common techniques are confrontation, reframing ideas, role playing, humor, homework assignments, guided imagery, and practice activities.

R.E.T. operates on the premise that emotions and behaviors are learned reactions. Because it involves cognitive structuring and restructuring, this theory will appeal to many teachers and counselors who want to teach students how to take more responsibility for their thoughts and actions.

Behavioral Counseling

Until the 1960s, client-centered and cognitive approaches dominated the counseling profession. Then, a revolution in counseling happened (Krumboltz, 1966) as learning theorists began to emphasize how their concepts could be applied through behavioral counseling.

The most recognized contributor was B.F. Skinner, who described operant conditioning as a mode of learning. B.F. Skinner had famous debates with Carl Rogers about counseling and therapy. In addition, Joseph Wolpe and Arnold Lazarus outlined behavioral procedures that could be used to relax and desensitize anxiety-producing situations. Albert Bandura posed a theory of social learning based on modeling, imitation, and reinforcement principles.

However, it was the work of John Krumboltz and Carl Thoresen (1969 and 1976) that inspired school counselors to take a closer look at behavioral counseling, with its focus on modifying behavior instead of such internal variables as self-concept or self-esteem.

Others, such as Bandura (1969), Blackham and Silverman (1971), and Krasner and Ullman (1965), also showed how behavioral counseling could be used. They advocated such methods as positive and negative reinforcement, modeling, contracting, behavioral rehearsal, role playing, and systematic desensitization.

Generally, the procedures of behavioral counseling evolve around precise steps, including:

1. Identify the problem in terms of behavior that can be observed and recorded;

2. Assess the problem by collecting baseline data and ascertaining any relevant developmental history;

3. Specify the goals, usually selecting one behavior at a time with which to work and remembering that little steps (successive approximations) lead to progress;

4. Select and apply the methods to be used, which are determined by whatever ethical means seem feasible to produce a change in behavior; and

5. Assess and evaluate the counselee's progress, making appropriate methodological changes until the desired goal is obtained.

Behaviorists such as Krumboltz and Krumboltz (1972) recognized the value of the facilitative conditions and relationships. But, they concluded that, although necessary, helping relationships are not sufficient in and of themselves, as client-centered therapists advocated. Rather, after a working relationship is established, behavioral techniques are needed.

One study, which involved personal interviews with more than 100 school counselors from elementary to high school, showed that counselors tended to favor behavioral counseling approaches. They still valued client-centered theory, but found its application in the schools to be too time consuming, slow, and impractical.

The pressure to show immediate results and to be more action-oriented has encouraged many counselors to use such techniques as behavioral contracts, role reversal, and simple positive reinforcement procedures. In addition, behavioral counseling approaches are easily accountable through the collection of baseline data and assessment of behavior later.

Reality Therapy

William Glasser (e.g. 1965 and 1969) used the term "Reality Therapy" to describe his approach to counseling and therapy. His experiences with institutionalized adolescents led him to conclude that the driving force for all behavior is the intrinsic goal of having a different, distinct, and unique identity. However, it is the acceptance of responsibility for uniqueness that is the central theme of his counseling approach.

All students want to believe that they are unique individuals and there is nobody like them. They all seek an identity. If they develop a "failure identity," then they believe that they have little chance of succeeding at anything. They claim that they are no good, worthless, and undeserving of anything positive. Consequently, they often have a distressing or negative attitude about school and life. They become critical of themselves and others, adopting irrational thought patterns in defense of themselves. They do not want to assume responsibility for themselves and frequently become apathetic, indifferent, uninvolved, and show little concern for themselves and others.

If students develop a "success identity," then they feel that they are good and can accomplish things in life. They are sensitive to others and they can assert themselves, assuming leadership when it is appropriate. Their positive attitudes are valued by others and they eagerly anticipate living their lives.

The key to putting this theory into practice is first building a positive relationship and then emphasizing that each person assumes responsibility for one's own behavior. While attention is given to behavior change, individuals are encouraged to understand themselves and others, to set goals, and to make responsible decisions.

Also, self-awareness is related to current situations or present behavior instead of plodding through the past or trying to guess what the future will be like. Therefore, irresponsible behavior is confronted. Counselees are encouraged to pinpoint what they will do and to make a commitment to action. Specific plans are formulated and then they implement their plans, with no excuses accepted or punishment administered. The counselor consistently and willfully conveys a feeling of hopefulness and persistence.

Teachers and counselors in the schools like Reality Therapy because of its many classroom and educational applications. Glasser (1969), for example, advocated "classroom meetings" where students and teachers can know one another better and explore their mutual interests and goals.

Middle and high school teachers working in TAP, and elementary school teachers in their regular classrooms, might have "open meetings" in which thought-provoking questions are asked and students explore issues that are relevant to their lives. Or, they could have an "educational-diagnostic meeting" where attention is given to evaluating student strengths and weaknesses, teaching techniques and concerns, and the value of ideas and information presented in the curriculum. "Social-problem-solving meetings" are a third type of classroom meeting where individual or group problems are discussed. Problem-solving is the priority in these meetings as students talk about issues and problems that play an important part in their lives.

Reality Therapy is a common sense theory for helping people. It fits into a developmental approach and it is specific about problem-solving when crises occur. It is a rational and cognitive approach based on "here and now," personalizing behavior, and accepting responsibility for one's self.

The facilitative model described in the next chapter often has been linked to Reality Therapy, perhaps more than other theories. Counselors like the combination of the facilitative responses with the general theoretical constructs and counseling principles of Glasser's model. It embraces a straight forward humanistic behavioral approach that is action-oriented and suited for the schools.

Other Theories

A few other theories have particular relevance for guidance and counseling in the schools. Their application is often more limited, but they can help the counselor to conceptualize behavior and develop some counseling strategies.

Psychoanalytic theory, for instance, has been around since Sigmund Freud explained his classic approach to psychoanalysis. It is a fascinating theory which suggests that behavior is the product of mental forces and impulses which have their origin in childhood. Nothing happens by accident and all behaviors are goal-oriented, which can be explained. However, we do not always have access to their antecedents because they are buried in the unconscious part of our personality.

Psychoanalytic or psychodynamic theories are important to understand because they are often used to describe deviant behavior. The *Diagnostic Statistical Manual III* features a new emphasis upon behaviors, but it is still replete with psychoanalytic language. It is the reference book used in most mental health centers and by private clinicians.

Transactional Analysis (TA) is an offspring of psychoanalytic theory (Berne, 1961; Harris, 1969). It describes personality structure in popular language (The Child, The Adult, and The Parent) and has received attention by school teachers and counselors, especially when they want to help students understand human behavior.

Adlerian Psychology also provides an interesting framework in which to conceptualize behavior. The behavior of students, for example, is assumed to be purposeful and goal-directed. By understanding a student's goal, one can understand the meaning of the student's behavior. Therefore, Adlerians focus on goal orientation within a social context, emphasizing that people must see themselves as unique individuals who have the capacity to make decisions and choices. Consequently, students are assisted to gain insight into behavior and alternatives for solving problems.

Adlerian Psychology has found a home in many schools because the concepts are so closely related to parenting and teaching young children and adolescents. In addition, there are several structured programs which incorporate the theory which are practical for use in school guidance and counseling programs.

For example, Don Dinkmeyer's *Developing Understanding of Self and Others (DUSO)* kit is a widely accepted guidance program in the elementary schools. Published in 1970 and revised in 1982, *DUSO* helps children learn about themselves and others through group activities, songs, role playing, and classroom discussions. It is a structured program that has set an example for the development of guidance units and sessions at all grade levels. In addition, *Systematic Training for Effective Parenting (STEP)* and *Systematic Training for Effective Teaching (STET)* provide training for parents and teachers in basic Adlerian principles (Dinkmeyer, McKay, and Dinkmeyer, 1980; Dinkmeyer and McKay, 1976).

Gestalt theory (e.g. Perls, 1969) has appealed to many school counselors because it is based on perceptual psychology and the assumption that people respond according to various levels of awareness. Awareness can shift, giving some things more importance than others and this depends upon personal needs and choices. The active, confrontive, and creative techniques of "here and now" Gestalt counseling are intriguing because they focus on personal congruence, non-verbal behavior, and the use of imagery to cause change. Techniques such as talking to an empty chair or drawing attention to incongruous statements and behaviors have been incorporated into many counselors' styles of helping.

Lazarus (1971) coined the term "multimodal" to describe a broad view of looking at behavior and counseling interventions. Keat (1974) showed how the basic modes of such a theory (behavior, affect, sensation, imagery, cognition, interpersonal relationships, drugs-diet—the BASIC ID) could be used to work with parents and children. He added education and learning modes (BASIC IDEAL) to emphasize the role of the school learning environment. These mulitmodal approaches are attempts to draw upon several resources.

A Personal Theory

Most counselors and therapists look to the theories described above, and others, for general leads. Some use combinations of theories and strategies (e.g. Hutchins, 1979). They like to have something with which to identify, or "to hang their hats on." A theory can be comforting, as it provides some understanding and direction.

However, few people seem to be comfortable with just one theory. They might experiment with the use of a theory for an extended time, but soon they begin drawing upon other theories and related techniques. Drawing upon ideas and strategies from different theorists has led to the term "eclectic."

There is no eclectic theory, per se. But, counselors do pick and choose from things that seem to work for them and others. Selecting and using various techniques can be very much like moving down a cafeteria line. There are many choices and those who make wise choices undoubtedly have a basic theory about nutrition and balanced diets. Those who do not hold to such a theory may select only entrees, or only liquids, or only desserts. Working without a theory is interesting, but it can be risky.

In addition, it seems that developing a "personal theory" is also appealing to many counselors. When pressed to identify a theory of counseling, most say, "My own, which I have developed from my experiences." When pressed to continue, they began to draw upon basic theories, such as the ones discussed above.

The Need for New Theories and Strategies

The premises of classic theories of counseling and therapy are stable enough that they will be used for many years to come. However, knowledge of human behavior increases every day and this new knowledge will inevitably influence our thinking about teaching, counseling, and therapy. For example, the mystery of the brain and how it functions is still being unravelled. Perhaps future neuropsychologists will develop theoretical models which incorporate more biological data to assist us in gaining new insights into human behavior.

Many of the classic theories have proven to be valuable starting points. Yet, many school counselors have been frustrated when they tried to adapt them to a school setting. There is a need for some new counseling theories, ones that are school based. They would, most likely, be short-term approaches which focus on the particular needs and interests of students.

Likewise, psycholinguistics may provide us some new insights regarding how language development affects our thinking and behaving. We know that certain cultural experiences predispose us to perceive experiences in different ways. With the help of sophisticated computers, it may be possible eventually to diagnose language and thought patterns and learning styles, which influence behavior.

We also need new counseling theories that are related to special populations. Think for a moment how students are different in age, sex, and ability. Yet, it is assumed that what works for one group of students will work for all students. In fact, students come from different cultural backgrounds, hold different religious beliefs, are influenced by different family experiences, grow up in different economic and social environments, have different intellectual levels and abilities, and have progressed through some common developmental stages at a different pace and with different success.

Some students have the verbal skill and personal inclination to respond to some of the more intellectual approaches to counseling, such as cognitive restructuring or self-insights. They may have the verbal capacity to work with counselors in traditional ways. Other students who are less verbal need a more concrete and operational form of assistance, one in which they learn by doing instead of talking. Some students have learning disabilities that cannot be ignored. Still other students need to be motivated and to identify with the positive aspects in their schools. Special school populations may need to be singled out for counseling theories and techniques which are practical for them.

There is also a need for theories and strategies that focus on "contextual counseling." Some new theories in family counseling, in which a "systems approach" is applied, might lead us to discover how behavior can be changed and personal growth can be fostered within other family-type systems, such as those in the schools.

Time is precious. Time for counseling students is often difficult to obtain and it can be wasted if not managed carefully. There is a need to develop "brief counseling" approaches which can be used in schools, where time is limited and the demand for services is high. The basic philosophy of a theory may remain the same. But, goals may have to be limited and techniques may have to be condensed, intensified, reorganized, and presented within a time limit.

School counselors need a comprehensive theory. The theory needs to be practical and simple enough for many people to understand and to apply. It was Stefflre (1965) who said:

> "We make the best of theories... by remembering that they will not long remain useful. Since they are bound by space and time and the present level of our knowledge, the best theories will not long serve. If we should accept this limitation, we should teach our students not only presently held theories but ways of building new ones" (p.9).

All theories, traditional and personal, play a valuable role in counseling and guidance. They help us conceptualize our goals, develop interventions, and influence our style of working. Which established theories will you draw upon? What is your own personal theory?

The Professional Counselor

Part of being professional means being a member of the state and national counselor associations. Perhaps the primary organization is the American School Counselor Association (ASCA) which is a division of the American Association for Counseling and Development (AACD). In 1986, AACD had approximately 50,000 members, all of whom belonged to one or more of the following divisions:

American College Personnel Association
American School Counselor Association
Association for Specialists in Group Work
Association for Counselor Education and Supervision
National Career Development Association
American Rehabilitation Counseling Association

National Employment Counselors Association
American Mental Health Counselor Association
National Association for Ethnic Minority Concerns
Public Offender Counselor Association
Military Educators and Counselors Association
Association for Multicultural Counseling and Development
Association for Measurement and Evaluation in Counseling
and Development
Association for Humanistic Education and Development

A school counselor may belong to more than one division. In addition, these same divisions are usually found at state and local levels, each with a special interest and purpose (Garfield, 1985). Some divisions and regional affiliations, depending upon counselor membership, are more active and influential than others.

Members of AACD and ASCA receive newsletters and journals (AACD's *Guide Post, ASCA Newsletter,* AACD's *Journal of Counseling and Development* and ASCA's *School Counselor* and *Elementary School Guidance and Counseling* journals). They also have the option for other services and benefits, including insurance, travel, and some promotional programs. They can attend state and national conferences sponsored by the association and its divisions. More information can be obtained by writing the AACD Membership Division (5999 Stevenson Avenue, Alexandria, VA 22304).

Professional Preparation

Helping school counselors define their profession and gain respectable recognition is a continuing challenge. Professionalism assures the public that certain standards are being fulfilled. Counselors at all school levels need to receive the best kind of professional preparation.

The American Association for Counseling and Development (AACD) currently recognizes three professional credentials: (1) accreditation; (2) certification; and (3) licensure. What is counselor certification? Should school counselors be licensed? Should they be licensed at a national level? How is licensure related to the current practices of state certification? Where are the accredited counselor education programs?

In 1967, the American School Counselor Association (ASCA) issued guidelines for the preparation of secondary school counselors. In the following year, additional guidelines were adopted for elementary school counselors. By 1979, the Association for

Counselor Education and Supervision (ACES), another division of AACD, adopted standards for preparation of counselors by universities and colleges.

In 1981, the Council for Accreditation of Counseling and Related Educational Programs (CACREP) was established by the Board of Directors of AACD and charged with the evaluation of four types of counselor preparation programs: (1) school counseling; (2) student personnel services in higher education; (3) counseling in community and other agency settings (entry level); and (4) counselor education (doctoral level). As of 1986, more than 70 of the 600 counselor education programs in universities across the nation have been favorably reviewed, many others have been granted provisional approval, and several have been disapproved. CACREP is now a legally separate organization, but affiliated with AACD and its divisions, including ASCA (Wittmer and Loesch, 1986). The list of college and university programs accredited by CACREP is growing and can be obtained by writing AACD.

All of these efforts emphasize how the relatively new counseling profession is becoming solidified and how, until recently, it was possible for many school counselors to enter the schools with minimal or inadequate training. New standards require school counselors to graduate from approved programs with at least 48 semester hours. Many institutions, recognizing the complexity of preparing counselors and the difficult nature of their work, offer full two-year programs, ranging from 64 to 72 semester hours and ending in either a master's or educational specialist degree. Others, because of tradition and lack of resources, have struggled to meet the standards and their future could be in doubt, since students want to attend fully accredited programs.

As accreditation is to university programs, certification is to individuals. Certification is professional recognition granted to a school counselor when certain predetermined qualifications have been met. Most states have certification programs which grant guidance certificates, enabling a person to be employed in a public school. However, the requirements for certification among states can vary considerably. Some states require as few as 24 hours beyond a teaching certificate. Others require two years of teaching experience and then a master's degree in school counseling. Sixteen states do not require previous teaching experience but do require a master's degree with extensive field experiences.

Certification of school counselors is still done by state governmental agencies, who are responsible for affirming that an individual has the necessary credentials and related qualifications to be granted a standardized certificate for employment. These state agencies review college transcripts and rely on universities to set and measure the standards that are needed to be a school counselor.

A new counselor certification process was initiated in 1982 by AACD when it created the National Board for Credentialing of Counselors (NBCC). NBCC concentrates on generic counseling competencies applicable to all professional counselors and does not attempt to certify types of counselors or counselors for specialty areas, such as school counseling. However, NBCC appears to be building a reliable foundation which could be used by school districts and state divisions of education as a certifying agency because of its national scope and national testing procedures. As some states consider procedures for giving merit to counselors and teachers, a national standardized test is almost always part of such procedures. The NBCC examination may provide a valuable service to state or district groups who must provide evidence of competence for counselors who are to be hired or who are to receive merit. Because the NBCC also publishes a national registry, or list of counselors who are certified by the organization, it could also be used by potential employers.

Certification by NBCC does not imply that a counselor can do any particular type of counseling, but that the counselor knows about fundamental counseling activities applicable to a variety of settings. To obtain certification, a person must provide evidence of academic and experiential activities (minimum requirement is a master's degree) and successfully complete a written examination. Many school counselors have obtained this professional certification in order to be part of a national registry and to emphasize their professional potential.

Licensure, as it affects most school counselors at this time, is designed to help regulate the practice of mental health counseling outside of school hours. School counselors who want to be in private practice with paying clients may obtain licensure in some states, which enables them to open offices and to charge for their counseling services. Ethically, school counselors in private practice do not meet with students or parents in the school systems where they they are assigned or employed.

Continuing Education for Counselors

The preparation and training of school counselors reached a crisis in 1986. There were fewer students enrolled in graduate counselor educaton programs pursing school counseling, despite the increased demand for more school counselors. Currently, there are more jobs available than there are students graduating from accredited university programs in almost every state. As more retirements occur in the future, the shortage may become acute.

One alternative is for counselor education departments to recruit more students for school counseling. However, this is not easy to do, especially in those states where counselor certification is dependent upon at least two years of teaching experience. It is difficult to convince some teachers to return to a two-year graduate program at a university, giving up or substantially reducing their incomes during that period. It is more of a sacrifice when school systems do not pay counselors an extra stipend or a salary which makes it worth an individual to attend graduate school and earn a degree in counseling.

To complicate matters, within the past several years the vast majority of counselor education programs in the United States have been geared toward mental health and agency counseling. They are not as well prepared to accommodate teachers who want to pursue a counseling degree as they once were. It is not likely that they will change in the next few years without some substantial incentives, such as extra funding from national or state sources. The concept of "counselor institutes," such as the NDEA of 1958, may need to be revived in order to avoid a national crisis.

Another alternative, although a discouraging one, is to reduce the entry requirements for counselors, allowing teachers to take few counseling courses beyond their bachelor's degree to meet minimum state standards for employment. However, this is risky business. First, it could mean that many schools would employ counselors who were not knowledgeable nor skilled enough to build and implement a comprehensive developmental guidance and counseling program. Once a position is filled, it is very difficult to remove a person, even if a more qualified person is available. Second, it circumvents professional standards and accredited university programs. If this kind of alternative became a reality, a massive staff development effort would be needed in the school districts.

Some universities are attempting to offer more off-campus courses and degree programs through continuing education services. However, university programs are sometimes unresponsive to the cry for relevancy and on-site training opportunities are missed.

Professional organizations have become more responsive to counselors' needs for skill development and offer extended training workshops as part of the conference proceedings each year. Yet, most staff development programs are typically one-time meetings and there is a lack of follow-up. Staff-development training for counselors should be a continuing process.

Professional Ethics

A school counselor's conduct is governed by a set of professional ethics. Professional organizations (AACD and ASCA) have published ethical standards by which counselors function.

One of the first ethical obligations of counselors is to determine whether or not they are qualified to provide a particular service. If they do not have the training, skill, or perhaps experience, to assist a counselee, then they are obligated to refer the person to someone else. This is usually not a problem for school counselors, but on occasion a difficult case (e.g. suicide, dysfunctioning parents) may be encountered where consultation, direct assistance, or a referral is needed.

In general, precautions are taken to protect individuals from physical or psychological traumas resulting from the work of a counselor. The counseling relationship and confidential information are considered private, unless a counselee's condition or situation indicates an imminent danger either to the counselee or someone else. In this case, the counselor is obligated to take reasonable action and to inform responsible authorities. Some state laws (e.g. regarding child abuse or suicide) may dictate some professional actions. Even then, however, a counselor must inform the counselee and assume responsibility for the procedures that are followed. Ethical responsibilities respect the integrity and welfare of counselees.

If a student is involved in a therapeutic relationship with a therapist in the community, it is assumed that school guidance and counseling activities will not interfere with that process. School counseling, although focusing on personal and social issues, is related to learning in school and general development. School counselors and therapists are not obligated to confer with one another or to receive approval from whoever first started working with a counselee. School counseling is not therapy. However, with the counselee's permission, there are many times when consultation between a therapist and a school counselor would be appropriate and practical.

Counselors must also be aware of their ethical responsibilities regarding student records and parental authority. Students have rights which have been extended to them through various court rulings. There will probably be other court decisions in the future to further define and clarify the rights of students in regards to parental and school authority. If some school procedures seem questionable, it is the counselor's obligation to confront and challenge those procedures, reaching some agreement whereby the welfare and integrity of a student is protected. Respect for the rights of an individual and professional ethics set the tone for a counselor's work.

Determining the Counselor Role

Who determines the role and function of school counselors? Practically speaking, school counselors usually decide their roles and functions. This may involve some negotiation with administrators, but it is typically the counselors themselves who help others learn and make decisions about what they do.

The American School Counselor Association (ASCA) has some printed statements which help parents and administrators identify common roles and functions. These general guidelines can provide a base on which to build a developmental guidance program, to identify priorities, and to gain support for a professional role. In addition, some school boards and school administrators have adopted specific guidelines and procedures which affect counselors. District policies need to be studied and those that restrict counselors or are in conflict with professional guidelines have to confronted. Counselors must be assertive and take responsibility for clarifying ideas and bringing about changes when they are needed.

Recently, state legislators have become concerned about the roles and functions of school counselors. Legislation has been proposed in some states which outlines and dictates what counselors would do. Professional organizations have lobbied long and hard against such legislation. Most legislators were never privileged to have experienced a comprehensive developmental guidance and counseling program in the schools which they attended and many never have worked closely with school counselors, especially those who implemented the role and function as described in this book. They simply did not exist in many places. Therefore, it behooves counselors and their professional organizations to take the lead in determining their own destiny rather than one dictated by law.

A Practical Approach to the Counselor's Role

In a comprehensive developmental guidance and counseling program, a counselor's work is based on job functions or tasks. These job functions vary from one school to another and often depend upon different expectations and circumstances. As the job functions or tasks performed by the counselor become evident, it is possible to have an idea of the counselor's role. Hopefully, the role that emerges is comparable to the one advocated by professional organizations and educators.

The term "role" is an illusive one. It generally refers to the part that one plays in a given situation, such as the role assumed by a professional worker. Function, as differentiated from role, refers to the way in which the worker carries out one's part. Function gives attention to various behaviors or tasks that might be performed in the role.

Over the years, many studies have attempted to examine the counselor's role. They concentrated primarily on student, teacher, parent, and administrator perceptions, and they also compared these perceptions to one another. However, taken together, the studies seem incomplete and ambiguous because of varying and limited samples, questionnaires, and research methodologies.

Some unanswered questions are: How do role perceptions develop? Which comes first, role perceptions or job functions? How do role and function interact? What have school counselors been doing which contribute to current perceptions? Who determines the counselor's functions and role? How can a person's role perception be changed?

For many years, especially during the formative years, the counselor's role was a frequent topic of conversation and debate in the profession. There was much confusion. Books and articles were written, papers and programs were presented at conferences, and committees and commissions were appointed to study the role issues, but the counselor's role was still not fully understood.

Counselor educators, for example, argued for a role that might be compared to a counseling psychologist or a mental health counselor. The counselor, in this case, was to provide a unique relationship to students by virtue of not being aligned with authority. It was assumed that students would be more inclined to communicate openly and honestly with counselors who refrained from passing judgments and who were permissive and unconditionally accepting. Thus, the counselor was to set up interviews where students could talk about their problems and concerns. The counselor, often following client-centered counseling theory, tried to enter the student's frame of reference and provide assistance by being a good listener.

Most administrators, on the other hand, saw counselors in a different light. Many school administrators had never taken a course in guidance and were unfamiliar with counseling theories or procedures—a problem that still exists (Lampe, 1985). They needed help in managing the school, disciplining students, meeting and communicating with parents, and organizing curriculum. There were many day-to-day problems that needed attention and counselor time was flexible. Teachers were less available to help because they were assigned classes that met at regularly scheduled times. It seemed inappropriate to interrupt teachers, especially when counselors were ready and willing to assist. Although they liked the idea of counseling and having a guidance specialist in the school, most administrators saw counselors as their assistants.

Professional counselor organizations, such as ASCA and ACES, tended to align themselves with counselor educators. They took the position that counseling students was the primary responsibility of counselors. Although some unrelated guidance tasks would be a part of a counselor's job, counseling was a unique service. Avoiding specification of duties and performance standards, professional leaders often spoke in generalities when emphasizing how counselors were to assist students in decision-making, career choices, and personal development. In addition, test interpretation, career information, educational placement, and consultation with teachers and parents were frequently mentioned as counselor responsibilities.

Counselors themselves seemed unsure of their role and most mistakenly assumed that someone in the school system would know what they should do and tell them. When counselors were the "new kids on the block," nobody in education was sure what to expect from them. Since most counselors were minimally prepared, it followed that most were also skeptical about their abilities and skills in counseling. They were uncertain about how to establish a guidance program in which they functioned as specialists. Although the idea of providing counseling services to students was appealing, they had difficulty putting counseling theory in practice.

Counselors often found it easier and more expedient to advise, or even lecture, students on their behavior, instead of taking the role of a listener to help students behave in responsible ways. For many counselors, performing administrative duties seemed one way of justifying their jobs and this in turn accounted for the lack of time to engage students in counseling.

In addition, the issues of privacy and confidentiality were prominent as counselors talked about their unique role in the school. Counselors were to be "student advocates" and holders of confidential information. They increasingly secluded themselves in their offices, forming an inner chamber within the school where students could unload their secrets and reveal their problems. Such a position inevitably created the image that counseling was a hidden and mysterious process. It also placed counselors in an adversary role with many teachers who believed that counselors always sided with students.

Wrenn (1957) reported that people in the profession did not agree on the role of the counselor in a school. Ten years later, according to Bentley (1968), the situation had not changed. Now, twenty years later, the same issues are being discussed and there is still concern about the role and image of the school counselor.

Can and should the counselor's role be defined? Some suggest that it has already been defined by virtue of what counselors have been doing for the past thirty years (Van Ripper, 1971). In this case, the role is a restrictive one, especially in the secondary schools. And, if we studied the weekly schedules of counselors and compiled a list of their job functions, it is likely that we would conclude that most have become administrative assistants or clerks. The exception might be elementary school counselors, who usually have had more training and who have had more latitude in developing their role and functions.

Peters (1962) was concerned and cautioned, "If we (counselors) do not define our duties, we will be saddled with tasks and responsibilities that not only take away from our primary concerns, but actually interfere with the guidance function." And, even more, if those who are involved in the counseling profession do not take responsibility for defining the counselor's role, then others will, or the role may be eliminated all together.

If counselors know their role, then they have a reference point to help them understand the issues related to their job. They can then communicate their role to others more effectively, especially to those with whom they work. This, in turn, clarifies expectations, opens doors for creative innovations, and improves the chances that counselors will be seen as part of the team of educators in the school.

While there have been some attempts to differentiate the school counselor's role by grade level, very little seems to be gained by such an approach. It evades the fundamental professional issue: What is the job of a school counselor? In addition, the only way that a comprehensive guidance and counseling program, kindergarten through high school, can be implemented is to have some agreement on the fundamental role of a school counselor.

For many years the generic roles of a school counselor (ACES-ASCA, 1966) have been counseling, consultation, and coordination. Within these there seems to be a specialist's role related to specific kinds of job functions and interventions. The nature of student problems, guidance topics, and focuses of discussion may change from one grade level to another. However, the way in which counselors define their roles and manage their time around basic job functions and interventions will not change significantly from one grade level to another.

Generally, there are six fundamental interventions that most counselors will provide in their jobs. Because counselor time, behaviors, skills, and activities can be related specifically to these interventions, they can be used to develop a picture of the role or image of a developmental school counselor.

Six Basic Counselor Interventions

The six basic counselor interventions are shown in Figure 4.1. The interventions outline the work of a school counselor. They have been described as counselor functions, services, approaches, tasks, activities, or jobs. Sometimes they have been referred to as roles themselves. For our purposes, the term "intervention" is preferred because it describes what a counselor does or can do in a comprehensive guidance and counseling program.

Figure 4.1

Counselor Interventions

(Weekly Scheduling Plan)

Counselor Intervention	General Caseload	Weekly Time Commitment
		(Hours)
(Direct Services) INDIVIDUAL COUNSELING	4-6 "cases," including high priority or target students meeting no less than twice a week during one grading period.	2-6
SMALL GROUP COUNSELING	4-5 "groups," preferably meeting twice a week for 6-12 structured learning sessions in 3-6 weeks.	4-10
LARGE GROUP CLASSROOM GUIDANCE	2-3 "large groups," usually meeting once but sometimes twice a week.	2-3
(Indirect Services) PEER FACILITATOR PROGRAMS AND PROJECTS	Trainer/Coordinator of PF program and/or projects (class, club, etc.)	1-5
CONSULTATION	(Group) — Teacher or parent group meetings (30 minute seminars or conferences)	Variable
	(Individual) — Teachers or parents (about 30 minutes or less)	1-2
COORDINATION OF GUIDANCE SERVICES	Other guidance related duties (e.g. orientation, testing, career information, educational placement)	Variable

TOTAL = 10-26 HOURS

Each of the interventions is discussed in greater detail in other chapters of this book. However, take a brief look at them now, including some related concepts and general recommendations. In addition, consider how these interventions are associated with counselor role and image.

Individual Counseling

Individual counseling involves a personal interaction between the counselor and a student when just the two of them are working together on a problem or topic of interest. It is one-to-one. This ratio of helper to helpee tends to intensify the counseling experience and provides an opportunity to interview a student in greater depth than most other interventions.

Working with individuals was once thought to be the only way to do counseling. The private, face-to-face meeting was considered to be the best situation in which to form a close personal relationship and to solve personal problems. It was assumed that in individual counseling, counselees would "open up" and disclose more than if they were in a group.

Even if individual counseling were the most desirable intervention, there are too many students. Counselor-student ratios are high in the schools. One elementary school counselor, for example, might be assigned to a school with 700 to 1,000 children. Middle and high school counselors typically have ratios of 1 to 500 or more. In a few "ideal" cases, counselor-student ratios have been known to be as low as 1:250. If the ratio were 1:100, the task of providing individual counseling to all students would still be formidable. It is simply unrealistic and impractical to rely on individual counseling as the only counselor intervention.

Individual counseling by certified professional school counselors is becoming a luxury in most schools. It cannot be provided to everyone. Some students, more than others, require it because of the nature of their concerns or their inability to work in groups.

As a counselor, you might think of individual counseling on a caseload basis. More specifically, about six to eight students might be seen individually for a given period of time. Individual counselees, targeted for your caseload, might meet you for as many as 12 sessions in a six-week grading period, or about two times a week.

This caseload would be reflected in a weekly schedule or plan for managing your time. The estimated individual counseling session is about 30 minutes, although it could be longer or shorter, depending upon the problem and the type of counseling procedures that are being used. This also varies from one counselor to another because of counselor personality, working style, and school situations.

Individual counseling time on your weekly schedule is not the "crisis hour;" rather, it is for students with whom you are working regularly and who have scheduled appointments. These are students on whom you are concentrating and taking more time to provide assistance.

As part of your job, you would continue to have "one-time" interviews with other students. They might drop-in for a quiet chat or to explore something quickly. Sometimes a brief individual meeting is scheduled as part of a follow-up to another intervention. Some students simply want to say a friendly "hello." These one-time sessions vary in seriousness and intent, but they usually lack continuity. Each one has its own purpose and moments of closure. Follow-up may or may not be appropriate, depending upon a situation. But, one-time, drop-in, spontaneous sessions are not considered a part of a working "case load." These meetings are simply part of the business of being a counselor in a school, but they must be considered in terms of how they affect your time.

Small Group Counseling

Small group counseling involves a counselor working with two or more students simultaneously. Small group counseling in the schools most often happens with five or six students. This provides group members an opportunity to explore ideas, feelings, and behaviors as they relate to one person or to all group participants.

Those people who think that it would be ideal to see all students on an individual basis, assume more positive things can happen when a counselee receives the undivided personal attention of a counselor. This position, however, underestimates the power of group dynamics and ignores the fact that most learning happens in the context of groups (e.g. families, classrooms, and social groups).

When children reach school age, peer influence plays an important part in reinforcing and discouraging behaviors and building self-concepts. This influence increases as students become older and more socially conscious. Students want to be liked and accepted by their peers. They frequently turn to their classmates and friends for assistance before seeking an adult. They are interested in what their peers think about them.

If all students are to have an opportunity to receive counseling, then group work must be part of the counselor's job. Small group counseling, for example, makes it possible for you to see several students at one time and, eventually, more of the students assigned to you. In addition, group relationships offer a different dimension to counseling that is needed and beneficial.

Some students go to extraordinary and inappropriate measures to be recognized and accepted by their classmates. These students may be rejected or thought of as "weird." Since their behaviors are intended to receive attention, they need honest reactions from others about their attitudes and behaviors, especially from their peers. Because behavior is generally reinforced or extinguished by the reactions of others, a group of people responding to a person's feelings, ideas, and behaviors is potentially more powerful than the response of one person, especially if the group members are viewed as significant persons in one's life.

Common concerns and interests can provide a foundation for most groups. When there is a feeling of mutual support and a sense of belonging, a group identity emerges which enables group members to risk exploring ideas, feelings, and behaviors at deeper levels. Honesty and genuineness permeate small group counseling sessions. There is a realization that one is not alone and that people do care. These are powerful healing forces and they contribute to the learning process.

Rushing ahead without considering the consequences was a problem to Sarah, a ninth grade student. Parents lectured and teachers criticized, but when a group of peers gave her some personal feedback on her behavior, she listened attentively. She did not want to be perceived as someone who was irresponsible and lacked control. With a heightened sense of awareness, she set about trying to change.

Group counseling provides an opportunity for several students to be part of an interpersonal process that is directed to the four facilitative processes of self-disclosure, feedback, increased awareness and decision-making, and responsible action. If the facilitative conditions, such as trust, caring, understanding, and acceptance, are part of the group climate, then students will explore their feelings, ideas, and behaviors with the group.

Group counseling will be discussed in more detail in Chapter 7. However, a few factors need to be noted here as we consider the counselor's role in a comprehensive developmental guidance plan.

Small group counseling is time limited. Students are usually not available for more than ten or twelve meetings, and even this may not be realistic in some secondary schools where academic schedules make it difficult for counselors to have access to students. Students are usually willing and responsive, but the daily schedule in a school can dictate the way in which small group counseling is organized.

It is recommended that you meet with your small counseling groups no less than four sessions, and preferably six to eight times. It is also preferable to meet the group twice a week, although once a week is typical. The group sessions are usually completed during one school grading period. Thus, it is possible to provide a series of six to eight group sessions within three to four weeks.

On occasion, if students are accessible, you might meet with a group for ten or twelve sessions, but seldom beyond this number. If students are taken out of their academic classes, small group counseling in some schools might be limited to four sessions. Any less time makes it difficult to create a close working relationship within a group and more time can penalize students because of class absences.

Limiting the number of counseling sessions also enables you to meet with more students. Although most students would probably benefit if they met more often, it is more realistic to take whatever gains have been made and move on to another group. There are always exceptions, and you may want to meet with a group for a more extended time. Getting some group closure within ten or twelve sessions is considered practical. The group could always meet again later for some follow-up sessions.

Small group counseling is usually structured. While there will be times when group sessions are spontaneous and free-flowing, most school counselors lead groups where members participate in structured learning activities. These group activities are designed to encourage participation and to promote self-disclosure and feedback. Although similar activities may be used, each group has a special uniqueness of its own and may react differently.

Target students can be identified for participation in small groups. Some students are difficult to work with individually and may respond better to counseling in a group. Small group counseling, especially when it has a developmental focus, can make them feel more accepted and less like a problem. In addition, you can use small group counseling to build a personal working relationship with individual students, so they might later be more responsive to other counseling interventions if needed.

As part of your weekly schedule, you might meet four to six small groups of students a week, preferably twice a week for about 30 to 45 minutes each time. This means budgeting about four to ten hours a week for small group counseling sessions (See Figure 4.1). Some counselors prefer to work with more groups and are able to do so because of their personalities, interests, and stamina. Most counselors, on the other hand, find it too difficult to work with more than ten groups a week, even if small group counseling were the preferred mode of intervention and time were available.

Large Group Guidance

Meeting with individuals and small groups of students is still not enough, considering the high student-counselor ratios. There are too many students who need guidance and counseling services. Therefore, you will also want to meet with students in larger groups.

Large group guidance consists of meeting 15 or more students in a group. Many counselors consider anything above eight students to be large group work. Typically, a classroom group of about 25 to 30 students is the basis for this kind of work. However, it is also possible to meet and work with as many as 150 students or more.

Classroom guidance, for example, is a typical counselor intervention at the elementary level. A counselor may meet with an entire class and work with the classroom teacher in providing group guidance activities. These can be integrated into the daily or weekly schedules of classroom teachers.

Students are familiar with working and learning in large groups. This can be a problem if students have experienced teachers who depend primarily on lecturing or independent study and who are unfamiliar with group procedures which encourage students to interact. Most teachers, for example, seat students in files or long rows of chairs. Group participation and discussion is limited because of this seating arrangement. Even when classes have been organized for more discussion, teachers tend to talk too much and students talk with one another through the teacher.

In large group guidance, cooperative learning methods are used in which students work together in small groups, and with the total group. This helps personalize and individualize activities. It also encourages all students to participate.

Large group guidance, for the most part, has been ignored in the secondary schools. Sometimes occupational materials have been disseminated or general information about college or vocations have been presented to large groups. Yet, even in these situations, counselors have relied on meeting students individually as their customary mode of intervention.

The infrequent use of large group guidance in the secondary schools has been blamed on lack of teacher cooperation, lack of space, and the difficulty of organizing large group meetings. The problem, however, seems more related to crisis, instead of developmental, approaches. Far too many counselors are uncomfortable with large groups and unprepared to work with them.

Although large group guidance has not been a common practice in junior and senior high schools, it has been a part of most middle schools. Teacher as advisor programs (TAP) provide an organized guidance curriculum for all students, much like that in the elementary schools. Again, there are still too many teachers and counselors who are unfamiliar with how to work with students in large group guidance.

Meeting with students in large groups makes common sense. The activities that take place in the meetings must be personalized and this requires careful planning. As a counselor, you will need to give attention to the topics to be discussed, group participation, cooperative learning activities, and time available.

Currently, elementary school counselors schedule more large group guidance than do other counselors. Therefore their weekly schedules may show them working with as many as five or six classes. However, most counselors at all levels will typically schedule two to three large groups for guidance (See Figure 4.1).

Large group meetings are generally scheduled for 20 to 30 minutes in the elementary schools and 30 to 45 minutes in the secondary schools. Some counselors in high schools meet for a class period (45 to 55 minutes), because it is convenient to be scheduled that way with a teacher or within the school's daily schedule. TAP provides a regular large group meeting time.

Peer Facilitator Training and Projects

Students as helpers to other students is a valuable concept that has been in education for many years, and it has received special attention within the past decade. Many young people are now learning how to help others through peer facilitator training programs.

As we shall see later (Chapter 9), most of what peer facilitators do can be classified into four roles: 1) student assistants to counselors and teachers; 2) tutors; 3) special friends; and 4) small group leaders. Students learn how to help others and participate in supervised projects where these roles are used.

Peer facilitators can assist counselors in a guidance office with many routine tasks, and they can also be assigned as special tutors to work with students who are having academic problems, perhaps because a student is new to the school or was sick and absent. Counselors who take time to train and organize tutoring projects win support from teachers and parents.

In addition, counselors cannot see all the students in the school who need individual attention. Sometimes students prefer to talk with peers instead of adults. When peer facilitators work as special friends, they are matched with students who need to talk with someone who will listen to them. Peer facilitators are not trained to be counselors, but they can assist other students to think about their problems, concerns, or special interests and to assist them in finding help when appropriate.

Peer facilitators can work as small group leaders too. Working together, counselors and peer facilitators can make large group guidance a practical approach to meeting many of the guidance and counseling needs of students. Five peer facilitators worked with six students each in a large room where a counselor was able to supervise all six groups. The counselor began with a general presentation about coping with stress. Students were then organized into five small groups. Peer facilitators, working as small group leaders, helped group members share ideas. Instead of a few assertive students dominating a large group discussion while others listened, all 30 students actively participated.

Peer facilitators do not take the place of counselors. They help extend guidance services throughout the school by working closely with teachers and counselors in supervised projects and activities. Consequently, counselors—with peer facilitators as their helping hands—can reach more students who need guidance.

As Myrick and Erney (1979) explained,

"Very few students can learn to *counsel* other students. Counseling is a special skill that takes extensive training, study and practice. However, all students can learn to *facilitate* other students. Some will be more effective than others, especially those who have received training in communication skills and interpersonal relationships, who are participating in a *peer facilitator program*" (p.1).

Peer facilitator training programs of all kinds have developed over the years. Some have been successful despite very little planning and this is often attributed to the personalities and styles of the students and program coordinators. They have energy and enthusiasm, and they are committed. They show interest and a caring attitude which makes their programs work.

There are other programs, however, that are more consistently successful because they have developed a systematic approach to preparing students as peer facilitators and they have some well-organized projects in which the peer facilitators can participate. Students learn about facilitative conditions and helping characteristics. They develop peer facilitator interventions around them. It is this approach that has appealed to so many educators and students.

Who should be responsible for such programs? Who should train and supervise students in helping projects? Ideally, this person is a school counselor.

There are many places throughout the United States where school counselors did not pick up the challenge and where peer facilitator training is left to teachers or other support personnel. Sadly enough, it often happens in schools where counselors are not held in high regard. After all, school counselors should be, by training and professional specialization, in the best position to develop and organize peer facilitator training programs.

Peer facilitator programs vary in terms of the time required of a trainer. For instance, in some high schools, the counselor teaches a peer facilitator class which meets about one hour every day of the school week. While many projects can happen during this class period, some projects require a commitment of other times during the week. Some counselors meet their groups two days for one hour each. Other counselors have trained their peer helpers outside of school hours and meet with them over lunch on different occasions for planning, supervision, and follow-up training.

A few schools have designated teachers as peer facilitator trainers because an elective class is offered to students through the regular social studies curriculum. In this case, successful counselors work closely with those teachers, both in presentations to groups and helping them identify projects in which their peer facilitators can use their skills.

As TAP becomes more accepted in secondary schools, the TAP periods (about 30 minutes each day) could be used to train peers and help them with their projects. But, generally, counselors need to plan between one and five hours a week to work with peer facilitators as either a trainer or a coordinator of peer facilitator projects, or both.

Consultation

Consultation with teachers, parents, students, administrators, and community helpers is part of the counselor's job. Generally, it is the process of helping someone to think about a work related problem. More specifically, the counselor-consultant helps a consultee talk about problems that one is having with a third party.

Consultation is an essential part of developmental guidance. Wrenn (1962) emphasized its importance in his historic report. Later, he said that it should have been given even more emphasis by the state and national commissions which were trying to define the role of school counselors (Wrenn, 1973).

One teacher was experiencing problems with a disruptive girl in her class. The girl was talking loudly and at inappropriate times, making sarcastic remarks to the teacher and classmates, and refusing to follow classroom procedures. The teacher was frustrated and annoyed. This situation led her to seek out one of the counselors in her school and talk about the problem. In this case, the teacher became the consultee as the counselor acted as a consultant. They talked about the girl and tried to find some solutions for the teacher.

Perhaps the reason that consultation is given so much emphasis in a developmental approach to guidance is that the total learning environment of the school is always the first consideration. Consulting with teachers helps improve learning environments in classrooms and throughout the school. Moreover, consultation with teachers enables a counselor to benefit more students since helping one teacher who is responsible for thirty or more students is an efficient use of time, perhaps more than trying to see all thirty students individually or in small groups. Sometimes student problems arise from ineffective teaching procedures or a lack of understanding between teacher and student. The counselor may not need to counsel a student about a problem if teacher-student relationships are improved through consultation.

The same thing might also be said about parent-child relationships. Parent education can be part of a counselor's responsibilities and some counselors are very active in this respect. For instance, they might provide or arrange for parent education courses and seminars to be offered in the evenings at their schools. They might meet privately, usually upon parent or teacher request, with parents during school hours to discuss concerns about their children. Sometimes the counselor/consultant acts as mediator. At other times, difficult situations are facilitated so that some action steps can be taken by parents, teachers, and others.

Counselors as consultants are part of exceptional education staffings and child study groups. They offer their observations and contribute their knowledge on a case that is being considered. They consult with administrators and teachers about many matters. This might include discussions about curriculum, evaluations, or referrals. Counselors also consult with resource personnel who work outside a school. It is not uncommon for the principal of a school to rely upon an effective and supportive counselor to be a confidante. "I need to talk with you about a matter...." was one way a principal alerted the school counselor that it was time for some consultation. The counselor was the consultant.

Consultation can take place with individuals. Many counselors mark times on their weekly schedules when teachers and parents can meet with them to discuss special concerns or interests. These times are usually immediately before or after school. Teachers also have planning periods when consultation could happen. Most counselors try to accommodate teachers who have less flexible time.

Consultation can also take place in groups. Teacher seminars, for instance, offer opportunities for counselors to consult with teachers in small or large groups. These meetings are often scheduled before or after school; but they can also take place with a team of teachers during school. In most cases, the counselor as a consultant will facilitate a discussion instead of offer expert advice.

A group of teachers decided they wanted to meet and talk about academically talented students who were disruptive and acted as "class clowns." They met once a week for three 30-minute sessions after the last class of the day on Wednesdays. The counselor, as consultant, started the meetings, focused the topic, encouraged teachers to share their thoughts and feelings, summarized ideas, and ended the meetings on time. The teachers felt supported and understood in an accepting group. They had an opportunity to learn about how others worked with such students and, subsequently, they had new ideas to try.

Consultation is a viable counselor intervention and it needs to be scheduled as part of a counselor's work load. However, just because it usually involves adults is no reason that it should take priority over other counselor interventions. For instance, it is not advisable to cancel a small group counseling session with students to consult with a parent who happens to drop by the school. To excuse or cancel the group would communicate that whatever you are doing is not important and that student interests are superseded by adult interests.

There are several consultation approaches which might be used by counselors. Consultation as a counselor intervention is described in more detail in Chapter 10.

Coordination of Guidance Services

Finally, we come to the sixth counselor intervention—guidance coordination. The counselor is a coordinator and administrator of guidance services in the school and this involves many activities.

You might, for example, be involved in coordinating a school's standardized testing program, although you do not administer tests. You could administer individual or group tests, but this is preferably done by teachers and other support personnel. Yet, many counselors schedule standardized tests, arrange for their administration and interpretation, and handle the routine procedures and paper work. It might be one of the most visible aspects of your job.

Some counselors are responsible for coordinating the data that go into cumulative folders, although this responsibility is primarily given to teacher aides or a registrar in most schools. It is possible that, as a counselor, you could be assigned to coordinate the procedures and oversee the storage and retrieval system, especially if there is no registrar or other support personnel available. Clerical assistance is essential if you are to avoid being entrapped in coordinating duties.

Counselors usually help coordinate the educational placement of students. This might involve coordinating staff meetings. At the secondary level, especially, it might mean working with class schedules to meet student needs. Counselors across the nation complain about how much of their time is "wasted" in scheduling procedures.

Working as a liaison between the school and social agencies, such as mental health centers and health services, is also a coordinating function. For instance, if you suspect that one of your counselees is a victim of child abuse, most states have laws which require you to inform state health and rehabilitation agencies so that they can follow up with an investigation. A social worker may consult with you and ask your assistance in coordinating a meeting with the child's teachers.

Coordinating staff-development or in-service meetings can be a counselor's responsibility. Counselors can help identify staff-development needs and appropriate resources. They might also arrange meetings and work closely with external consultants who provide seminars and workshops for the school faculty.

Obviously, this coordinating function or intervention is the "catch all" category. Counselors are expected to do many things in a school, often because there is a shortage of administrative personnel and there are so many administrative tasks that must be done. Coordinator is a better term to use in describing this function than administrative assistant. However, the plight of most counselors is that too much of their time is spent in administrative and coordinating tasks.

One way to avoid being overloaded with certain duties is to arrange your own weekly schedule so that some coordinating tasks are dealt with on certain days of the week and within specific blocks of time. For instance, changing class schedules by a high school counselor might be limited to Fridays only, or Fridays and noon hours on other days. This would enable a counselor to schedule other interventions and experience fewer interruptions and distractions, especially as students and teachers learn when a counselor is available.

The coordination of guidance services takes time. Unfortunately, many unrelated guidance and counseling tasks can become a part of a counselor's job. Administrative expectations, and the guidance needs of a particular school, can influence how much time a counselor gives to administrative and coordinating tasks. Administrator and teacher expectations can be negotiated, especially if you have a plan for how you will be using your time.

To avoid being overwhelmed by administrative tasks, you will want to educate or remind others about counseling and guidance interventions, the nature of a developmental guidance program, your weekly schedule, and the priorities you have set. Otherwise, it may appear that you are always available to "pick up" and "go for" a host of things, many of which are unrelated to your work as a counselor in a developmental guidance and counseling program.

The largest proportion of time in a counselor's weekly schedule (Figure 4.1) is given to coordinating guidance services. It is coded on a schedule as "Flexible Time," since tasks are so varied from day to day and, ideally, coordinating functions are worked in and around other interventions. For many counselors, this is still not enough time and they begin to steal time from other interventions, such as individual counseling and group counseling. When this happens, counselors can be guaranteed that their images with students, teachers, and parents will not be one of a developmental counselor.

Managing Counselor Priorities

There will never be enough school counselors to meet all the guidance needs of students. School budgets are limited and administrators prefer to look for less expensive ways in which to better manage existing programs and personnel. They expect counselors to work within the limits of their abilities, the resources that are available, and the time they have available.

Considering the range of guidance services and the different counselor interventions that are possible, identifying priorities is essential when planning a comprehensive developmental guidance and counseling program. It is also a practical means for personal and professional survival.

As a counselor, you will be asked to do many things, some of which are directly related to counseling services and some that are not. You will meet many people who will place demands on you. You will not be able to meet everyone's expectations. To feel a sense of control and to gain some satisfaction from your work, you have to set priorities and manage your time carefully.

How do you set your priorities? Should you give most of your attention to students who voluntarily come to your office and ask for help? Or, should you work primarily with students who have been referred? Should you concentrate your work on a few students who especially need assistance? Or, should you try to distribute your time equally among all the students who have been assigned to you? Should it be a first-come first-serve basis, or are there certain students who, above all others, should be assisted? Do you wait to see what administrators and teachers have in mind for you, or should you have your own plan?

If you want control of your work and your time, then you will need to approach your work schedule systematically. To start, here are a few ways to think about how priorities can be set.

Priority-setting by Guidance Needs

One way to begin is to ask the students and faculty to help you identify the guidance needs in your school. This might be done by interviewing teachers and administrators, noting their awareness of the problems facing students in the school. It might be helpful to identify some students who, because of their personal circumstances, need extra help, beyond what might be given by most teachers.

A needs assessment in the form of a written questionnaire could be distributed to students and teachers. Students, for example, might check their most important concerns on a list of common problems and issues. They could suggest guidance topics of interest to them and their classmates. When a middle school counselor administered a one-page survey to students, it was learned that many students wanted to talk about "Girl-boy relationships," "How to get along with teachers," and "How to make friends."

A guidance committee, composed of teachers and counselors, can also be helpful. This committee, for instance, might informally interview other teachers or listen for special needs as they emerge in team meetings. The committee might work with curriculum committees to see how guidance could be integrated into classroom activities.

Parents and community members can help identify priorities. They might suggest things about which they are concerned. Parent-teacher organizations could survey parents and report their findings.

In addition, state and community reports by governmental agencies may provide some clues regarding student needs. One community was especially concerned about a drug abuse problem that was increasing in the area. Another community experienced several unexplained teen-age suicides, while still another community was aware of the high number of "latchkey" children who attended their schools. In each of these communities, it was thought that schools provided a base where the issues could be addressed.

A list of guidance needs could be elicited from teachers and parents, focusing on both developmental and problem-centered concerns. Those needs could be matched with the developmental needs and interests that are a part of the school's developmental guidance curriculum, such as the objectives of TAP. It is then possible to see where the needs might be addressed in the regular program and where special guidance services might be added.

Priority-setting by Crisis

There are times when a student or teacher experiences a personal crisis and immediate attention must be given to the situation. There are also occasions when an intense situation happens in a school or community and counselors react by giving it high priority.

When a tornado ripped through a small community, many families suffered hardships. Death and economic depression suddenly became a part of the students' lives. This called for urgent action and priorities were shuffled as the school and community began the process of adjusting and rebuilding. The school counselor and some counselors from the mental health center consulted with teachers and parents. Small group counseling was done with students who had experienced severe losses. Large group guidance activities in classrooms helped the school's student body think about the needs of the community, their classmates, and what they might do to make things better for everyone.

When the space shuttle *Challenger* exploded, many counselors and other guidance personnel changed their schedules to respond to a national crisis. It was a time to help students through the shock. The nation grieved. It was also an occasion for timely teaching when students could talk about life, death, and how people respond to grief. For some students it was an opportunity to talk about some unresolved feelings and experiences in their own lives (Myrick, 1986).

In another case, a brother and two sisters were being neglected by their parents. They had inadequate lodging and little or no food. The parents were alcoholics and they sometimes became abusive of the children. When this came to the attention of a teacher, the counselor in the school met with the children and talked with personnel in community agencies to get help. The nature of the case required special and immediate attention, and it was given high priority.

Students have many kinds of problems and some are critical. A crisis-intervention may be needed. Crisis-interventions are a part of a counselor's job, but sometimes the stressful events in a student's life can be met through developmental guidance. Events and circumstances do not have to escalate to a crisis before help can be obtained and they do not have to be confronted directly. Sometimes developmental guidance activities, taking a less direct approach, can help students to focus their attention on a problem that is developing in their lives and to take responsibility for doing something about it.

A school counselor was aware that Ron, a seventh grade student, was worried about his parent's pending divorce. There was a lot of stress in the family and Ron was unsure about his future. He was "targeted" for special attention within the context of a developmental guidance unit that was being offered during TAP. The unit focused on communication with adults and problem-solving. Students were asked to think of how they might apply the ideas that were being discussed and experienced. The counselor and the teacher were particularly alert for opportunities to help Ron during this unit.

Priority-setting by Counselor Intervention

Priorities can also be set according to the interventions that a counselor can deliver. This places an emphasis upon the kinds of guidance services that are offered and on the counselor's role and image.

Some professional writers have advocated a "hierarchy of services" approach to setting priorities. They give the highest priority to working with groups of people instead of working with individuals alone. Dinkmeyer and Caldwell (1970), for example, ranked the following as major areas for counselor intervention: 1) Pupil Appraisal and Child Study; 2) Teacher Consultation; 3) Counseling; 4) Classroom Guidance; 5) Parent Consultation; 6)

Curriculum Involvement; 7) In-service Education for Staff; and 8) Administration and Coordination.

Faust (1968), on the other hand, listed first and second level priorities in terms of roles. More specifically, a developmental guidance counselor is first concerned with consultation, and in the following order: (First Level Hierarchy) groups of teachers, with an individual teacher, with groups of children, with an individual child; and (Second Level Hierarchy) curriculum development, with administrators, with parents, with school personnel specialists, and with community agencies. Faust believed that consultation was the key to a counselor's work since the rationale for developmental programs was based on improving the learning environment. He also suggested an order of other counseling interventions: counseling teachers in groups, counseling teachers individually, counseling children in groups, and counseling children individually. This hierarchy of counseling roles for counselors was an attempt to maximize counselor time and counseling relationships.

Actually, it is difficult to prioritize counselor interventions beyond the emphasis that group work is preferred over work with individuals. If interventions are equally effective, then group work deserves more priority, especially in schools where the number of counselors is limited.

Priority-setting by Time-Management

There is only so much time in a school day. Though you may arrive early and leave late, a regular school day is about seven hours, from approximately 8:00 AM until 3:00 PM. The starting and ending times vary from one school to another and are frequently affected by bus schedules, classroom space available, and administrative preferences. Regardless, there are only so many hours in your regular work day which can be allotted to various kinds of interventions.

One way of prioritizing counselor time and energy is to decide how much time might be spent delivering each of the six basic counselor interventions during a typical week. That is, if you work in a school 35 to 40 hours a week, how much of your time should be spent doing individual counseling? Small group counseling? Large group guidance? Peer facilitator training and projects? Consultation? Coordination?

You might decide, for example, that the maximum number of times which you want to meet with small groups for counseling is 10 sessions a week. This averages to two group meetings a day. You might also decide that you want to arrange the meetings on two days a week. Therefore, you could schedule five groups for Tuesday and another five on Thursday. The frequency has been set and the time of each meeting limited to perhaps 30 to 45 minutes.

Likewise, the other counselor interventions might be scheduled accordingly. For instance, if you decided upon a caseload of six students for individual counseling and decided to meet each one for 30 minutes twice a week, then those 12 half-hours of individual counseling time would have to appear on your weekly schedule.

The advantage of scheduling interventions by the time you have available is that it assures you of a balanced program, one in which you are not consumed by any one particular guidance service or intervention. It enhances your image if you are seen providing all six basic interventions. Without a balanced program in which all six are represented to some extent, the faculty, students, and general public may get a distorted picture of your job.

Because priorities are eventually based on how much time you have in your job, you could begin by drawing up a weekly schedule showing the time available in a school day. Then, the six basic counselor interventions can be put on the schedule by blocks of time, until a realistic schedule has been developed.

Managing Interventions

It is the management of interventions within the time that is available which can determine whether you have a realistic and practical program in your school. It is what you do, more than what you want to do, that determines your role and image. To help manage your interventions, you might organize them into a weekly schedule. This schedule must also reflect events on the annual guidance calendar.

The Counselor's Weekly Schedule

The basic planning outline is shown in Figure 4.1. Counselor interventions are listed on the left and some minimum time commitments are suggested on the right.

You might begin by making yourself a weekly schedule similar to the ones found in Figures 4.2, 4.3, or 4.4. First, you will see that a school day has been divided into half-hour blocks of time. The time periods could just as easily have been divided into whatever times a particular school has scheduled for class periods.

The next step is to place a set of counselor interventions on the schedule. For example, the weekly schedule in Figure 4.2 shows an elementary school counselor meeting with five individuals, twice a week for one half-hour each. Individual counseling is provided for students IC1, IC2, IC3, IC4, and IC5. In your own schedule, the names of students could appear instead of numbers, but you could also assure the anonymity of your caseload by continuing to use the numbers or some other code. The essential consideration is that you have target students and scheduled five individuals for individual counseling.

These individuals are given high priority in your caseload. That is, they are seen regularly, usually for one grading period. They could be scheduled for once a week, but since it is preferable to see them twice a week to have a more intense intervention and more continuity, the schedule in Figure 4.2 shows a counselor meeting Student 1 two times during the week. The middle and high school schedules (Figures 4.3 and 4.4) also show individual counseling, some twice a week and others once a week.

The three weekly schedules each show four groups that are targeted for small group counseling: GP 1, GP 2, GP 3, and GP 4. In Figure 4.2 the four groups are scheduled to meet with the counselor twice a week and they will be completed within three weeks. Other groups of students then will take their place in the schedule at the same or different time block. Groups might be scheduled for once a week over a longer time. Instead of twice a week for three weeks, a group might meet once a week for six weeks (Figure 4.3). Or, a group might meet once a week for ten weeks, depending upon the purpose of the group and the counseling strategy.

The weekly schedule for the elementary school counselor also shows how classroom guidance was scheduled for a one-half hour period four times a week. The counselor, in this case, decided to meet with four different classes during the week, but the decision could have been made to go to one class four times in one week.

The allotment of large group guidance or classroom time depends upon arrangements that are made with a teacher or group of teachers. However, seeing two groups or classes twice a week instead of four once a week usually requires less counselor and

Figure 4.2

Elementary School Counselor Schedule

Time	Monday	Tuesday	Wednesday	Thursday	Friday
7:30 - 8:00	Consult	Consult	FT	Consult	FT
8:00 - 8:30	Consult	FT	FT	FT	FT
8:30 - 9:00	FT	FT	FT	FT	FT
9:00 - 9:30	IC1	IC4	IC1	IC4	Class 3
9:30 - 10:00	FT	IC5	FT	IC5	FT
10:00 - 10:30	IC2	FT	IC2	FT	FT
10:30 - 11:00	FT	GP2	FT	GP2	FT
11:00 - 11:30	GP1	GP3	GP1	GP3	FT
11:30 - 12:00	FT	FT	FT	FT	FT
12:00 - 12:30	Lunch	Lunch	Lunch	Lunch	Lunch
12:30 - 1:00	Class 1	Class 2	ESE	Consult	Class 4
1:00 - 1:30	FT	FT	ESE	Consult	FT
1:30 - 2:00	FT	GP4	ESE	GP4	FT
2:00 - 2:30	IC3	FT	ESE	IC3	Peer Pj.
2:30 - 3:00	FT	Teacher	ESE	FT	Peer Pj.
3:00 - 3:30	Consult	Seminar	FT	Consult	Peer Pj.

IC = Individual Counseling
FT = Flexible Time
GP = Group Counseling
Class = Classroom Guidance
ESE = Exceptional Student Education
Planning Team
Consult = Teacher/Parent Consultation
Peer Pj. = Peer Group, Training, and Projects

Figure 4.3

Middle School Counselor Schedule

Time	Monday	Tuesday	Wednesday	Thursday	Friday
8:00 - 8:30	Consult	FT	Consult	Consult	FT
8:30 - 9:00	TAP	TAP	TAP	TAP	TAP
9:00 - 9:30	GREEN	FT	FT	FT	FT
9:30 - 10:00	TEAM	IC4	FT	IC4	Staff
10:00 - 10:30	FT	FT	IC2	FT	Meets
10:30 - 11:00	FT	GP1	FT	FT	FT
11:00 - 11:30	IC1	FT	RED	GP4	IC7
11:30 - 12:00	FT	GP2	TEAM	FT	FT
12:00 - 12:30	Consult	Consult	Consult	Consult	Consult
12:30 - 1:00	Lunch	Lunch	Lunch	Peer	Lunch
1:00 - 1:30	IC2	IC5	GP3	Proj.	BLUE
1:30 - 2:00	FT	ESE	GP3	FT	TEAM
2:00 - 2:30	IC3	ESE	FT	FT	FT
2:30 - 3:00	FT	FT	IC6	Teacher	Consult
3:00 - 3:30	Consult	Consult	Consult	Seminar	Consult

IC = Individual Counseling
FT = Flexible Time
GP = Group Counseling
TAP = Teacher-Advisor Group Meetings
ESE = Exceptional Student Education Planning Team
Consult = Teacher/Parent Consultation
Team = Grade Level Team Meetings
Staff = Counselor and Student Services Team

　Developmental Guidance and Counseling

teacher preparation and is less personally demanding. Classroom guidance by teachers, of course, is scheduled on their own schedules and would not appear on the counselor's schedule, unless the counselor was scheduled to participate.

The middle and high school counselors' schedules are similar to the elementary school counselors' schedule, except TAP happens at the beginning of each day. Teachers, working as student advisors, present guidance units during TAP time, perhaps twice a week (e.g. Tuesdays and Thursdays). But, a counselor might develop a special guidance unit that could be delivered during TAP time, either by the counselor or in collaboration with TAP teachers. The counselor could also pull together two or more TAP groups to present some general information or a guidance activity.

Peer facilitator training could take place when TAP is scheduled, perhaps as a special TAP group for peer facilitators. Later, during that same time period, peer facilitators could work with other students and teachers. For instance, after nine weeks of training during a TAP period, meeting five days a week, peer facilitators might assist teachers or counselors with small group activities in their TAP groups. Or, the peer facilitators might be asked to meet with individual students during a TAP block of time for tutoring or special friend projects.

In some high schools, peer facilitator classes are a part of the academic curriculum. This regular class, perhaps 45 to 55 minutes, may be taught by a teacher or a counselor. If the counselor teaches the class, then that time commitment should appear on the counselor's weekly schedule, as shown in the high school counselor's schedule in Figure 4.4. In other schools where an academic class is not available, counselors could train peer facilitators in a one-day workshop, or in a week-end retreat, and then follow-up time with peer facilitators might appear on a schedule. As peer facilitator projects are developed and implemented, organization and supervisory times would also appear on the weekly schedules.

Consultation with students, teachers, parents, and administrators happens at various times. However, the counselor can identify times during a day which are most likely to be used by those who want consultation. For example, the first and last 30 minutes of the school day are often marked for consultation, since these times are most convenient to teachers and parents. It will be helpful if teachers and administrators have some scheduled times for meet-

Figure 4.4

High School Counselor Schedule

Time	Monday	Tuesday	Wednesday	Thursday	Friday
7:30 - 8:00	Consult	Consult	FT	Consult	FT
8:00 - 8:30	TAP	TAP	TAP	TAP	TAP
8:30 - 9:00	FT	FT	FT	FT	FT
9:00 - 9:30	IC1	IC5	ESE	IC5	Staff
9:30 - 10:00	Consult	FT	ESE	IC6	Meets
10:00 - 10:30	Consult	FT	ESE	FT	FT
10:30 - 11:00	IC2	GP1	FT	GP1	FT
11:00 - 11:30	Peer	Peer	Peer	Peer	Peer
11:30 - 12:00	Facil.	Facil.	Facil.	Facil.	Facil.
12:00 - 12:30	FT	FT	FT	FT	FT
12:30 - 1:00	Lunch	Lunch	Lunch	Lunch	Lunch
1:00 - 1:30	IC3	GP2	GP3	GP2	GP3
1:30 - 2:00	FT	GP2	GP3	GP2	GP3
2:00 - 2:30	IC4	FT	GP4	FT	GP4
2:30 - 3:00	Consult	Teacher	Consult	IC4	FT
3:00 - 3:30	Consult	Seminar	FT	Consult	FT

IC = Individual Counseling
FT = Flexible Time
GP = Group Counseling
TAP = Teacher Advisor Program
ESE = Exceptional Student Education Planning Team
Consult = Teacher/Parent Consultation
Peer Facil. = Peer Facilitator Class and Projects
Staff = Counselor Meetings

ing with you. They may request to meet at another time, such as during their planning periods or perhaps during lunch, and you will want to build your schedule to accommodate them as best you can. Therefore, try to avoid student conferences or small group counseling at times when most teachers can meet with you conviently. Scheduling consultation time can cut down on interruptions, especially if teachers use the time that you have made available to them. It also communicates that you are busy at other times of the day and not wasting time.

Group consultation with teachers is also recommended. Teachers can voluntarily meet as a group to talk about some mutual interests or concerns. As a consultant, you might arrange for interested teachers to talk about parent conferences. The middle school Teacher Seminar in Figure 4.3 was scheduled for 3 consecutive Thursdays, with each session lasting about 30-45 minutes. In one instance, the counselor facilitated a discussion about successful techniques in parent conferences.

Aside from Teacher Seminars, you might do group consultation with teams of teachers. The middle school counselor, in our example, found it helpful to attend the planning meetings of the Red, Blue, and Green teacher teams, which met at regular times during the week.

Scheduling consultation time can help clarify your role and inform people about times when you might best be available. Therefore, some "best times" are usually noted on a schedule. When the time is not used for consultation, it automatically converts to flexible time.

Flexible time (FT) is shown in all three sample schedules. This is time which has not been committed to the six basic counselor interventions and may be used for different purposes. It is the committed time for each intervention that maintains the balance of the counselor's schedule and it is this time that needs to be protected against interruptions and changes.

Even flexible time can be a time when a counselor provides one of the basic interventions, depending upon what is scheduled for that day or that week. When flexible time appears on a schedule, a counselor might meet with an individual student who happens to want an appointment that day or with a parent who happens to stop by the school.

Flexible time might also be used for follow-up with students, going to a classroom or an area in the school where the student might be.

It could be used to call in a group of students, to meet with a social worker, to make a telephone call to a community agency or a parent, or to work with a school's computer to call up some records. It might be used to talk informally with students who are in the Career Resource Center or to observe students in a class. The time could be used for responsibilities related to coordinating the guidance program in the school.

The term "chunking" is used by some time management experts to describe a technique for grouping similar job tasks which could be performed within the same time block. For instance, the return of telephone calls might be reserved for a particular hour in the afternoon. Another time period might be set aside for writing notes or recommendations, or working with the school files. In this respect, you might try to identify a few times during the day or week when some related tasks can be completed. Although labeled "flexible time" on your weekly calendar, there might be some routine or typical activities which often occur at a particular time.

Instead of "free time," the term "flexible time" is preferred, particularly when you are blocking out your schedule on a piece of paper. Teachers or counselors may perceive themselves as having some extra or free time during a planning period or when they are not scheduled to meet a class, a group, or a student, but such time is still considered "flexible time" to professional counselors.

Some counselors use a master weekly schedule as a general guide, editing it as needed to show the actual events that happened during a work week. This "working schedule," with its deletions, substitutions, and notes, can be filed as a permanent record for later reference.

The management of counselor interventions and time involves building a weekly schedule in which a minimum set of the basic six counselor interventions and services are arranged and noted. The number of commitments that appear on your weekly schedule will depend upon your special interests, the circumstances in your school, and the needs of student and teachers. However, in a comprehensive developmental guidance plan, approximately 10 to 26 hours of your time will be scheduled for five of the basic counselor interventions. If we assume a 40-hour work week, the remaining 14 to 30 hours are given to the sixth basic intervention—coordinating guidance services or flexible time. It is this remaining time which threatens the image and role of all school counselors and must be kept under control through careful and systematic planning.

The Annual Guidance Calendar

The same concepts for building a weekly schedule also apply to an annual guidance calendar. This calendar shows school-wide events, such as when standardized tests are to be given, when orientation meetings are scheduled, and applications for college are due. Seasonal events and holidays which lend themselves to guidance units or special school traditions are also noted.

One guidance calendar for a high school highlighted such events as test weeks, when standardized tests were administered; College Night, when representatives from different universities came to campus; Career Week, when several vocational guidance activities took place; Educational Planning, when students planned for next year's courses; Orientation Week, when middle school students visited the high school and scheduled their classes; Parent's Night, when parents were invited to an open-house at the school; and Deadlines, when various applications or forms were due.

An annual guidance calendar can identify events around which some related guidance units could be developed, such as those which focus on orientation to the school, career guidance, educational planning, friendship, and study skills. The calendar can suggest times when readiness activities might be appropriate, such as some test-taking skills units before standardized test week.

Annual guidance calendars for a school and counselors' weekly schedules coincide a great deal. They can be changed as a need arises. Weekly schedules are representative and are usually designed for one grading period. The schedule might be posted in the guidance office or given to administrators and department heads so they are better informed about what counselors are doing. The annual calendar is usually prepared before school starts and additions take place at staff meetings.

A junior high school principal reported that the three counselors in his school were not very busy. The counselors denied this, of course. He continued by saying that he sent different tasks down to the guidance department, as a favor to give them something to do.

After the counselors' initial anger and disappointment receded, they recognized that they were operating out of a crisis-based model. They saw students as they were self-referred or referred by others. The counselors were reactive more than proactive. Therefore, they decided to implement a developmental guidance program and to change their visibility and image. They began by outlining weekly schedules.

The principal, who was given copies of their new weekly schedules, later remarked that his counselors were now too busy for some of the clerical and administrative tasks which he formerly assigned to them. Personnel in the front office now completed many of the tasks. He also tried to help the counselors protect their "schedules" so that they might work more with students and teachers. He was proud of what the counselors had accomplished and told other principals what the counselors were doing. It was probably the first time the principal had a clear understanding of what counselors could do for students. The schedules clarified counselor roles and functions and improved communication between the principal, the counselors, and others in the school. The administrator, in this case, was unable to speak with much confidence about the work of his counselors until he had a visual picture of what they were trying to do and how they were spending their time. The weekly schedules had done more to describe the work of counselors than any professional publication or written role statement.

Schools are also finding it useful to employ counselors in a flexible schedule. For instance, one high school in Fort Lauderdale, Florida released one of its counselors during the day to meet with students and parents on Wednesday nights. Many more working parents were able to avail themselves of counselor assistance at that time. In addition to the school counselor, a mental health counselor, and a counselor assigned from the sheriff's office also worked in the school the same evening. The three counselors provided family counseling and consultation services and met more needs of students and their families.

Counselors are being challenged to think of new ways of scheduling their time. Finding new ways to have access to more students can be difficult. One group of high school counselors recognized that students had time to see counselors during lunch period, if counselors were available. Therefore, counselors took turns shifting their lunch schedules to accommodate times when students could see them without missing academic classes.

Factors to Consider

There are some other concepts and strategies that can help you be effective in the limited time that you have available at school. Some of these are discussed below:

The Law of Parsimony

The Law of Parsimony suggests that you work with students in large groups first. For example, you may be concerned with student attitudes about school. Classroom guidance or a guidance unit in TAP is the first strategy to be used in effecting a change of attitude with students. Those students who do not respond to large group guidance might be targeted for small group counseling at a later time. Likewise, if a student fails to respond to small group counseling, then individual counseling might be in order. If individual counseling is ineffective, then a referral might be made to another counselor or agency.

The Law of Parsimony encourages you to think about reaching all students. It helps you implement guidance activities and strategies that otherwise might not be available to students. In addition, the sequence of moving from large group guidance to an outside agency referral provides a systematic approach to interventions and services. These can be documented and you can then have a base from which to talk about any next steps that need to be taken.

Multiple Interventions

Experimental research on counselor interventions is limited. There is a need for more studies in which a counselor intervention is implemented with one group of students and then compared to another group of students who did not receive the intervention. There is also a need for more single-case studies, in which baseline data is taken and then measurement is continued with one person throughout the time a counselor intervention is administered. The studies that are available have not only been limited but they have also tended to prejudice our thinking toward using a single counselor intervention.

Doctoral dissertations, master theses, and other exacting and rigorous research isolate variables for study. For instance, if individual counseling is to be studied, then efforts are made to control extraneous variables by not combining it with other treatment modalities. If you mix individual counseling with group counseling, as part of an experimental treatment, someone might ask, "But, which one made the real difference, the individual or small group counseling?"

The legacy of single counselor interventions was born out of research studies and has been sustained because most published research focuses on single treatments or interventions. Practically speaking, a multiple intervention approach can be used as part of your work. It involves the use of more than one of the six basic counselor interventions, simultaneously or in sequence.

A student who has been referred to you for counseling, for example, may meet with you in small group counseling, working with others who have similar problems. In addition, you might on occasion talk with the student on an individual basis (individual counseling) and talk with a teacher about the student (consultation). You might even want to telephone the parents (consultation) before asking a peer facilitator to be a special friend or a tutor for the student. In such a case, several counselor interventions are being brought into play, with the assumption that they will intensify the helping process and change might be expedited. It seems practical to have as many helpers as possible involved in working with a student, especially if the nature of the case allows for it.

When a multiple intervention happens by chance, it is because the circumstances seem to dictate that type of involvement and you make the best use of them. However, when a multiple intervention is carefully orchestrated to maximize impact and increase the chance of making positive changes, then you are more likely to have more satisfying results.

When a multiple intervention is planned, you avoid a "fragmented approach," in which people are trying to help but sometimes working at cross purposes because they are not communicating and working together. This wastes energy and is analogous to a football team having its players run around in different directions without any plan or rationale. It may work. But, when everyone understands the goal and works together on a similar plan, then chances of success are greater. Multiple interventions invole teamwork and they take time to construct. They are more likely to occur when you have control of your time and concentrate on a few students in a caseload.

The Caseload

Given high student-counselor ratios in almost every school in the nation, it makes sense for counselors to develop a caseload of students who will receive high priority. These students might be selected for any number of reasons. They may not be the students who have the greatest need or who are the most troubled. While such students are good candidates to be part of a counselor's caseload, one's caseload is often determined by such factors as accessibility, time restraints, availability of other helpers, specific requests by teachers or administrators, and the probability of making a positive difference.

In a developmental guidance program, some of the students who are seen as part of a counselor's caseload will be in the normal range of functioning and have concerns, needs, and interests that are not as intense as some dysfunctioning students. However, who is to say that these students are any less deserving of a school counselor's time?

The purpose of the caseload is to help you manage your time. It also gives you an opportunity to focus your work, and you will feel less torn than if you take whatever comes your way, day by day. Students in a caseload receive special attention because they are part of your weekly schedule and you see them regularly. This can make your job, and your time, manageable. You simply cannot be available to all your assigned students at all times.

There was a time when school counselors were told to see all their "counselees" at least once each school semester. This meant that some counselors scheduled 500 individual interviews, which lasted about 15 minutes each. One counselor in this situation said, "I just wanted the students to get to know me and to find out how things were going for them.... I wanted them to know that I was available, if they needed me." It was a tragic waste of time to line up students outside a counselor's office for a quick interview that was often rushed, stiff, and meaningless to either counselor or student.

Your caseload may be determined several ways. However, let us assume you have decided to meet individually with eight students. Further, you have decided to meet with them twice a week for 30 minutes each time. This accounts for a total of eight hours of individual counseling time to set aside each week. Next, you might decide how many students you will see through group counseling and schedule the groups on your schedule. These students might also be considered part of your on-going caseload, although some counselors prefer to think of caseloads only in terms of individuals being seen in counseling.

Counselors who use the caseload approach report that they feel more in control of their schedules and that individual counseling, particularly, is more productive and rewarding. By highlighting a caseload of students, there is a better chance that more systematic procedures will be used in working with them.

Target Students

A target student is one who has been singled out for special attention by the counselor. Target students receive the highest priority and tend to occupy most of the thinking and planning time that you have to give in your job as a counselor.

All individual counseling cases are probably target students, except some students who meet briefly with the counselor and who do not take much of a counselor's planning time. When counselors have a few targeted students at a time within their caseload, they are much more likely to consult with other counselors or professionals about them, to do some professional research on them, to read a book or journal article about their problems, or to chart their behaviors and evaluate their progress. It is impossible to give that type of attention to all counselees.

Some target students are seen in group counseling sessions, perhaps with other students who are not targeted but who are there to benefit from the group experience. For example, if you are meeting with a group of five students, one may be a student whom you particularly want to receive attention. Maybe you want to help that student to self-disclose more or to receive some extra high facilitative responses. Or, you may want the group to eventually use this student's situation or problem as a focus for discussion. While all group members are part of the learning process, you are keenly aware of target students and you seize upon timely opportunities to help them within the group.

How can you identify target students? Of all the students who need help in the schools, which ones should be targeted for special attention? Here is one simple way to identify a group of target students.

Let us suppose that you are one of six high school counselors working in a school that has 2,400 or more students. You and the other counselors might ask the building administrators and department heads to use a computer print out list to identify students who need special help, beyond what classroom teachers can give them. This list averages between 150 to 200 in a school of this size, probably because the administrators will think about students who have the most visible needs.

Next, ask the administrators to cut the list in half by identifying those students who might be most responsive to counselor help within a grading period (i.e. six or nine weeks). Or, you might ask,

"Which ones do you think we can make a positive difference with, in some way, during the next grading period?" There is no need for discussion or debate, as time is usually limited and it is the paring down of the list that is essential. Thus, you will have about 100 student names.

Now, you and your counseling colleagues look over the new list and again cut this list in half by identifying those whom you think might respond positively to a counselor intervention. The list is now down to 50 students.

These are your target students. It might be appropriate to divide the names among the six school counselors, giving each approximately eight students to work with closely during the next grading period. Use any one of the counselor interventions, or a combination of them (a multiple intervention), or anything else that you believe will work to help your target students adjust to school, resolve their personal problems, or become better students.

Do whatever you can to make a positive difference. Making a difference within one grading period with half the list (25) can affect the climate of the school. Some of the students only need a little boost, while others may be targeted again later. Most important, with the help of others, you can identify students who need special help, and you can manage your efforts and time in light of an overwhelming number of students with whom you could work.

Target Populations

Aside from the target students, there are target populations of students within a school who need special attention. For instance, some target populations might be: students who have poor study habits and skills and who do not know how to manage their time; students who experience high anxiety and stress when they take tests and perform poorly; students who have experienced a recent death or separation in their families; students who are "at risk" and potential dropouts; students who are frequently absent from school; students who are unsure about their job goals; students who are frequently rejected by their peers; and so forth. Target populations might be identified by the faculty or students.

Career Development and Life Style

The term career development has been used to describe several lifelong processes, all of which form an individual's life style and patterns of career identity. How these patterns evolve is based on one's values, interests, skills, abilities, personal and educational experiences, and environmental influences. Life style and career choices characterize one's life (Herr, 1986).

The most recent position statement on career development affecting the work of school counselors was issued by the American School Counselor Association (ASCA) in 1984. It was suggested that counselors should concentrate on the delivery of a series of common, core experiences, which should lead to career maturity. They include:

- Clarifying work values and developing coping and planning skills.

- Assessing abilities, personality traits, and interests through formal and informal measures.

- Providing occupational and career information, linking community resources with guidance.

- Helping students learn interviewing and job-hunting skills, and increasing their awareness of educational and training opportunities, including financial aid.

- Encouraging training, goal setting, and decision-making related to a tentative career path.

- Integrating academic and career skills in a school curriculum.

- Reviewing and evaluating student action plans.

The foundation for career development and the motivation for career goals and career-related behaviors is laid in the early school years. Beginning in elementary schools, children learn about work-related behaviors and feelings. Field trips, videotaped programs, and in-class experiences, for example, are designed to increase children's awareness of the world of work. More importantly, children have an opportunity to learn more about the value and importance of work and how it can give special meaning to their lives. As children get older and move through middle and high schools, their interests become more prominent and career development experiences are extended and grounded in decision-making and planning.

Life-style and career development will remain a central focus for most school counselors, but some related issues challenge counselors to do more than what has been done in the past. More attention must be given to the career development of women, ethnic minority groups, and the economically disadvantaged. This inevitably involves confronting some traditional thinking, values, stereotypes, prejudices, conventional programs, and methods.

Counseling and Learning Styles

In the future we will know more about learning styles, their effect on personal and academic development, and how they affect a student's participation in learning activities. Presently, learning style assessment measures are limited and often unreliable. Yet, it is generally recognized that some students have a predisposition for visual learning approaches, while others prefer auditory and kinesthetic modes. Some students take socially active roles in learning while other students are more introverted and passive. This insight is not new to counselors who have appreciated, measured, and interpreted individual differences for many years. However, it is surprising that counselors, like many teachers, have been slow to adapt their strategies and techniques to student learning styles.

Counseling is primarily a talking process. For some students, this kind of learning situation is workable. Their verbal and conceptual abilities are drawn upon in the process of counseling. Other students, with different learning styles or slower rates of cognitive development, may find themselves hopelessly inundated with words when being "counseled." They may feel overwhelmed, insecure, or lost in the intellectual efforts that seem to form the basis of most school counseling and guidance. Perhaps this is one reason why some students are unresponsive to counselor activities and why sometimes counselors feel frustrated and defeated when working with some students. Counselors who have different learning styles than their counselees may experience less success than usual, unless they are flexible, adaptive, and learn how to use different counseling approaches.

This book, like so many others, has emphasized the verbal process of counseling, through examples and recommended procedures. First, it is the most popular and practical approach, as the vast majority of students can work with this counseling process. Secondly, there are few, if any, innovative counseling approaches which do not rely on words and that are feasible for school settings.

Play techniques have been popular with child therapists and counselors for many years. Play media are often used by elementary school counselors to supplement their counseling work. Puppets, art materials, guided fantasies, music and movement, creative dra-

The Counselor: A Developmental Guidance Specialist   131

matics, and games are part of almost every elementary school counselor's repertoire. Yet, it has only been recently that play counseling has moved beyond the traditional Axline (1947) approaches, which are considered inappropriate for school counselors who do not have a lot of time for individual cases. Play media may be used at all grade levels, but there is a lack of proven activities and almost no research to support their use with adolescents in the schools. Some new developments are needed in play media to accommodate learning styles in counseling. One solution to meeting students' needs who have different learning styles and rates of cognitive development may be found in high technology.

Using High Technology

Computers will help revolutionize much of the work of school counselors. Presently, most computer technology is being applied to information storage and retreval. Counselors can work with students regarding career decision-making and immediately access information about the world of work on a microcomputer sitting in a guidance office. A computer program might provide data about job opportunities, educational requirements, skills and interests needed, and some appropriate references. Programs such as *SIGI, DISCOVER,* and *CHOICES* enable students to interact with a computer in search and explore activities.

Counselors often feel burdened by clerical tasks which must be performed as part of their job assignments. Computers can make clerical duties easier and more efficient. One small high school, using a personal microcomputer, was able to schedule all students for classes within a shorter period time and with less personnel involved. The savings amounted to over $3,000 a year, most of which was saved by reducing the time that counselors formerly needed to schedule students (Strong, 1983).

Because computers make more information available at a counselor's fingertips, data might also be used to study groups of students targeted for guidance and counseling. Patterns and trends with a population of students might be identified. Final reports, with graphs and summary data, could be easier to construct.

Networking among counselors, with the assistance of computers, will likely increase in the future. Some school districts with mainframe computers can easily transfer a student to another school within a district, since a student's records can be displayed on a terminal in any of the district schools. The use of modems will increase, enabling counselors and students to go beyond a mainframe computer and share information through personal micro-computers. It will be possible for a group of counselors in a school district to relay forms and details associated with a certain counselor intervention, perhaps within the same school district or to other counselors in another community or state. It will also be possible to have a computerized network which might serve as a clearinghouse for ideas and activities.

In addition to computers, high technology is providing counselors with other ways to match or accommodate students' learning styles. Video cassettes, some which interface with computers, can provide experiences in which students gain new information, explore alternatives, and learn skills. Video cameras and monitors are becoming more affordable and might be used as a tool to assist students in guidance and counseling activities, perhaps providing unique opportunities for more decision-making, feedback, or the study of interpersonal relationships. Using video tapes and role playing situations, a counselor might coach students in communication or problem-solving skills.

The marvels of high technology are typically implemented in the military services and business enterprises before they reach schools. However, there is a trend for sophisticated electronic equipment to become less expensive and more available to counselors. Their own imagination and innovative practices will determine how helpful high technology can be. Many counselors will be challenged to enter the 21st century of counseling by learning more about computers and high technology.

Share the Responsibility for Guidance

Counselors and teachers need not be the only providers of guidance services. They can teach others basic helping skills which can be used in guidance related activities.

There are people who, without professional training, seem to have a natural talent for helping others. Their personalities, interpersonal skills, and positive attitudes make it possible for them to accept some guidance roles in which they provide direct and indirect services to students. However, because they are not professionally certified nor formally trained, they are often referred to as paraprofessionals. Their roles are limited and supervision is needed.

Systematic preparation of paraprofessionals can make a positive difference in a school. An effective training program introduces participants to their working environment, roles and functions, and provides practice with interpersonal skills which can be used with students and adults in a school. Without such preparation, paraprofessionals feel less like team members and more like tag-along workers.

If paraprofessionals such as parent and community volunteers assist counselors in their work, then more students can receive guidance services. There is more time for attention to details and follow up. They create more opportunities for differentiated staffing. Well-trained and enthusiastic paraprofessionals can add a positive element to the working environment.

There are many helpers within a school and community (e.g. Big Brothers and Big Sisters, church groups, neighbors, and relatives) who can help a young person with a problem. While the burden of responsibility for personal choices and changes always rests with the student, the responsibility for caring and being helpful can rest on the shoulders of many people.

Working with Legislators

There was a time when counselors did not concern themselves with the work of national and state legislatures, but that time has passed. Counselors now must take an active part in working toward legislation which affects them and their programs.

Financial support for counseling and guidance started two decades ago from the federal government (e.g. NDEA Act, 1967) and the funds helped train and employ more counselors and improve counselor education programs. This early, federally supported thrust had a significant impact on the development of the school counseling profession and the role of school counselors. Likewise, *P.L. 94-142* (1976) not only appropriated millions of dollars to help children, but it influenced many procedures and activities that are used in the schools. It also determined how some personnel would function in their work and forced them to reorder their service and time priorities.

Elementary school counseling in Florida resulted from state legislators being convinced that early intervention was the best way to help improve the academic, personal, and social development of students. Specific legislation was passed which marked funds for the employment of elementary school counselors. This kind of categorical funding protected the counselor from encroachment of other needs in school systems, of which there are many. It has given counselors time to build programs and to provide some accountability studies to justify legislative action. Over the years since 1972, elementary school counselors in Florida have firmly established themselves and their developmental guidance programs as a regular part of the school system. Almost every elementary school in the state now has at least one full-time counselor and this would never have been possible without the support of state legislators.

Legislators can give funds and create opportunities, and they can take them away. Some promising programs have been discontinued in some states because time ran out and they were never established independent of federal or state funding. Some of these programs had the potential to be exemplary models for other school systems, but when funding was reduced or lost, the programs melted away.

Counselors, usually through their state professional organizations, can form legislative task forces which work with legislators. These task forces, sometimes with the help of paid lobbyists, help keep legislators and their aides informed about the guidance and counseling needs of young people and the value of guidance programs to meet those needs.

For instance, the Florida School Counselor Association and the Florida Association for Counseling and Development develop a written legislative platform for each meeting of the state legislature. The associations help raise funds to employ professional lobbyists. They organize groups of counselors to visit and talk with their local state legislators, prior to the time when the legislature meets, in order to be informative and to build positive relationships. Consequently, Florida legislators, in general, have a good idea of what counselors are trying to do and what they have accomplished.

Take Your Gains

"Take your gains where you can get them. Then, move on." Look for positive differences and do not expect to get dramatic reversals every time you work with students. It is not easy to turn someone's attitude around 180 degrees or even to raise a student's grade point average. When students have problems with a teacher, you are unlikely to do anything overnight to help them become good friends. In these situations, you probably need to take a few small steps in the right direction.

Some counselors have lofty goals for themselves and their coun-selees. They feel unsuccessful, or even defeated, unless they reach their general objective. They fail to consider the difference that a few little things can make and to take credit for helping a person have the courage or the skill to take a first step. While we all hope for some quick turnarounds, most progress is slow and sometimes goes unnoticed.

Intervention and time management plans are based on the assump-tion that you work toward and take short-term gains. There is little doubt that six small group sessions are only a start to helping some students learn to communicate more effectively or to explore a problem that is facing them. But, time restraints emphasize that you "take your gains" where you find them and then work with other students.

The Developmental Counselor

Counselors in developmental guidance programs are often de-scribed as human behavior and relationship specialists. They focus on the developmental needs, stages, and tasks of students in the elementary, middle, and high schools. They adapt the best of counseling theories to educational settings, relying primarily upon brief counseling and short-term approaches.

Developmental school counselors work with a caseload, which they can manage within a given week or few months. Target stu-dents are singled out for study and given special attention. The concepts of target students, target populations, and caseload make a counselor's work manageable and realistic.

Counselor interventions are scheduled in a representative work week, and a master weekly schedule can be shown to others. The counselor's job is defined by what counselors do, not by what counselors or the counseling profession think or wish they could do. Counselor interventions and time management eventually define counselor role and image.

Developmental counselors base their work on helping students learn more effectively and efficiently. Counselors are concerned with the personal problems of students because they can detract from learning. More effective and efficient learning is the essence of counseling and guidance, no matter the counseling theory or in-tervention.

Chapter 5

The Counselor as Facilitator

School counselors and teachers have often been described as facilitators. A facilitator is someone who is adept in the use of interpersonal skills and who can assist individuals or groups to move toward their goals. Facilitators help people explore their ideas and arrive at responsible decisions.

Many books and articles have been written for counselors, teachers, and therapists by qualified professionals. They have contributed ideas which have led to some innovative practices. Yet, school counselors and teachers continue to look for simple ways to describe their work and for practical plans to give them direction when they are helping others.

The Facilitative Model

The Facilitative Model consists of a few basic interpersonal concepts and related skills. This model has evolved over the years, as practitioners have helped make it a practical and feasible model from which to work. Although it may appear similar to what others have presented (e.g. Carkhuff, 1983; Egan, 1975; Ivey and Simek-Downing, 1980; Wittmer and Myrick, 1980), close examination will show that the model is a unique package of selected concepts and skills that are systematically organized and linked together. The Facilitative Model is easy to implement because complex concepts and skills are simplified for easy reference.

The model can be used with students, parents, administrators, and others. It is meant to be a practical guide, something to keep in mind as you manage counselor interventions. It is not an attempt to replace other counseling theories or strategies that you may already find useful. The Facilitative Model emphasizes certain aspects of helping relationships and facilitative processes that can help you become more effective in your work. In addition, it identifies and clarifies the essential interpersonal skills needed in developmental guidance and counseling.

The Facilitative Model consists of four parts: 1) the facilitative conditions of the helping relationship; 2) facilitative processes; 3) facilitative responses; and 4) facilitative activities and tasks.

The Facilitative Conditions of the Helping Relationship

Sometimes close relationships between people just seem to happen, without any apparent reason. Some people just "hit it off." From the beginning, there is a friendly bond between them—a bond which feels comfortable and secure. These people like each other almost immediately and enjoy being together. When asked to explain it, they often struggle to find the exact words to describe the friendship or the closeness they feel, but they know that the relationship is special.

Then, there are some people who have unfavorable impressions of one another when they first meet; yet, eventually they form a close relationship. Sometimes they are not even aware of one another until they are placed in a situation where they have to take note of each other. Then, the relationship starts to grow because they listen to each other and find mutual interests. Eventually, they learn to value the friendly relationship that develops.

There are also some relationships between people that seem adverse. These people dislike being in each other's presence. They seem ill at ease and find it difficult to be attentive to what the other person is doing or saying. They are insensitive to each other's needs and interests. There is usually no bond between them and, consequently, they have little positive impact on one another. Unfortunately, there are cases in which such unproductive relationships have existed among counselors, teachers, and students.

Teachers and counselors want to establish good working relationships with students. But, close relationships do not always come easy. They depend on how people interact and communicate with each other, as well as upon first impressions.

We have known for a long time that certain relationships are more helpful than others. Carl Rogers (e.g. 1957 and 1962) was a pioneer in drawing attention to the importance of "the helping relationship." He assumed that if certain conditions existed between people, then a process would be set into motion that would be productive. He said that these personal conditions were essential and sufficient to produce positive changes in personality, attitudes, and behaviors.

Although not everyone has agreed that these conditions alone are sufficient and that nothing else is needed (e.g Krumboltz, 1966), they are still seen as essential ingredients in the helping process. Despite theory or method, the characteristics of a relationship will make the critical difference when it comes to helping students take responsibility for themselves and making desired changes in their lives.

More specifically, if you are perceived as a friendly and caring person, then students are more likely to be drawn to you. If they also experience you as an attentive listener who is respectful, understanding, accepting, and interested in what they are thinking and feeling, then they will tell more about themselves and explore ideas and choices with you. If you recognize the pain and joy of growing up, while patiently helping them look at realities and the positive side of life, then a personal working relationship can be established.

Teachers frequently find themselves in situations that have potential for conflict. They cannot always be responsive to individual interests and needs when assigned to teach large groups of students. Classroom procedures, which are usually aimed at managing groups of students, can cause some individuals to feel ignored or treated unfairly. Likewise, group teaching methods may make it difficult to identify or respond to individual problems. Many teachers feel trapped in a system where decisions are based on what is best for most students and teachers. They also feel pressured when time is limited and so much academic work needs to be done.

School counselors have more flexibility to work with individuals and small groups than do teachers. However, counselors can feel in a bind when it comes to following school rules and procedures which are aimed at managing large numbers of students in a complex school environment. Sometimes easy access to students is denied to counselors. Time is so limited that many feel rushed, and they fail to form a positive working relationship with students before pushing ahead with an agenda. Some counselors have complained about being seen as "enforcers" more than "friends" by students because they are charged with reminding students of school rules and policies. Others worry that they are strangers to their students because they see them so seldom.

Six Facilitative Conditions

For our purposes, the facilitative relationship is characterized by six conditions. These facilitative conditions are: 1) caring; 2) understanding; 3) acceptance; 4) respect; 5) friendliness; and 6) trustworthiness.

Caring suggests that you are personally interested and concerned about a person's well-being. It also involves a sense of personal commitment to the person because you give something of yourself in the relationship. You value the person enough to psychologically reach out and be attentive.

Understanding is a term used to describe the phenomenon of perceiving and acknowledging what another person is experiencing. There is an empathy for the person in which an awareness of feeling is communicated. It goes beyond a knowledge of events in a person's life and touches on emotional experiences.

Acceptance focuses on a willingness to believe in and acknowledge the personal worth and dignity of a person, despite the circumstances. We can be accepting of someone and still not agree with the person's ideas or behaviors. In this case, it is assumed that one's behavior can be challenged or ignored, if necessary, but the value of the person as a human being is always present.

Respect suggests that common courtesies are given to people, including the right to express their own ideas and feelings, to be responsible for their own decisions, and to shape their own lives.

Friendliness communicates a warm personal style that invites others to reciprocate mutual interest and warmth. It is a factor which often comes from some of the other facilitative conditions. But, in its own right, friendliness is best characterized as a kindly attitude in which there are amiable exchanges and a genuine sense of comfort and support.

Trustworthiness involves being entrusted with confidence or a sense of security. It often inspires faith and reliance, but it is primarily founded on a prediction that someone will act in an honest and forthright manner so that an individual's well-being is not hurt.

No doubt the learning climate of a school is directly influenced by the interpersonal relationships between students and their counselors and teachers. Facilitative or helping relationships are ones in which students explore their ideas, feelings, and behaviors. These relationships are needed in a developmental guidance and counseling program (Kurpius, 1986).

The Facilitative Processes

"Okay," you may be thinking, "but if I'm friendly and have a good working relationship with students, then what happens?" The answer to that question can depend upon the situation or the problem that has been presented and the processes which receive special attention.

If you are counseling a student, for example, you will want to build a helping relationship by creating the facilitative conditions of trust, understanding, and so forth. This is done through mutual self-disclosure and feedback. As the relationship continues to develop and awareness increases, it is then possible to think about how decision-making and problem solving skills can be activated so that the student will take some responsible action toward desired goals.

One boy wanted to improve his grades. This general result was further delineated and one goal was to reduce his test anxiety in order to improve his examination scores. In another case, a girl decided that she wanted to feel better about herself as a person and to have more self-confidence when she played basketball. One of her desired counseling outcomes was to reduce the number of negative thoughts she had about herself. She also wanted to reduce the panic she felt when someone guarded her closely in a basketball game.

Three students, two boys and a girl, disliked a teacher. They resented the homework that was assigned and described it as trivial busy work. They became upset when the teacher threatened to lower their grades or remove them from class because of their attitude. After some discussion with a counselor, the students decided to work on paying more attention in class, starting their homework at school, and stopping their inappropriate talk in class.

In these cases, counselors and students had general and specific goals when they met together. Likewise, teachers, as advisors, might have goals in mind as they present a guidance activity. Yet, it is the way in which counselors and teachers work with students that frequently determines successful attainment of goals.

The facilitative processes that happen in counseling or guidance sessions refer to the interactions that take place and the dynamics of the interpersonal relationship. Each facilitative process has its own special attribute which contributes to the events that happen in counseling. In addition, these processes tend to emerge because of the reciprocal reactions of counselor and counselee. The facilitative processes are also interactive, with one process influencing another. They are unique products of the communication of ideas, feelings, and behaviors in a helping relationship.

This leads us to consider the four basic helping processes of the Facilitative Model: 1) self-disclosure; 2) feedback; 3) increased awareness and decision-making; and 4) responsible action.

Self-disclosure

Self-disclosure involves revealing one's self to others and it is the primary process in counseling. As the trust relationship builds between a counselor and a student, there is more sharing of personal information and there is greater depth in exploring private ideas and feelings.

All of us have had experiences in our lives which made a significant impact on us. Sometimes we remember the events vividly and at other times we can only recall the general effect that they had on us, but strong feelings and impressions linger. The events may not be nearly as important as the meaning that we give them. Talking about our feelings and ideas can be useful as we examine situations and attempt to understand others and ourselves more.

Borrowing from Harry Luft and Joe Ingram's famous Johari's Window (Joe and Harry's window), it is possible to illustrate several things about the Facilitative Model. A few liberties have been taken with the original illustration (Luft, 1984). For our purposes, we will refer to it as the Relationship Quadrant (Figure 5.1) since it features four distinct areas that are involved in analyzing individual or group relationships and the facilitative processes.

Let's see how this might be applied to you and your relationships with others. For instance, there are some things which are known to you and known to others (Quadrant I). This shared knowledge

Figure 5.1

Relationship Quadrant

	Known to Self	NOT Known to Self
Known to Others	Open I	Blind III
NOT Known to others	Closed II	Potential IV

makes it possible for you and others to have a base from which to relate with each other. It is an open area and free to comment. It is within this open area that ideas and feelings are explored and it is from here that awareness, decision-making, and actions eventually spring.

If some parents know, for example, that you are a counselor and that you have taken courses in family counseling, they may talk with you about some parenting matters. If students know that you jog at the school race track every day, they may use this information to talk with you about exercising or maybe some athletic events. Knowing something about you may invite them to talk more freely with you, especially on topics about which they have some information.

Information known to self and to others can be a departure point for further discussion. Although limited at first, Quadrant I is where you start. It is the area that you want to expand and develop as part of guidance and counseling relationships.

At the same time, there are some things about yourself which others do not know much about. These things may be hidden or undisclosed for various reasons (Quadrant II). This is not necessarily because you have deep, dark secrets and you are afraid to disclose them, but it may be because you have not had a chance to tell certain things about yourself.

To reveal your favorite television program to someone, or to share your likes and dislikes about sporting events, is a form of self-disclosure. They become part of the open area, just as much as telling what you remember most about your parents and how they influenced your life. The circumstances of a situation, time, energy, and the invitation to talk about ourselves and our experiences can determine how much we disclose to others.

Some sensitive topics are more likely to be disclosed when we perceive the presence of the facilitative conditions in a relationship. It matters not whether it is with an individual or a group.

Student self-disclosure. Some counselors claim that self-disclosure has a strong cathartic value for students. Many therapies are based on this premise. There may be times when your students need to blurt out their feelings or "pop off," just to drain away some tension. They might talk rapidly and impulsively with you, just to "get it out"—to hear how their ideas sound to themselves as much as to you. One way of helping students sort out their ideas and feelings is to encourage them to disclose more and explore with them their ideas. Such a process can help them to gain a better picture of themselves and how a situation is affecting them.

You might be thinking, "But students are always talking about themselves. They disclose continually." That is probably true, especially when you consider non-verbal communication. Yet, when students talk with others casually about their interests and needs, they seldom are in a situation where they can share their feelings and ideas in depth. They rarely have a chance to discuss a topic to any great length because somebody is changing the topic or taking the focus away from them.

Systematically helping students disclose their ideas and feelings about school, and the things in their lives that affect their learning at school, is part of a counselor's job. Some students will not "open up" to adults. They are accustomed to being evaluated or "put down." Some quickly learn to clam up after they have started to reveal things about themselves because they begin to receive subtle, or blatant, messages which warn them to be careful and cautious. This is especially true when they are not experiencing the facilitative conditions of a helping relationship.

It is difficult to help students assess themselves or to change their ideas, attitudes, and behaviors if you do not know what they are thinking or feeling. Therefore, when providing guidance and counseling services to students, you will want to create situations and an atmosphere in which students can self-disclose and talk about matters.

Counselor self-disclosure. There was a time when counselors and teachers were told that they should not reveal much of their own personal ideas, feelings, and values to students. It was assumed that students would be unduly influenced by teacher and counselor ideas, feelings, values, and decisions. Some early client-centered theorists, for example, believed that counselor self-disclosure would influence the counseling process in an inappropriate way and make it less productive, since clients would try to please their counselors (Patterson, 1959). There appears to be some truth to this idea. Students may say things that they think will please a counselor, especially if they are not experiencing the facilitative conditions.

Johnson and Matross (1977) described a trust-enhancing, self-disclosure sequence in which the counselee first discloses personal information about needs, problems, history, and relationships. The helper then responds by offering the facilitative conditions, and reciprocates in self-disclosure by revealing such information as views of the counselee, reactions to the unfolding counseling situation, and personal information.

Several investigations have shown that helper self-disclosure does function to elicit client self-disclosure and ratings of greater helper trustworthiness (e.g. Bierman, 1969; Sermat and Smyth, 1973; Simonson and Bahr, 1974). But research is still inconclusive regarding what and how the helper might self-disclose to be effective.

In a sense, everything that you do while you are with others reveals something about yourself. Your choice of words, for example, may tell how you feel and what you value. Or they may reveal your attitude or a hidden agenda that you are carrying into a meeting. You cannot avoid revealing some things about yourself in counseling, even if you try. The point here, however, is what and how you self-disclose. What is the most facilitative way to disclose things about yourself?

First, most students have heard parents and teachers tell about their student days, "the good old days." "When I was a kid, I had to...." is an opening line that is a sure bet to turn students away. Similarly, students have heard such things as, "If you think it's tough now, well I can remember when I...." Or, "When I was your age, I...." For the most part, students have a difficult time imagining adults, especially teachers and counselors, as young people their age. It does not compute well with them.

In the second place, most adults usually go too far when they self-disclose things about themselves. They tell too many details and they do not share enough of their feelings. They seldom miss having a moral to the story. The bottom line is usually, "So, I understand what you are going through, and therefore...." It may even have the ring of that's what happened to me, here's what I did, and this is what you can do (or should not do). Students frequently hear more advice than a genuine shared experience.

To avoid falling into old cliches and boring students with stories about days past, remember to self-disclose more of your feelings than the details of the event or situation. Be cautious when telling students how you solved a similar problem or how you turned a potential disaster into a smashing success. Rather, emphasize what you were feeling during those times.

For example, consider the following self-disclosure by a school counselor, working with a high school senior who was trying to make a decision about college:

> "I was unsure about what college I wanted to attend, too, when I was your age. There was a lot or pressure on me to make a decision. Those were confusing times."

Notice how the counselor, in this case, communicated what was thought to be a similar experience. In contrast, the following would probably be less effective.

> "I remember when I was trying to decide between two colleges. I finally decided on the one closest to home because that is where my friends were going and I could get home easier when I needed to. Today I would look more at what courses were offered; but, I guess your first college major does not make any difference. Most people change. I know I changed my major three times. Now, if I were you, I would...."

Interesting, no doubt, but this self-disclosure runs the risk of being only tangential to what the student is experiencing. Most attention events add credibility to the advice that is about to follow.

If you focus primarily on the feelings that you experienced in a situation and less on the event itself, then you are likely to build a bond that cuts across differences. This is particularly true as you begin to work with students of a different race, sex, economic, or cultural background. Similar feelings bridge communication gaps more than similar events or situations. Self-disclosure will be a mutual experience for you and your students as you work with them. The appropriateness, timeliness, and the extent of personal disclosure will result from your professional judgment and skill.

The self-disclosure process is the first priority in counseling and guidance and it sets the foundation for other facilitative processes. As students disclose more about themselves in guidance and counseling activities, they can receive feedback from others about their ideas, feelings, attitudes, and behaviors. The two facilitative processes of self-disclosure and feedback interact together to create a free and open relationship as the facilitative conditions continue to grow (Quadrant I expands). It is in this facilitative relationship that people can begin to explore their ideas in greater depth, to evaluate their goals more honestly, to examine alternatives, to make responsible decisions, and to find solutions to their problems.

Feedback

Feedback is a term that probably had its origin in electronics and aerospace engineering. It implies that a circuit is looped back to its original source and this flow back allows for a modification of an effect that produced the results.

For example, the thermostats in your home use information about temperature to activate air conditioning or heating units. Commercial airline pilots use guidance systems that involve feeding information into computers and then confirming or correcting the airplane's flight pattern.

In a similar sense, personal feedback is helpful to us as individuals. It sometimes validates our attitudes and behaviors. At other times, it helps us modify or make changes in our lives. Feedback from others can help us stay on track or chart a new direction. As seen in the Relationship Quadrant (Figure 5.1), there are some things (facts and perceptions) that are known to others but not necessarily known to us. This area (Quadrant III) has been called a blind spot or a blind area, which can only be reduced by the process of feedback.

What do you know about your friends? What do they know about you? If you know the same things about each other, then you can talk about these matters and they may often be a subject of conversation with one another (Quadrant I). You may have told some of your friends things about yourself that others, with whom you are less acquainted, do not know (Quadrant II). In other words, you moved some things from the closed to the open area (Quadrant II to Quadrant I) as you found the occasion and time to talk with your friends. Similarly, they may have done the same with you.

There are also things that your friends know about you but may not have shared with you. They have observed you in several situations and have noticed how you behaved. They have also experienced certain reactions to things that you have done. They have formed impressions of you and have reached some conclusions about you as a person. Unless they have taken time to tell you, much of this information is still blind to you (Quadrant III). Feedback from those who have observed you can add to the open area. When done in a positive way, it can open the relationship even more and provides you some valuable information.

As one of the three facilitative processes, feedback is an essential part of guidance and counseling services. First, any useful data that is collected can be used by students to assess their development and progress. It can help them determine if they are accomplishing their goals or objectives. It also reinforces some behaviors and provides a stimulus for changing others. In addition, counselors need feedback from students and teachers. They need to know how they are being perceived in their work. They also need to know what kinds of counseling interventions are working and which ones are not.

Feedback in the Facilitative Model can be equated with personal information that is received about one's self. There are several possible sources of data, including tests and inventories. But, personal information from other people, including reactions of peers, is the most valuable and useful of all.

Increased Awareness and Decision-making

The third facilitative process in the Facilitative Model is that of increased awareness and decision-making. It is this process that most people want to experience when they seek a counselor for help. Decision-making or problem-solving are not always seen as products of self-disclosure and feedback. However, these processes are closely related.

Most people want their problems solved immediately. They want to tell their story in brief and be told what to do, or at least it seems that way. They want to learn more about themselves in a few quick steps. They prefer everything to be as painless and effortless as possible. It is human nature to wish for an easy and satisfying process that does not take much time or commitment. Yet, it usually takes time to establish a facilitative relationship. It takes time and energy to disclose and explore ideas and feelings. It also takes time and commitment to receive and give feedback. Finally, it is hard work to identify goals, weigh alternatives, set priorities, and take some action steps.

Again, the Relationship Quadrant helps us gain insight into the process of decision-making or problem-solving. As Quadrant I increases in scope and depth, people talk openly about matters. The processes of self-disclosure and feedback help Quadrant I grow and become meaningful. The potential for a relationship (Quadrant IV) also grows as Quadrants II and III decrease in size as self-disclosure and feedback take place. It is in the context of Quadrant I that people experience a greater awareness of themselves and others and they feel more confident in making decisions and solving problems. This third facilitative process, then, is a product or outgrowth of Quadrant I, despite its size and scope. The more limited the open relationship, the more limited the communication and, consequently, the ability to become more aware of self and others and to make decisions. These three processes are directly related to the action that a person takes as a result of working in a helping relationship. Responsible action is the final process and final goal.

Responsible Action

Considering alternative courses of action happens with increased awareness and the decision-making process. As students think about what they can do and the consequences of any action they might take, they gain a clearer picture of their own rights and responsibilities. Eventually, they are encouraged to take some action to make a decision or solve a problem.

The person ultimately responsible for taking any action is the counselee, who has had a valuable counseling or guidance experience with a counselor or teacher-advisor. While helpers have to resist the urge to rush in to advise and act for the student, students must learn to form their own courses of action and then to implement them.

In general, the best way to implement a course of action is to develop a plan and search for some step-by-step procedures which will lead to success. Moving toward a goal through small steps tends to assure students that they are moving in the right direction and that they are making some progress toward achieving their goal.

Sometimes an action step involves developing a skill or practicing one. This might be done in individual or small group counseling. It also might result from guidance activities that are part of TAP. It could be an outcome of a student having had an opportunity to talk with another student about a decision that one is trying to make.

Despite the plan of action, students learn that they are responsible for implementing the plan and its consequences. It is the fear of having to accept the consequences or the fear that they will fail which often prevents people from taking action, even a first step. As students take action, they also learn to evaluate their outcomes and to make new choices. They elicit feedback and explore their feelings, perhaps their indecision. They seek new understandings of themselves because of the actions that they took and consider new alternatives. They examine details and find new courses of action. In the process they become more mature and responsible.

Professional counselors and teachers know that they must help create and participate in the four processes of self-disclosure, feedback, increased awareness and decision-making, and responsible action. They also remember that they are not working alone in making these processes happen, but that it is a joint effort between helpers and helpees.

The facilitative processes during counseling and guidance are directly related to what people do and say in the time that they are together (Figure 5.2). Therefore, special attention needs to be given to how people talk with one another as they attempt to produce the four facilitative processes and the facilitative conditions.

Figure 5.2

Facilitative Processes
(Individual or Group)

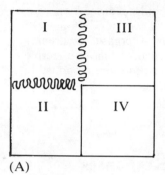

(A)

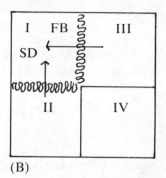

(B)

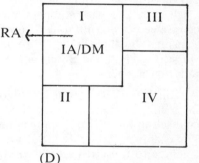

(C)   (D)

SD= Self-disclosure
FB= Feedback
IC/DM= Increased awareness/Decision-making
RA= Responsible Action
〰〰 = Barrier

(A) The barriers around the open area (I) can be broken through
     facilitative responses and facilitative activities, or both, in
     order to enhance the facilitative processes.

(B) Through self-disclosure (SD) and feedback (FB), the open
     area (I) is expanded; there is more freedom to discuss and ex-
     plore issues in this area.

(C) As the barriers are reduced, the open (I) and potential (IV) areas get larger and the blind (III) and closed (II) areas are reduced. This is true for both individual and group relationships.

(D) When the open area (I) is expanded and developed, there is more opportunity to gain increased awareness about self, others, and special issues or concerns. Increased awareness by itself may be valuable, but it also leads to more effective decision-making. This, in turn, can lead to more responsible action on the part of an individual or group.

The High Facilitative Responses

About 25 years ago, researchers began to take note of how people talked with one another. They were particularly interested in how teachers talked with students and how counselors responded to counselees. It was not long before it was concluded that even relationships which are intended to be helpful can be for better or for worse (Carkhuff and Berenson, 1967), depending upon the type of talk that happens.

Although Carl Rogers never advocated or outlined specific talking techniques when he described his client-centered approach to counseling and therapy, some of his colleagues and supporters did. For example, Arbuckle (1950) was among the first to encourage teachers to use client-centered concepts of the helping relationship. He described how teachers could be better helpers if they listened carefully and adopted a student-centered attitude.

Flanders (1965) reported fifteen years later that 95 percent of all teacher talk in the classroom is in the form of advising, judging, giving opinions, reporting facts, and providing information. Not much has changed since then. Most classroom interactions, despite grade level, are situations in which the teacher talks and the students listen. This may be appropriate occasionally, but when it dominates a teacher's style, then the working relationship is one-sided and less productive than it could be.

More recently, Wittmer and Myrick (1980), among others (e.g. Dinkmeyer, McKay, and Dinkmeyer, 1980; Ginott, 1972; Gordon, 1974), expressed concern about teacher-student relationships and tried to help teachers view themselves as facilitators. They wanted teachers to play a more significant role in helping students grow personally and socially, as part of the academic process. They emphasized that meaningful learning was a product of facilitative teaching and described how classroom communication could be improved.

Likewise, communication between counselors and clients has been highlighted as a critical factor in the helping process. While acknowledging non-verbal communication, most writers have concentrated on verbal interaction (e.g Carkhuff and Berenson, 1967; Benjamin, 1969; Brammer, 1973; Ivey and Simek-Downing, 1980). All contemporary authors of books about counseling and therapy suggest ways that counselors might talk with their clients.

You will find no exception here. Counselor talk is such an important variable that everything else pales when compared to it. Even one's attitude is conveyed through how a person talks and the words that are chosen to express an idea.

The Facilitative Model is based on the assumption that personal relationships are the basis for effective teaching and counseling. In turn, personal relationships are built on selective listening and responding. Certain verbal responses, and non-verbal behaviors, increase the probability of a helper being perceived as friendly, caring, understanding, accepting, and trustworthy. Facilitative responses help create the facilitative conditions and enhance the helping relationship.

There are six basic responses that are the foundation of the Facilitative Model. You will want to increase the frequency of them in your work. They are: 1) the feeling-focused response; 2) clarifying or summarizing response; 3) open question; 4) facilitative feedback, as a compliment or confrontation; 5) simple acknowledgement; and 6) linking.

The Feeling-Focused Response

The feeling-focused response is one of the three highest facilitative responses you can make to others. It is an attempt to surpass the events or ideas that are being expressed and to capture the essence of a person's experience. It directs attention to what a person is feeling.

Some writers have referred to this type of response as "reflecting understanding," knowing that people feel better understood when someone senses what they are feeling in a situation and mirrors back those feelings. There is a feeling of being understood when others communicate that they have grasped the essence of your experience.

Here are some examples of feeling-focused responses:

"You're really angry, John."
"Jennifer, you seem confused."
"That was exciting for you."
"You're feeling more relaxed now."
"It hurts to think about it."

Feeling words are the key ingredients in these empathic statements. A feeling word has to be present in this type of response. It cannot be assumed that you understand and know what the person is feeling. You have to say or do something to show it.

You have probably heard the old adage, "Put yourself in the other person's shoes." It suggests that by doing so you will be more understanding. You could also ask yourself, "How would I feel if I were to say something like that?" Or, "How would I have to feel to do something like that?"

The answer to these questions might give you some insight to what the person is experiencing. They might lead you to be more empathic. However, the problem with this approach is that it sometimes traps you into projecting your own feelings on others. We often assume others experience things the same way we do, whereas this may not be true.

Being perceived as an empathic listener, one who responds accurately to what a person is experiencing, requires you to tune into the person's feelings and respond to them. It is not enough to identify the feelings and say nothing or to think you understand and not verbalize that understanding. It is never enough to say simply, "I understand what you are experiencing" or "I know what you are going through." Neither of these statements communicate understanding.

Pleasant and unpleasant feelings. One helpful method which can make you a more empathic person is to listen for the feelings that exceed the literal sense of the words. Ask yourself: "Am I hearing pleasant feelings, unpleasant feelings, or both?" This will give you some clues regarding what the person is experiencing.

To assist teachers and counselors in their work, it has been suggested that pleasant and unpleasant feeling word lists be developed with students (Wittmer and Myrick, 1980). These lists could be posted for easy reference by everyone. Helping students develop a feeling word vocabulary is a part of guidance and counseling and is just as important as teaching them some problem-solving strategies.

A list of some pleasant and unpleasant feeling words is presented in Figure 5.3. Review the list. Which words are most familiar to you? Which ones do you tend to use the most in your work? Which ones are likely to be present in certain situations? Which ones are unfamiliar to you or sound strange? What are some current slang expressions which students use to tell about their feelings which could be added to list?

If you are looking for a key to being a more empathic counselor, then begin by increasing your feeling word vocabulary. This enables you to be more sensitive and to respond more accurately to what people say and do. Be as precise as you can, choosing the best word to grasp the person's feeling.

There are many feeling words that are closely related. Sometimes you might choose one that captures a shade of the basic emotion (e.g. "You're annoyed," instead of "You're mad.") It acknowledges the unpleasant experience and may not evoke as much defensiveness as some words which are less socially accepted. If you are wrong, or if people want to use even stronger words to emphasize their emotions, then you can substitute or add another word.

Making a feeling-focused response, even when it is not exactly on target, will usually get you credit for being an understanding person. You are trying, and most people appreciate the effort. You can always be corrected. But, meanwhile, your attempt emphasizes how much you want to understand. You can hardly lose when you make feeling-focused responses. Even when corrected, if not accurate, your effort tends to put you in closer communication with the other person and your understanding is enhanced.

Many people are unaware of their feelings. In times past, people frequently ignored or suppressed them. "Don't get emotional" is an expression that most of us have heard, especially when we were trying to make a decision or to solve a problem. The assumption is that logical and clear-headed thinking is without personal feelings. This is nonsense.

Figure 5.3

Feeling Words

PLEASANT	UNPLEASANT
enjoyment	defeated
satisfied	suspicious
excited	doubtful
loved	threatened
happy	offended
contented	disgusted
delighted	guarded
proud	angry
hopeful	hateful
accepted	rejected
bright	unhappy
peaceful	sore
calm	cramped
warm	worried
close	troubled
strong	shocked
optimistic	depressed
joyful	disappointed
pleased	discouraged
cheerful	pained
stimulated	abused
refreshed	uneasy
trusting	uncomfortable
confident	sad
secure	gloomy
interested	tired
needed	bored
powerful	fearful
relieved	confused
relaxed	irritated
special	annoyed
important	angry
uplifted	concerned
inspired	empty
successful	overwhelmed
appreciated	defensive
welcomed	pressured
satisfied	fragmented

Our feelings have a powerful influence on our behavior. Feelings are a part of living. There are a few people who are so unresponsive to their environment that the scope of their feelings is limited. These unfeeling people are dysfunctioning. If a student is without feeling or affect, the counselor knows that extensive help and therapy, probably beyond school resources, are probably needed. The person should be referred to a doctor or mental health professional.

Most of us experience many kinds of feelings during a day. We take some routine events in stride while others are unsettling. Generally, there is a very low level of awareness of our feelings as our thoughts and images seem to take precedence in most situations. As people respond to our feelings, our awareness increases. Feelings complete the pictures that we have of ourselves.

Feeling-focused responses will help you be perceived as someone who cares, who is interested, and who is an attentive listener. They help people feel more comfortable and relaxed with you, as you demonstrate your empathic abilities and show that you are trying to understand how they see things.

To begin a sentence with "You feel...," does not necessarily mean that you will focus on a person's feelings. For instance: "You feel that the basketball team will win tonight." This statement is not a feeling-focused response. It is really directed to the person's opinion or idea. It might be stated, "You feel excited about the game... and think the team will win tonight." The first part focuses on the feeling and the second part goes on to emphasize the person's thoughts or ideas about the game. To receive credit for this type of response, feeling words (pleasant or unpleasant) must be in the context of the statement.

Another response that is not feeling-focused is: "I feel that you should study more." This is an opinion. It suggests what the person should do. The response is not person-centered; it is a form of advice coming from someone else's experience.

Feeling-focused responses can echo feelings that may or may not have been expressed overtly. You follow the lead of the person. Nothing new is offered except your own perception of the feelings that are being expressed.

We talk and behave with feeling. We always feel something, although we may not be aware of the feelings that complement the experience. Both our verbal and nonverbal behavior reveal these feelings to others, especially if they are attentive observers and tune into our experiences.

Non-verbal behavior and communication. Non-verbal communication is a part of the interaction that happens between you and the person you are helping. It does not receive much attention in most counseling texts. We need to know more about it and how to use it in our work. We typically acknowledge its importance and sense its strength and power, but we still neglect it.

Nonverbal communication comes through in the tone of one's voice, the speed at which one speaks, the pauses, and the hesitations that happen as an event is being described. It includes stammering, stuttering, shouting, whispering, and other vocal expressions. It also includes facial expressions, hand gestures, foot movements, and body position.

Body messages are part of the communication process. Often the position or the movement of one's body will communicate whether one is experiencing pleasant or unpleasant feelings. A turn of the lip, a frown, a grinding of teeth, or a rolling of the eyes can be valuable clues as to what someone is thinking and feeling. Although an awareness of non-verbal behavior can be helpful in counseling and teaching, there is no reliable reference book which helps us analyze and interpret this type of behavior.

Eventually, the person with whom you are working will be assisted to see how feelings and behaviors are related. Feelings and behaviors play a significant role in decision-making and problem-solving. Yet, in the general scheme of life, feeling-focused responses are uncommon to everyday talk. Many people, consequently, complain that nobody understands them. Feeling-focused responses are often times considered the most critical response in the counseling process. They communicate understanding and add to the other facilitative conditions.

The Clarifying or Summarizing Response

If you are like most listeners, when a person is talking you will attend to the events or the ideas that are being talked about. They are the basis of the conversation and provide the framework for accurate understanding. Although emotion is part of expressing ideas, the thoughts and the story that are being communicated must also be understood.

After listening attentively, you may want to clarify a significant idea or summarize some themes that you heard expressed. For instance,

"You aparently have already made your plans."

"Let's see then, you plan to enter the military service after graduation."

"You and your parents disagree about what you should do after graduation."

Clarifying or summarizing responses attempt to capture basic ideas or events. When so much is being said in a free-flowing conversation, many things are communicated. One statement might express a key idea, such as plans after graduation, while other statements support the idea. Sometimes the person who is talking will veer off course and begin talking about something else, maybe introducing more key thoughts, which may or may not be relevant to the first idea expressed. Being an attentive listener is not an easy job, especially when a person is rambling along about many things.

It can be helpful to make a clarifying or summarizing response when you: a) are not sure if you are following the person's train of thought; b) are not sure if you heard something correctly; or c) want to draw attention or emphasize something that was said. Such responses focus on the content of the discussion or the events of the story. There is no attempt to use feeling words, although feelings may be heard when the ideas were expressed.

As you try to focus the conversation or highlight a few ideas, use fresh words when you clarify or summarize. This helps you avoid parroting. You can use some of the same words, but turn the basic phrases around, unless you deliberately want to repeat the phrasing for emphasis. Some people have referred to this type of statement as paraphrasing, which is a rewording of the meaning expressed in something written or spoken.

When used at appropriate moments, clarifying or summarizing responses help communicate that you are interested in following the thoughts that people are expressing and that you want to understand them. These responses also give people an opportunity to hear their ideas and to think more about what they have said. In a sense, they can provide a focus to the discussion, almost serving as a checklist of ideas that are receiving attention.

If you have misunderstood, the person to whom you are talking can correct you or add information that could increase your knowledge. Then, you are back on track and can again follow the lead of the person as the story continues.

Unfortunately, the clarifying and summarizing responses have been spoofed by a few people who associate them with a lack of genuineness. They might think that you are using a phony technique by mirroring back ideas, especially when they hear some typical lead in phrases such as:

"If I hear you correctly...."
"You seem to be saying...."
"If I am following you, you are saying...."
"In other words, you are trying to...."
"Correct me if I am wrong, but...."
"What I hear from what you have said is...."
"It strikes me that you are primarily...."
"I have heard these key ideas, 1)...."
"Let me see if I understand, you have said...."
"What is emerging from all that you said is...."
"Let's see, you are thinking that...."

There is nothing wrong with such introductory phrases. In fact, they can be useful. They alert the person that you are trying to focus the conversation. They also provide a little "wiggle room" or a simple qualification of what you are planning to clarify or summarize. Moreover, they can provide you a lead as you attempt to express your thoughts.

Suppose that a student came to your office and began talking about a test which was to be given in the near future. You might respond to the person's feelings (e.g. "You're worried about the test;" "It makes you uneasy and nervous to think about it"). You might clarify or summarize (e.g. "This test is coming up soon;" "You're planning to spend tonight studying for the test"). In both cases, you follow the lead of the student, rather than give advice or reassuring remarks, and this facilitates more communication.

The Open Question

Questions can be either open or closed. Closed questions only require simple yes or no responses. They are sometimes experienced as a "just give me the facts" approach. On the other hand, open questions ask for more information and encourage answers with more explanation. Look at these examples:

"Do you get along with your teachers?" (closed)
"What can you tell me about your teachers?" (open)

"Did you talk with your teacher?" (closed)
"What did you say to your teacher?" (open)

The open question provides a broad base from which to respond. There is some leeway and how the person responds may provide valuable clues and information. The closed question is narrow and only interested in the basic fact. Closed questions also tend to be couched in terms of your perspective, whereas open questions elicit student points of view.

Note the examples below. Which do you find more inviting?

"You don't like school, do you?" (closed)
"What do you dislike about school?" (open)

"Is this task confusing to you?" (closed)
"What is it that's confusing to you?" (open)

"Are you going to go to college?" (closed)
"What do you think about going to college? (open)

Open questions are more facilitative because they invite additional self-disclosure. They encourage people to express themselves more. Closed questions, however, also have their value, especially if you are trying to get some specific information or confirm some thoughts or facts about something. There will be times when you can speed up information gathering by using closed questions, if that is what you want to accomplish.

The most facilitative open questions tend to begin with "What" or "How" instead of "Why." The latter is risky since it tends to ask people to explain or justify themselves. The infamous "why" question deserves special attention.

Most people do not know the reasons they do the things they do. Yet, they might be asked, "Why did you do that?" Many students respond to such a question with a quick, "I don't know." They look away or shrug their shoulders. They feel on the spot. Look at these questions:

"Why don't you study more?"
"Why did you hit him like that?"
"Why are you always late for class?"
"Why do you play your music so loud?"
"Why didn't you talk with your teacher?"

How would you feel if such questions were directed to you? What kinds of answers are possible? What kinds of impact do you think they might make on students?

We may never discover or understand all the reasons we do the things we do. A rational explanation of some things seems almost impossible. In addition, the "why" question has also come to mean something else besides a question. It is often an opinion. Look again at the examples above. Behind each of the questions is advice: Study more; Do not hit; Be on time for class; Turn down the music; Talk with your teacher.

When students hear the "why" in a question, they also hear criticism. They frequently get defensive, even when it is a legitimate question of interest or concern. Therefore, facilitative counselors and teachers limit their use of this open question, knowing that it is not as productive as turning it into a "what" or "how" question. For example:

"Why did you cut school yesterday?"
"What made you want to cut school yesterday?"

"Why don't you like math class?"
"How could math class be better for you?"

"Why don't you study more?"
"What keeps you from studying more?

"Why don't you like school?
"What's your biggest complaint about school?"

The what and how questions are more specific and they are easier to answer. The why questions, although they may produce some insightful thought and comments, are usually less productive because they tend to elicit rationalizations and defensive postures.

Clearly the wording of a question, the way in which it is phrased or posed, can make a difference in the response that is received. Tone of voice can also make a difference. A question is a response to someone and it communicates your values and interests.

Finally, students frequently say that teachers, counselors, and parents ask too many questions of them. Out of habit and social custom, more than anything else, it is easy to ask questions. We have heard and used them more than other kinds of responses. It is easy to fall into the trap of asking questions and failing to listen to the answers.

Behind every question is an assumption. The basis of the question is likely to be found in what the person said. Therefore, questions can easily be turned into statements, which are either feeling-focused or clarifying responses. For example,

Closed Question:
"Do you listen to rock music?"

Statements:
"You listen to like rock music."
"You enjoy rock music."

Open Question:
"What feelings do you have about the war?"

Statements:
"The war is on your mind a lot these days."
"You worry about the war."

Turn questions into statements to reduce the number of questions you pose to students. This can be especially helpful if you find yourself asking a lot of questions. It is also effective to ask an open question and follow it with a feeling-focused or clarifying response. This kind of interaction keeps the focus on the students and facilitates conversation.

Facilitative Feedback: Complimenting and Confronting

Feedback, as a process, involves reducing blind areas in a relationship, as presented in the Relationship Quadrant (Figure 5.1). When you use a feedback response, you will be telling another person the impact that person is having on you. The response is a personal one in which you are expressing your own feelings about a person's behavior.

Students want feedback. They want to know how they are coming across to others. This includes both the personal and academic aspects of their lives. While they may be skeptical of flattering statements or leery of criticisms, they nevertheless are curious about how others experience them and the impressions that they make.

How can you give people feedback without judging them? How can you compliment or confront people without making them feel defensive?

Facilitative feedback consists of a three part response. It can be either a compliment or a confrontation, depending upon what you want to communicate.

Part 1: Be specific about the behavior. What has the person done? Give an example and be descriptive.

Part 2: Tell how the person's behavior makes you feel. Is your experience a pleasant or unpleasant one? Or both?

Part 3: ***Tell what your feelings make you want to do.*** Being in the presence of the person's behavior and feeling as you do, how do you want to respond?

The three high facilitative responses mentioned earlier (feeling-focused, clarifying or summarizing, and open questions) are powerful tools which keep the focus of discussion on the students with whom you are working. Feedback still keeps the focus on the students, but it also discloses some things about yourself. It is an honest response that can be presented in an organized manner so that your message is clear.

See if you can identify the three parts of feedback, as we have defined them, in the following response:

> "Richard, I remember you telling me about your
> getting a morning job before school and how rushed
> you were going to be, but I've noticed that you've been
> to school on time every day this grading period. I'm
> proud of you and it makes me want to support you in
> anyway that I can."

Now, try this example:

> "Jennifer, I'm interested, but I'm also confused. I'm not
> sure what to say to you. You came in the office today,
> sat down, and haven't said anything. You're just staring
> at me."

In the first example, a compliment was paid to Richard and the three parts of facilitative feedback were presented in the order of parts 1, 2, and 3. In the case of Jennifer, however, the parts appear in a different order (2, 3, and 1). They are also the basis of a gentle confrontation.

The order of the feedback parts in a statement is not particularly important, unless their placement may create a different emphasis. In fact, the order of the parts can be mixed easily. Sometimes only the first two parts are relied upon to provide a basic feedback response.

The three parts of the feedback model help us to organize our thoughts and to communicate them. They provide a format, just as though you were writing a thoughtful letter and you were using your best knowledge of English grammar and paragraphing.

The difference between a compliment and confrontation can be found in part 2, regardless of where it appears in the feedback statement. Your pleasant feelings will be perceived as a compliment, while your unpleasant feelings will probably be received as a confrontation.

Both compliments and confrontations can be difficult for people to receive. Most people are not used to them. They may feel defensive, especially when confronted. Feedback statements are sometimes dismissed in an off-hand way because they are so personal. Few people have experience in how to respond positively to them. However, the words are likely to be heard and the impact felt.

Students will especially like to hear about how they have affected you in a pleasant way. They will enjoy hearing your compliments. It creates warm feelings for them and they will be drawn to you, although first they may feel a little uneasy to hear positive things about themselves. You can help others feel important by tuning into some of the pleasant feelings that you experience when they do certain things.

On the other hand, we have learned that when we share our unpleasant feelings, there is a tendency for people to be defensive. They may initially pull back and take a second look at you, then probably at themselves. Therefore, there are three guidelines that may be helpful when confronting.

First, do you have any "chips in the bank?" This is another way of asking, "Have you taken time to listen to the person?" Have you tried to be understanding? Every time that you are an attentive listener and use feeling-focused responses, clarifying or summarizing responses and open questions in your talk with students, you are putting some "chips in the bank." In essence, you are building up a reserve that can be drawn upon when it is time to confront. Some counselors have reported that they intended to confront students, but after listening to their stories and after making an effort to make other facilitative responses, there was more understanding and less unpleasant feelings. There was no need to confront.

Secondly, is your unpleasant feeling a persistent one? Nobody likes a grouch or someone who "pops off" at every little turn. Life is full of conflict and you do not want to confront everyone who has created some unpleasant feelings in you. However, it is neither healthy nor wise to let things build to the point that they "boil over." That can be messy and hard to clean up. When persistent feelings are left to simmer and boil, then a relationship suffers. Timely confrontations are valuable and have a place in a facilitative relationship.

Finally, which words best communicate your ideas? If you are too intense and choose words that are loaded with heavy emotion, you run the risk of not being heard. The impact of the feedback response could be diminished, if not dismissed.

There are many words which describe unpleasant feelings and that could be used in a confrontation. Some are similar but have a slightly different shade of meaning. For instance, it may not be helpful to tell a person how much "hate" you feel. It might be better to tell how you feel "irritated" or "annoyed." Words that are too intense can miss the target. Obviously, your choice of words depends upon the situation, your judgment, and your own personal style.

Facilitative feedback, whether a compliment or a confrontation, is systematic. It offers you a degree of control over your own emotions. It can generate energy and release tension. After you give feedback to people, then it is time to carefully focus your attention on them and tune into any reactions. It is time to continue making facilitative responses to enhance the relationship.

Like the other responses, compliments and confrontations are most effective when the timing is right. Again, the more "chips in the bank" that you have, the more receptive the person will likely be. If you are working with a student who is in a shell and does not want to spend time with you, then your words will probably bounce off, like water off a turtle's back. On the other hand, if you use facilitative responses to have an open and positive relationship, then your time together will be more productive and you will feel like you are a counselor.

Suggestions or advice, if any, may be included as one aspect of the third part of the feedback model, but it is qualified. It is also linked to the source—your feelings. Those who receive feedback are ultimately responsible for whether they want to continue or to change their behavior. But, they need to know how their behaviors affect others. It is part of the facilitative processes.

Facilitative feedback may be *direct* or *indirect*. The direct approach can be seen in the examples provided above. Direct feedback is straight-forward and relies upon the a clear choice of words to draw attention to the person's behaviors and to your reactions. The indirect approach uses metaphors to describe the impact that behaviors have on you. Inanimate objects, animals, or fantasized ideas can be used to help communicate your experiences.

For instance, something like this might be said:

"Derrick, you remind me of a book. It is brand new and it is never been opened. I don't know much about it, except what I have heard from others. The cover is interesting and I find myself wanting to open it, turn a few pages, and get a better idea of the book before I recommend it to others."

Or, "Renee, you remind me of a fast race horse. You have so much energy and you plunge right into things. I envy your ability to get things done so quickly. It makes me want to be around you more, because I think you'll win many races and you are fun to watch."

Do you have any ideas about these two people? Do you think that this feedback would be helpful to them? In both examples, the speaker is being descriptive. You can do the same. Tell size, color, location, and unique qualities. Include your feelings and what you want to do with the object when you are in its presence. All three parts of the facilitative feedback response are included. Also, the parts could have been put in a different order.

Indirect feedback may have a lighter tone, but it can be just as effective as direct feedback. It sometimes allows us to say things that would otherwise be difficult to say through the direct approach. It is dramatic and creative. It appeals to some students and catches their attention more than other kinds of responses.

Facilitative feedback, the art of complimenting and confronting, is an essential skill for counselors and teachers. It enhances the helping process. In addition, we also learn more about ourselves through feedback to others because we invariably disclose some things about ourselves.

Simple Acknowledgement

People like to be acknowledged for their contributions. They might be embarrassed or feel awkward if what they say is ignored. Therefore, a simple acknowledgement can be facilitative, especially in groups.

Here are a few common simple acknowledgements:

"Thank you for sharing that."
"Okay."
"Thanks."
"All right."

These responses, and others like them, help avoid the "plop experience," when someone says something and nobody responds before moving onto someone else. It is easy enough to recognize that you heard the person without discussing or making reference to any specific ideas. In addition, such a response is effective in bringing closure to someone's comments. It acknowledges but does not encourage the person to talk more—at that time. It is a polite way of telling a person that you are now going to move on to another topic or another person.

Linking

The linking response is especially facilitative in groups. Although it could be used to refer to another person who is not present, it is effective when a group leader identifies similarities (and perhaps differences) that are occurring among group members. For example:

> "Juan and James, you both seem to have a special interest in soccer." (Linking content).

> "Juan and James, you're excited about trying out for the soccer team." (Linking feeling).

As a group leader, you can look for opportunities to "link" events that students have in common or their ideas or general experiences. On the other hand, you can also link feelings. You listen for unpleasant and pleasant feelings as they are being expressed by group members and, on occasion, try to show how these feelings are shared.

Linking responses help develop a sense of togetherness in a group and add to group cohesiveness. They accentuate relationships by linking information or feelings from one person to another. They enhance the facilitative conditions within a group and, therefore, are listed as one of the six facilitative responses.

The Low Facilitative Responses

While all responses—at one time or another—might be helpful, some are likely to be less facilitative than others. Three common responses that are generally considered to be low facilitative are: a) advice/evaluation; b) analyzing/interpreting; and c) reassuring/supportive. Let us see how these fit into the facilitative model.

Advice/Evaluation

Advice/evaluation is a category which describes responses that tell people how to behave or which judges behavior. For instance:

"Don't drop geometry, you'll need it later to get into college."
"Instead of arguing, you should try to see his point of view."
"If you'd make a study plan, then you'd get more homework done."
"What you need to do is to talk with your teachers about your concerns."
"One of the best things you can do now is to apologize and ask to get back in class."

Advice is cheap and it is given by almost everyone. Just tune into a group of people for awhile and you will soon hear some form of advice creeping into the conversation. Students hear a lot of advice from their parents, teachers, and counselors. It is easy to recognize and follows such lead-ins as:

"You should...."
"If I were you, I would...."
"The best way is to...."
"If you do not..., then...."
"If you would only...."
"You need to...."
"The thing to do is...."

When advice is relevant and practical, it can be helpful and it might facilitate people toward their goals. This is especially true when it is offered at an appropriate time and is in the form of a suggestion instead of a directive or command. Students will look to you for some timely advice and you will want to advise them on occasion. But, remember that it shifts the responsibility for decision-making and is usually perceived as less respectful, understanding and accepting.

Evaluative statements are judgmental, whether positive or negative. They are unlikely to be facilitative. Even when used as a secondary reinforcer, as advocated by learning theorists (e.g. That is great! Good!), evaluation often closes the door to open communication. People are less inclined to self-disclose for fear of being rejected. Praise and criticism, although well-intended, communicate that you are judging the person.

Advice and evaluation are rated as the least facilitative of responses for building a helping relationship. Yet, they do have their place in the work of counselor and teacher. It is the timely use of them that will make the critical difference.

Analyzing/Interpreting

Analyzing/interpreting responses probably gained their popularity from the theory there is always a logical reason people do the things they do. And, if people only had more insight about their behaviors, they could change. Look at these responses:

> "Don't you see that being critical of school is just another way of expressing your unhappiness with your family's situation?"

> "You want to be an engineer because your father wants that for you."

> "You don't participate in class because you're a shy person and afraid of failing."

> "You want to be in Mrs. Johnson's room because she was your sister's teacher."

The intent is to explain the reason behind the person's thoughts or behavior in the hope that this will provide insight. These responses are marked with "because" terminology and suggest what the student might or should think. There is an attempt to provide some meaning to a situation, but most people do not like to have their behavior or ideas interpreted.

An interpretation may be accurate, but most of the time it is only a guess, a hypothesis at best. Too often interpretative statements are textbook cliches (e.g. "You threw your pencil at her because you wanted attention.") This may or may not be true, but is it facilitative?

Interpretations tend to discourage self-disclosure by confronting people, who then become defensive and hesitate to share their thoughts. Want to slow down rapid and long talking bores? Interpret a few of their statements or behaviors and watch what happens.

Reassuring/Supportive

Reassuring/supportive kinds of responses are intended to tell people that we believe in them. These responses are meant as encouragement, but they can easily dismiss someone's feelings and fail to facilitate self-disclosure. For example:

"Everyone feels like that at your age."
"Things will turn out okay."
"You remind me a lot of another boy, Chris, and he did real well in that class."
"I know how you feel."
"It looks bad now, but things will be better tomorrow."
"There's nothing wrong with you that a couple of year's of growth won't help."

Unfortunately, most of the time reassuring statements miss their mark, probably because they imply that individuals need not feel as they do. They suggest that one's feelings are common, normal, or tentative. They are often followed by advice, or advice is implied. They suggest that one should not be concerned and should feel differently.

To test the impact of the three high and three low responses on the facilitative relationship, three discussion leaders were each assigned two different groups of eighth grade students who were matched for age, sex, academic achievement, and attitude about school. The groups met twice with their leaders, who were counselor education students, to first talk about school and then pet peeves about adults. The groups were very similar, except each leader was instructed to respond to one group with three high facilitative responses (feeling-focused, clarifying/summarizing, open questions) and to the other group with low facilitative responses (closed questions, reassurance, interpretations, and advice).

Tape recordings validated the leader's use of responses in each group. After the two meetings, the students completed a relationship inventory. Results indicated that students who experienced the high facilitative responses described their leaders as more empathic, caring, interested in student ideas, and respectful of students, among other positive helping characteristics. The study was repeated three different times with similar results (Wittmer and Myrick, 1980).

Because many counselors want to push things along in their busy schedules, they have a tendency to use too many low-facilitative responses. Impatience and a press for time often causes counselors to rush in with low facilitative responses. Low facilitative responses have their place in counseling and guidance activities.

You are going to give advice occasionally. You will give reassuring statements and occasionally you may make interpretations. But, it is timely advice, timely interpretations, and timely reassurance that makes the critical difference.

Facilitative Responses in Groups

The six high facilitative responses described earlier are effective with students when you are meeting them individually. You are the only listener and you are totally responsible for responding to the individual. The six responses can also be used with groups of students. In this case, you can still respond to an individual in the context of the group or you can respond to the total group.

For instance, you may notice that a group member is apparently fatigued and struggling to be attentive. You might make a feeling-focused response such as, "Debbie, you're tired and it's not easy to be a part of the group right now." Or, if the group is experiencing fatigue, you might say, "As I look around I'm sensing there is a loss of energy in our group. It seems like we've hit a snag and it's dragging us down."

Likewise, it is possible to clarify a group member's point of view, or some of the ideas that have been expressed by the total group could be clarified or summarized. For example, "If I followed you, Roberta, you think that the school policy should be changed." Or, "Let's see now, in this past half-hour our group has suggested at least four different ways of changing the policy. First, you said...."

Questions can be directed to an individual or to the total group. Simple acknowledgements are usually made to individuals, but could be directed to the whole group. Linking events and feelings tends to be used in the "here and now" as a group works together.

Compliments can be paid to an individual in a group or to the total group. For instance, "I was pleased and encouraged to see that we could start our group on time today, especially knowing that it's not easy for you to get here. It makes me want to make the most of our time together today." Another example might be, "Jessie, I was impressed with the way that you told us about your situation. You shared some personal information and you were not afraid to talk about your feelings. I'm touched by your trust in us and I want to honor that trust and confidence."

When a counselor makes all the responses after each group member has shared something, the process tends to look like individual counseling before an audience. It chokes off communication among group members, the very strength of the group. Group members need to talk with one another, not just to the counselor.

Eliciting the six high facilitative responses from members of the group makes them more responsive to each other. It enhances the facilitative relationship in the group and builds greater cohesiveness.

For instance, you might elicit a feeling-focused response by saying something like this, "Jessie's been telling us about some things that are important to her. Let me ask the rest of you in the group, are you hearing pleasant or unpleasant feelings as she talks?" Then, using a "go around" procedure, each member tells the feelings that were heard.

The same might be done with a clarifying or summarizing response. "What basic ideas have we discussed so far in our group?" Or, "Who can summarize what you heard Jessie say to this group?"

Likewise, questions can be elicited. "Who can ask Jessie a question that will help us think some more about what she's been telling us?" "What's a question that needs to be asked at this point?"

You can also elicit a linking response by asking the group to take note of similarities among members. For example, "Who in our group has some things in common when it comes to the type of jobs they want to have someday?" Or, "It seems that some of you have had some similar experiences or feelings when interviewing for a job. Who remembers the feelings that some of our group members shared in common?"

Thus, you can respond to individuals within a group or to the group as a whole. You can make the facilitative responses or you can elicit them from group members. Consequently, the original six facilitative responses can be doubled when practiced in groups.

Increase the frequency of the facilitative responses. They are not representative of a particular theory. They can be incorporated into whatever theory you find useful, or whatever role you want to play. They are not a panacea by themselves. Taken out of context, they may even appear contrived or phony to you. However, in the context of a guidance and counseling session, and in the time, they can be comforting. They provide a focus and help build close working relationships. And, within those relationships, they also help create the facilitative conditions of self-disclosure, feedback, and decision-making. They help you accomplish the goals of guidance and counseling.

The Facilitative Activities

The facilitative responses are powerful tools and may be adequate alone to facilitate your students. In one group counseling session, for instance, participants might be invited to share what is on their minds, followed by an open discussion of matters. You hope there will be a spontaneous flow of ideas and feelings, as you and your students move toward some guidance and counseling objectives. The movement and direction of the group, in this instance, might depend entirely on the dialogue that happens between you and your students.

However, facilitative activities can also be used to build relationships and expedite the facilitative processes. These activities are considered structured learning experiences, which may be used with individuals or groups. Some activities, for example, are designed to elicit self-disclosure and increase self-awareness. Others encourage self-assessment and feedback. Still others focus on decision-making and problem-solving.

The term "activity" is often used to generally describe a planned structured experience. Each activity has a set of "procedures" which outline the steps to be followed. Counselors pay particular attention to procedures since they structure the flow of the session. In addition, participants in an activity are given "tasks" which call for their responses. Some counselors use these terms interchangeably, but it can be useful if they are viewed in more precise terms.

Facilitative *activities* are structured learning experiences which tend to elicit the facilitative processes of self-disclosure, feedback, increased awareness and decision-making, and responsible action. Some counselors and teachers think of them as exercises. An activity might also be viewed as a composite strategy with procedures and tasks.

Facilitative *procedures* are the sequence of steps to be followed. They describe a course of action or a way of doing something. They are the general guidelines which outline a manner of proceeding in a structured experience.

Facilitative *tasks* are more specific assignments. They request specific action from participants. They may call for certain behaviors or responses and are usually posed as a question or some type of directive.

For example, in group counseling, it is common to begin with introductions (an activity). You might first put group members in pairs (procedure) where they then interview each other (procedure) before introducing one another to the rest of the group. One direction that might be given to each pair is: "During your interview, find out the name of a famous person whom your partner admires and would like to visit" (task). The task, in this case, focused on a specific area for self-disclosure, making it easier for group members to reveal something of themselves. This introductory activity, with its procedures and tasks, aided the facilitative process.

In an individual counseling session, a counselor used an activity to help a student begin talking about future plans. A piece of paper which contained some unfinished sentences (e.g. What I want most is....; Happiness is....; When I am under pressure I....; One thing I want out of life is....) was given to the student, who quickly penciled in some responses which came immediately to mind. Then, the student and counselor talked about the list and some of the responses. In this case, the activity consisted of using some unfinished sentences. The procedures described the stages and steps within the activity (e.g. give the student a paper with unfinished sentences and some directions; talk about the experience) and the task was completing the unfinished sentences themselves.

Facilitative tasks are specific assignments which direct a person to do something. They may be given alone or as part of some group procedures. One task might request a person to "Tell one thing that you do well." Another might be "Tell one thing you would like to improve upon." These tasks focus on self-disclosure.

A person might also be directed to "Tell something positive that you have noticed in one of our group members." Another might be "Tell one thing you have noticed about how we work together." Both tasks focus on feedback.

As you might imagine, tasks can also be directed toward decision-making or problem-solving. For example, "List ten things you want to accomplish this year and then rank order the top three." Or, "List three things that you can do to resolve the problem and then discuss the consequences of each one."

Many of the activities and tasks used in guidance and counseling grew out of human relations training and the group movement of the 60s and 70s. Sensitivity groups, encounter groups, growth groups, and other kinds of groups evolved around certain exercises or procedures. These interpersonal groups increased opportunities for self-understanding and human awareness.

Some of these human relations groups and their related procedures were integrated into academic and guidance programs. A few teachers quickly adapted some for use in their classrooms. However, most teachers and counselors were scared of them or were unsure how to "process" them. Some activities were more facilitative than others and some were entirely inappropriate for the schools. But, we have learned a lot since those soul-searching days and now we borrow the best ideas to make our work easier.

Activities and tasks can be organized in a sequence, as part of a guidance or counseling session or unit. Activities can be arranged so that they are likely to lead students sequentially through the facilitative processes. Self-disclosure is usually the first step, followed by feedback. After a few activities along these lines, it is assumed that the counselees are more open to exploring and making decisions, with the help of some more activities.

Activities and tasks can elicit behaviors and responses from people. They can help focus a discussion, keeping individuals on task. They expedite matters; however, they are not an end to themselves. They do not do the work of the counselor.

You must be selective of activities and make decisions about the best procedures to follow. After giving counselees a task, you must still be the facilitator to move them toward their goals. The activities you choose will fail or have only marginal success without your selected use of high facilitative responses to "process" the experience that results from, and during, the activity.

Facilitative Counseling and Teaching

The Facilitative Model, then, consists of building interpersonal relationships in which students experience the facilitative conditions of trust, understanding, acceptance, caring, respect, and friendliness. These conditions develop as you and your students self-disclose to each other, reducing some of the hidden areas that block communication.

These conditions are also fostered through the process of feedback, where an honest exchange of perceptions help students know more about their impact on others. Interestingly enough, as the these two facilitative processes happen, the helping relationship is further enhanced and students become more open to exploring ideas, feelings, and behaviors. Finally, as the first two processes occur within the relationship, increased awareness, responsible decision-making, and problem-solving can happen.

176 Developmental Guidance and Counseling

Chapter 6

Individual Counseling as a Counselor Intervention

When most people think of counseling, they think of two people sitting across from one another and talking about a personal matter. The counselor is settled back, relaxed, and listening attentively as the counselee describes a personal event. After a time, the counselor offers interpretations, insights, advice, and encouragement as the counselee reflects and considers their meaning. It is a scene of two individuals—one a professional—working together to discover causes and solutions to problems.

Not surprisingly, it is the intensive nature of individual counseling which attracts persons to counseling. It is also this same scenario which appeals to many people who want to enter the counseling profession and to become counselors. At the same time, this same scene can be intimidating to young people, who think that they will be psychoanalyzed and treated as "mental cases."

The early history of guidance in the schools suggests that individual counseling consisted primarily of interviews about occupational plans. Students explored their vocational interests and abilities. Test results were interpreted to them. They received occupational information and suggestions about job placement. Vocational counseling, the foundation of all school counseling, was generally an individual counseling process. As the years passed, a greater emphasis was placed on helping young people with their personal and social problems, which involved meetings between a counselor and a student. It was often called personal counseling.

Individual Counseling Defined

By definition, individual counseling happens when a counselor meets privately with a student for the purposes of counseling. It is this dyadic interaction between counselor and counselee that many think is the essence of the counselor's job.

Many young people are reluctant to talk about personal matters or their personal concerns in classroom discussions with teachers. Some hesitate to talk in front of small groups. Therefore, individual counseling in the schools, taking its lead from psychotherapy, was based on the assumption that a counselee would prefer to talk alone with a counselor.

Furthermore, confidentiality was always considered the cornerstone of counseling. Consequently, it was assumed that students needed a private meeting with a counselor to confide their thoughts and to be assured that their disclosures would be safeguarded. Nothing appeared safer than individual counseling.

Individual counseling as an intervention gained its popularity from theoretical and philosophical premises which emphasized respect for individual worth, differences, and rights. The counseling relationship is a personal one. It allows for some distinct kinds of communication to happen between counselor and counselee, protecting the integrity and the welfare of the counselee is protected.

Counseling has been considered so intricate, with each word, gesture, inflection, and silence being considered significant, that it could only happen between a skilled counselor and a willing counselee. Together they search for hidden meanings behind behaviors. Such a personal examination necessitated permissiveness and freedom to explore ideas in depth, under the watchful eye of a counselor. For many years, it was assumed that this experience could only happen in a two-person interaction.

Individual counseling is popular in the schools for many reasons. First, most school organizations are structured around classes and classroom teachers. Teachers are more inclined to release one student at a time from their classes because it is less disruptive of their classroom routines. Individual counseling is easier to schedule than other interventions and may seem more practical. Subsequently, it is the most frequently used counselor intervention (e.g. Peer, 1985; Wiggins and Mickle-Askin, 1980).

In addition, many school counselors acquired a preference for individual counseling through their graduate studies in counselor education. Counseling theories and techniques, for example, are most often illustrated through individual case studies. Many of these have emerged from the long history of psychotherapy, where many individual case studies have been recorded. Because individual counseling seems easier to understand and to manage, most beginning counselors start with that kind of counselor intervention in their practicum experiences. Counselor education programs have expanded their course offerings to include group counseling, consultation, and other interventions; but, individual counseling is still the primary focus for counselor preparation.

For these and other reasons, individual counseling is a primary counselor intervention in the schools. It is a valid job function and it will always be a unique and important part of the counselor's role.

Stages of Counseling

Most of us like some order in our lives. Among other things, we organize our days, our households, our personal belongings, and our work. We envy those people who seem to be systematic and efficient.

Unfortunately, counseling is not always an orderly and logical process. We would like, for instance, to have counselees start their stories from the beginning, touching on only the most relevant details as they proceed step by step to relate significant events and circumstances that have led to their concerns. Likewise, it would be convenient if they would clearly articulate their dilemmas, alternatives, and consequences, and then systematically arrive at some insightful meanings or plans that would solve their problems. Counseling does not often seem to follow such an easy path. First, counselees are frequently distressed and full of emotion. They are confused or frustrated and cannot think clearly. Typically, they avoid critical issues and resist examining ideas, as their rambling dialogues become part of their defensive postures to change.

Nevertheless, close observation of many counseling sessions has revealed some common patterns. The easiest place to begin is to think of the three basic parts of a counseling interview: 1) initiation, or statement of the problem or situation; 2) development or exploration; and 3) closing. These three parts indicate movement and direction in an interview. The actual amount of time given to any one part may vary extensively, and sometimes parts are difficult to identify. In many respects, the totality of counseling with all its sessions is parallel to an individual session. There is a beginning, a working, and an ending period.

Although counseling topics change and can merge, and the sequence of events are sometimes unpredictable, it is possible to identify some representative stages of counseling. These stages can provide a convenient checklist and, occasionally, suggest some directions in which you might work.

Let us take a look at eight stages which characterize the general nature of counseling.

Stage One: Beginning and Orientation

The first stage of counseling is characterized by getting acquainted, gathering some background information, forming a helping relationship, clarifying roles and expectations, making some initial assessments, and setting some goals. Counseling is initiated and the counselee is given some orientation to the nature of the counseling process. While this stage might be completed in one session, it may take as many as two or three sessions, even in short-term counseling.

The first stage is when you and your counselees discuss what you will do together and mutually agree upon some roles and procedures. These may be stated in general terms, but there is an attempt to identify some parameters for the sessions.

No matter the setting or the occasion, the first meeting sets the tone for the rest of the counseling sessions. First impressions are formed immediately as counselor and student meet. The student might be thinking, "Can this person help me? How much can I trust this person? What's going to happen? Should I really do this?" Meanwhile, the counselor might be thinking, "Will this person trust me? How can we best work together? How can I make the best use of our time? How serious is the problem? Where do we begin?"

This is a get acquainted time. Both you and a counselee might exchange some friendly greetings and words that reach out and invite the student to talk. Relationship building begins from the first time that the two of you set eyes on one another and it continues to grow as you exchange ideas. Therefore, the general rule is to follow the lead of the counselee, helping the counselee self-disclose as you "put chips in the bank" (building the helping relationship) by responding with high facilitative responses.

Non-verbal communication during the early minutes of the first meeting plays a significant role and could be more important than anything which might be said. For instance, a counselee's eyes will examine your demeanor, looking for personal clues which will suggest how to act in your presence. They scan around the room, searching for things which will tell how comfortable and safe the environment might be. For that reason alone, it is common to see students spend time looking around the room instead of speaking directly to a counselor. Stealing close glimpses of the counselor is common among students who are generally insecure around adults, especially authority figures. The eyes soak up unspoken information and influence the counseling process.

Some tension is usually present as you and your counselees test one another and move toward a working relationship. Therefore, like most counselors, you may want to begin your first meeting by asking students, especially if it is counselee-initiated, "How can I help you?" or "What's on your mind?" or "What did you want to see me about?" All these are straight-forward questions, although counselees may not know what to say, where to begin, or what particular reasons brought them there. It gives them an opportunity to tell you what has led them to see you. Such questions may make some people feel on the spot, but they are reasonable inquiries and have the advantage of letting counselees begin wherever they are most comfortable. It is always better to let people state their reasons for wanting to see you, although you might already have an idea.

When counseling is a result of a self-referral or is self-initiated, small talk or "ice breakers" are not usually needed to get things going. The person has something in mind and is anxious to get started. As long as you do not confuse the issue with a lot of unnecessary reassuring words, the person will usually begin to talk, even when unsure of how counseling works.

If a first meeting is not a self-referral but is counselor-initiated, then it will be your responsibility to clarify the reasons you called a student into your office. Even then, in the beginning you will want to ask open questions and avoid any long speeches or lectures. Some counselors make the mistake of quickly telling students that they are in trouble with a teacher and the possible consequences if the problem is not resolved. This only makes students think defensively and tends to create a picture of the counselor and teacher conspiring as a team against them. The task is to get students to talk as much as possible about their situations, perspectives, and to avoid speaking for teachers or others.

An English teacher referred Allen, a ninth grade student, for counseling. His classroom behavior was described as uncooperative and inappropriate. Apparently, he paid little attention to class lectures, made aside remarks to classmates, and became sullen when confronted. He was considered disruptive and the teacher did not want the boy back in class.

The counselor began by asking a series of open-ended questions such as: "How's school going for you, Allen?" "How would you describe your English class?" "How do you get along with your teacher in that class?" Each of these questions, of course, were followed by clarifying and feeling-focused responses.

Some counselors may prefer to begin by revealing the motivation for calling the student into the office, such as: "Allen, I had an opportunity to talk with your English teacher this week. She's concerned and has asked me talk with you. How's it going for you in that class?" This gives the discussion a focus and, while it could elicit some initial defensiveness, it identifies the reason for the meeting. It is assumed that a candid and straight-forward approach encourages counselees to be honest and open.

Most counselees are unfamiliar with the counseling process. It is usually a new experience for people to talk with a trained professional who helps them think about their ideas and feelings in depth. Most counselees will not know what to expect from counseling or from the counselor. They are unsure of what roles are played by each person. They enter the counselor's office with more hope than knowledge of how to get the most out of counseling.

It is risky to assume counselees know who you are and what counseling is about, even if they have had some counseling experiences with other counselors or therapists. It might be foolheardy to assume others work in the same manner as you, or share the same philosophy, theories, and skills. In fact, they may be different, using other approaches and forming contrary impressions. If a counselee has had some previous experience with other counselors, then it may be appropriate to ask how counseling worked out and how they experienced the counseling process. This again follows the lead of the student, gives you information which might be helpful, and buys some time as you decide how you might best be of help.

After hearing the initial thoughts and feelings of your counselees, and their requests and expectations, it is time to explain and clarify counseling, as you see it. What is counseling? What is your job or role? What services do you provide? Who else is available to support you in your work or might also be available for assistance, if needed? How does the counseling process work? What are your expectations, ground rules, and limitations?

The first interview is a critical aspect of counseling. Some call the first session an "intake interview," drawing upon the work of mental health counselors and therapists. The term is not commonly used in school counseling, but, it has been used by some counselors to describe the first experience that a student has in a counseling center.

Intake interviews with students may or may not be with the counselor who will be assigned to them. For example, some mental health centers and counseling agencies have intake specialists who gather general information from each new client before any therapeutic experience. There are routine procedures and then, based on the intake information, assignments are made to counselors or therapists. School counselors conduct their own "intakes" because they are usually assigned to a designated class or population of students.

In addition, there is less need for traditional intake procedures and information since most background data are available in student records and cumulative files. Drawing upon data which have followed students through the school years can save you time and reduce the need to ask general background questions. However, it is always valuable to hear how students describe their situations instead of depending totally on school records.

Regardless of circumstances or settings, the first meeting is the beginning of counseling. When you meet a student for the first time, first impressions come into play. Opinions are formed, subtle decisions are made, and personal perceptions begin to influence the interaction. The first meeting usually sets the direction of the counseling for other sessions—for better or for worse.

During your first counseling sessions with students, preliminary hypotheses are formed as you look for clues which suggest what the problem might be and the best direction to take. If the first interview is seen as a fact-finding question and answer period, despite the reason, then counselees might conclude that counseling is a process of answering questions, which will eventually lead to their being told what to do to make things better. Consequently, you may want to look for some effective ways to collect information without falling into a "just give me the facts" type interview.

Collecting some general and specific information in the first meeting can clarify the reason a person is seeking counseling and some of the resources available to that person. Background and history might be useful in diagnosis or in making decisions on how to proceed. How and when this information is collected can vary from one counselor to another.

Some counselors prefer less formal methods, following the lead of the counselee and noting information as it emerges from a relatively unstructured interview. Others prefer to expedite matters and use more structured procedures, gathering particular information to use in formulating a counseling plan or contract. One counselor said, "Without some basic information, a counselor is not only delaying the formulation of a counseling strategy but could go off on a tangent and waste a lot of time." Others have countered by saying, "Yes, but there is no need to rush and push things along. The basic referral information is all that is needed at first. The highest priority is to build a working relationship."

By the end of the beginning and orientation stage, the counselees should know more about you, your roles and functions, the general procedures you follow, and the services that you can give, including your limitations and expectations. You should know what help you can and might give, in light of your current commitments, and some idea of your next step. The next step might be to schedule the person for more sessions, or for a small group. It is also possible to mutually agree to stop at this point. The orientation and introduction stage needs special attention if you and a student are to make the most of your time together.

Stage Two: Building the Relationship and Assessment

If you decide to work with the counselee beyond the orientation and introduction stage, then it is likely that you will engage in some assessment procedures and continue to build the helping relationship. Assessment of a counselee's situation or problem is a continuous process, one done jointly. Sometimes you may want to administer a brief form or inventory to obtain baseline data as you start counseling, so that progress can be assessed. There are two types of assessment: *formal* and *informal*. Both can provide valuable information and each in its own way affects both the counseling relationship and process.

Formal assessments consist of standardized measurements to which a student responds. Such instruments provide norms for comparison and can enable both the counselor and the student to gain some idea regarding how one compares to others. They might focus on intelligence, attitude, values, achievement, interests, concerns, skills, and aptitudes. Standardized tests and inventories are explained in greater detail in other books, but it is important here to recognize their impact at this stage of counseling.

Formal assessment usually takes more time than informal assessment. Data is collected through recommended administrative procedures. Students often feel as if they are taking tests, although it may only be an interest or career inventory. Tests and inventories are usually paper and pencil devices. This puts some distance, although temporary, between the counselor and student. Sometimes students assume, after completing the "exam," that you now have all the information that is needed to help solve any problem.

Formal tests and inventories are impersonal and it takes a skilled counselor during interpretation to reduce the threat, suspicion, and personal distance that most instruments create. Students have been conditioned about the nature of tests and how they are used. Few students support them, even among those who always perform well. Tests are considered a "necessary evil" in school and there is no reason to believe that tests and inventories administered in the guidance office will be perceived any differently.

Informal assessments are those that rely upon first hand observations, a simple checklist, or counselor intuitiveness. While formal assessments, such as standardized tests, might provide some valuable information and insight, many counselors are moving toward getting as much information as possible through informal assessments. The biggest criticism of the less formal assessments is that they lack reliability and validity. However, experienced counselors have developed an idiosyncratic set of norms that enables them to use informal assessment procedures with confidence. Some counselors have developed their own school norms.

Assessment (both formal and informal) typically focuses upon seven areas:

1. *Physical.* The manner in which a student physically presents oneself can be the first clues to help assess a student's situation or problem. How is the person dressed? Groomed? What about physical posture? What do the eyes tend to say about the person? Is this an energetic or fatigued individual? What outward signs of stress are evident? What evidence is there about overall health? Does the person have any hearing or vision problems? Do medical records suggest any unusual

health problems (diabetes, etc.). Is the person taking any medication?

2. *Social.* How well does the person relate to you and to others in the office or immediate area? Does speech flow easily or hesitantly? Is the person's demeanor generally positive or negative? What attitudes are expressed in both verbal and non-verbal behaviors? Does this person form social relationships easily or is it difficult? Does the individual have any friends or fit into groups around the school?

3. *Cognitive.* How well does the person conceptualize ideas? Do words flow easily or falteringly? Is there a logical flow to discussion, or does the person jump from one topic to another? What about the tone of voice, the pitch and speed at which the person talks? Is the individual taking any medication or drugs that might affect the thinking processes? How well is the person's testing of reality and is there an understanding of the consequences of behaviors? What kinds of values tend to influence the person's thinking and behavior? Is there any evidence of appropriate affect and the ability to think logically about matters?

4. *Cultural.* What religious, cultural or environmental factors have influenced the person's thinking, feeling, and behaving? Are there any special pressures or difficult to control circumstances in the individual's life that make it difficult to make choices? Does the person feel stigmatized, isolated, persecuted, or rejected because of cultural background? Can the person appreciate cultural differences or is there a tendency to think in terms of disadvantages or being less valued?

5. *History.* What general and specific history is relevant to the situation or problem? Have there been any particular events in the person's life that may have contributed to any problems of difficulties (e.g. traumatic events, frightening episodes, unstable family, migrant history)? What particular circumstances have and are contributing to the person's present state of mind and patterns of behavior?

6. *Future Perspective.* Does the person have any goals for the future? Is the future seen as positive or negative? Is the person hopeful, although the situation is difficult? Can problems be seen as solvable and as part of life's process? Is the person fatalistic or is there a a sense of control over one's destiny?

Can goals and objectives be described in realistic terms? Is there a sense of how past, present, and future are related and that the future can be affected by current behaviors? Does the person seem willing to take control and responsibility for one's future?

7. *The Presenting Problem.* What is the situation or problem that has been given as the reason for counseling? The level of awareness will vary from one person to another, but does the person have some idea of what has led to counseling? Of all the problems that might be presented, which is the one with the clearest theme? It is called the presenting problem because it is the place where you are starting. It may be not be the most serious problem or even a problem, but it is a place to begin.

Some of the assessment information might be obtained by simply asking the counselee a list of questions. However, most can be obtained by being a careful listener as you help counselees talk about their situations. It is during this time that you are also building your working relationship. Following the lead of the counselee by using high facilitative responses is still appropriate counselor behavior in this stage.

Stage Three: Exploring and Discovery

This stage is described as a working stage by some writers. It is a time when the counselor and counselee explore events in an attempt to find some special meanings, discover some new ideas, gain insight, and consider alternatives. It is a time to think and feel freely about a situation without restraints, and it is frequently characterized by spontaneous talk. Sometimes a structured activity can help stimulate thinking and feeling or help identify patterns of behavior, self-pictures, influential values, and significant others.

In this stage, you provide the counselee the luxury of weaving through images, collecting ideas, sharing fleeting thoughts, and momentarily gaining glimpses of past, present, and future. You assist the counselee to move from an external to an internal frame of reference and understanding. It is a time for patient and attentive listening and gentle structuring.

This is a difficult stage since you or the counselee are often eager to move ahead toward some satisfactory solution, and the two of you may grow impatient, especially if the sessions tend to ramble.

Although stimulating, exploring ideas and feelings can lead one through confusing mazes of thoughts and deadends in terms of personal insight. Yet, the process is, more often than not, considered productive.

It is as though counselees are searching for treasures. They may not find what they are looking for, but the experience can provide valuable information about themselves and it can be an exciting adventure. This is especially true if they are making the journey with a trusted friend who has, at the right times, provided some timely guidance, reassurance, insights, and encouragement.

Stage Four: Centering and Setting Goals

Eventually, the time will arrive to take what has been learned in the previous stages and put it to use. This usually requires that a focus be given to the discussions. This might come because of patterns, which clarify a person's attitudes and behaviors. Or, it might come through general themes that keep recurring in discussion.

As counselees get a focus on what they want to happen in their lives, some personal goals might be identified. They are clarified and made more meaningful. They are described generally and in specific terms to obtain an image or picture of desired outcomes. In this sense, the process of counseling is much like working with a camera. It takes some fine tuning to get a clear image and the camera's eye only takes in so much of the landscape. However, this fine tuning makes counseling manageable. In addition, as the camera begins taking snapshots to be studied, new scenes are developed and explored. Some scenes receive particular attention, and it is possible to focus on some things later.

Stage Five: Planning and Taking Action

During this stage, a counselee identifies a specific goal and arrives at a plan of action. This plan is primarily a "next step." It may have several parts, but the most immediate course of action is identified.

One of the human conditions that is intriguing is our ability to have fantasies—to dream about things we would like to see happen. How often have you thought about doing some things but did not do them? We can think about what we would like to have happen, but sometimes we fail to take any action and so nothing happens. In a some cases, this is not so bad. In other instances, the lack of action reduces energy and commitment and the goal slips away into fantasy or is forgotten altogether.

It is assumed that a first and next step will trigger other related positive behaviors, if a next step is carefully planned. While other goals and more plans may be sketched out in detail later, preparing for some immediate responsible action is given high priority in school counseling. Discussion of consequences, alternatives, role-playing, and skill-development might be included in this stage.

Stage Six: Collecting Data and the Interim

In the counseling process, it is usually appropriate to identify a starting point. This may be done in the first stage and first meeting. Or, it may come after specific goals have been identified (e.g. more homework completed or improved attendance record) and some baseline data are collected and examined. Data collection can continue as the plan of action is implemented.

It is the responsibility of the counselee to begin the plan, to note any consequences, and to make decisions. The time when the counselee is implementing some course of action is considered an interim period. Sometimes supportive sessions are needed to help a counselee keep focused or to practice skills; but, for the most part, this is a waiting period for the counselor.

Stage Seven: Follow-up and Evaluation

The follow-up and evaluation stage is a time when the counselor and counselee look at what has been accomplished, assessing any progress that has been made and the effectiveness of any plan or behavior. Some counselors choose only to follow-up cases where the counselees need more help or where things have not gone according to plan. Yet, it is just as valuable to hear a counselee tell a success story as it is to focus on parts of a plan that did not work out or that need improvement. Having a follow-up listener is reinforcing to counselees and gives them an opportunity to clarify what happened, to identify the parts of their plan that contributed to success, to think of how the results might be generalized to other aspects of life, and to start thinking of new goals and objectives.

"How did it go?" "What happened?" "How did things work out?" "Tell me how you started." "What did you like best about what you did?" "If you were to change things, what would you do differently?" "How would you approach it now?" "What did you learn or relearn from your experience?" All these open-ended questions are possible entry statements for this stage, as you follow the lead of the counselee. You might also listen for behaviors that can be reinforced and generalized.

Based upon a joint evaluation with the counselee, it is possible to make such decisions as whether the plan of action should continue as it is, be modified, or be terminated and another plan developed. An evaluation may suggest that counseling is ready to end. It is during the last part of this stage that you make plans to phase out the counseling process or to make a referral.

Stage Eight: Closing and Separation

In this final stage, you help fashion an end to the contracted counseling arrangements and bring closure to the counseling relationship. It is time to separate because counseling is over.

Ward (1984) discussed some concepts and strategies related to termination, or the end of counseling for a counselee. He believed that it should be managed effectively to maximize counseling outcomes and to minimize abrupt endings and negative reactions. He acknowledged that parting may be a sad and difficult experience for both counselor and counselee.

Although some interesting ideas or issues might be introduced during the final stage, it is usually best to avoid any new counseling material. If necessary, another contract for counseling services can be agreed upon, perhaps for another two or three sessions. "If we had some more time to spend together in counseling, how could we best use that time?"

During closure, you will want to end on a positive note. Perhaps you will want to summarize any progress that has been made, even celebrate the gains. Or, you may want to ask the counselee to think about what has been learned or relearned. Final impressions might be in order. Some counselors end by using some of the time to compliment the counselee about something, using the feedback model.

One counselor would always remind her elementary school students that although the counseling sessions were over, she would be around the school and continue to see them on occasion. She would tell them that while they would no longer be meeting regularly, they were free to visit with her again. She would make every effort to visit the counselees' classrooms and give a friendly "hello," as way of letting the young students know that she was still around and available if needed. Without some limits, however, this popular counselor found that students did not want to end their counseling sessions. The counselor provided a warm, caring environment that was difficult to terminate. Therefore, she took some precautions in helping students find closure to counseling.

Almost all counselors forewarn their counselees about the number of counseling sessions that remain. For example, you might say to a student, "We have two more meetings or sessions together. How do you think we might spend that time?" Or, "Next week is our last session, so what can we do today to make the best use of our time?"

Even in a one-time counseling session, closing remarks can make a lasting impression. As time comes to a close, you might ask, "Our time is about up, is there anything else you'd like to say?"

One favorite way of terminating counseling is to ask counselees to summarize what counseling has meant to them, from their point of view. Or, you might take the lead and provide a summation of the sessions. Then, ask the counselee what might be added. Any final statements are positive and you conclude by wishing the person well.

Probably no two counseling cases are same. Every counseling session is different. Yet, these common stages seem to appear in one way or another. They are intended as a practical guide and should not be considered a concrete path to success.

Factors to Consider

There are a few factors to consider in a practical approach to individual counseling. Some beginning questions might be: Who? When? Where? and How?

Who should receive individual counseling?

Some situations are especially suited for individual counseling. For example, there will be students who lack self-confidence and who are hesitant to participate in other kinds of counselor interventions, such as small group counseling sessions. They cannot imagine others understanding their situations or even caring. Speaking in front of a group is unthinkable to them, as they struggle to find the courage to talk to one person.

There are other students who lack social skills and are quickly rejected by others. Their lack of personal sensitivity sometimes leads to socially inappropriate remarks or behaviors, which can make it difficult to obtain group support. One student, for example, had an offensive body odor and dressed in odd clothes which tempted other students to joke about him. They made every effort to avoid his presence. It was not practical in the beginning to put him into small group counseling, although he and other students could learn from each other. He needed individual attention, as part of preparing him for group counseling, where he could receive feedback and help from his peers.

Some students have problems that are intensely emotional and they need the privacy of individual counseling to risk talking about their situations. Some topics are so confidential and sensitive that it may be questionable to work on them in a group. A young girl, in one case, worried about her older brother who was selling illegal drugs to buy a motorcycle. She was unsure of what to do, particularly since he had been unresponsive to her pleas to "stop pushing drugs" and her warnings that he might be caught. She did not want others to know for fear that they might turn him in to the police. She needed to think through some of her thoughts. She needed individual counseling because her problem threatened the welfare of her brother and she was uncertain how others might respond.

Child abuse, teen-age pregnancies, family violence, and drug abuse are other examples of situations where individual instead of group counseling may seem appropriate. However, there are many skilled counselors who can form supportive counseling groups in their schools where almost any topic can be discussed by a group of counselees in a responsible and confidential manner. Therefore, topic sensitivity is a general guideline instead of a steadfast rule for determining who should be seen in individual counseling.

Individual counseling also appeals to some students because of their developmental needs. For example, some teen-agers may be afraid of being perceived as different, or they may be afraid of what others might say. They do not want to be described as "weirdos" and think it would be impossible to be open and honest with their peers in group meeting.

You will find that almost any topic can be discussed in individual counseling (e.g. study habits, test anxiety, family problems, depression, how to get along with a teacher, and fear of failure). While the same topics could also be discussed in group counseling, individual counseling might be the first step for some students. It is especially valuable for those who need more self-confidence or social skills, or those who need to experience being accepted by at least one person who will provide undivided attention.

Sometimes the urgency of a problem makes it necessary for you to meet alone with a student. This often occurs in a crisis-intervention. The problem needs immediate attention and circumstances suggest that you talk with the person privately. For instance, a report came to a guidance office that a girl was staggering in the hallway and seemed disoriented. After reaching her classroom desk, she sat quietly and stared out the window with a fixed gaze. Her school counselor went to find the girl. Then, the two of them sat together in the privacy of an alcove near a classroom where they talked about the girl's behavior and what she was experiencing. As it turned out, the girl had taken an overdose of a prescribed medication.

This might be a good time to emphasize that one student should not necessarily be given preference over another, although crisis-interventions may sometimes call for an exception. Suppose that a student is having a very difficult time at school and has suddenly reported to the guidance office for help. If possible, instead of canceling your other counseling commitments, try to schedule the student around them. This does not mean that you do not care about the student. It says that the time that you are spending with the students you are seeing at that moment is important and that, when you meet with students, you value your time with them.

One counselor was scheduled to meet with a group of students who were in their fourth session together. Another of the counselor's counselees, a young girl, showed up in the guidance office and said she needed to see the counselor immediately. Her problem had become more difficult and needed attention. The girl was at a loss of what to do. The counselor was concerned and decided to cancel the group meeting to respond to her situation. Eventually, the girl's problem was resolved, but it came at the expense of the group. Group members received the message that the girl's problem was more important than their own. Could the counselor have met with the girl after the group finished meeting? Was the girl's situation so urgent that she needed immediate attention? Was there no one else who could help the girl until the counselor finished meeting with the group? Do students have to be in crisis before they can gain and maintain a counselor's attention?

Similarly, individual counseling may be happening and a parent of another student unexpectedly arrives in the guidance office and asks to see her child's counselor. Should the counselor interrupt or cancel the session with the student to immediately give attention to the parent? If this is the case, then what is the message to students?

To the parent? Most important, what is the message about the work of the counselor? If it happens regularly and as a matter or practice, then the strongest message is that whatever the counselor does is probably not important.

Therefore, interruptions and cancellations should be the exception instead of common practice. Principals, teachers, parents, and students can be assisted to understand this policy, especially if your work schedule is available to them and it identifies times when they can see you. This also means that someone in the guidance office, maybe another counselor or guidance aide, must help protect your counseling time by working with whomever has walked into the office or by identifying the next time when you will be available.

Of course, exceptions are rooted in professional judgment. One guideline for interruptions might be the same that a principal would apply to a teacher who is responsible for a class of students. Would this teacher be interrupted and called out of session? If so, what would happen to the class of students? Flexibility of counselor time is not meant to imply that the counselor is always available to respond to every crisis or adult whim.

The development of your schedule, with special attention to when you will meet with your caseload of individuals, will do a great deal to communicate your role and image. Periods designated as flexible time on your schedule will be used for individual counseling when appropriate, but unless you guard your blocks of times, there will be no time for counseling.

Where does individual counseling happen?

Like most school counselors, you will probably have a small office where you can hold individual counseling sessions. Ideally, this room is in a guidance center and will be suited for private conversations.

Be careful about the arrangement of furniture in your room. The order and appearance of a room can influence counseling interactions. For instance, one counselor was given a traditional, bulky, business-like desk for her small office and conversation could only happen across the desk. This fostered an impersonal relationship and tended to communicate authority. The counselor had the desk removed and replaced it with a small table. She also removed the large filing cabinets and brought in a small couch, an easy chair, an end-table, and an attractive table lamp. She wanted a more relaxed atmosphere in which to counsel and was aware of how distant and impersonal formal office furniture can be.

Individual counseling need not always take place in the counselor's office. Dyadic interactions have the advantage of being able to happen in many small spaces throughout the school. For instance, one counselor knew that a certain hyperactive boy, who was often disruptive in classes, felt caged-in when he was in the counselor's small office. Therefore, the counselor asked the boy to walk with him around the school. They walked and talked, occasionally stopping to sit in secluded corners of the building. They sometimes walked to the gymnasium where they sat on the bleachers and talked about matters. This occasional reprieve from the confines of the counselor's office seemed to make meetings more productive.

No doubt you will have your own preferences for room arrangements and places to talk with a counselee. While space and room arrangements are not critical, they can contribute to your image and working atmosphere. Trust your judgment and do not be afraid to be creative, especially when the occasion calls for some unusual approach to reach students.

When does individual counseling occur?

Individual counseling can occur at almost any time during the school day. Experienced counselors who want to implement a comprehensive developmental guidance program try to schedule their individual counseling sessions during times when it is not practical to meet with groups of students. Because it is easier to gain access to one student, group counseling times always take precedence when developing a weekly schedule.

As you look over your week, there will be times when individual counseling appears to be most practical because of the school's daily schedule. Try to schedule individual appointments for those times. Individual counseling is usually scheduled by caseload, as described in Chapter 4, but crisis-interventions are unpredictable and come at various times. Such interventions are obviously not scheduled or shown on your weekly calendar, although they may happen often because of circumstances in your school or the nature of the student body.

The famous fifty-minute hour on which psychotherapists traditionally based their work was quickly adopted by many people in the early days of school counseling. It was assumed that it took that long, at least, to get down to business. Now, it seems that 30 minutes is a feasible and practical time in which to do individual counseling.

Half-hour time blocks reduce the time that a student is out of class, although some teachers may prefer that a student remain with a counselor an entire class period (e.g. 45 to 55 minutes) instead of entering late and disturbing the class. You will need to know each teacher's preference, although you may not always be able to honor it.

Some counselors have learned that individual counseling may be as few as 15 to 20 minutes and that quick follow-up sessions might be only 5 or 10 minutes. One middle school counselor who had met with a group of five boys regarding their study habits and classroom behavior decided to follow up group counseling with some individual sessions. Each boy was assigned a day to meet with the counselor at the beginning of the school day for about 5 to 10 minutes. Discussions usually focused on a boy's plans for that week and concluded with a quick progress check. It was a supportive effort and not intended as a time to explore matters in depth.

Again, the scheduling of classes or the bell schedule in your school will help determine the best times to meet with students and how long you will want to meet with them on an individual basis. You may find it practical to meet with some students longer than others. But, try to avoid seeing students individually for long sessions, such as for more than 45 to 50 minutes. This has rarely proved productive and is usually reserved for special kinds of crisis-interventions.

How often does individual counseling happen? Practically speaking, it seems best to meet with individual counselees at least twice a week. There will be more continuity in the sessions and the students often need more concentrated focus and support than once a week. However, many counselors find it workable to meet once a week.

As recommended earlier, individual counseling students, who are a part of a caseload (about 6 to 8 individuals), might be met twice a week for one grading period. The grading period is a convenient time around which to organize counseling interventions. Therefore, in a six-week grading period, a counselor and a counselee might meet for a total of 10-12 times. As a rule, six individual counseling sessions are considered practical for most students, which means that if a student is seen twice a week for three weeks, it would be possible to see 18 to 24 students in individual counseling as part of your caseload in one nine-week grading period.

Obviously, this type of individual counseling precludes extensive in-depth counseling and lends itself toward cognitive and behavior counseling theories. This is usually a more direct and guided approach, with an emphasis on clarification of ideas and feelings, goal setting, and behavior management. In addition, individual counseling in the schools is considered to be "brief counseling," in which goals and techniques are more focused and limited.

It is a mistake to think that a student who has a serious problem can only benefit from long-term counseling, or therapy. Unfortunately, old models of counseling and therapy continue to dominate our thinking. Some counselors have reported that they feel guilty when they are unable to provide extensive counseling and they believe that their short-term work with students is not really counseling. Yet, short-term individual counseling can be very effective, depending upon how it is done.

How is individual counseling done?

There is a tendency for counselors who have been schooled in one approach or theory to be attentive to certain dynamics, symptoms, counselee behaviors, and counselor techniques. But, there is a need to reconceptualize counseling theories, especially their applications to school settings. The effectiveness of any counseling approach or technique will always rest in the ingenuity, talent, and capacity for caring of the counselor, instead of the theory or techniques themselves.

Part of being an effective school counselor is knowing a school system and how it works; understanding the expectations of administrators, teachers, and parents; and teaching some simple procedures that can make life easier for students. It is knowing how to make school more palatable to students who do not want to be there, helping them find ways to cope with day-to-day situations, that makes the difference.

In some cases, it is helping students cope with a particular concern or issue outside school, something that distracts them from their school work. But in most cases, it is a matter of coaching students through the system helping them to adjust and to get the most out of school—perhaps the central mission of school counseling.

Individual Counseling as a Counselor Intervention   197

More brief-counseling or short-term counseling theories need to be developed and applied to school counseling. Such theories and techniques are usually more structured and the counselor plays an active part. Typically, one important problem is clarified at a time and relevant behaviors are identified. Priorities are set. It is a systematic approach, pecking away at one symptom or problem-behavior at a time, and then another.

The most common steps of individual counseling are: 1) Identify and assess the problem; 2) Define goals and objectives; 3) Develop a plan; 4) After the student has implemented the plan, evaluate the progress that has been made; and, finally 5) Terminate the counseling relationship. This general outline characterizes the large majority of individual counseling cases and is closely matched to the counseling stages discussed earlier.

But, there are no short-cuts to some problems. There is not always a sure step or an easy road to follow. You might, for instance, work with a young person who has some serious family problems that are frequently displaced on people at school. You might feel powerless to do anything about the family situation. Or, recognizing that the person needs more extensive help than you can give, you might feel guilty for not giving more of your time or not having the ability to make things better. These unpleasant feelings can paralyze you to the point that nothing is done for fear that things would only get worse.

Without minimizing the severity of any problem, you can make a positive difference with even the most dysfunctioning of students by focusing on those aspects or symptoms that are school-related and proceeding to work in those areas. You can, for instance, work on the child's personality and life-style as it is manifested in school. Most troubled students, unless placed in a residential treatment center, continue to go to school and participate in school events although they are being treated by professional therapists, social workers, and medical personnel outside school. While the student is in school, it is the structure of the school that takes precedence over the structure of the family.

Let's look at two examples of individual counseling approaches which might be helpful to you in your work. The first is an interview procedure which has been called the systematic problem-solving model. It encourages the counselee to do most of the talking and thinking. It is especially helpful when you are limited in time and do not have access to all the facts of a case. The second example is that of a behavior contract. It will identify behaviors which are contributing to a problem or a solution. Using methodology founded on principles of behavioral counseling, a plan is articulated and implemented. Both approaches are examples of short-term counseling. They can be applied to many different situations and they are appropriate for use in elementary, middle, and high school settings.

The Systematic Problem-Solving Model

Everyone has problems. Some need immediate action; others need careful thought and time before they can be resolved. Regardless, school counselors are seen as experts in problem-solving.

The art of problem-solving need not be the exclusive domain of the counselor. There are many resources within a school who can assist people. Students themselves can even be trained in problem-solving skills as part of their academic training and then be assisted to apply those skills in their personal lives. However, by training and by job description, a school counselor is considered a resource to be drawn upon.

A review of professional literature suggests that problem-solving and decision-making involve several steps. First, the problem is identified. What is the situation? What has happened to cause the problem? Who is involved and what parts do they play in the problem?

Identifying the problem can be a difficult task, as the "presenting problem" may not be the "real problem." The presenting problem may only be a symptom or a manifestation of the source of the problem, but it is a place to begin. And, it is safe place in the minds of most counselees. Later, other related problems or behaviors may emerge during the process of counseling and these might receive attention. They might even take precedence over other issues that were first introduced.

Problem-solving can be tedious work. It is not always easy to know where to begin once the problem has been identified. Some problems are particularly stressful and frustrating. They can cause some anxious moments for both you and your counselees. There is an uncertainty that permeates most beginning counseling relationships after a problem is presented, especially if there is no obvious solution.

A second common step is to define the problem. As you explore the situation, you will want to break down the problem into areas that can lead to further understanding. Defining the problem in specific terms and behaviors is especially helpful. For example, if a student complains that a teacher is bigoted and insensitive to ethnic minority students, then it is best to specify actions and behaviors that have led to this conclusion. Or, if a student is worried about receiving a passing grade in a class, the problem might be defined in terms of teacher expectations and assignments, study habits and behaviors, and current grade status.

After a person has a clearer picture of the problem, it is possible to have a better understanding of what might be done. Alternative courses of action can be considered. This may involve the exploration of values and some possible next steps. For instance, some counselors have assisted students to build a "value hierarchy" chart in an attempt to identify factors that influence decision-making. Ideas or values might be listed and given a positive or negative weighing of their significance. They might then be ranked from most to least important and then related to possible courses of action.

One high school girl was having a problem deciding whether to attend a college in her local area or go to one out of state. She wanted to be close to her family, but she also wanted to meet new people and be more independent. In another instance, a younger girl was having trouble choosing between two groups of friends, each of whom liked to do different things. One group was very athletic and involved in sports while the other group spent more time in the arts, such as dance and a creative crafts club. She liked both groups, but realistically knew that time was limited and that she could not join in all the activities. The values chart was a starting place for both girls.

The final steps are selecting a course of action, developing a plan, and then acting upon it. After ideas and values are clarified and goals are identified, courses of action are considered. Obviously, this involves choices and with each choice there are some consequences.

Suppose that a student, perhaps a girl in the eighth grade, has asked you for help because she was dismissed by a music teacher for being disruptive and inattentive in class. Her return to the class is on the condition that she talk with you, her counselor, and work out her "problems." Otherwise, she will be dropped from the class. The girl is defensive and immediately she talks about how unfair the teacher is with her, emphasizing that others in the class take more advantages and do not receive the same reprimands.

What are your choices in this case? Where do you start? How can you help? Perhaps it would be helpful if the girl first clarified her situation and identified the specific problem that led to her being excused from the class. It might then be helpful to think about what she has done and could do to take some positive action.

As you help others solve problems, one practical framework from which you can work is the Systematic Problem-Solving Model. It is an organized approach to thinking through a problem and finding a possible next step. It places responsibility on the counselee or the person who has the problem. It assumes that a person will benefit by being coached through a thinking process, whereby it is possible to put the problem into perspective and to arrive at some action which can be taken in the near future. The experience with the process also enables the counselee to learn how to approach problems and to apply the same process with other problems. While it emphasizes that responsibility for solving the problem rests with the individual, it also gives you an opportunity to give timely suggestions or advice.

There are four steps to the model. These are couched as four open-ended questions. They are arranged sequentially according to a natural flow of thinking which tends to occur when people systematically try to solve a problem. More specifically, they are: 1) What is the problem or situation? 2) What have you tried? 3) What else could you do? 4) What is your next step?

You might think of the four key questions as "trigger questions." They trigger off the imagination of the counselee, guiding the person into a particular area of thinking about the problem. In addition, the counselor is in charge of pulling the trigger on each question when it seems appropriate to move onto the next area to be explored.

The decision to trigger a question is governed by such things as the nature of the problem, the emotional intensity with which a counselee describes a problem, the ability to identify the problem, the degree to which relevant feelings and behaviors are explored in each of the question areas, and the time-frame in which the counselor and counselee are working. The model has been used successfully within a 15-minute counseling session as well a 50-minute session. It has also been used over more than one counseling session by giving some of the questions attention in different counseling sessions.

Because the model is flexible, it can accommodate most counseling theories and techniques that are used in school settings. It gives direction. In that sense it can be comforting to you as a counselor because you have some idea of how your time might be spent and where a counselee is headed. It can be used in situations where you have only a limited amount of knowledge, since most of the work is being done by counselees as they think about their problems. Counselees will have the most pertinent details and information in their minds. It is the counselees who assume responsibility for bringing information to a session, exploring what has been done and what alternatives remain, and identifying some actions that might be taken.

The four questions only provide the parameters of a counseling session. The questions lend themselves to several follow-up responses. As you ask each question, and after a counselee responds, you will have an opportunity to use high facilitative responses. For instance, you might listen for pleasant and unpleasant feelings, maybe responding with a feeling-focused response. Or, you might also demonstrate that you are following the counselee by clarifying or summarizing ideas or events that were described. In the same sense, you might also ask more questions, either closed or open-ended ones, which will help the person to disclose more information. In addition, compliments and confrontations are possible at each step. Similarly, the model might be used with a group of students. In this case you would be able to use and elicit all the high facilitative responses, including linking.

Let's take a closer look at each of the questions since they suggest four important steps in problem-solving. The Case of Bill will help illustrate.

The Case of Bill

"What is the problem or situation?"

When you start by asking this simple open-ended question, you encourage counselees to begin by telling you what they are thinking and feeling. It is especially important to be alert to opportunities to show your understanding and respect by responding with some high facilitative responses. You are not only helping them to identify the problem, but you are fostering the facilitative conditions of the counseling relationship by letting the counselees know that you care, that you are interested in what they are experiencing, and that you want to help them explore the matter further.

Counselor:
What's your situation, Bill?

Bill:
I'm having a lot of trouble with a friend of mine. He's doing some pretty stupid things and he's going to be in some deep trouble if he doesn't shape up real soon.... It's just plain stupid.

Counselor:
You're worried about your friend.

Bill:
Yeah. You see, he's dating this girl and they are getting pretty close, if you know what I mean. He's a senior, right? He wants to go to college and he's got good grades. No problem there. But his girl friend is talking about getting married, saying he doesn't need to go to college. She's saying he can work for her father, who has a business in town. Marriage is all that she can think about. And, she's afraid that if he goes to college, she'll lose him to some other girl. I honestly think he wants to go to college and we were planning on going together, but he's so involved with Michele, his girlfriend, that he doesn't know how to deal with it. I know, because he's talked with me, lots of times.

Counselor:
You're concerned for your friend and uncertain what you should do.

Bill:
That's it. He really needs help and if she gets pregnant, then it's goodbye college, goodbye future.

Counselor:
You don't see a future for your friend unless he goes to college.

Bill:
Well, I guess he'd have a future all right, but it sure isn't the one he's been talking with me about all this time. I really don't think he wants to get married right after graduation, but she does. I know he doesn't because he tells me that he still wants to go to college with me, together as we always planned. What would you do in a situation like that?

Counselor:
I'm sensing that you're frustrated, wanting to help your friend go on to college but seeing him involved in something that could change his plans... and yours.

Individual Counseling as a Counselor Intervention   203

Bill:
Yeah, it bugs me. It really does. She just wants to keep him at home. She doesn't care if she get's pregnant and he's not ready to be a father. He's younger than me and I know I'm not. I don't understand how he could be so caught up with her.

Counselor:
You just can't imagine yourself in his position... and the situation irritates you.

Bill:
Yeah, it sure does. Andrew, he's my friend, keeps asking me what I'd do and what he should do. He's a mess. I'm not sure how to help.

Counselor:
You really want to help your friend, Andrew.

Bill:
Uh, uh. I really do.

"What have you tried?"

After a counselee has described a problem or situation, and defined it enough to have some type of focus, this second open-ended question inquires about any action that has been taken. There is no use to make a suggestion or give some advice if it is something that has already been attempted. Or, if your idea has already been tried, you would at least like to know how it is different from what the counselee did or how the same idea might be modified to make it a possible alternative.

For example, you can follow up the key question with another open-ended question such as "And, how did that work out?" "Okay, and how did you go about doing that?" These kinds of questions provide the counselee with an opportunity to discover if what was tried seemed reasonable and might be workable with some changes.

Surprisingly, this second key question in the problem-solving model often catches people off-guard, especially students who expect somebody else to solve their problems. Asking a young man about what he has done to resolve a conflict that he is having with his teacher can be thought-provoking and help him see that he has some responsibility in the situation. Too many students prefer to complain instead of take some positive action to make matters better.

Counselor:
Well, Bill, what have you tried in helping Andrew?

Bill:
I don't know. Lots of things. We talk about it all the time. It always comes up whenever we are alone, like when he spends the night at my house. But, he never listens to me.

Counselor:
So, you've talked with him about it and on several occasions. But those talks haven't been very satisfactory to you.

Bill:
Nope. He listens to me... you know, just like he's hearing me, but then nothing.

Counselor:
For instance, what things do you suggest?

Bill:
Well, for one thing, I told him he'd better not depend upon her for birth control. She wants to get married and getting pregnant is a sure way of that.

Counselor:
So, you've cautioned him about taking responsibility for birth control. What else have you done with Andrew?

Bill:
I've told him I think he should break it off with Michele, right now, before it's too late. But, he tells me he really loves her.

Counselor:
You've advised him to break up with Michele, but that's unacceptable to Andrew. He really cares a lot for her. Any thing else that you've done in trying to help him?

Bill:
I told him to think about his future and to think about what college can do for him, but he is starting to think that maybe he can do without college and that worries me. If he gives up the idea of college, then it's all over.

Counselor:
You've encouraged him to look to the future, especially college and what it could mean for him. But it's been discouraging to you when he says he's also thinking that he may not need to go to college.

Individual Counseling as a Counselor Intervention   205

Bill:
Yeah. He says there is a future in her father's business. But, ...

Counselor:
Anything else that you've tried?

Bill:
That's about it. Maybe there is something else but I don't know what it is. Do you have any ideas?

Counselor:
Well, let's see, you've.... (Counselor summarizes Bill's attempts at helping Andrew before asking the next key question.)

"What else could you do?"

This third key question encourages people to think more about their situations in terms of some other courses of action—some new possibilities. It focuses attention on other alternatives, or even previously tried actions that might be attempted again.

As counselees think about their situations, some ideas might come to mind that they have not thought of before, especially as you guide them through a systematic process of talking about the problem. The process helps organize one's thinking and places events in perspective.

Notice again, this question also places responsibility on the counselees, encouraging them to search their minds for more ideas. As they explore ideas with you, and as you continue to use high facilitative responses, they gain additional insight. They feel supported. Moreover, here the process is also setting the stage for timely advice or suggestions.

As each possible action is considered, you might ask related open-ended questions such as, "And, how do you think that might work?" "What might result from your doing that?" This kind of follow-up question is aimed at helping the person to think of what it takes to complete such action and what the consequences might be.

Consideration of the consequences for every possible action can be a wearing procedure on both counselee and counselor. It is laborious and fatiguing to review each alternative and the consequences. You may decide not to comment on some alternatives, assuming as you work on others a counselee will learn the process

of thinking about actions. Some seemingly illogical or inappropriate possibilities can just as easily receive no response or maybe,
"Okay, and what else could you do?"

After a counselee has offered as many ideas as possible, you might
suggest other alternatives, if you can think of any. These are
usually not offered as advice; they are simply other possibilities for
consideration. They might even be a result of brainstorming, without weighing their value.

Counselor:
Anything else that you could do, Bill?

Bill:
I suppose I could get him to talk with someone besides me... maybe
you... or some other counselor. And, then, maybe it would help if
we took off and went to see the college campus, so he could see
what he would be missing. That's a real possibility.

Counselor:
Anything else that you could do?

Bill:
I'm not sure. Maybe... I could talk with Michele but... nah, that's
not too good of an idea since she thinks I'm trying to break them
up anyway... and I guess I am. I'd probably make things worse.

Counselor:
So, you could talk with Michele but that doesn't appeal to you
right now. You don't think you could be very objective. Alright,
what else could you do?

Bill:
Well, let's see. It is hard to see her point and to keep from thinking
he's so foolish. But, that's just the way it is.

Counselor:
You sound so convinced that Andrew is making a serious mistake
with Michele and that continues to annoy you. Although it's
Andrew's who has to make the decision about his life, you still
want to do something.

Bill:
Yeah, it's really Andrew's problem... but... but... well, let's see....
Maybe they could go together to talk with someone... you know, to
make some decisions about their future. I know that neither of
their parents want to see them get married now.

Counselor:

So then, another possibility is to talk with them about seeing a counselor or someone who would help them explore their situation and what they want to have happen in the next year or so. How would you go about doing that?

Bill and the counselor continued to think about things that Bill could do to help his friend. Although not reported here, the counselor also asked what might happen if Bill acted on some of his ideas.

There are many things that can be done with a list of alternatives, besides look at the consequences. They might be reviewed in terms of one's values, skills, energy, commitment, or time. They might be rank-ordered in terms of feasibility. Role-playing might be tried with some, as a counselee attempts to see how an idea might be implemented. Some alternatives might be examined in terms of their components, segments, steps, or procedures.

"What is your next step?"

Finally, after some thinking about different courses of action that might be taken, and possibly their consequences, it is time to help the person take some action. It is not enough for most people to simply think about a problem, to analyze it, and to obtain some insights. In fact, many people are willing to talk about a problem, and in the process lessen their concern and anxiety. Some hope it will go away by itself. Others leave a counselor's office and may still be undecided as to what they want to have happen, where to begin, or what to do next.

Most counselors want to do something that will start counselees moving in a desired direction. It is possible that a next step is to wait a period of time before doing anything. After that, another decision can be made about what to do next. A decision to wait, however, is preferably part of a planned course of action.

Counselor:

What then, Bill, is your next step?

Bill:

I suppose that the next thing that needs to be done is talk with Andrew and Michele... to get them to talk with someone else who could talk some sense into them.

Counselor:
You want them to talk about their situation with someone who can help them think things through. How would you go about that?

Bill:
I don't know, just tell them what I think I guess. It won't be easy, knowing how Michele thinks but I guess I'd say, "Hey, you guys got a problem and you should talk with...."

Counselor:
All right, so although it's going to be difficult and you're a little skeptical about how it might turn out, you want to encourage them to see someone, perhaps me. Well, let me see, Bill, what would happen if you told them first of your feelings and then suggested that they talk with me.

Bill:
What do you mean?

Counselor:
Perhaps you might say something like, "I know that you two care a lot for each other. But, I care about you, too, and I can't help but think you should see one of the counselors, just to talk together about your future plans." Now, Bill, that may be a little wordy, but perhaps the key is to share with them your feelings instead of emphasizing that they have a problem. How does that sound to you?

Bill:
That sounds pretty good. I can do that.

Counselor:
Then your next step is to talk with them and to express your concern, suggesting that they see a counselor.... Alright, when do you see yourself doing this?

Bill:
Probably this week.

Counselor:
Better the beginning of the week or the last part of the week?

Bill:
Probably tomorrow sometime.

Counselor:
Better in the morning, the afternoon or at night?

Bill:
Tomorrow night. We plan to meet after football practice and I can ask them to hear me out then.

Individual Counseling as a Counselor Intervention

The next step is often broken down into other thoughts, such as what, how, and when. "What will you do?" "How will you do it?" "When will you do it?" These additional questions give a focus to a next step that grounds it to reality. It clarifies and calls upon a commitment. It elicits a public statement, in a sense, that has a way of encouraging some action. Even if the person does not follow through with the idea as discussed, there is a greater probability that something will be done. If the step is not taken, then it can become the focus of the next counseling session when the counselor asks, "How did things go?" "Okay, what kept you from taking that step?" "Alright, what now?" Or, "What else do you need before you can take that step?"

Counselees are always responsible for taking any next steps; therefore, they have the power to change their minds, modify their plans, or try something else. The process of thinking through the problem is considered the essential part of counseling, although a reasonable and responsible plan of action is a desirable outcome.

On occasion you may be asked by a counselee to do something as part of a plan. For example, one girl wanted her counselor to go with her as she talked with a teacher about a grade that seemed unfair. Another girl wanted a counselor to talk with her parents about her progress in school and to participate in a plan in which a weekly progress report would be given to her parents, so she could be rid of home restrictions. A counselor was part of a plan of action when a letter of recommendation was written for a student who was applying for a job after school hours.

In all these cases, the counselors were part of the plans of action. They collaborated with the students. There is nothing wrong with this, but the counselors have to accept responsibility for their own actions and parts in the plans.

The Systematic Problem-Solving Model can also be be used with students who have problems but who are resistant to doing anything about them. You may find it necessary to bring a problem to their awareness and then lead them through the model.

For instance, suppose that Christy, an eighth grade girl, is having a problem completing her class assignments. A frustrated teacher asks you to talk with Christy about the situation. You might begin by saying, "Christy, there seems to be a problem developing in your English class, at least according to your teacher. I'm curious, what's the situation there?" When Christy has shown an awareness of the problem and clarified the situation from her perspective, you might proceed in sequence with the other key questions ("What have you tried so far?" "What else could you do to make things better for yourself?" "What do you see as a next step?"). This approach confronts the girl, prompts her to think about her situation, coaches her through a thinking process, and motivates her to take more responsibility and action.

The model's success is directly related to the facilitative model discussed in Chapter 4. The high facilitative responses are integrated within the four key steps. As the facilitative responses are used with the problem-solving model, you will become increasingly more aware of their value, including their simplicity, directness, and flexibility. You may be surprised how creative you can be with them, as they allow room for all of your counseling skills. Most important, they can make you more effective in your work and make your job easier.

Contingency Contracts

It is common to hear educators talk about student problems in terms of self-concept, attitude, or intelligence level. Some problems are even excused to some extent by referring to a student's unfortunate home life.

But, problems can also be discussed in terms of observable student behaviors. It can be helpful, occasionally, to ask: What has a student done that allows us to conclude that person has a low self-concept? Lacks motivation? What behaviors allow us to infer that the person has a poor attitude about school? And, if a student's self-concept or attitude were to improve, how would we know? What behaviors would be different?

There will be many times when you will find it useful to focus on specific behaviors when a problem is presented and to help students learn to manage the contingencies which affect their behaviors. Learning theorists have provided us with some effective counseling strategies which are particularly applicable to school settings.

Behavioral counseling approaches have found their way into school counseling because of their efficacy and because they lend themselves to brief counseling. The major assumption in behavioral counseling is that behavior is either strengthened or weakened by its consequences. This is reinforcement theory in its simplest form. Subsequently, if one can manage the factors that elicit behavior and the consequences that follow behavior, then behavior can be changed.

The terminology used in behavioral counseling (e.g. positive and negative reinforcers, shaping, successive approximations, chaining, reinforcement schedules, modeling, and punishment) can help you conceptualize counseling strategies. For our purposes, we will focus only on how a behavior contract can be used in individual counseling.

Contingency contracting is a technique in which the counselor and counselee work together to first identify desired behaviors and then to manage the reinforcing consequences that control the performance of those behaviors. It usually involves some form of agreement in which a student is promised rewards in return for performing some desired task or behavior. Behavior or contingency contracts can be used at any grade level and with various problems.

There are seven basic steps in contingency contracting: 1) Identify the behavior; 2) Introduce and discuss the contract idea; 3) Develop a contract and present it to all involved people; 4) Outline supervisory or follow-up procedures; 5) Initiate the program or plan; 6) Record progress and evaluate outcomes; and 7) Modify the contingencies, terms of the contract, and reinforcement schedules as needed to obtain or maintain desired behavior.

The Case of Deborah will help illustrate the steps.

The Case of Deborah

Counselor:
Well, let's see, Deborah, you say that your teacher thinks you are lazy and don't care about your school work. What do you do that might give her that impression?

Deborah:
I don't know, she just has it in for me. She picks on me all the time.

Counselor:
You seem discouraged. It's not easy to attend class when things aren't going well.

Deborah:
That's right... it's makes me wonder if it's worth it all. Sometimes I feel like quitting.

Counselor:
You're so disappointed that you don't even know if you want to continue.... (Pause) You're frustrated.

Deborah:
Yeah, I am.

Counselor:
(Pause) Okay, one more time, what is that you do in class which causes so much conflict between you and your teacher?

Deborah:
I don't know.

Counselor:
Suppose I could talk with her, what would she say?

Deborah:
Oh, she'd probably say that I've got a rotten attitude and that I'm uncooperative... you know, the usual stuff.

Counselor:
Be more specific. What do you do that lets her reach that conclusion.

Deborah:
Nothing, I guess.

Counselor:
You do nothing.

Deborah:
Well, I don't do my homework and what I do finish, I don't turn it in. She's unfair. She....

Counselor:
Okay, but what else would she say?

Deborah:
Oh, she'd say that I talk too much. I do talk a lot with Ann, she's my best friend. But, the class is so boring and that's how I stay awake, talking to Ann.

Counselor:
So you don't do your homework assignments, you often don't turn in those that you do, and you talk with Ann. What else?

Deborah:
I know one thing that bugs her is that I chew gum and she is forever asking me to spit it out. It's one of her stupid rules. Yet, other kids do it and it's okay.

Counselor:
You feel treated unfairly, although chewing gum is breaking a classroom rule.... Okay, what else get's you in trouble?

Deborah:
That's enough, don't you think!

Counselor:
What do students have to do in that class, Deborah, to get along... to improve their grades? What would be your advice to a student who is new to the school and just starting that class?.

Deborah:
I'd tell them not to let her get on their case or she'll never let up.

Counselor:
It's important to get off to a good start with her, but be more specific. What does a student have to do to survive, to do well?

Deborah:
Take notes and listen to her lectures. Her tests, every Thursday, are based on them. And, then, always do the Friday writing assignment, since class discussions are based on that.

Counselor:
Well, let's see, Deborah, you've noted several things that one might do in that class. Look at this list. (Counselor shows list of items that were written down as Deborah mentioned them: 1) Attends class on time; 2) Removes gum before entering class; 3) Starts home work assignments; 4) Completes homework; 5) Turns in homework; 6)Talks at appropriate times; 7) Completes Friday written assignment; 8) Take notes on class lectures; and 9) Reviews for Thursday tests.

Now, Deborah, where would you rate yourself on each of these items as they stand now, using a 0 as low and a 5 as high? *(Deborah rates each behavior.)* Now, let's think of a way to help you improve on these items. Which two do you particularly think you can improve on immediately? *(Deborah points to 1 and 2).*

How can you go about getting some improvement in those two? *(Deborah says she can talk less between classes and spit her gum out in the basket by the door when she enters the classroom.)*

Now, let's see. If you can improve on these two items this week, what is a special reward that you might give yourself?

Deborah:
What do you mean reward?

Counselor:
(After describing possible rewards and the principle of positive reinforcement) So, what do you like to do after school?

Deborah:
I usually go to Ann's house and we talk, sometimes do our homework together, and just listen to music.

Counselor:
Do you think Ann would help us put together a contract, an agreement, that would help you do better in class?

Deborah:
(Nods yes.)

Counselor:
Okay, let's start by keeping track of how often you can attend class on time and without gum in your mouth. If you can do these two things each day, for four days, then on Thursday you can both come to my office during study hall and listen to the radio while you study for Friday's class. We've got a small room in the back that's not being used right now. However, the teacher has to sign a progress report showing that you did complete our agreement. Okay?

Deborah:
Yeah, okay, sounds like fun. But, I do get to bring Ann on Thursday, right?

Counselor:
Right! Now, let's make this more formal. *(Counselor writes out terms of contract and both sign at the bottom.)*

There are a few guidelines for making a behavior contract. These include the following:

1. The problem should be diagnosed and stated in terms of behaviors. Be specific. Use examples to illustrate if needed.

2. The premise of the contract must be clear and explicitly stated. It is honest and fair.

3. Initial contracts call for small bits of behavior which are frequently rewarded. Reinforce small approximations. Or, focus on one small problem behavior at a time so that some degree of success can be experienced.

4. Rewards should be agreed upon and given immediately when progress occurs, not before. Tokens can also be used to build toward a special reward. In addition, rewards can come in many forms, but they must be acknowledged as desirable to the student and in the contract.

5. Be systematic and follow through.

6. Be positive and focus on accomplishment instead of obedience. Negative contracting involves a threat: "You'll be punished if you don't...." And, "If you don't..., then you won't get the reward." Instead, it might be worded: "If you accomplish..., then you will receive...."

For example, to get an "A" grade, a student must do many tasks that may seem simple to a casual observer, but it involves several things—starting home work, turning homework in on time, having a pencil in class, being attentive to the teacher, following directions, and participating in class discussion. Each of these, and others which might be listed, could be isolated for special attention. You might encourage a student to select a few items or behaviors and take a few steps, instead of flooding the person by focusing on all them. After some discussion, some possible reinforcers (rewards) might be identified and then linked to one of the desired behaviors. A contract also specifies the frequency of the behavior that must be obtained and the form of the reward. Conditions of the agreement are spelled out in a contract, including what part (behaviors) each person involved is expected to play.

The final objective of any contingency contracting arrangement is to help a student learn more about managing one's own behavior through self-contracts. If contracting is always in the hands of teachers, parents, or counselors, then a student does not learn how to be independent and is always looking to someone else to account for life's problems. On the other hand, self-contracting encourages people to identify their goals in behavioral terms, to devise plans that consider successive approximations and adequate rewards, and then to implement and monitor the plans by themselves.

One counselor, after a few contracts with a sixth grade boy, suggested that the student think of something that he wanted to improve upon, either at home or at school. Then, without revealing the desired goal to the counselor, the student was asked to undergo the same steps that had been used in the other contracts and to develop a personal contract. The plan was written down and put into an envelope, which the counselor held in his office. Two weeks later, the student was called in to talk about the plan. The envelope which contained the self-developed contract was opened. The counselor began with, "How did it go?" The boy reported that things had not gone as well as expected. The counselor and the young man proceeded to identify parts of the contract which were successful and those which needed more attention. It was decided that the boy should try the exercise again, since self-discipline and self-management of behaviors were the goals of counseling.

Helpful Hints

Here are some special issues and helpful hints which are related to individual counseling.

Voluntary and Involuntary Counselees

In many schools and families, young people have few choices or rights. Because they are dependent, they are limited in their options and they usually refrain from challenging adults. They have to adjust to adult rules and expectations. Sometimes adults have unrealistic expectations or their personal styles clash with student personalities. Therefore, the focus in many school counseling sessions is how to help young people get along with others, especially parents and teachers.

Most students learn how to cope with adults. These students are sensitive and know how to modify their behavior when it is appropriate. They can adjust to different situations. Less able students frequently have conflicts with these same adults and are seen as undisciplined, uncooperative, and incorrigible, among other things. The question is: Who has the problem? Is it the adult or the student?

Some students will know the kinds of services that they can receive from counselors and will voluntarily seek out a counselor for help. They are self-referrals. Consequently, they are motivated and appear to be an easier group with which to work. However, self-referral alone does not mean that a person is committed to change or to taking responsibility.

Other-referred students are those who have been sent to the counselor by a concerned teacher, parent, or administrator. These students may or may not want counseling. They may not see any need to talk with a counselor, since it is someone else who has concluded there is a problem. These involuntary counselees can be difficult to engage in counseling, especially at first, but they can become willing participants (Ritchie, 1986).

Regardless of whether or not students see you on a voluntary or involuntary basis, some questions must be answered for them, at either a conscious or unconscious level, including "What's in it for me?" For some it will be temporary relief from whatever else they were doing. For others, it will be a challenge. Still others will enjoy playing the devil's advocate and they will try to be argumentative, maybe insisting that they have been treated unfairly and that nobody really cares about them. Resistance to introspection can run high, especially when they do not know what counseling is about, who you are, and what you are trying to do.

Counseling and Discipline

Counselors are involved in school discipline. You will work with students who have broken school rules or who have conflicts with school personnel. However, the way in which you are involved can influence your image and work.

When a troublesome student is sent directly from a classroom by a teacher to the guidance office, students see school counselors as disciplinarians, even if it is just a place for the student to sit and wait until class is over. One teacher sent a boy to his counselor with the following note: "He's out of control again, just keep him until the bell rings. I don't want him in here." This is an inappropriate use of the guidance office.

Schools have rules and procedures, and students are expected to adjust to them. Teachers also have their own sets of classroom rules and procedures, and students are expected to adjust to them. In addition, students themselves live by their own codes of conduct.

A list of student offenses in school could include: "chewing gum in class," "talking at inappropriate times," "refusing to follow a teacher's directions," "fighting with another student," and "using profanity." Sometimes students provoke one another by teasing, calling names, and making insulting gestures. The result is conflict, which may lead to a disciplinary report.

When students receive disciplinary reports, they should report to a building administrator. This person talks with the students about their cases and then administers some form of discipline, depending upon the offense and school policies. Reprimands, restrictions, conditions, and agreements are usually parts of the discipline process.

Counselors become involved in discipline as part of a referral process. That is, administrators in charge of school discipline may encourage, but not require, students to meet with their counselors and talk about their problems. Counselors, in turn, might talk with the students about their situations, how they are proceeding, and the meaning that it has for them. While some students will voluntarily want to meet with their counselors and talk willingly about their situations, others will only come on an involuntary basis, perhaps assuming counselors will reprimand them again. Being a sensitive listener is a prime condition for following up with a discipline case.

Thus, you will probably be involved in school discipline as part of a team. You will want to work out some procedures with your administrators regarding the way in which discipline cases are handled and referred. There is no need to give the same lecture, set the same limits, or offer the same advice that has already taken place in the administrative offices. Put yourself in the position of being a student advocate, the follow-up person who encourages students to talk openly about their situations.

Introducing the Counseling Game

The student is not necessarily a logical, rational consumer of counseling services. A common misunderstanding is that students know what guidance and counseling is about. It is practical, in the first counseling session, to explain the nature of counseling and your role as a counselor. You need to tell counselees how the counseling game is played.

Most students will not have had an occasion for individual counseling, unless brief one-time interviews are called counseling sessions. If this is the case, they may have a wrong impression and expect you to do all the work, ask a few questions, and give them information. Having never experienced in-depth counseling, they will tend to behave like they usually do with adults—be quiet and listen.

You may have to sell the idea of counseling to some students. They maybe not only unfamiliar with counselors and counseling, but they may also enter with skepticism based on previous experiences with adults. Initially, most students will not be able to describe the counseling process or to know how they can participate. They seldom explore their ideas and feelings, beyond a few statements with friends or family members. You are providing them a unique experience. Therefore, you will want them to learn about counseling.

You might say,

"Well, let me begin by explaining how our work together might go.... As a counselor, I want to provide you an opportunity to think about some of your ideas, feelings, and behaviors. As you take a look at those kinds of things, you can gain a better picture of yourself and your situation. My job is to help you think aloud, to listen carefully, and to help you clarify your thoughts and feelings.... What you say here is between us and no one else. We will probably meet four or five times, for about 30 minutes each time. This will enable us to think about several things, and perhaps help you decide what your next steps might be. What happens in our sessions, of course, depends a great deal on how much you are willing to share your ideas and to let me help you think about them. You are not going to be asked to share anything about yourself that you do not want to talk about.... Now, what questions or comments do you have at this point?"

You may then need to answer some more specific questions about your job and what you have in mind for the scheduled counseling sessions. You might also ask, "How did you feel about coming here today?" This is an excellent place to start, especially if the student was called in and is not there on a voluntary basis. Or, "What were some of your thoughts as you were on your way to my office?" "What have you heard about what I do?" "What do you know about counseling?"

This will give you an opportunity to learn what the student is thinking and some initial feelings about being in counseling with you. It will provide some clues about purpose, motivation, and commitment to counseling. Listening to a student's choice of words will also give you an idea of what misperceptions or misinformation need to be corrected at sometime in your work. Clearly, such questions focus on first impressions and the initial helping relationship. Perhaps most important, they also give you an opportunity to use some high facilitative responses which focus attention on the counselee and to establish yourself as a caring and interested person.

With a much younger child, perhaps one in kindergarten or the first grade, you would be careful to use words that are appropriate for the age level. You might begin by saying, "Do you know who I am?" And then continue with, "That's right, I'm a counselor and part of my job is to help students like you. Sometimes I go into classes and sometimes I meet with children one at a time, talking with them about such things as how to get along with others, how to get along with teachers, and how to get the most out of going to school. Tell me, what do you like best about school?"

Another question that must be answered for students is: "Okay, now that I'm here, what do I have to do?" Students want to know what is expected of them. Perhaps the initial statements about counseling, your role and how counseling works will help them figure out their own role. But, the question runs much deeper than that. It addresses such student thoughts as: "Who am I?" "How do I act with this person?" "What do I have to do to survive here?" "What's really expected of me?"

Students have learned to look for clues from parents and teachers regarding how to behave. Their common sense tells them that adults set the rules and not to upset the system. Many have learned to do what has to be done, but not to volunteer extra information as it could be met with criticism, advice, or be dismissed as unimportant. This defensive posture is common among students and they bring it with them when they enter counseling.

A fourth grade boy was in his second interview with a school counselor. The counselor noticed that before the boy would say something, he would raise his hand about shoulder high. During a quick exchange of ideas between the counselor and the student, this provided almost a comic routine of rapid hand raising behavior. Finally, the counselor said, "You don't have to raise your hand in here when you want to speak." And, that was the end of the hand raising. It was either a conscious or an unconscious habit that the boy brought with him from his classroom experiences.

Even when students understand how the counseling game is played, do not be surprised if they are still hesitant to share their ideas. Some may be resistant or reluctant to talk openly. Others may talk, but they talk about irrelevant things and avoid talking about themselves. Regardless, part of counseling readiness is "knowing how the game is played."

Dealing with Resistance

When a student is told to talk with you about an attitude problem, you can expect some defensiveness during counseling. You will probably be seen as part of the establishment or "one of them." Many students see school and family systems as disrespectful of their wishes, inconsiderate of their needs, and unfair. That can put you in a hole when you start your first counseling session.

If students are verbal, even argumentative, you have a place to start. You will, of course, try to draw them out by using high facilitative responses. You help them disclose more and more, maybe facilitating them to talk through their anger, their disappointment, and their discouragement. Resistance can then melt away.

Many students who are sent to see counselors have had trouble before in school, and probably at home. These troublesome students have learned that passive aggressive behavior, such as sulking or staring but saying nothing, is annoying to adults. "You can't make me say anything; you can't make me do anything. I refuse to play your game, just so you can put me down like all the others." With these thoughts, students find the silent treatment works best. It puts them in control. It frustrates adults and ends a confrontation before it begins. It is the ultimate in defiance and defensiveness.

Highly resistant students frequently shrug their shoulders, look away, and avoid eye contact. They shut you out and dare you to invade their domain, knowing that you are powerless to do so. They know from classroom experiences that mumbling "I don't know..." and then saying nothing else can have a powerful impact. It puts them in control. They also know that most teachers will take the pressure off by quickly moving on to someone else. It is an easy way to avoid being center stage and having to perform, to produce, or to be accountable.

Rarely, will a classroom teacher say, "That's okay. Take a little more time and think about it. We can wait." To do so seems to jeopardize control of the class, as others would have nothing to do and would become restless. Or, rarely do teachers say, before moving onto another student, "All right, nothing is coming to mind right now. Think about it some more and we will come back to you in a minute." Then, make it a point to go back to the student. Students bring this knowledge, their learned behaviors, and coping skills with adults, into counseling.

One resistant young man would not talk at the beginning of counseling. The counselor responded to feelings, such as "You're not sure you want to be here," and then paused for awhile. "You look like you feel uncomfortable, perhaps uncertain about what's to happen here," and paused again, before saying, "It's not easy to talk." The boy continued to sit with his arms crossed, looking away, saying nothing, with only occasional shrugs. Next, the counselor said, "That's okay, you don't have to talk. You may want to just sit and think to yourself for awhile." The counselor waited. Still nothing. The counselor continued with, "I have some work to do here on my desk, let me know when and if you want to talk with me. Unfortunately, it looks like it's not possible for you to go to class until the bell rings."

This student did not talk the first session. He was full of anger and it was displaced on the counselor, who was a convenient symbol for a world run by adults. Perhaps the boy's personal survival system was cautioning him not to talk for fear that he would say things which would put him trouble. Besides, he might have been thinking: Who is this person? Why should I say anything?

Interestingly enough, in this case, the counselor later requested another meeting with the boy and the student was more receptive to talking, eager to tell his side of a classroom incident. The facilitative conditions and relationship had really begun in the first session but could only be expedited later.

Here and Now vs. There and Then

A close examination of some of the responses used as a means of dealing with resistance, in the example above, will show a focus on the "here and now" feelings of the counselee. Here and now statements emphasize the present moment, what the counselee is experiencing when with the counselor. There and then statements refer to events and feelings that occurred outside the room in which counseling is taking place.

Some examples of "there and then" responses include:

1. "So, you felt like hitting back when he pushed you in the cafeteria this morning."

2. "You talked with your teacher and her comments only discouraged you more."

3. "What were you feeling when that happened?"

4. "It made you uneasy to talk with people you didn't know very well."

5. "Think how you might feel if you did something like that."

In each of these five examples, the choice of words and focus are not in the present moment but refer to feelings and events that have already passed and that happened elsewhere or, as in the last example, are hypothetical and somewhat removed from the reality of the moment.

Using these same five examples, it is possible to make "here and now" responses.

1. "You're still angry and feel like hitting back."

2. "It's discouraging to think about your meeting with the teacher. You look really down."

3. "As I listen to you talk about what happened, you seem so excited, you're just bubbling with with enthusiasm."

4. "We don't know each other very well and you're feeling uneasy right now."

5. "It's fascinating you right now, just to think of the possibilities."

These statements have a more immediate focus, giving attention to feelings and events that are present. They are usually perceived by people as more intense, more intimate, and more personal, although there and then responses also focus on personal feelings and events. The present moment is dynamic and self-disclosure is at its most vulnerable state. Here and now responses, although very powerful, are more exciting and more threatening. There is more comfort when there and then responses are used, as they are less real, perhaps more into the mind's fantasy of the past or the future. Consequently, the excitement and the intensity of the present moment is diffused.

When things appear to be boring, increase the use of here and now responses. When things are too intense, increase the use of there and then responses. When you are first getting started with a person in individual counseling, both of you may find it more comforting to use more there and then responses. When you are searching deeper and exploring matters in greater depth, here and now responses will add a significant dimension.

Diagnosis and Assessment

Some students call counselors "shrinks" and assume the guidance office is where they are tested, analyzed, and evaluated. While the office may be associated with standardized testing programs and personal and career assessment measures, testing may or may not be a part of individual counseling.

Currently, there are no diagnostic manuals for school counselors to help classify counselees and their problems. While some students may have been diagnosed by a psychiatrist or mental health worker according to the *Diagnostic Statistical Manual, Third Edition (DSM III)*, few school counselors, if any, use this classification system in their work. Yet, they are frequently called upon by school personnel to help assess a student's personal and social functioning. It is done within the context of the school setting and by observation more than by formal inventories or tests.

There are some formal standardized measures which you can use to assess a student's intelligence, achievement, attitude, classroom behavior, and goals. There are also some informal inventories and general records which can be used. Together they can provide useful information for counseling. They might be used as baseline data, providing information about where you are beginning with a student. They can be used again after counseling, as a means of assessing outcomes. They can also be used during counseling as a means of helping students to gain insight, to assess their progress, and to make decisions.

When used in counseling, assessment measures must be considered part of the counseling intervention. Sometimes this can facilitate matters and sometimes it might not. One student assumed that, after taking a battery of tests, the counselor had all the information needed to provide some good answers to some problems and looked to the counselor for specific directions. Another student assumed that since the tests probably revealed everything, there was nothing to hide and began talking more freely than before.

Diagnosis and assessment is always happening, although no formal measure, such as a paper and pencil test, may be used. As a counselor, you will look at various forms of formal and informal data to assess the general functioning level of a counselee.

Functioning or Dysfunctioning

If you want to know how serious a problem might be or whether some behaviors are beyond what might be expected of a particular age group, the following four guidelines might be useful: 1) Frequency; 2) Duration; 3) Intensity; and 4) Appropriateness of affect. Or, how often does the behavior about which you are concerned occur? How long has it been going on? How much energy is invested in the behavior? Are the person's feelings and expressions socially appropriate?

These four guidelines can be used to help you identify and assess dysfunctioning students. Judgments can be based on your professional observations without the use of assessment instruments, which could be used later to confirm your initial diagnosis. The guidelines have proven practical to many counselors who do not have immediate access to profession personnel or resources to decide whether an individual is dysfunctioning or not.

A middle school girl, Rachel, had a history of being successful in school. Her academic records showed that she made A and B grades and that teachers liked her. She was well-groomed and respected by other students. She took part in after-school activities. Then, one day a teacher suggested to Rachel's counselor that the girl might be having some problems and the counselor called her into the guidance office.

It was learned that Rachel had missed at least two days of school each week for the past three weeks and she had not completed any class assignments for two weeks. This was unlike her. When confronted with this information, she exploded in anger and said that she did not care. Then, she withdrew and refused to talk. The next week, the same behaviors occurred and when approached by the counselor, Rachel leaned against the wall, sighed deeply, and choked backed tears. An intensity was there. The unusual pattern of school behavior suggested that something had happened to distract her from her school work. She began telling about family violence in which her alcoholic father abused her mother and threatened to move the family out of the state. She dreaded going home and worried about her own safety, and the safety of the other family members. She was dysfunctioning. Her coping mechanisms had broken down. She felt overwhelmed and it seemed her world was crashing down on her. Rachel received some individual counseling and was later referred to a counseling agency for more help.

Gary was a boy in the same school who skipped school for two days. He and his friend decided to go to a shopping mall where there was a game arcade. They played games until on the second day an attendance officer brought them back to school. It was Gary's first time to leave school without an excused absence. He talked with his counselor about the matter and seemed remorseful. In retrospect, he thought it was poor judgment on his part.

The intensity, duration, and frequency of Gary's behavior did not suggest the same seriousness as that experienced by another boy, Randy, who had a history of skipping school for two years. He came to the counselor's attention because he had missed several days of school during the previous grading period and was failing his classes. When he was brought back to school by an attendance officer, he said he did not care and would probably skip again in the future. He seemed defiant and rebellious. Randy was considered to be more dysfunctioning than Gary, although both were guilty of breaking the same school rule.

You can look for patterns of behavior to help you assess the degree to which a student is having a problem. You will have to make some professional judgments according to how much counseling a student needs and whether you are in a position to provide the counseling. You will also need to know both the student's limitations and your own.

Depth of Exploration

It is frequently assumed that individual counseling provides the best avenue for students to self-disclose and explore their thoughts and feelings. It has also been assumed that counseling differs from other kinds of helping services in the topics discussed and the depth of their exploration.

What does it mean to explore something in depth? Is it related to time or the information that is disclosed? Or, is it reflected in the personal meaning that results for the counselee? Are there levels of communication, some of which are more valuable than others?

It is not possible to answer these questions in detail here, but it can be useful to conceptualize the counseling process as facilitating the counselee to talk about matters according to three different levels of personal exploration. The first level (See Figure 6.1) is characterized by intellectual ideas and superficial talk. This talk is focused on other people and what they are thinking and doing. For example, "You know my friend, Helen? Well, she's planning to move away in two weeks. She is not very happy about it. They are going to south Florida somewhere. She's never been there before and...." There is little information about the person who is talking, only about her friend.

In another case, a counselee said, "I suppose that I should go to college. College is a good way to prepare for life, even if you do not know what you want to major in. It cannot hurt a person. On the other hand, there are many people who have gone to college later, after they have had some work experience. That might be a good idea." Again, this first level of communication might be interesting, but there is not much depth in the exploration. Look at the counselee's language. There is no personalization. There are no personal feelings expressed, although the topic is of interest to the counselee.

Figure 6.1

Depth of Self-Exploration

L   Talk of Others and Things: As Related to Self
E   General events and ideas
V   1   Intellectual concepts
E   Universal and public issues
L   "There and Then"

O   Talk of Self and Ideas: As Related to Others
F   Personal events and opinions
    2   Personal goals, future, interpretations
              "There and Then"

D   Talk of Self and Feelings: As Related to
I   Self-Experience
S   Personal experience and meanings
C   3   Personal feelings and perceptions
L   "Here and Now"
O
S
U
R
E

--------------1--------------2--------------3--------------4---------------

A COUNSELING SESSION / OR
SERIES OF COUNSELING SESSIONS

A second level of communication emphasizes talk about self. You hear the pronoun "I" used more often. There is an attempt to reveal personal information, but personal meaning and experience are lost in the event that is described or the ideas being shared. For instance, "I want to get better grades in English and it's a class that I could do better in if I tried. I know that. It's something that I must do and just can't put off any longer. I know that my teacher is thinking I can't do it, but she's got the wrong idea about my ability. If she sees me as a C student, then that's what I am going to get. I know, I can tell."

While this student is talking more about a situation from a personal viewpoint, the language focuses on general ideas about the class and the teacher. You should not be fooled by all the references to self, as they are limited and only in context of the event.

The third level centers on the impact that an event has had on a person and its personal meaning. Counseling theories tell us that this is most likely to be expressed in feeling words or personal statements which indicate what a person is experiencing. This invariably has to do with pleasant, unpleasant, or both kinds of feelings. It is the subjective core of the person's life experience and is directed to the person's values, perceptions and attitudes.

For example, "I'm so discouraged right now. You see, I've tried hard in that class, but I come up short each time. It's really getting to me. It just seems hopeless and I'm not sure what to do about it." In this case, the words not only provide information about the topic or event but they reveal personal experience and meaning behind the words that tell of ideas or events. They are penetrating thoughts or feelings which go to the depth of the experience.

One way to determine whether you are facilitative in your individual counseling is to look at the impact of your responses. Do they help a person explore matters in depth or do they steer the conversation to a more superficial level? How much time in counseling is spent at the more superficial levels? Is the absence of exploring matters in depth a consequence of counselor skill or counselee resistance? The facilitative model assumes that you will need all the high facilitative responses to encourage counselees to explore their situations in depth.

In counseling, you encourage students to explore their ideas, feelings, and behaviors at all three levels. Sometimes it is comforting and easier to talk about a topic at an intellectual level before looking at its personal meaning. A review of counseling typescripts suggests that most students jump from one level to another, and back again, as they attempt to talk about themselves. Those counselees who understand the counseling process, and who are experienced with it, can probably stay at a deeper level of self-disclosure and exploration for longer periods of time.

Perhaps one more concept might be helpful, especially as you consider what is and what is not facilitative. The facilitative model is built upon probabilities. That is, high facilitative responses are more likely to elicit the facilitative conditions. When high facilitative responses are used, there is also a higher probability that counselees will move through the facilitative processes of self-disclosures, feedback, increased self-awareness, decision-making, and responsible action. Moreover, high facilitative responses tend to encourage counselees to explore matters in depth.

Yet, perhaps the real test of whether or not a response or an action is facilitative—moving the counselee toward a desired goal and through the facilitatiave processes—is how the counselee acts or responds to whatever you do. For instance, eight critical points in terms of facilitating the depth of exploration are shown in Figure 6.2. Regardless of the issue or topic, or what was said or done, these points indicate that something happened to move the counselee (or perhaps a group) in a different direction, toward a different level of self-exploration. An analysis of a recorded typecript, for example, might reveal what happened at those points. It would then be possible to designate a counselor action or response as either facilitative or not.

Facilitative responses and actions are related only to general expectations and probabilities. By themselves, they mean nothing. It is in the context of counseling that their value must be demonstrated. Therefore, it is suggested that you increase the frequency of the high facilitative responses to help counselees explore matters in depth. Take note of the impact that your language and behaviors have on a counselee and then decide what you want to say or do next.

Finally, while in-depth counseling focuses on personal feelings and meanings and emphasizes the value of insight and awareness, identification of related verbal and non-verbal behaviors is an essential ingredient in counseling. People are what people do. This includes both their overt and covert actions, both of which can be a focus of counseling.

Figure 6.2

Facilitating the
Depth and Direction of Self-Exploration

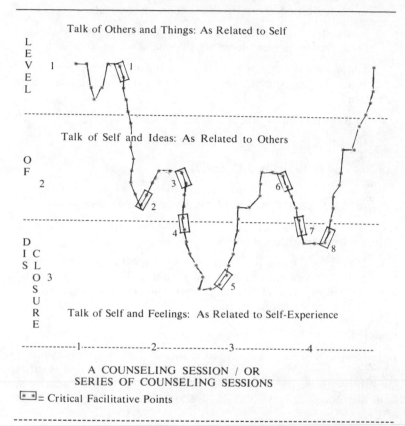

Talk of Others and Things: As Related to Self

Talk of Self and Ideas: As Related to Others

Talk of Self and Feelings: As Related to Self-Experience

A COUNSELING SESSION / OR
SERIES OF COUNSELING SESSIONS

[* *] = Critical Facilitative Points

Advantages, Limitations, and Conclusion

Advantages of Individual Counseling

1. There is a base of knowledge that supports the use of individual counseling and much of counseling theory is founded on work with individuals.

2. Most training institutes prepare counselors for individual counseling and, subsequently, counselors are usually most comfortable with it.

Individual Counseling as a Counselor Intervention   231

3. It is easier to gain access to one student for counseling than groups of students, especially at the secondary school level.

4. Counselors frequently feel more in control of the dynamics of counseling because it is easier to concentrate and focus on the behavior of one individual than on several.

5. Some students disclose more thoughts and feelings about their problems when meeting privately with a counselor.

6. Some socially sensitive topics, including some crisis-interventions, lend themselves better to individual than to group work.

7. Individual counseling is a place to start.

8. Confidentiality is easier to safeguard.

Limitations of Individual Counseling

1. Counselor-student ratios are too high to enable counselors to see all their assigned students in individual counseling.

2. It is a less efficient use of counselor time than meeting with students in groups.

3. Counselors work harder in many respects, as they are the only ones present to listen and respond. The counselor is the only interpersonal resource at the time of couseling and this limits the perspectives that might be given.

Conclusion

Individual counseling is a valuable and respected intervention. It is the most favored approach by school counselors and it is often considered to be the only mode of counseling by many teachers, administrators, and parents who are less familiar with other forms of counseling.

However, individual counseling is a luxury in the schools. Most schools do not have enough personnel to provide all the counseling services needed if counselors only meet individually with all students. Moreover, individual counseling must be thought of in terms of brief counseling. Perhaps the average number of students who are being seen by counselors for individual counseling, as part of their case load, will be six to eight, and they generally will be seen in six to ten 30-minute sessions. Individual counseling is usually more direct, tends to focus on behaviors related to achievement, and uses progressive steps toward personal goals.

Chapter 7

Small Group Counseling
as a Counselor Intervention

People are born into groups, live and work in groups, become dysfunctioning in groups, and can be helped in groups. Family groups, peer groups, social and school groups, and other groups are part of a student's life. Therefore, some young people are more comfortable and willing to participate in group counseling than in individual counseling.

Group counseling in the schools appeals to many students, especially as they learn how they often share common interests and concerns. They like knowing that others have feelings and thoughts about the same things. They enjoy the support of group members, who are all working together toward both individual and group goals. Group counseling in the schools is a valid counselor intervention that can meet the needs of many students.

Group Counseling Defined

Small group counseling is a unique educational experience in which students can work together to explore their ideas, attitudes, feelings, and behaviors, especially as related to personal development and progress in school. A counselor facilitates the interaction among participants in a special learning experience where helping relationships are formed. Members self-disclose, listen carefully, and give feedback to one another. While the content or topics of discussion may, at times, appear to be similar to other educational activities, the counseling experience is more personalized and intense.

Attempts to differentiate group guidance and group counseling have focused on topics, size of the group, leadership, and kind of group interaction. Group guidance is usually done with larger groups of students and discussion is less personal. Participation is more limited and it is not as easy to give individual attention to all members. Some writers have also suggested that group guidance involves more information-giving and teaching, and that a counselor plays a more active role in structuring the learning experience.

Small group counseling, on the other hand, is usually done with a smaller number of students who form a close working relationship in which they can explore matters in depth. The group usually requires and attains greater levels of trust, understanding, and acceptance than in group guidance, which affects the degree that members feel free to express themselves. In addition, group counseling has been characterized by greater privacy, personal involvement, and a willingness to investigate more sensitive issues and situations.

However, as counselors and teachers have become more skilled facilitators and group managers, the differences between guidance and counseling often rest more with the size of the group and the extent of personal risk that is taken. Some of the distinctions are arbitrary and it is not easy to see them, especially when group guidance is personalized.

Three Small Group Counseling Approaches

Group counseling might involve three kinds of approaches: 1) Crisis-Centered; 2) Problem-Centered; and 3) Growth-Centered. All these have their place in a comprehensive developmental guidance and counseling program.

Crisis-Centered

Crisis-centered small group counseling is concerned with an urgent problem. There is a need to give immediate attention to some incident or circumstance. If the group has already been meeting and has established a group cohesiveness, a crisis-situation might easily be worked on within the context of a problem-centered or growth-centered group. After the crisis has passed, the group would return to its original focus. Yet, some groups are formed and start their relationships as a result of a critical event or situation.

Six high school students were having a conflict with a teacher and walked out of class in protest. They believed that they were being treated unfairly and they wanted some changes. The school administration, to support the teacher and to show disapproval of the way in which the group dealt with the problem, suspended the six students for three days and requested parent conferences. Instead of attending the class, the group met with a school counselor to talk about their situation and to explore ways to resolve some of the problems. It was crisis-centered group counseling, as the students first vented their angry feelings and then moved to finding a reasonable solution for their predicament. After the students returned to class, they continued to meet with the counselor once a week for three more weeks.

Other times when crisis-centered small group counseling has taken place include: conflicts between student groups; conflicts that happened on a school bus; and conflicts that resulted from racial slurs. One group was formed of eight students who were receiving failing grades in a required class. A crisis was at hand since they needed to pass the class in order to graduate. Group counseling provided them a means to examine their situation and to think together about some possible solutions.

Problem-Centered

Problem-centered small group counseling also focuses on problems that are concerning students. But, the nature of a problem is usually less urgent and has not reached a critical point. Emotions are usually not running as high as when a crisis is at hand. Sometimes a problem-centered group will focus on a remaining problem after the intensity of a crisis has passed.

A high school counselor provided small group counseling to some teen-age girls who were pregnant and who still wanted to finish school. Another counselor worked with a group of students who wanted to rid themselves of the excessive stress and pressure that they experienced in their daily lives. Still another counselor worked with a group of students who had conflicts with their parents and who were considering running away from home.

An elementary school counselor organized a problem-centered group which focused on problems which were occuring in kickball on the playground at recess and during lunch period. Apparently, two boys were too aggressive, arguing and fighting with those who did not follow their wishes. They were "bossy" and would cheat in order to be on the winning side. The two boys needed counseling and were put in a problem-centered group with others who played in the same games and disliked the boys' behaviors. The group focused directly on the problem, encouraging each member to talk about what they liked and didn't like about playing kickball together and how they could get along better in the future.

In the problem-centered approach, the purpose of the group is clear. It is based on coping with a common concern or situation that is causing students discomfort or unhappiness. The problems distract students from learning well in school. The group members identify a problem and commit themselves to doing something about it. Groups which meet to resolve such problems are motivated, they know their problems, and try to find ways to resolve them before they become more critical and lead to a crisis.

Problem-centered groups have a central focus. A problem is identified, explored, and decisions are made. Members often pursue a direct approach when talking about the problem; there is a candid discussion about the issues. Confrontation and probing type questions are seen as an essential part of the group process. Sometimes group members might discuss a general problem, using it as a spring board for personal meaning. Specific details related to a personal situation or event may not be needed. The group might look at the problem area in terms of prevention, for example, in which case hypothetical situations might be discussed and role-played.

Typical kinds of problem-centered groups are: achieving better grades; resolving conflicts with teachers and peers; making career choices; coping with stress; finding a job; getting along with parents; coping with peer pressure; and avoiding the abuse of alcohol and drugs.

Growth-Centered

Growth-centered groups focus on the personal and social development of students. A crisis or a particular problem need not be the only reason for group counseling. A group can concentrate on learning more about self and others through some close and friendly interpersonal experiences (Gazda, 1978).

Growth-centered groups are designed for all students and they give attention to the general needs and interests of young people at various developmental life stages. Growing up and going to school are usually fraught with problems, some more serious than others. It is assumed that students need to talk about specific concerns related to their personal development. Small group counseling gives them this opportunity. Students do not have to wait until a problem arises before they explore some of the personal and social issues of their lives, such as accepting responsibility, changing behaviors, learning to communicate with others, assessing self, setting goals, and solving problems.

Common anxieties and dilemmas are frequently explored in growth groups. For example, one group of elementary school students met together to talk about what it was like when they went home after school to an empty house, knowing that their working parents would not be home for two or three hours. They explored their worries and their worst fears. They talked about ways to use their time at home and what to do if an emergency should develop. They shared ideas and learned that they were not the only ones who had to manage for themselves after school.

Another elementary school group met to talk about friendship. They discussed what people look for in friends and the things about themselves that would make them a good friend. They also considered things that they needed to improve upon to make them even better friends. One activity in the group was to think of ways in which friends supported each other.

Some people do not see personal and social growth as a subject for small group counseling. They argue that such growth activities and experiences might preferably be conducted in large groups where more children can be reached. There is some validity to the argument and we will examine this concept more in the next chapter when large group guidance is discussed. However, some students are more responsive to small group experiences where the activities enable them to be more involved. They also cannot obtain the same closeness or the degree of trust to risk exploring some issues in a large group.

Moreover, growth-centered groups provide a counselor an excellent opportunity to meet with a random selection of students on any number of different topics. There is no pressing problem. Problems are presented and discussed, but only as they emerge from whatever the group is exploring. The focus is frequently on "here and now" experiences that are inherent in growth group activities. That is, students participate in an activity and then talk about what they experienced and learned. Eventually, experiences are linked or generalized to life situations outside the group.

A counselor worked with a boy who was having problems getting along with teachers and other students. The boy had a negative attitude, a difficult home life, and was sullen and unsociable. He was called to the guidance office to be part of a "friendship group." There were five other students and the group met for four 45-minute sessions. Although friendship was the subject to be explored, the counselor deliberately put the boy in the growth-centered group as a "target student" to get to know him better. The boy was not confronted about his behavior around school nor was he singled out for individual counseling in the group. It was assumed that he would take what information and personal meaning that he could from the group activities and discussion. The group was less threatening than other approaches. His problems were not the focus of the group, except as he chose to disclose them.

Later, after the group ended, the counselor talked with the boy informally in the hallways and continued building a friendly relationship. Still later, the counselor called the boy into the guidance office to initiate some individual counseling which seemed an appropriate next step. The counselor believed that the growth-centered group had help put "some chips in the bank" so that individual counseling was not as threatening and there was not as much resistance.

Putting target students into growth-centered groups is a common practice among experienced counselors who want to avoid direct confrontations with students and who see the need to ease into counseling relationships. In addition, such groups also allow students with problems to work with peers who are models or who have had success in avoiding or solving similar problems.

The crisis-centered, problem-centered, and growth-centered approaches are general descriptors used to organize small group counseling. However, small group counseling approaches can also be titled according to such things as: a) a counseling theory that is primarily used; b) the topical content (problem area) of the group; c) the counselor function and activity; or d) the population of students drawn to participate. Duncan and Gumaer (1980), in their book on developmental groups for children, provided several examples, by different contributors, of groups titled along these lines.

Almost all small group counseling experiences described in the professional literature can be categorized into one of the three basic approaches described above. No doubt other names might be used. However, it is practical to think of groups in these fundamental ways because the terms suggest a general focus around which to organize small groups for counseling and some possible goals. It may also give you an idea of your primary leadership responsibilities and the activities that might be used. The actual interaction that takes place in small group counseling, the group activities that might be used, the particular emphasis that might be given, and the outcomes that might be obtained are totally dependent upon facilitative skills and choices made by you and the group members.

Stages of Small Group Counseling

It could be argued that the same counseling stages outlined for individual counseling, discussed in Chapter 6, are true for small group counseling. The counseling process in both cases tends to move along the same lines. Some writers, however, have abbreviated the stages to help us grasp the evolution of a group.

Mahler (1969) was among the first to describe how group counseling could be used effectively in the schools and he outlined four stages: Involvement, Transition, Working, and Ending.

The basic purpose of the involvement stage is to help members clarify their reasons for being in the group, to get acquainted, and to begin building a climate of trust and acceptance. During the transition stage, group members continue to learn how to share their ideas and feelings in greater depth, patterns of behavior begin to emerge, and some understanding of behaviors begins to increase. Most important, resistances to looking at self, working through some defenses and initial anxieties, and learning to facilitate one another are given attention. The group continues to build cohesiveness and there is a sense of belonging.

When the working stage is reached, members know more about how the counseling process works and the rules of the group. They have more confidence in the group and there is more effort to give and receive feedback, to learn more and help one another, and to discover some ways to take responsible action on life's problems and situations. Caring and support by members is high, as each person learns more about self and others. Finally, the ending stage is when everyone is thinking of how to apply what has been learned or relearned in their lives and to gain some closure on issues before the group is disbanded.

Besides gaining a general idea of the kinds of counseling groups that you want to provide students and the recognition that the group will move through different process stages, you will want to think about how the organization and structure of groups can influence group dynamics.

Factors to Consider

As in individual counseling, several factors need to be considered when organizing and structuring small group counseling approaches. Among these are:

How do you organize a group?

In organizing a group for counseling, you will want to think about such things as: 1) purpose, 2) accessibility of students, 3) member motivation, 4) peer relationships, and 5) member abilities and interests. After that, you will give more attention to who you will select, where and when you will meet, what approaches you will use, and how you will proceed.

The purpose. The purpose of the group is the prime consideration since it can affect other organizational decisions. Groups can be organized to meet a variety of student needs. What will the group try to accomplish? What individual and group outcomes might be expected? After the group has ended, what will the members probably say about the group? What is it all about?

The rationale for meeting the group is not only important to gain student cooperation and participation, but it can be valuable in obtaining teacher and parent support. Even an unstructured group needs a reason for meeting. Once a general or specific purpose is identified, then it is possible to think about the other factors which influence group interaction and process.

A practical approach to organizing groups is to think about target populations and target students. Though schools typically classify students by grade levels or subject matter classes, it is also possible to identify student populations according to special needs and interests.

The eighth grade class in a middle school, for instance, will have students who might be organized into such target populations as: students who are low-performers, yet who have high ability; students who are at risk of dropping out of school; students who are uncertain about career plans; students who have been referred to the school office for discipline; and students who are shy and withdrawn. Such a list seems endless, since grouping is based upon some common need or interest.

From a large target population, such as high school students who have poor working relationships with teachers, some students could be identified for small group counseling. In a sense all the students in the small group would have a need in common: to improve their relationships with teachers. This becomes a central purpose of the group. It is also possible to assign some of these students to several groups, where they might be, in the counselor's eyes, "target students" who are working on a problem within the context of a group.

Safran and Safran (1985) emphasized the importance of focusing on target behaviors within a group. They believed that behavior awareness should be taught in groups as a requisite for changing behavior and recognized the value of "peer group participation." They suggested that students might first be guided through some desensitization experiences designed to define and identify disruptive behaviors. These behaviors are then rated generally before a self-rating is applied. Finally, consequences and alternative behaviors are discussed.

One middle school counselor formed a "Girl Talk" group composed of all girls who wanted to talk about boy-girl relationships and other interests and problems related to being an adolescent girl. Another middle school counselor formed a group of all boys who resisted dressing for physical education classes and who were being failed for the course. An elementary school counselor organized a group of latchkey children, all of whom were having problems in school and who seemed to lack parental guidance.

Sometimes it may seem more appropriate to form a heterogeneous group, perhaps a random selection from a class, because the purpose of the group might meet the guidance and counseling needs of students at a developmental stage. For instance, all students can benefit from learning communication skills through a personal growth group. Even within this type of group, however, it is possible to have a target student in mind, one whom you want to experience the group in a special way or to whom you want to give particular attention.

Cassandra was a below-average student in school, although she had above-average academic ability. Her teachers reported that she was insensitive to classmates, rude to teachers, and had a negative attitude most of the time when in class. She did not complete her homework assignments.

The counselor decided to put Cassandra in a small growth group with students randomly drawn from her school class. It was assumed that this would reduce the girl's defensiveness, since she had been unresponsive and even defiant when confronted by teachers and administrators about her attitude. She was not identified as being in the group because of her problems. The purpose of the group was to develop some general communication skills. The counselor knew of Cassandra's problems and needs and she was a target student. The counselor seized upon opportunities to give her special attention, such as encouraging her to participate and reinforcing her efforts. When group activities and tasks were related to her problem, the counselor made an effort to respond to Cassandra more.

In this sense, the heterogeneous grouping in the communication skills group provided an indirect and safe approach to working with the girl, who needed a less confrontive form of assistance. The group experience also benefited the other members.

Accessibility. Accessibility or availability is the second major consideration when organizing a group. After you have identified potential group members, the next question is: "Can the students meet together as a group regularly?" If not at the same time for each session, can you and the selected members negotiate meeting times with teachers and administrators so that you can meet consistently as a group? It makes practical sense to identify and work with those groups of students who are available to you. You will probably have many students who could benefit from group counseling more than you can possibly meet during a school year. Therefore, if some students whom you would like to meet in a group are not available, meet with those who are.

You may find it helpful to "contract" with teachers to get students from their classes. The contract explains the general purpose of the group, the time it is meeting, and the total number of sessions which have been scheduled. Teachers sign the contracts, excusing the group members from their classes. The contract is an agreement, but it also has the advantage of alerting teachers to how much time will be missed from class and reducing conflicts between teachers and students in your groups. Sometimes a verbal contract is all that is needed, but busy teachers frequently forget. A written agreement can be a friendly reminder.

Recently, teachers and administrators have taken measures to reduce interruptions and keep students in academic classes. Some state laws prescribe the number of classroom hours that students need to be present in a classroom before they can receive credit for a class. However, most of the same laws recognize that counseling and advisement time is a legitimate reason for an excused absence and do not penalize a student who works with a counselor during an academic period. Nevertheless, high school counselors in particular have found it difficult to organize small group counseling sessions because of various restrictions and teacher reluctance.

Many counselors have learned to meet with groups of students on a class period basis, rotating meeting times through the school week. In one case, a counselor met with her group of high school sophomores during the first period of the day on Monday, the second period on Tuesday, and the third period on Wednesday. The following week, the group met two more times—fourth period on Thursday and fifth period on Friday. Students missed only one period from their regularly scheduled classes.

Counselors have used variations of this arrangement to contract with students. During the first meeting, students are given a calendar showing the group's changing meeting times and teachers are notified of the days that the students will be out of class. It works. However, although this procedure is practical when considering loss of academic class time, it tends to be wearing on most counselors when it comes to making arrangements for the group. It is not an easy system to manage for most counselors. In addition, a rotating schedule of meetings results in more absenteeism and tardiness, as many students get confused about the changes of times or they forget. And, those are usually the students who most need the group counseling experience.

One time to meet students is before and after school. This time of day may be unavailable for some students, especially those who ride a school bus. You might take students from your target list, for example, who are within walking distance to school and organize a series of four 30-minute group sessions for five students who need assistance.

Still another time to meet students is during lunch period. When arrangements are made, students can bring their lunches to the guidance office. While this may have some limitations, such as less eye contact and some minor disruptions from the noise of eating, it has proven to be a practical meeting time when counselors have access to students.

Middle school counselors often have more access to students during the regular class periods than do high school counselors, as class credits have not yet begun to accumulate for high school graduation and the same class attendance restrictions do not usually apply. Still, middle school teachers dislike having their classes interrupted. Elementary school counselors appear to have less trouble in arranging small group counseling, especially in the afternoon of a school day when teachers are finished with the morning academic lessons. But, meeting times can be a problem in all schools.

Therefore, the value of TAP (Teachers as Advisors Program) cannot be ignored by school counselors. When schools have regularly scheduled TAP periods, such as the first half hour of each school day, then counselors have more access to students for group work and there is less need to pull groups of students out of academic classes during the day.

Motivation. Motivation plays an important part in the work of a group. We know that voluntary or involuntary participation can make a difference, just as it does in individual counseling. If a group is involuntary, as many of them are, then you may need to work harder at selling or motivating the members on the purpose and benefits of the group. They will surely be thinking, "What's in it for me?"

Although you may initiate the counseling process, each person must voluntarily participate. People might pass on a discussion topic, if asked, and wait until a later time to comment. Resistance can usually be overcome by using "go-around" procedures, in which warm-up tasks are given and encouragement can take place. Start with some topics that are relatively less probing and sensitive. This can stimulate participation which can then be reinforced.

Students who are skeptical, uncertain, or reluctant to be in a group can be more responsive after they understand the purpose of the group and take part in a few activities which build group cohesiveness. The same facilitative conditions that are helpful in individual counseling are also needed in group counseling. Once the facilitative conditions are experienced by members, motivation and interest increases.

Peer relationships. Relationships between students can be affected by many things, including age, sex, social status, prior acquaintance, similar experiences, and personal styles. Because of personal and social likenesses, some groups are immediately more compatible and form quicker bonds. Other groups can develop a group cohesiveness as they come to know each other; but, it can take more time.

Many counselors find that similar age is an important variable when working with students in school. Although students from grades six, seven, and eight can be grouped together for academic experiences in a middle school and can take part in similar group activities, eighth graders are less tolerant of sixth graders and sometimes they will take a cool, reserved approach in counseling. Sixth graders, on the other hand, because of developmental stages, can sometimes feel intimated by the older eighth graders who are usually physically and socially more mature. While there are exceptions, working with a two-year age span is generally a comfortable arrangement.

Gender does not seem to make a difference in how groups function, unless a boy and girl who are "going together" are in the same group. Then, there seems to be more guardedness and role-playing. Sometimes a topic related to physical growth can be more sensitive when both boys and girls are present and can inhibit group participation. But, in today's world, boys and girls can learn to talk openly about most things and can be of valuable assistance in giving feedback to one another.

Abilities and interests. Similar abilities and interests provide a homogeneous group that can work well together almost immediately. While social maturity and skill come into play, perhaps verbal ability is the most critical factor. If a group has one or two slow, deliberate speakers, there is a tendency for the group's energy to sag. Group process is usually dependent upon group talk and this requires some social skills such as listening, attending, responding, conceptualizing ideas, and being sensitive to others. While some of these process skills can be taught to members, a group member who is clearly deficient in these areas may first need tutoring and individual counseling before becoming a group member.

In a similar vein, when group members have extremely varied interests and experiences, it is sometimes difficult for them to attend to others. They can lose interest and find the group boring, especially if there is no attempt to personalize group experiences.

One counselor met with a group of high school students who were uncertain about career plans and were anxious about what they were going to do following graduation. Some of the students in the group had very low grades and were not interested in pursuing any more formal education. A few others were undecided about which college to attend since they were unsure about their career goals. Exploring the interests and needs of these two groups stagnated the group's cohesiveness until the counselor began to pose questions and provide activities which affected all group members (e.g. "List three goals you hope to achieve someday." "Name a personal strength that you have going for yourself and then something about yourself you need to improve upon." "Tell about someone who has supported you in your decisions and what you like or admire about that person.")

Some other students were in group counseling because they were unable to obtain passing grades in a social studies class and all the participants needed to pass the class to graduate. Two students in a group of eight were negative and said that they did not care if they passed or not. The presence of these two members prevented the other members from exploring their needs, interests, and the barriers which they had to overcome to graduate. It was difficult to facilitate interaction because there was no agreement on the value and purpose of the group.

Friendships and prior acquaintances can sometimes inhibit some group participation, as small cliques might rely on each other for support or form some sense of exclusive loyalty to each other. Yet, you can also let friends start their own groups by identifying topics that they want to discuss with a counselor and finding a mutual meeting time.

A middle school counselor recommended that two girls who were experiencing test anxiety and excessive pressure to do well in school find four other girls or boys who were experiencing similar concerns and who could meet with the counselor for some group counseling activities. The girls took the responsibility for recruiting the other members and finding an afternoon time when they could be in the guidance office.

What should be the size of the group?

The answer to this question has varied over the years. Most people who have had a course in group counseling will give the standard answer of ten members, although a few would be willing to go as high as twelve or even fifteen. However, experienced school counselors prefer to work with about five or six and no more than seven or eight. The trend is to meet for shorter periods of time and with smaller groups. Having fewer members allows for more participation by each person in the group.

When counselors have six group members, most small group activities can be used, including go-around activities. A go-around is when the counselor gives the group a task (e.g. "Tell about what you look for in a friend") and then, usually starting on the counselor's immediate left, the first person speaks to the topic. Then, the next person to the left speaks, going around in a circle until all have responded to the task or topic, including the counselor. If the group has more than six members, such a procedure can become tedious and time consuming. It would not be practical.

Groups of eight or more rely on spontaneous contributions and participations. The topic or tasks may remain the same, but group dynamics are different. Some members participate less while others tend to dominate. Some receive inadequate attention and tend to withdraw. The counselor's leadership function is affected. Interactions are more complex and there is more group behavior to which to attend. One problem with large groups is a tendency for them to become more like a regular school class than a counseling group.

It may be possible to have too small a group, especially with high school students. That is, the counselor and two other students can make up a group, but this number can also be fatiguing as the interaction is intense and focused. Elementary school counselors, however, often work with three or four primary grade children in a group. It is practical and effective because of their attention span and lack of social skills.

How often should groups meet and for how long?

Generally speaking, one session a week per group is the average for most school counselors. It is preferable to meet twice a week and sometimes more. The purpose of the group and the urgency with which you are trying to accomplish some objectives can influence how often you meet. Most developmental counselors like the idea of meeting twice a week for three weeks and building group counseling around six sessions. If more sessions are needed, then a new contract is drawn. Rarely do school counselors meet students in small group counseling for more then 10 or 12 sessions.

The length of the session varies among counselors, but many middle and high school counselors prefer to meet for the duration of a regular class period. Generally, this is about 45 to 50 minutes. It is uncommon for counselors to meet more than one period, unless a crisis-intervention is taking place. Typically, elementary school counselors choose to meet for 20 minutes with primary grade children and 30 minutes with upper grade children.

You might think about using 30-minute sessions. While they are typically more structured than longer sessions, this time frame allows counselors and students an opportunity to meet without taking too much time away from academic studies. It seems better to meet for two thirty-minute periods a week than one hour period. This also will depend upon your leadership style and the kinds of group activities or experiences you want to provide.

If meetings are held infrequently, once a month or once every two weeks, group cohesiveness tends to wane, if it ever develops. There is less personal commitment by counselor and students, as the group is an event which seems almost out of context. There is often a lack of continuity and the group must begin anew each time it meets. Sometimes such stretched-out meetings are unavoidable and you will have to decide what skills and activities are needed to keep the group involved and moving through the counseling stages.

What is the duration of the group?

Some experts suggest that a minimum of ten sessions is needed before most small group counseling can be effective and that may only be a start. Practically speaking, however, ten sessions is about the limit for most school counselors. Six to eight sessions seem more ideal. Some counselors typically make plans for four sessions before ending the group or recontracting for a few more sessions.

Obviously, the longer you meet with your students, the more opportunities you will have to build a solid helping relationship and to talk about more matters in depth. But, this is a luxury and students are not often available for long-term counseling. Therefore, counseling groups organized for a specific purpose and with limited goals tend to be the choice of most school counselors.

Where does the group meet?

Not surprisingly, considering the history of school guidance and counseling, the vast majority of school counselors have offices that are too small and inadequate for small group counseling. Counselors usually need more space for group activities, especially those that involve movement. A conference room might be used. If there is no conference room, you might use an unoccupied classroom. But, space is often at a premium in today's schools and you may find yourself meeting in some unusual places. Counselors have found meeting places in storerooms, auditoriums, cafeterias, media centers, hallways, and coatrooms.

Ideally, the group counseling room should be small enough to provide intimacy but large enough to be comfortable. It should provide enough privacy so that group members are not distracted or feel inhibited by outside observers. Although students are accustomed to sitting in desks or around tables, it is best if you can arrange the chairs in a circle without the presence of desks so there is a greater feeling of openness, and each person's personal presence can be felt. A few students will want to sit behind a table, as it provides a sense of security and something to lean on. They feel less exposed. While they might be able to write ideas down better if they are seated around tables or in desks, the general rule is try to avoid them. Another guideline is to have all members sitting in similar fashion—all on the floor, or around a table, or in desks that are arranged in a circle.

How do you end a group?

The same closure problems that confront you in individual counseling are also present in small group counseling. Some groups will resist termination and think of reasons for continuing. If the reasons are legitimate, and if you want to continue, then renegotiate and recontract with group members and their teachers. Otherwise, resistance to ending the group might be viewed as a healthy sign that the group has enjoyed the experience. Since most school counseling groups meet for a short duration, it is understandable that most groups will have some unfinished business which could be addressed if more time were available.

Groups can be called in for a follow-up meeting, but this is rarely done in the schools. Tapering-off sessions might be in order for some groups, but this can usually be done in the next to the last session, as you prepare the group for closure.

In most cases, group members will have full knowledge of the overall plan and be aware that the group counseling sessions are limited. They will know that the group is meeting for a specific purpose and most will be pleased to have had such an opportunity. Most students accept the last meeting as the end of the counseling group.

An elementary school counselor told how a group of fifth grade girls enjoyed meeting together so much that they began thinking of other problems that they were having or could have. In the two weeks that followed the end of the group, two girls regressed from the progress that they had made. Some old and new disruptive behaviors began to appear in the classroom. When confronted, the girls responded with, "But, we need to meet more as a group and work out our problems." When the fact that the group was over finally was accepted by the girls, disruptive classroom behaviors also declined.

Almost all counselors like to end groups on a positive note; therefore, part of the last session is usually aimed at "celebrating" the group's accomplishments and having had an opportunity to experience something special together. A common activity used by counselors focuses on "strength bombardment," where members tell each other some of the positive things that they have noticed. Another closing activity asks each member in the group to make a final statement, perhaps using a go-around procedure. There is no attempt to discuss the statements or elaborate on them. After everyone has had a turn, including the counselor, the group is ended.

Communication Labs: A Growth Group Experience

One way of providing a small group counseling experience to many students is to offer a series of group sessions which focus on communication skills. The group might be called a communication lab, since it is a type of laboratory experience in social skills.

The two purposes of this type of group are: 1) to provide a brief experience in learning and practicing communication skills, and 2) to increase self-awareness about self and others. The group members learn to listen more carefully, to ask facilitative questions, to give and receive feedback, and to think about problems.

In addition, the group allows you to form some close working relationships with students before other counseling situations that may arise during the year. Therefore, one or two target students can be included in a group of about six students.

This type of group usually meets for an established time, perhaps six sessions. The sessions are structured in an order that considers the basic group counseling stages. The group members participate in various activities and the interaction of the group members makes each group experience unique. The counselor is the leader and gives directions to provide structure. The counselor also takes a turn with the students in the activities and tasks.

An illustration of a structured group experience for communication skills is diagrammed in Figure 7.1. The titles of the sessions, general focus, and some of the activities are outlined briefly. These can give you an idea of the flow and focus of the group and the sessions.

More specifically, group movement is outlined horizontally across time from left to right and group interaction and focus of each session is shown vertically from top to bottom. In the first phase—sessions one and two—there is an attempt to establish group identity. Also, through self-disclosure activities, the facilitative conditions such as trust, understanding, acceptance, and caring are learned. Group members learn to be sensitive listeners, which includes a focus on feelings and an awareness of self and others. Some simple ground rules help tell the members how they will function in the group.

The second phase consists of sessions three and four in which more attention is directed to here-and-now situations where feedback (complimenting and confronting) is introduced and practiced. The third stage is more flexible, depending upon the interests and progress of a group, and may include problem-solving, role-playing, non-verbal communication, or a group member's problem. It is often used to explore typical problems that students their age might have. The final session always involves some positive feedback activity and typically a "strength bombardment."

The case of Jennifer and Andrew will help illustrate a small group counseling effort which followed a growth group approach and also included target students.

The Case of Jennifer and Andrew

Jennifer and Andrew were eighth grade students. They had above average intelligence, but they did not perform well in school. Their motivation and interest had been questioned by teachers and both appeared on a list given to the school counselors as students who needed more time and attention than teachers could give

Figure 7.1

Facilitating Groups
(Communication Labs)

	1 "Getting Started"	2 "Self-disclosing Flag"	3 "Secret Pooling"	4 "Indirect Feedback"	5 "I've Got A Secret"	6 "Strength Bombardment"
F O C U S	Begin the group Structure the process Feelings/behaviors Self-disclosure Build cohesiveness	Self-disclosure Building cohesiveness Increased awareness	Self-disclosure Increased awareness Feedback Member exchange of information	Increased Awareness Feedback	Decision-making Problem-solving Responsibility Increased awareness	Feedback Positive impact Action Plan Closure
A C T I V I T Y	Introductions Ground Rules Pantomime Feelings Words List "Go-Arounds"	Sharing symbols High facilitative responses	Pooling impressions Guessing identities Eliciting feedback	Using Metaphors Feedback "Go-Arounds"	Pooling secrets Exploring problems and actions Hypothetical cases Role Playing	Giving Feedback Next Step Final statements Summary End the group

them. Both students were put into a "communications skills group" with four other students, who were available to participate in the group and who did not appear on any referral list to the guidance office. The group met six times. Below is an outline of those sessions.

Session 1: "Getting Started"

The group members were first asked about the kinds of groups that they had been in before this time. The counselor then went on to explain that this was going to be a different group and that they would be doing some things to make it a special learning group, one in which they would work closely together to learn more about communication skills.

The group was also told that they would meet six times, or twice a week for three weeks, for about 30 minutes each session. The positive focus of the group and the emphasis upon learning ways to communicate with one another reduced the pressure that often is associated with "being counseled because of a problem," especially with Jennifer and Andrew.

Group members were paired and requested to interview each other, trying to learn things that they did not already know. After about three minutes for each interviewer, members introduced their partners to the rest of the group. The counselor then introduced the idea of talking about and listening for feelings as one of the things to do in the group. Members thought about times they could "hear" someone else's feelings or thoughts, even when they were not saying anything. Some nonverbal expressions were role-played to help get the group thinking, as members tried to guess the feeling. Then, a list of feeling words were elicited from the group as the counselor wrote them on a large piece of paper under "pleasant" and "unpleasant" headings. The list was posted for easy reference.

Students took turns telling something that had happened to them during the past week, as others listened for unpleasant, pleasant, or both kinds of feelings. After everyone had a turn, the counselor talked about how the group might work well if it had a few ground rules and suggested the following:

We talk about our feelings and ideas.
We listen to what others are saying and how they are feeling.
Anyone can pass on a turn to talk.
What happens in the group stays in the group (confidentiality).

Because the counselor liked to use "go-around" procedures, starting on the left, Jennifer and Andrew were seated in the third and fifth places in the circle. They would have a chance to hear others participate before their turns. It was important that they say something in the first session and that what they said be accepted by the group. Using high facilitative responses, the counselor encouraged everyone to participate.

Session 2: The Self-Disclosing Flag

After going around the group and calling each person by name, members were asked to review some of the communication skills that had been learned in the first session. Each member then drew a flag, divided into four parts, on a sheet of paper. Group members filled in four quadrants on their personal flags with little symbols or pictures according to: 1) Something I Like About School; 2) Something I Do Not Like About School; 3) What I Would Most Like to Be Someday; and 4) Something I am Good At Right Now.

Next, members took turns sharing one of their symbols. Questions were asked and ideas were clarified. Feelings were identified and put into sentences by group members as they practiced their listening skills. After all had shared one symbol, a second round took place in which a second symbol was shared.

Jennifer had drawn some numbers for her second symbol and said that she hated math class. The counselor asked her what she liked least about it and she said that it was uninteresting and boring. The counselor responded, "You say that like it's so tedious and weary for you." "That's right," Jennifer continued, "and I just hate going to that class." The counselor then commented, "It not's easy for you to attend math class and you don't look forward to going there each day.... Okay, John (the next person), tell us about one of your symbols."

When it was Andrew's turn, he said that he was good at football and it was a lot of fun to play on the school team because they had a winning record. The counselor turned to the group and said, "As Andrew told us about his symbol, were you hearing primarily pleasant, unpleasant, or both kinds of feelings?" The group was encouraged to look at the feeling word list that they had made during the first session. The counselor elicited such words as "proud," "happy," and "excited" to reflect Andrew's self-disclosure. After a minute or so, the next member took a turn.

The counselor used this opportunity to give and elicit some high facilitative responses to the two target students, knowing that some "chips in the bank" would build a positive relationship. Group members did not discuss their symbols in great detail or explain why they used the symbols. No attempt was made to interpret art work or evaluate contributions. In addition, no one person was asked to talk (self-disclose) at great length before the next member took a turn and, subsequently, no one felt pressured or on the spot for very long.

Session 3: Secret Pooling

After reviewing briefly what had happened in the first two sessions, members individually wrote on pieces of paper three words that they believed classmates might use to describe them. The counselor collected the papers, shuffled them, and read them one at a time. Members tried to guess who would use such words about themselves.

The procedures were structured so that a person who was guessing spoke directly to the person being guessed. For example, to the words "Big, not smart, and likes sports" one person said, "I think that it's you, Andrew, because you think all us see you as a big, dumb athlete and that's all.... Which isn't true, of course!" The counselor picked up on the statement and an opportunity to elicit feedback. "What is it about Andrew that makes you say it isn't true?"

When someone was being guessed, that person remained silent as part of the activity, encouraging others to continue the guessing, identifying which words led them to their guesses, and giving more specific observations. The papers were only a vehicle to promote feedback. The counselor also wrote down three words and participated, just the same as when the self-disclosing flag was used in the second session.

Session 4: Indirect Feedback

In this session, group members learned how to give indirect feedback through metaphors. They took turns describing each other as an animal or an object. A simple lead-in model was used: "(Name), I see you as a ...." Then the person added some details such as color, size, where it was located, what might be done with it, feelings about it, and what those feelings made the person want to do. In this case, members did not proceed through a go-around as in previous sessions, but everyone took a turn. The counselor kept the three-step facilitative feedback model in mind while encouraging members to be descriptive.

All members liked this session. It was fun and had a game-like quality. Yet, the feedback were valid statements about how students were being perceived and experienced by others. Special efforts were made to assure that members spoke for themselves and that a group consensus was avoided. When a similar animal or object was used, the details provided the uniqueness and added the perspective that was needed.

"Jennifer, I see you as a star, hanging on a tree. You have so much potential to sparkle and shine so bright, but sometimes it is hard to see you hanging on that tree, as though you're hung up and can't really do your thing." The counselor facilitated the person by saying, "And, what are you feeling when you look at the star and what do you want to do?" The person continued with, "Well, I don't know... maybe, a little sad, but then I'm happy when I think of how the star could be real bright, if it wanted to... and... and... I guess I want to reach up and wipe off some of the dust from the star... maybe untangle it so that we could see it better."

Some group members were more creative than others in describing people, but when facilitated with a few open-ended questions, all made their animals or objects take on special meaning. People receiving feedback learned more about themselves and the impact that they were having on others. People giving feedback learned the power of reaching out to communicate to someone about things that they noticed. Excitement was high and some group members wanted to take another turn, or have another round.

Session 5: I've Got A Secret

After a brief review of the communication skills that had been learned (listening and personal feedback), the counselor began the session by asking members to think of a problem that they had or one that someone else their age was having. Next, the members wrote down one or more secrets or problems on pieces of paper, without signing their names. The counselor said there were some problem statements from other groups that would be added to the ones from the group.

The pieces of paper were collected. The counselor shuffled them and read the first one. It said, "My problem is that my parents won't let me stay out late or stay overnight with some of my friends." The group was asked how they might feel if they had that problem and, later, how they might act if they had those feelings. After a brief discussion, a second problem was read aloud, "My problem is that I have a teacher who doesn't like me." Again, the same discussion procedures were used.

The counselor, knowing that Jennifer and Andrew would benefit from a discussion of student-teacher relationships, made sure that such a problem was a part of those put in the pile of papers and that it was discussed. Jennifer and Andrew were particularly asked to share their thoughts when it was introduced.

Not all problems were discussed in detail. Some discussions stopped after feelings and related behaviors were explored. Some were carried to the point of thinking about different alternatives and possible solutions.

Session 6: Strength Bombardment

The sixth and final session was a positive one in which each member in the group took a turn sitting in the middle of the circle while other members told what they saw as personal strengths and best qualities. The bombardment was given to the person in the middle, with every group member giving at least one or more positive comment. After all members had a turn in the circle, reactions and questions were encouraged.

The session and the group meetings ended as the members told what they had learned from the group experience. A summary was made of the communication skills and implications for outside the group. Finally, using a go-around procedure, each member took a turn making a final statement to either someone in the group or about the group.

Before leaving, group members completed a group evaluation form. All evaluations were positive and the part which members liked least was that the group was too short and coming to an end.

The communication skills group described here has been used with considerable success at all grade levels. There are different variations which you can use, depending upon the members in the group and the target students you want to experience a growth group. For example, some counselors have chosen to make session five more flexible and to focus on problems that are of general interest to the group, including some role-playing activities. Other counselors have chosen to teach the direct feedback model to students in session four or sometimes introducing it in session five, after the group has experienced indirect feedback.

Figure 7.2

Group Evaluation
(Communication Labs)

(In terms of percent)

MIDDLE SCHOOL (N = 104)	SA	A	U	D	SD
The Group Increased My Understanding of Others	42	49	8	1	0
The Group Had No Affect On Me	1	8	5	26	60
The Group Had Some Affect On My Behavior Outside The Group	19	48	18	10	5
I Disliked Being A Member Of The Group	0	0	3	19	78
The Group Increased Understanding Of Myself	36	44	12	5	3
I Would Recommend The Group Experience For Others	66	23	7	1	3
HIGH SCHOOL (N = 103)	SA	A	U	D	SD
The Group Increased My Understanding of Others	25	70	0	5	0
The Group Had No affect On Me	0	3	5	41	46
The Group Had Some Affect On My Behavior Outside The Group	16	68	13	0	3
I Disliked Being A Member Of The Group	3	0	5	27	65
The Group Increased Understanding Of Myself	32	46	14	8	0
I Would Recommend The Group Experience For Others	73	21	3	0	3

After completing a school district workshop on small group counseling, six middle school counselors agreed to provide the communication lab group experience to students in their schools (grades 6-8). Each counselor met three groups, with six students per group (N = 104). Likewise, nine high school counselors, who attended the same inservice workshop, each led two groups of about five or six students (N = 103). A post evaluation only took place one week after the groups were completed. Data were complete on 104 of the 108 middle school students and 103 of the 108 high school students. As shown in Figure 7.2, results were favorable at both grade levels. The group experience apparently made a positive difference in no less than 92% of the cases. In particular, 67% of the middle school and 74% of the high school students reported that the group had some affect on their behavior outside the group. Most agreed that it increased their understanding of self and others and that they would recommend the group to other students. Positive results have also been found in similar group experiences in the elementary schools.

Group Counseling for Negative Attitudes

Students with negative attitudes have learning problems. In addition, they often disrupt other students from learning. They distract or annoy teachers and make their work difficult.

Myrick and Dixon (1985) reported a small group counseling approach that was problem-centered which was designed for sixth grade students who had negative attitudes about themselves and school. The approach has since been used successfully at other grade levels. It consisted of a series of six structured small group counseling sessions of about 30-45 minutes each. In this case, all students in the group knew from the beginning that they had been asked to join the group because teachers were concerned about the feelings that they had about themselves and school.

A brief description of the six sessions is provided below. Notice the parallel structure that the problem-centered group has to the growth-centered group (communication skills) described above. The members for the group were selected from a list of students given to the counselor, all of whom were viewed as having negative attitudes.

Session 1: Feelings About School

The counselor began by asking the six members to introduce themselves, including one thing that they like to do when not in school.

The purpose of the group was explained as one to help students think more about themselves and school. The students seemed resigned to be in the group and no questions were asked.

A hand-made set of cards with feeling words written on them was distributed randomly among the group members. Using a go-around procedure, members read the words on their cards and a discussion about each word took place. For instance, "Okay, your word, Jason, is disappointment. What does that word mean to you?" Then, to Jason or the group generally, "Is it a pleasant or unpleasant feeling?" "How can you tell if a person feels that way?" "Have you ever seen anyone who felt that way?" "Have you ever felt disappointed?"

The questions were sequential, moving the discussion from a general to a more personal focus, always beginning with the nature of the feeling word before focusing on specific behaviors related to a particular feeling, and giving the person with the feeling word the first opportunity to self-disclose before asking for the feelings and ideas of the rest of the group. This general procedure had a way of easing the group into talking about personal matters and gave each person an opportunity to participate.

The words were also listed on a large piece of paper under categories of pleasant and unpleasant as they were discussed. As other words came out in discussion, they too were added to the list. In addition, at one point the counselor asked if the group could quickly think of other words to add to each of the lists, although time did not allow a discussion of them. This list remained in view for all sessions and other words were added from time to time.

Ground rules for this group were not announced in advance. The counselor chose to introduce ground rules as they seem needed. It was thought that the group members might interpret ground rules negatively and become resistant to the group process.

Session 2: Illustrated Tee Shirt

In the second session students drew symbols on a paper which represented a "tee shirt." The tee shirt was chosen because slogans on tee shirts were a fad. There were five sections: 1) Tells something about this school; 2) Represents something you would like to change about school; 3) Tells something that you like about school; 4) Shows one thing about yourself that you would like to change or improve upon; and 5) Three words that teachers might use to describe you.

Using a go-around procedure, each member took a turn, including the counselor, telling about one section of the tee shirt. Go-arounds continued as group members shared their ideas and feelings. The counselor used the high facilitative responses, often referring to the list of feeling words and adding new ones when appropriate.

The students liked talking about school, especially being able to express their negative thoughts without being corrected, put down, or asked to account for their feelings. The counselor was careful not to probe or ask too many questions. The basic strategy was to encourage students to talk, clarify ideas, and respond to feelings. No one was forced to talk nor did anyone talk for very long before the next person was asked to share a symbol. By design, each person participated in a friendly atmosphere where ideas and feelings were respected and where persons were not forced to defend themselves.

The group continued to think about how feelings and behaviors are related, whether in or out of school. When students told how teachers might describe them, the counselor sometimes said, "What do you do that makes them see you that way?" Also, "If you wanted to be described differently, what would you have to do?" Such questions were not directed at everyone, but they were used in a timely way so as not to provoke defensiveness and resistance. The counselor assumed that after one or two times, the others would come to understand the relationship between classroom behaviors and teacher perceptions.

Session 3: Dear Abby

The group activity for this session began when the counselor said: "Think of a problem that you are having in school... or perhaps a problem that someone else you know is having... or maybe some problems that students your age might have in school which would be interesting to discuss. Now, write a problem (or more than one) down on these small pieces of paper and do not sign your names. I'll collect them and then we'll discuss some of them in our group."

To each problem read aloud, the counselor began by saying, "If you had a problem like this, how would you feel? Then later, after some discussion, "Well, then, if you had these feelings (or feeling), how might you act or behave? Still later, "Okay, what could a person do in a situation like this?"

Group members learned that they were not alone in their feelings about school. They continued to learn that feelings and behaviors are related and how problems often resulted from the consequences of inappropriate behaviors. They explored alternative actions to a few of the problems. The counselor made sure to avoid advice-giving while concentrating on understanding the dynamics involved.

Session 4: Giving and Receiving Feedback

Group members learned the three-step facilitative feedback model: 1) Be specific about the behavior you see or hear; 2) Tell how it makes you feel (or what you experience when in the presence of that behavior); and 3) Tell what your feelings make you want to do. Members first practiced the model by thinking of examples and identifying people outside the group who might be recipients of feedback. An empty chair was used, as members imagined talking to someone while trying out the model.

After the members saw how the model could be used to compliment or confront someone, each person thought of someone outside the group, perhaps a teacher, parent, or friend, to whom positive feedback (a compliment) might be given during the coming week. Everyone was to try the model and be able to talk about the experience at the next session.

This session encouraged students to think positively and to learn an effective way to be positive with others. It was assumed that students in the group were used to criticism and, unfortunately, modeled the behavior which was most often directed toward them. In addition, it was assumed that the students needed to learn some positive ways of behaving and to take some positive action before they could begin receiving more favorable responses from others.

Session 5: Some First Steps

Reports of how the feedback model was put into practice were first heard. Then, each member was asked to respond or complete this statement: "One thing about myself that I want to improve upon is...." After a quick go-around in which areas for improvement were identified, each person (the counselor participated too) talked about a possible next step that might be taken. Group members listened and offered suggestions regarding how a person might get started. Finally, members were encouraged to begin their first step during the coming week.

Session 6: Being Positive

The last session began by members describing what had happened to them during the week that they tried to take their first steps for self-improvement. Next, group members, including the counselor, took turns sitting in a "cool seat" while members who were sitting in the "hot seats" bombarded them with positive statements. The statements were based upon things that were noticed both in and out of the group. Finally, the group concluded when each member gave a final statement, focusing on what they had learned or relearned in the group.

An experimental study (Myrick and Dixon, 1985) compared students who received the group counseling unit with those who did not. A significant difference was found in favor of the counseling group regarding classroom behavior and general attitude, according to teacher reports. In addition, students in the group were asked to evaluate that experience. Results showed that 72% believed that the group had increased their understanding of themselves and 86% said it helped them gain a better understanding of others. In addition, 62% indicated that the experience helped them change their behavior outside the group and 60% said that they liked school better because of the group. Eight out of ten recommend a similar group to other students.

It was concluded that the group was effective across sex of student and across schools, suggesting that both boys and girls benefited despite the school or the school counselor. It appeared that students liked the opportunity to share their ideas and feelings and to learn about themselves and others. The group enabled them to disclose feelings about themselves, others, and school and it provided some feedback. It encouraged them to think about their behaviors, including some of which they wanted to improve in school.

Not everyone who experienced the group experience liked it. As expected, some students not only have negative attitudes about teachers and classes, but about other things related to school, including counseling and guidance activities. Some students disliked some of the operational activities which were used to bring the group together and others described the group as "pushy" and "trying to get me to change." However, the large majority complained there was not enough time when asked what they liked least about the group. Although all the counselors in the reported study thought the group sessions had a positive affect on most of the students, they also identified students who needed more individual attention or further group work.

Obviously, some of the sessions could be changed by substituting other activities. Or, the sessions could be more flexible, perhaps without a planned activity. It is also possible to extend the number of sessions. Moreover, the sessions could be adapted to almost any age group.

Helpful Hints

There are many things that you might do to help make your group counseling efforts successful. You can find more detailed ideas in other texts that are specifically written about small group counseling or group work. However, the following hints may be helpful:

Open and Closed Groups

Open groups are those that allow new members to be added to the group from time to time, perhaps as some members drop out. These are usually on-going groups and are not very common in the schools, except as support groups.

Support groups are unique since they are composed of members who have a common problem or concern and who need a base to touch on occasion. One school had a support group for students who were new to the school. The "newcomers" group met each Friday. It was an open meeting where students worked through feelings of awkwardness, confusion, and loneliness. They shared ideas and met new friends. New students were added each week as they registered for school. Others were free to leave the group as they felt less like newcomers.

Four girls in a middle school were discussing the issue of dating older boys in small group counseling. The boys came to the school and were asked to leave the campus by the administration. The girls were first upset and expressed their unhappiness in the initial session of a problem-centered group. Then the focus shifted to the impact that the dating had on their self-concepts, school work, and personal values. All the girls thought it was flattering to have the attention of the boys, but dating them also created some problems. They wanted to keep meeting as a group and to continue their discussions. Two other girls, who were friends, asked to join the group, since they had similar concerns. The counselor met with the group for four more sessions.

In this case, the problem for the counselor and the group was to form a "new group," building on the previous one. The challenge was to build a new sense of group cohesiveness and trust. To begin, the purpose of the group was clarified. The counselor thought it was similar to taking two steps backward, while the other two girls caught up, before taking four steps forward. This is always the problem of open groups.

Most school counselors prefer to have closed groups. There is more continuity when the membership remains constant. Given the limited number of sessions available for group counseling in most schools, a closed group can move toward its goal faster and with greater purpose than one that is repeatedly starting and stopping to accommodate new members.

When a member drops out of a closed group, the group continues after discussing the impact of the absent member. Since the dynamics of the group are changed, the group is realigned and a new group emerges. However, the group members have a shared experiential base from which to build. Sometimes an outside person might be invited to attend a session, perhaps a teacher or student. This change or intrusion is always discussed with group members and the person's attendance is a mutual decision.

Ground Rules

Every group needs ground rules for making it a special learning experience. These rules or procedures are general suggestions which help members function in the group. For example, here are the three most common ground rules:

1. Only one person speaks at a time.
2. You can pass, if you do not want to speak.
3. What is said in the group is private.

In an elementary school, the following additional ground rules proved to be useful with some primary grade children:

4. Raise your hand when you want to speak.
5. Listen carefully so that you can remember what was said.
6. Keep your hands to yourself and remain seated in the group.

All these ground rules give direction to group members. Most important, they are all stated in the positive, suggesting what a group member is to do.

Generally, it seems best to avoid negative statements such as, "There will be no putdowns or name-calling in the group," "Don't interrupt when someone else is speaking," "Avoid gossiping," "No killer statements," "Don't give advice," and "Don't tell others what happens in our group." Each of these ground rules emphasize obedience and foster a negative feeling. All the concerns behind them can be stated in the positive to suggest how a person might behave in a group.

It is also advisable to avoid long lists of ground rules. Keep them short and to the point. You might find it helpful to post the ground rules for easy reference. Some counselors have a set of cards with each rule on a card and these are set in view of the group. When students have trouble all talking at once, for example, the counselor may look at the list and say: "Which one of our ground rules is not being followed right now?" That rule is then reviewed. New ground rules might be added as they are needed.

There are three ways to form ground rules for a group. First, you can decide upon the behaviors that you want and make the list of rules yourself. These are announced to the group in the first session. The group discusses and clarifies them. Or, you could ask the group for suggestions. Their ideas might be written on a large piece of paper as the group discusses and clarifies them. Finally, you can begin a group without any rules and then build a set of guidelines as situations or problems develop. For instance, if several people are talking at the same time, you might say: "We have a problem here. What is happening in our group? ...Okay, perhaps we need a ground rule that will help us."

Indirect and Direct Approaches

Some students are very sensitive about their problems and would prefer not to discuss them with anyone, especially their peers. They may feel pressured or on the spot. They might fear that others would not understand or accept them. They often believe that to have a problem is a sign of weakness and they are embarrassed at the idea of others knowing about their situation. These students can benefit from group experiences that focus indirectly on a problem.

A major goal of group counseling is to develop relationships among students to meet developmental needs. Each member in a group is encouraged to think for oneself, to share perceptions, to seek understanding of self and others, and to accept responsibility for one's own behavior. But, this does not mean that a problem must be dealt with directly and that members must examine a specific problem that they are having in their lives.

An indirect approach to group counseling is one in which students learn about themselves and others through a discussion of ideas and events that are not based specifically on problems which they are having. That is, a student who is having trouble with a sibling might gain some ideas by participating in a group where members talk generally about conflict resolution, perhaps as part of a growth group. If the person chooses to bring up the sibling problem as a point of reference or an example, it is usually done briefly. The student draws one's own conclusions and implications from the group's activities and discussion.

When a direct approach is used, the counselor or the group may be more confrontive. One counselor opened a group meeting that was counselor-initiated by saying, "Look around our group. What are some possible reasons for our being here together? ...That's right, all of you are have been late to school a lot this year. Perhaps, it would be helpful to think about this problem together, which is the reason I asked you to meet with me. How do you feel about being here and talking about the problem of school attendance?"

Some direct approaches are student-initiated. It is assumed that such groups can expedite matters, getting to the heart of a problem faster. However, this may not always be true since direct approaches also tend to invite defensiveness and resistance, even when members are committed to pursuing solutions to the problem.

The indirect approach is primarily used in growth groups. It has been effective in pulling resistant students into the counseling process because it is generally less threatening, especially at first. Such an approach depends on each individual to apply what is being learned in the group.

Working with Target Students

As suggested earlier, one practical approach to working with a target student might be in a growth group situation where the focus is more indirect. The idea, of course, is to help the target student become more involved, to experience facilitative conditions from you and the group, and to make some personal gains by being a participating member in the group.

You can lead the group as you usually would; however, you can also give some special attention to target students by doing such things as:

1. Ask them an open-ended question about something to which you think they can respond.

2. Use their names frequently, as you comment to them and the group. This helps personalize the process.

3. Always acknowledge their contributions, finding some way to associate them with their task if they are off-task. If you want to draw the person out some more, you might say, "I really like what you said about..., but I'm wondering if you could think of something else that goes with our topic (or, tell us how that relates to our topic). Or, you might say, "Let's see now, you seem to be saying...." Then tie the contribution to the topic or theme being discussed.

4. Comment on and use non-verbal behavior, especially if it is not too sensitive and something that you want to reinforce (e.g. eye contact, alertness, body posture).

5. Pair or link the feelings and the content of their contributions to others in the group.

6. Encourage people in the group to talk with one another (e.g. "Could you please say that to....")

7. Be positive and acknowledge contributions with "Thank you."

8. Use feedback responses. If a target student makes or receives a negative comment, you might elicit a feedback response by saying, "You said that you dislike.... Tell us what it is that you dislike (behaviors and examples)." And, "How does that make you feel?" And then, perhaps, "Can you tell (the person) what you do like? Or, "What would you like (the person) to do?" And, "How would that make you feel?" You can also turn to group members and elicit their reactions, using the feedback model. "How do the rest of you feel, right now?" "What's happened to give you that feeling?" Perhaps you might turn to a person who was put down and say, "How did it make you feel when you heard...?" "What did it make you want to do?" The person making the putdown will get some feedback on the undesirable behavior.

9. Give tasks ahead of time so that the students have an opportunity to think about a response and are not caught off-guard.

10. Use go-around procedures to get some initial involvement from everyone in the group. Avoid putting target students on the spot for too long a time. Let them become comfortable with the group before extending their ideas or asking them to probe deeper.

Finally, it is your own professional judgment that will tell you when a target student has become a regular participating member of a group and how much risk that you can take in focusing on that student. Sometimes the extra attention is not even necessary, as the group membership and group activities will have the desired influence and impact in its natural progress.

Contracting with Teachers and Students

A common complaint by teachers about counselors is that they interrupt scheduled classes and they pull students out of class after a class period has started. It irritates teachers to be disrupted without notice and some become uncooperative, refusing to release students or penalizing them if they are in the guidance office instead of class.

One way to avoid such problems is to contract with teachers who are supportive of your efforts and who will make students available to you. This is particularly helpful when working with groups. A contract, whether written or verbal, begins with your request of a teacher to release a student for counseling. Once that request is granted, the specific times and days for counseling are negotiated. These meeting times, and any conditions, are written down as a contract. Copies are given to the teacher, the student, and the counseling office.

When contracts are made in advance of group counseling, teachers can identify times when it is best to release students. For example, one teacher allowed students to report to the counseling office on Thursdays, which was when independent study was scheduled in her class. She told the counselors that no student would be released on Monday or Tuesday when new information was being introduced or on Friday when tests were given.

This concept is a courtesy that encourages teachers and others to work with counselors. Calling students out of class without consulting with teachers should be reserved for crisis-counseling. If counseling is to be extended beyond a critical first meeting, then contract with teachers.

Structure and Flow

After the group has started, the primary objective is to elicit self-disclosure. As the group moves along, feedback can take place. All this eventually leads to more openness and specific consideration of a situation or problem about which possible decisions are examined. As a rule, responsibility for implementation of an idea rests with each individual group member, although, on occasion, a group may decide to act together on something.

The facilitative model is basic to group process, with the six high facilitative responses both given by the counselor and elicited from the members. You might listen to a group member tell about an event and then clarify what you heard. Or, you could ask the others in the group to clarify or summarize what they heard. "Who can put into fresh words what you heard said?" Or, you can also elicit a feeling-focused response. "Eddie has shared a lot in that statement. Let me ask our group, were you hearing primarily pleasant, unpleasant, or both kinds of feelings when he was talking? ...Okay, what kinds of feelings did you hear from Eddie?" Likewise, you can also elicit open-ended questions, "Who can ask Eddie a question that will help us understand his situation better?"

Structure and flow can also be affected by group activities. Group activities have been presented in many books about group counseling and group guidance (e.g. Canfield and Wells, 1976; Gazda, 1978; Johnson, 1972; Simon, Howe and Kirschenbaum, 1972; Wittmer and Myrick, 1980). They should not be seen as an end to themselves; they are a means to an end. They are a vehicle which can provide a structured learning experience for group members.

Some group activities lend themselves to eliciting self-disclosure. For instance, members might be asked to complete a series of unfinished sentences such as:

If I were a ..., I'd....
One thing I did for a friend was....
If I had more money, I'd....
A famous person I'd like to meet is....
One thing that's hard for me to do is....
I'm proud of....

All these and other sentences when completed become statements about a person. You might ask each member to select one or two to share with the group. "Which one was the most difficult?" "The easiest?" "The most stimulating?" "The most surprising to you?" In the process, disclosure of self is happening and the group forms a closer bond as members come to know more about each other in a positive learning climate.

Group activities can also be used to elicit feedback. For example, members might take turns pretending that they have amnesia and that they do not remember things about themselves. Other members tell what they have noticed, perhaps around school, in class or in other situations. You could help members tell what they feel when in the presence of some behaviors and how they tend to respond.

An unstructured group does not feature any formal group activities. Any structure or organization is given spontaneously by you and the members. Yet, the flow of the group in terms of self-disclosure to feedback and through the different group counseling stages seldom varies.

Connecting Sessions

Some counselors worry about continuity among group sessions. One counselor, who met once a week with a group of counselees, said, "So much happens in these kids lives before I get a chance to see them again. There is such a lack of continuity that I feel I'm starting all over again each time." Another counselor complained about the number of times it was necessary to reschedule a group because of some events at the school which interrupted their schedules. "Last week I wondered if my group knew why they were there, although we were meeting for the fourth time." Admittedly, keeping a group focused on its goals and the purposes of a group may not be easy when meetings are spaced far apart.

The desire for some continuity and perhaps for some connecting of sessions might be accomplished by allowing a few minutes at the beginning of a session to get focused, perhaps to hear what members are thinking about the group and its impact on them. Using a quick go-around, here are a few "connecting stems" from which you might select to get the group started:

1. What I liked best about last time was....
2. One thing I learned from the last session was....
3. After the last session, I....
4. One feeling I had the last time we met was....
5. I hope today that....

Or, you might begin by asking someone to tell what was remembered from the last meeting, perhaps even saying, "If you could say something about our meeting together, what would it be?" Or perhaps, "How would you describe our last meeting?"

This is also a convenient way to obtain some feedback about the group, especially as it relates to the counselor intervention and your own goals for the group. After some comments, you can then clarify the purpose of the group, reinforce those behaviors which seem to be facilitative, and direct the group to the goals and activities of the current session.

Advantages, Limitations, and Conclusion

Advantages of Small Group Counseling

1. It is more efficient than individual counseling because more counselees can be seen at one time by a counselor.

2. Students can learn from each other by listening carefully and giving and receiving feedback.

3. Many of the problems that people experience are related to social interaction and the counseling group can be a place for re-enactment of the behaviors and feelings related to a problem.

4. Group members can offer support, encouragement, and help provide the facilitative conditions to a greater extent than can one person.

5. The sense of belonging and togetherness in group counseling creates a unique learning climate.

6. Group members can practice behaviors, receiving feedback and suggestions from others. Peer feelings and ideas often have more credibility than those of adults.

7. Most of what young people learn is learned in a group context; therefore, learning and relearning might occur with more results in a group.

8. The counselor may not have to work as hard at facilitating the group, because group members can learn to facilitate one another.

9. As group members facilitate one another, the counselor has more time to reflect on what a person is saying, how the person is responding and some possible alternatives.

10. Instead of the counselor being the only personal resource to a counselee at the moment, group members provide additional resources to draw upon. For example, various alternatives might come from the group before the counselor offers a suggestion.

11. Some students find it too intense to meet with an adult alone. The presence of peers helps reduce the tension and the feeling of being singled out for counseling.

Limitations of Small Group Counseling

1. It can take more time to establish trust and a close working relationship than in individual counseling since there are more relationships which come into play.

2. The counselor may feel less in control since there are persons who need special attention and there are more interactions to observe and manage.

3. Confidentiality is more difficult to safeguard, as more people share in the communication.

4. Some issues appear too sensitive, too emotional, and too complex to work with in a group.

5. Although everyone usually gets a turn, there may not be enough time for some people who need special help and attention.

6. The counselor must be prepared to counter some less than facilitative behaviors by group members.

7. The counseling process is more complex since there are more variables to which the counselor needs to attend.

8. It is more difficult to organize a group than to call in one student and continuity of topic and content is dependent upon more people to be present. Scheduling a group can a difficult task.

9. Sometimes school systems require parent permission if students meet for small group counseling in contrast to individual work. However, this is not a recommended procedure since the counselor is a school official and small group counseling is a part of guidance services. On occasion, because of the sensitivity of the topic or content, parent permission may be advisable, especially if it is difficult to see how the group's work is tied to learning.

Conclusion

Within the past decade, we have learned more about counseling people in small groups. School counseling groups are short in duration, organized to take advantage of time, and structured to expedite the facilitative conditions and processes.

As a group leader, you will find the six high facilitative responses useful. In addition to your making the responses, elicit facilitative responses from group members. Teach them communication skills that can be used in the group. This cooperative effort by participants makes the group more productive and makes your work less difficult.

Individual counseling in the schools is now a luxury. Because of high counselor-student ratios, more small group counseling is needed. Since students like to work in groups, and because peer relationships play such an important part in the development of young people, small group counseling is a valuable counseling intervention.

Chapter 8

Large Group Guidance as a Counselor Intervention

In times past, when there were no school counselors, students were dependent upon classroom teachers and classroom guidance for any personal help that they might receive. Students who needed personal counseling were referred to counselors and therapists outside the school. After counselors were employed in the schools, teachers continued to think of their personal work with students as guidance or advisement instead of counseling. They continued to see large group guidance as a way to work with the general developmental needs of all students. Counseling was a term reserved for more intense and private assistance.

Large Group Guidance Defined

When a counselor works with more than 10 students in a group, the intervention is referred to as "large group guidance." The number 10 is an arbitrary number and dividing point, as some counselors claim that they can do small group counseling with as many as 12 students. But, the vast majority believe that if a group goes beyond 10 members, the counseling process is diffused and the dynamics of multiple relationships and interactions change the group's character. There seems to be a point where the process becomes something other than counseling.

Beyond the size of the group, the differences between small group counseling and large group guidance rest primarily with the focus of the group and the way in which it functions. This difference includes purpose and objectives, leadership behaviors, and the interpersonal relationships that can be formed. This, in turn, affects the cohesiveness, trust level, and intensity of group interaction.

Large group guidance sessions in secondary schools were first arranged to pass out information on educational or career planning. It was more expedient than repeating the same thing over and over with individuals. Too often in large group guidance sessions, however, adults did the talking as students sat passively and tried to absorb what was being presented. There was little or no group interaction.

Teachers in elementary schools were among the first to demonstrate that meaningful personal discussions can happen with a large group of students and that such discussions may be as beneficial as individual meetings with students. They also showed that a structured learning experience was an effective way to integrate guidance into the curriculum. Large group or classroom guidance, delivered by teachers and counselors, is an important aspect in comprehensive guidance and counseling programs (K-12).

You can communicate general and specific information to students in large groups. But, it does not have to be an occasion in which you deliver speeches to an audience. You might use panels of students to help clarify or illustrate some of the points you are trying to make. You can also organize a large group into smaller working units so that more student interaction can take place. Whatever your school's organization or grade level, you will find large group guidance a valuable intervention.

Factors to Consider

How do you organize large group guidance sessions?

Large group guidance can be viewed as a helping process, one in which students meet together to work with a counselor, a teacher, or both. It can also be pictured as a series of lessons which are part of an organized guidance curriculum.

A guidance curriculum can be divided into several units, with each unit having a central focus or theme. There are general and specific goals. Units are further divided into sessions, each with its own specific objectives and activities. The units and sessions are placed in some type of sequential order, focusing on the developmental needs and interests of students.

Purpose and Objectives. Although students meeting in large groups can discuss the same topics they do in individual or small group counseling, large group guidance is seen as more structured, exploratory, and directed to the general needs and interests of the students. Each year high school students are given an orientation to the next grade level when they complete their registration forms. Most school counselors have found it feasible to work with large groups, perhaps classroom groups, to speed up the registration process. High school counselors have also found it easier to meet with all students who will enter the military after graduation from high school and to talk with them about the general procedures for entering the service. Recruiters from the different military services can make large group presentations and answer questions. Similarly, students going to a particular college or university might meet as a large group for special guidance.

Guidance units focus on the developmental needs and interests of students at different grade levels. A guidance unit on "How to Get and Hold a Job" might be particularly interesting and well attended in the secondary schools; whereas, "Beating the Bullies" might be appropriate for an elementary school group that is having trouble with people who are teasing and calling them names.

Some other examples of large group guidance units are:

> Human growth and development
> Choosing a career
> Study habits and time management
> Resolving conflicts with people
> How to be more assertive
> School orientation
> How to pick a college best for you
> Making new friends

Whereas some guidance units are considered standard fare and appear regularly each year because they are appropriate for all age groups, others result from some particular needs or events in a school or community. For instance, a counselor decided to meet with a group of students to discuss some problems that were happening on the school bus. One counselor called in 40 high school students who were failing English which was needed for graduation. As a large group, they talked about what was needed to pass the English course and what were some possible next steps they could take to improve their grades.

An elementary school was located in an area where several child abductions had taken place. School officials wanted to caution children and to teach them more about how to respond to strangers. Counselors were asked to develop a special guidance unit that could be presented to all students in the school. In another school, teachers and counselors were alerted to an increase in the use of illegal street drugs in the community and they were afraid that older brothers and sisters would bring it into the homes. A large group guidance unit was developed so that counselors and teachers could talk with students about the potential dangers.

When Christa McAuliffe, the New Hampshire teacher, died in the 1986 space shuttle explosion, there was a need in her school to talk about the tragedy. Students needed opportunities to vent their feelings, to explore their ideas, and to consider what might be done to cope with the loss of someone who was so visible and close to them. Large group meetings helped. For some students, this was not enough and they met with counselors in small groups or in individual sessions. Mental health counselors from outside the school also went to the school to meet with students individually and in groups.

Timely Teaching. Faust (1968) described how guidance lessons might be introduced into elementary school classrooms. He emphasized the value of "timely teaching" in which a particular event might stimulate thinking and stir the imaginations and feelings of students. He encouraged teachers and counselors to seize upon such opportunities and engage students in a guidance lesson in which ideas, feelings, and behaviors could be explored.

It seems that timely teaching and large group guidance are especially appropriate when local, national, or international events loom in the eyes of students and they are ready to talk about the personal impact of the events. For instance: when space shuttle *Challenger* exploded; when the nuclear reactor exploded at Chernobyl; when a local bank was robbed; when someone set a world record; or when a former student was honored for career achievement. All these might be moments for timely teaching and guidance.

The purpose of large group guidance may be to impart information, to help students explore the consequences of some action, or to learn some procedures for setting and achieving personal goals. You will want to think of ways in which you can personalize the experience for students.

Personalization. Drawing upon Faust's work (1968), some personal objectives for most classroom guidance sessions, regardless of topic, might be: 1) To help students become aware that human feelings exist and to help students develop a working vocabulary in which they can see how feelings, thoughts and behaviors are related; 2) To help students become aware that all people experience all kinds of pleasant and unpleasant feelings and that these feelings are part of life; 3) To help students be aware there is nothing wrong with having feelings, as they are part of being human; and 4) To help students learn that there are some socially acceptable ways in which to express feelings. Students learn that to have a feeling does not necessarily mean that they have to act it out and that respected social behaviors help people live together cooperatively and productively.

In addition to these more personalized goals, guidance units also can focus on the learning of specific information (e.g. graduation requirements or ways to organize a study schedule). They can feature exploratory activities in which students have an opportunity to talk about citizenship, friendship, or responsibility. They can be organized around activities such as a career fair, a music and art festival, or perhaps some valuable educational objective that is difficult to work into an already full academic curriculum.

Accessibility. When there is a regularly scheduled time during the school day or school week for large group guidance activities, you can also use these times to present a guidance unit. Otherwise, you will have to coax teachers into giving up some academic class time. The Teacher Advisor Program (TAP) for middle and high schools, discussed in Chapter 3, is based on the assumptions that teachers will provide some large group guidance to students and try to work individually with advisees. Guidance units form a guidance curriculum and TAP provides the structure through which they are delivered. Scheduled TAP periods in the secondary schools also provide a time when counselors have access to large groups, including the possibility of combining some TAP groups to work with 50 or more students. Schools without TAP must find alternative ways of providing large group guidance or it could lose its importance as a counselor intervention.

Elementary and middle schools typically build their school programs around the concepts inherent in TAP. Classroom or large group guidance is a part of the weekly schedule. For example, some elementary school teachers have 20 minutes a day for a classroom guidance activity, perhaps following the lesson plans provided in such materials as *DUSO—Developing Understanding of Self and Others* (Dinkmeyer and Dinkmeyer, 1982).

Peer Relationships. In large group guidance, you frequently work with students who represent the student body or a particular grade level. For many group guidance sessions, a random sampling of students might do. Classroom groups that are already scheduled to meet regularly with a particular teacher would be convenient. In other cases, a large group guidance experience could be organized for a targeted population (e.g. those students interested in medical careers). Selection of participants is, then, based on common interests and needs.

Some students may find a sense of security in large groups, perhaps hiding behind the participation of others. They listen but do not speak up. They count on others to take the lead and to keep the pressure of participating off themselves. They dislike talking in front of large groups for fear that what they say will not be accepted. The larger the number of members, the more unsure they are about the facilitative conditions.

Self-conscious and inhibited students prefer small groups before they feel secure enough to share their ideas in large groups. This tends to be the general rule for most students. Therefore, the larger the group the more difficult it is to engage members in a discussion. This dynamic often pushes counselors into talking too much at students or letting the group develop into a simple question and answer period, with the counselor answering the questions.

There is nothing wrong with this type of controlled interaction, if it serves a purpose. You will want to think of ways in which students can get to know each other better and to experience the facilitative conditions. Then they will want to participate more. For instance, by using cooperative learning and group management procedures, you can sub-divide large groups into smaller groups within the same room. By using structured learning activities, you can increase involvement and participation.

Who is the group leader?

In schools where comprehensive developmental guidance and counseling programs have been established, teachers and counselors work together to develop guidance units. The units are tailored to the school's population and students' general developmental needs and interests.

As a counselor, you can work in at least two roles in terms of large group guidance. As a coordinator of guidance, you can consult and collaborate with teachers in developing a guidance curriculum which involves classroom or large group guidance. As an expert in school guidance and counseling, you can be a resource to teachers and give some direction to the guidance curriculum. You can lead a group and present some units or sessions yourself. On occasion, you might co-lead with teachers or other counselors.

A developmental guidance program that reaches only a few selected students is not adequate. Therefore, teachers have to take an active part in large group guidance activities. They need to understand the philosophy behind developmental guidance, how guidance units can be organized and presented, ways to manage large groups so that all students can participate, and how to facilitate group discussion.

As a counselor, you can "coach" teachers in group guidance discussion skills. While many of the skills that teachers use in their academic classes will apply in large group guidance, there is a need to consider the leader's role and the purpose of the group. For guidance activities, teachers and counselors should think even more about creating the facilitative conditions through the increased use of high facilitative responses.

You can meet with teachers to discuss the guidance units that have already been developed and organized into a curriculum. They may need help in deciding when it would be best to present the units, if they are not already organized into some sequence. They might also want to review some of the activities, discuss some of the procedures, or consider alternative activities and methods. In addition, when you co-lead a session or a unit with teachers, model the use of the facilitative responses, and reinforce teachers for their efforts and skills.

There will be times when you will have your own "dog and pony" show. That is, you will develop a special guidance unit to take into classes or other large groups of students that you have organized. Teachers who are available might be invited to assist or to take a part in the procedures. There are many teachers who welcome the idea of working with students in guidance activities.

What size should the group be?

Certainly, the size of a group can affect the amount and type of interaction that happens, the nature of the topics introduced, the degree of personal involvement, and confidentiality. Yet, depending upon activities and procedures, participants in large group guidance can be given active roles and the topics for discussion may be very personal. Members may sense that they are getting personal attention from the counselor or teacher who is leading the group. It is not uncommon to hear favorable reports that large group guidance sessions had an influential impact on student lives.

There is probably no limit to size in large group guidance, as you could work with 100 or more. Size is not a problem if you have some assistance or helpers. Most counselors, however, think in terms of 25 to 30 students. This enables the group to be conveniently subdivided into five or six small working teams with about five or six students each. These teams can then be further divided into dyads and triads for some activities.

Where should the group meet?

The size of a group may be determined by the facilities or space that is available. The most common place to meet students in large group guidance is a classroom. Other meeting places might be in the library, cafeteria, media center, gymnasium, or auditorium.

You will want to avoid wall-to-wall people or places where you must work elbow to elbow. You want enough space to form at least five small circles, perhaps arranging them in the four corners and the center of a room. The number of movable chairs or desks in a room can also determine the size of a group, although occasionally it is possible to have students sit on a carpeted floor.

When large group guidance is aimed primarily at information-giving and when time is limited, then an auditorium might work. In this situation, representative groups of students ask questions, take part in panel discussions, or in some other way provide the dialogue that is needed in the group.

One large group of 80 high school students met in an auditorium to review the procedures needed to enroll in college, including how to complete forms for financial assistance, housing, and so on. After the counselors made some introductory remarks and provided general information with an overhead projector on a large screen, questions were asked by students.

An auditorium, however, is too restrictive. More flexible facilities are preferred to obtain more student involvement and participation. For example, with the same group of high school students as described above, the counselors could make their presentations and then divide the group of 80 into 10 teams of eight students each, positioning them around the room (media center, cafeteria, and so forth). The smaller groups could then be given the task of discussing the ideas that were presented, seeking clarification and, as a group, listing four or five questions that they would like to hear answered. The groups might even rank order their questions on a piece of paper. Next, counselors could interrupt, after some time had passed, and have the small groups reposition themselves for a large group question and answer period. More student interaction and involvement could be built into large group guidance. This procedure can be used with almost any topic.

How often and for how long?

Most large group guidance units are organized into sessions of about 20-30 minutes, although they may also be arranged for 45 minutes or longer. Sessions are quite often structured around a school's bell schedule, when students pass from one class to another. In the secondary schools, large group guidance is typically a regular class period, but it can be scheduled for less time. Sometimes, because of guest speakers or the availability of special demonstration materials, group guidance can last longer. But, that is an exception.

The value of a regularly scheduled TAP period has already been discussed. When TAP is part of the weekly schedule, large group guidance units and sessions are developed for that time frame. Generally, 30 minutes is the amount of time set for TAP meetings. Any less time makes it difficult or impossible to use some group activities and procedures.

In elementary schools where students attend self-contained classrooms and there is more flexibility of time, large group guidance can be scheduled for whatever time is convenient to teachers. This is usually in the afternoon of a school day and sessions frequently are between 20 and 30 minutes, although some counselors report that they prefer 45 minutes because it allows for more discussion and student participation. A practical approach is to think in terms of 30-minute sessions, which can be stretched to 45 minutes if the time is available. The extra time is used for more discussion or more activities.

A guidance unit can be organized into several sessions, but it is also practical to think in terms of six sessions per unit, with the sixth session being used primarily for evaluation and wrap-up. Some units might be organized around four sessions or perhaps as few as one or two. Other units might have as many as 10 sessions. It seems more feasible to have several guidance units which can be implemented and evaluated instead of one long continuous effort. Take your gains where you can, relying on student feedback to determine the next most appropriate unit.

Which activities should be used?

Several years ago there was a push in educational circles for "humanizing education" (Randolph and Howe, 1963; Simon, Howe, and Kirschenbaum, 1972; Weinstein and Fantini, 1970). While the philosophy behind the movement was aimed at creating a friendly and personal school climate, one in which students felt free to examine the personal meaning of learning, it was too often translated into simply leading students through some human relations group activities. Some of the activities were appropriate for students in school and some were not.

Group activities consist of a set of procedures in which participants take part in a task and then talk about their experiences. The activities are related to the four facilitative processes of self-disclosure, feedback, increased awareness and decision-making, and responsible action. But, activities alone are hardly effective in helping students and cannot be considered outcomes of large group guidance.

Each activity should be reviewed in terms of its relevance to the desired objectives of a unit or session. In addition, it should also be considered in light of what is appropriate for a particular age group and the school setting. For instance, "values clarification" was part of the humanistic education movement and there were many books written which described activities that teachers and counselors could use with their students (e.g. Canfield and Wells, 1976; Johnson, 1972; Simon, Howe, and Kirschenbaum, 1972;). However, in some communities, parents have challenged their use, worried that students are disclosing too much about themselves or that there is an unwarranted invasion of privacy. Their concerns might be related to someone misusing guidance activities.

When guidance activities are misused or inappropriate, it may be because they have not been carefully selected. They may not be closely related to guidance objectives. Activities that put people in the position of making negative choices (e.g. who will be thrown out of a boat in order for the rest to survive) have sparked a lot of controversy. It takes a skilled person to use this type of activity and, even then, its use might be questionable.

All activities can be modified to suit your purposes. Eliminate those that make you uncomfortable or that are difficult to publicly defend. Find a substitute or modify those activities that have been published or recommended by others, yet make you feel awkward or uneasy. Use your best judgment. The activity is only a vehicle, a means to an end.

How do you facilitate a large group?

Many of the same skills that you use in small group counseling will be appropriate for use with large groups. You will want to use the high facilitative responses and elicit them from group participants.

You will probably find the need to set more limits, to provide more structure, and to stay more on task in large groups than in smaller groups. This is not incompatible to being a facilitator or helper. It will not threaten your role as an understanding, accepting, and trustworthy counselor. But, you have more people who are demanding attention in large group and some will stray off course for lack of involvement or your attention.

The facilitative model can be applied to large groups easily. Think of what you can do to show that you want to hear students' ideas and feelings. Do something to show that you value their participation and respect their efforts. Try to be understanding and accepting, but also let them know that you expect them to work cooperatively within some unavoidable limits.

Consider the following ideas as you lead the group through activities and in discussion.

Accept all contributions. Acknowledge students for their efforts, even if it is a little off target. You might look for the major idea of something expressed and tie it to the topic, avoiding rejection. You might have to reframe or redirect the focus of the comment if necessary.

"Okay, that's interesting, but how does that relate to...?"
"Let's see, you seem to saying...." (Reframed idea)
"Okay, so you're thinking about... right now. But let's see if we can give attention to...."
"All right, you seem to be saying that.... Okay, and that suggests...."

Use eye contact. Eye contact is part of communication. It shows that you are attentive or that you are interested. Your eyes can tell students that you notice them. Eyes can give simple acknowledgements and elicit and reinforce contributions. They can also show disapproval or give signals of concern. They express your feelings and may communicate more than your words.

Use your eyes when working with teams stationed around the room. You can move your eyes to a section or to an individual. If you ask an open-ended question of the total group, you might use your eyes to elicit a response from one of the sections. You might even gesture with your hand and say, "Let me hear from some of you in this section." Give the students time to respond. Have patience and let your eyes do some talking for you, especially during a pause after you have asked a question. Eyes can be soft, encouraging, and inviting. Or, your eyes can be intense, intimidating, and threatening.

Participants are often uncertain of when it is their turn to talk. Some may wonder if they are talking too much. Your eyes, and your words, will communicate when it is time to talk. Some students who are unsure of themselves will avoid eye contact with you. They will turn away when you look at them, almost pleading for you to move onto someone else. You might say, "That's okay, take your time and think about it for a moment." Then, pose the question again.

Naturally, other non-verbal behaviors will play a part in facilitating the group (e.g. gestures, facial expression, tone of voice, posture, and physical proximity in the group). Be aware of what affect they have on your group, and take note of those that you can positively use to the group's advantage.

Reinforce participation. Just as your eyes can be used to reject or reinforce participation, so can your choice of words. Be careful not to use too many evaluative terms such as "Good," "Great," "Excellent," "Wonderful," and "Outstanding." You might be cautious also about using popular slang, although your personality may allow you to use it without putting down students or making you seem condescending (e.g. "Super duper," "Right on," "That's A-Okay," "That's cool,"). While they are intended to tell a person or a group that their performance or contribution is appreciated, it sometimes communicates that it is the best or correct response. In addition, evaluation, either positive or negative, runs counter to creating the facilitative conditions you want in a group. Evaluations are needed and inevitable, but they are also low facilitative. Therefore, the responses of "Okay," "All right," "Thanks for sharing that," and "Thank you" are favored because they tend to seem less evaluative and more acknowledging.

Feedback in the form of a compliment can be very reinforcing to an individual or a group. Most counselors and teachers do not give enough compliments. Think of ways that you can let individuals or a group know that you value their responses. Students like to be reassured that the group is going well and that their contributions are important.

Move to and away from students. If you are not getting the type of behavior that you think is helpful in a large group or you are meeting with resistance, you may want to use the feedback model to gently tell individuals or groups about the effect that their behaviors are having on you. This is after you have tried other means of getting them to work with you.

If you have a student in your group who is non-attentive or disruptive, you might use your physical presence to gain the person's attention. Move closer to the student. As you get into someone's territory or space, there is a tendency for the person to be more alert. Anxiety increases and attention to your movement and words will likely increase.

When students are tired or fatigued, or perhaps it is hot and at the end of a day, keep on the move. Do not station yourself in front of the room or in one place. Your movement breaks monotony and is stimulating. It forces people to shift their attention and to be attentive, especially as you move closer to them. For example, if you want a particular section of the large group to participate more, then move closer to that section and use your eyes and physical presence to invite them to participate.

In a similar fashion, if one student or section of students is dominating discussion, then move away. Move to another area, saying, "We've already heard from some members in our group, let's hear what the rest of you are thinking. How about from some of you in this section?"

Set limits. You may have some students in your groups who are disruptive or whose behavior is unacceptable. Set some limits with the students, by first responding to their feelings and then telling them what they can or cannot do. In principle, it is always best to focus on what you expect of people instead of asking them to refrain from doing something. The first requests something you want someone to do, while the latter requests obedience and fails to give direction.

For example, suppose that two students are laughing to themselves as others participate. It has become annoying to you and others.

You might say something like this, "You two are having a difficult time listening today and it's clear that something is striking you as funny or amusing. However, you're making it hard for us to keep focused and to share ideas. So, please, give us your attention."

If you have built up "some chips in the bank" from earlier experiences, you may want to go straight to the point and say, "You're having fun and finding something amusing, but we need your attention." There are fewer words. You can also say, "Please stop your side remarks and give us your attention." It is not a time to argue and it is not a time to discuss behavior, if you want to stay on task. On the other hand, some counselors deliberately let such behavior continue for a short time before saying, "We have a problem in our group. What's happening?" Then, the situation and behavior of the students is processed. This is more confrontive, but it can also prove educational, if it is timely and you use your facilitative skills.

Setting limits can also be used in a large group when a student is stimulated to talk too personally or self-disclose too much. Students who are under stress or full of anxiety are not particularly concerned about where they are or what group they are in, if they have an opportunity to get something off their minds. They often seize upon an opportunity to ease the burden by venting their feelings, especially in what seems to be a safe place.

If you are concerned that such self-disclosure is inappropriate for the group or too personal, you might interrupt and say, "This is really important to you and you're feeling like you want to talk about it now." Or, "I can see by what you've told us that you're feeling... and, it's not easy to think about something else. However, this may be something you and I could talk about as soon as our group is over." Or, "Our group discussion brought back some strong feelings in you—some sad ones, and you're remembering something that happened which had a big influence on you." Depending on your skill and professional judgment, you might continue with, "But, what you've told us is very personal. Do you want to continue? Or, is this something you might want to talk about later?"

You might remind the group that people do not have to share anything that they do not want to talk about and that, in this case, the person has trusted the group to be respectful of the situation. Or, you might shift the focus for a few minutes by interrupting the person and asking the group, "We've just heard a very personal statement by one of our group members. What do you think that person is feeling right now?" Then, "What is that person saying about us as a group?" Then, a discussion of the facilitative conditions of caring, trust, and so forth might take place.

Give tasks. It can be facilitative in a large group to give group members specific tasks. One such task might be: "All right, let's have this section (or team) listen to what this section (pointing to another team) has to say. See what you would add." This encourages the members to focus their attention on the topic and discussion. You might continue with, "Now, as you listen, think of a question that you might ask to help us learn more about their ideas."

Another task might be to have everyone write down the key words or phrases that are being reported, or to take note of key ideas. Still another task might be for everyone in a group to respond to a particular question, or to write a one word response, or draw a picture in response to a question or unfinished sentence. This alerts group members, directs their attention, and enhances their involvement.

If a group is not going well, change the task. For example, instead of plunging ahead with the outlined procedures, you might stop and say, "What's happening in our group? What are some of your feelings right now?" "What do you think is happening to cause some of those feelings?" "What are some things that we could do to make it more interesting?"

Sometimes a "here and now" task will create enough excitement to motivate the group and personalize the experience. A "there and then" task, such as "What do you think the student was feeling in that situation?" may be too hypothetical and too far removed from the group's experience to keep them involved.

If the students continue to struggle with their attention or motivation to discuss an issue or situation, you might re-examine the topic or the tasks that are being given. Students generally like to talk about their ideas and feelings in large and small groups.

Sometimes counselors are limited by time and must stay on task to complete the "guidance lesson." When it is important to lead students through a lesson or complete an agenda, you will be more time-conscious. You make decisions to keep the group on task, moving through the activities and procedures. Missed opportunities happen, not for lack of skill, but because professional judgments must be made according to the clock.

There is nothing wrong with staying on task. However, the trade-off is usually in terms of depth of discussion and the number of high facilitative responses that are made. In elementary schools, 30 minutes is becoming a common time for many large group guidance experiences. When an extra 15 minutes is available (for a total of 45 minutes), there is generally more discussion and more group participation. Counselors feel less rushed and more like facilitators when they have the extra time, but it may not be available.

Have a plan. There are some experienced counselors and teachers who can take a few leads and spontaneously begin a guidance lesson, drawing upon their vast knowledge of activities and their ability to facilitate a group. They know how to personalize discussion topics. They are familiar with typical questions and concerns. They recognize potential problems before they occur. They are master educators who, with a little study, can quickly involve a large group, such as a class, in a guidance lesson. But, few counselors or teachers rely exclusively on their experience and abilities to work on "automatic pilot" in unstructured situations. It is hard work.

It is more practical to have planned guidance units, each with a specific number of sessions that have been outlined for a given amount of time. There are always adjustments. Sometimes activities must be modified or procedures changed to accommodate the time and setting. On some occasions, discussion may take a turn in which there is an opportunity for some timely teaching. Then the remainder of the guidance lesson plan may be eliminated. But, when you have a plan and the option of changing it when you choose, instead of always depending upon your personal resources and faith that things will work out, your work is easier.

Some people like to sketch out a general plan with a few notes and then follow their intuition and experience. Others prefer more detailed plans. Regardless, the most effective counselors have a clear idea of the objectives they are trying to accomplish, have the materials that are needed, and know how they will start the group. They may have written down a few opening remarks for easy reference. They know which activities they plan to use and have thought through the specific procedures of the activities, especially as they are suited to a particular room or space in which a group is meeting. They have in mind a summary statement or a way to conclude the group discussion, with particular attention given to getting closure.

If leading a large group guidance session is new to you, then you probably will need a more detailed and structured plan. Try to visualize how the time might be spent, identifying an approximate number of minutes for each part of your plan. You will have to be flexible and recognize that facilitating a longer discussion in one part of the plan means reducing the time for an activity or discussion in another part. Your own personal interests, skills, and professional judgment eventually determine your decisions when leading a group.

One example of a large group guidance experience that was proven effective with fourth grade classes, referred to as the Florida Classroom Guidance Project, was developed in Orange County, Florida (Myrick, Merhill, and Swanson, 1986) and has been replicated in other school districts. It can be modified to fit your own needs and the interests of your students. The general outline can also be used to develop other guidance units.

The Florida Classroom Guidance Project

Attitudes about school, self, and others affect student learning. When students do not like school, they are ineffective learners. If they feel accepted, successful, and important in school, they tend to participate and achieve more. Helping young people to develop positive attitudes is an objective of all school guidance programs.

The Orange County Florida School District (Orlando, Florida) had 67 elementary schools in 1984, each with a full-time counselor, which were part of a large group guidance project. The county-wide project featured a guidance unit for fourth grade students and focused on attitudes about school.

More specifically, the unit was made up of six 30-45 minutes classroom guidance sessions: a) Understanding Feelings and Behaviors; b) Attitude Glasses; c) Helping Someone New to School; d) Making Positive Changes; e) I Am Lovable and Capable; and f) Looking for Personal Strengths. Two more sessions were used to administer pre and post measurements and to prepare students to work in group discussion teams. The unit is described in Appendix A.

This unit is an example in which some universal group activities were used, activities which were modified to fit the situation. In addition, some newly designed sessions were also included which were aimed directly at desired objectives. Each of the sessions had detailed instructions and was divided into four parts: 1) Introduction, including the opening counselor remarks; 2) Activity I, which involved a counselor-led discussion with the total class; 3) Activity II, in which five small groups were formed from the class and go-around procedures gave each student an opportunity to respond to a group topic; and 4) Closure, which included both a summary of the session and an assignment for students.

Management and arrangement of students was important, as each classroom was organized into five small group discussion teams. These teams were first positioned in semi-circles around the room during the introduction of a session. The counselor spoke with the entire class via their teams in Activity I. During Activity II, the teams closed into small circle groups for specific tasks and discussions. The teams then quickly repositioned themselves into their semi-circles for the closure activities and final discussion.

This Florida project was later replicated by 30 counselors in the state of Indiana and favorable results were also reported (Myrick, Merhill, and Swanson, 1986). Both target students—those who teachers had identified as having negative attitudes about school—and top students—those who were seen as academically successful—benefited from the guidance unit, according to teacher reports. This was true in both the Florida and Indiana studies, which involved more than 1,700 students who were either in control or experimental groups. The 20 items which were used in the study to compare groups that received the unit and those that did not are shown in Figure 8.1. The indicators of significant differences in favor of the experimental group that received the unit are also shown. Students were given the same inventory, with a few changes. The results are shown in Figure 8.2.

This was a significant study because of its scope, research design, replication, and positive findings for both target and top students. It demonstrated that students who have negative attitudes about school can benefit from large group guidance. Just as important, students who are doing well academically (top students) can also gain from the same large group guidance experience. The unit, of course, is directed to all students and, in this case, is the first counselor intervention.

Large group guidance is the most parsimonious approach to students who have negative attitudes. Those students who appeared to need more help or who did not respond well to large group guidance could then be seen in small group counseling, perhaps experiencing the series of structured group experiences described in

Developmental Guidance and Counseling

Figure 8.1

Teacher Inventory Results:
Comparison of Treatment and Control Groups

Behavior in school:	Florida		Indiana	
	Target (n=623)	Top (n=403)	Target (n=350)	Top (n=381)
1. Starts school work as soon as assigned.	*			
2. Works hard on school assignments.				
3. Finishes assignments on time.				
4. Has materials ready to do work.				
5. Participates in class discussions.				
6. Follows directions and school rules.	*		*	
7. Accepts helpful corrections and suggestions.	*	*	*	
8. Says kind things about and to others.		*	*	
9. Gets along well with others.	*		*	
10. Likes teachers.	*		*	
11. Is liked by teachers.	*	*	*	
12. Others are interested in what student says.	*	*	*	
13. Believes oneself to be an important and special person.	*	*	*	
14. Likes coming to school.	*	*	*	
15. Likes oneself as a person.	*	*	*	
16. Is a good worker at school.		*	*	
17. Sees school as a friendly place to be.	*	*	*	
18. Sees school as contributing to feeling happy and successful.				
19. Tries harder when things don't go right the first time.	*		*	
20. Knows how to make friends.				

.05 level of significance

Figure 8.2
Student Inventory Results:
Comparison of Treatment and Control Groups

	Florida		Indiana	
	Target (n=623)	Top (n=403)	Target (n=350)	Top (n=381)
How I am in school:				
1. I start my school work as soon as assigned.				
2. I work hard on school assignments.	*			
3. I finish assignments on time.				
4. I have materials ready to do work.		*		
5. I participate in class discussions.				
6. I follow directions and school rules.				
7. I accept helpful corrections and suggestions.				
8. I say kind things about and to others.	*	*	*	
How I think about some things:				
9. I get along well with others.				
10. I like teachers.				
11. My teachers like me.	*	**	**	*
12. Others are interested in what I say.	*			
13. I am an important and special person.				
14. I like coming to school.				
15. I like who I am.				
16. I am a good worker at school.	*			
17. School is a friendly place to be.	*	**	**	*
18. School makes me feel happy and successful.				
19. I try harder when things don't go right the first time.				
20. I know how to make friends.				

.05 level of significance

Chapter 7. Finally, those who are unresponsive to large or small group work might then receive some individual counseling.

Each session in the unit was organized on the assumption that only a minimal amount of materials would be available and that the unit should be able to be implemented without additional expense beyond the typical resources of most counselors. This limited the selection of structured learning activities for this unit. The unit was aimed at fourth graders; however, middle school counselors have already reported that, with a few modifications, it has proven to be valuable in their work. Some high school counselors have also used it. You may find that other activities would better suit your purposes. You could modify the unit for your own interests and needs.

One group of counselors asked if the activities could be used in small group counseling sessions, doing away with the need for large group management arrangements. This is possible, but the group discussion teams positioned in semi-circles and circles may have been the most important aspect of the experience. The activities themselves were not that unique or special.

The school counselors who were in the original studies reported that all students who received the unit participated in class discussion. They could not think of a single student who refused to take part in the go-around activities. None withdrew or continually passed when it was time to speak to the group topic. This is an impressive finding and it surprised both teachers and counselors. Students, who seldom took part in class discussions, shared their ideas in each session.

Large group guidance, especially as outlined in the Florida Classroom Guidance Project, is a unique and valuable experience for students. As a type of counselor intervention, it has a special place in the services that counselors provide.

Helpful Hints

Some of the same helpful hints that were suggested for small group counseling might also apply when working with large groups. In addition, you will find the following of value.

Grouping Students

Room and space arrangements can influence the interpersonal dynamics of a group and the kinds of interactions that happen between you and the students and among the students themselves.

Generally, there are five basic arrangements in which students can be seated (See Figure 8.3). Each has some advantages and limitations.

Figure 8.3

Managing Large Groups:
Seating Arrangements

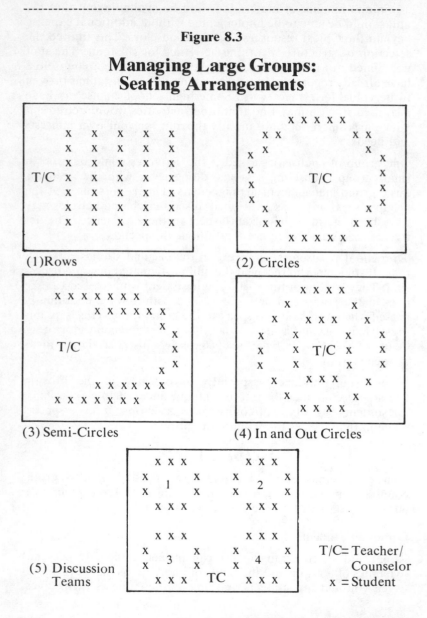

(1)Rows

(2) Circles

(3) Semi-Circles

(4) In and Out Circles

(5) Discussion Teams

T/C= Teacher/ Counselor

x = Student

Developmental Guidance and Counseling

Rows. The first arrangement features students seated in lines or rows. It is the most commonly used classroom arrangement in all schools. Chairs are typically set in five or six rows of about five or six, with six or seven chairs to each row. Sometimes tables will be added, but they are frequently placed in some line, with the teacher's podium or desk in front. Even in the most progressive schools, where efforts have been made to eliminate such traditions, one can see simple modifications of students seated in lines.

This is the ideal set-up for delivering a speech. The eyes of students are to the front of the room and it is difficult to focus attention elsewhere. Because eye contact among participants is so limited, there is a tendency, however, to have a minimal amount of discussion and a few students usually dominate. The lack of eye contact also hinders the feedback process and some students become hesitant to participate when they cannot tell how their contributions are being received by others. Therefore, if your intent is to address the students and have them listen to a presentation, then such an arrangement of chairs would be most appropriate.

Circle. In an attempt to gain more eye contact and to stimulate more participation, students are sometimes seated in a large circle. This enables everyone to see each other. It tends to invite everyone to participate more, as the circle appears to make everyone equal and positioned in such a way as to feel a part of the total group.

Sometimes the size of a group (e.g. 30 students) makes the circle so large that eye contact is still limited. Students must look a long way across the room to see others and the desired sense of being part of a group can be lost. In addition, some rooms do not lend themselves to a circle and students end up sitting in a rectangular set, or two long lines facing one another. With 15 to 20 students, a large circle works well; otherwise, different group arrangements may seem more advantageous.

Semi-circles. In a semi-circle arrangement, eyes are still to the front, although students can now see each other better and discussion is more likely to involve everyone. However, as the group increases in size, maybe 20 or more, the semi-circle gets larger and there is less a feeling of being a group. Recognizing this limitation, some counselors and teachers have arranged students in two or three large semi-circles, keeping the group closer and avoiding crowding. This, too, might be considered a variation of rows or lines since their eyes are toward the front of the room.

In and Out Circles. Sometimes two concentric circles or ovals can be arranged. The inner circle is smaller in number than the outer circle. This "fishbowl" arrangement is a popular one when demonstrations are made or when it is important to work with a group within a group.

If you seat yourself in the inner circle, you will have a sense of closeness with that group, almost shutting out the participants in the outer circle. This is also true for the students who, after a few moments, become less self-conscious of being in the spotlight and who may forget about being in the middle. The volume of their voices may drop and people seated in the outer circle may have a difficult time hearing what is being said by people in the inner circle. Members in the outer circle are usually asked to observe and not to interrupt as they listen to the comments made by members of the inner circle. This can become tedious and boring, unless you give them a task, something for which to watch or listen. Or, you may momentarily stop the work you are doing with the inner circle group and speak to those in the outer circle, eliciting their comments briefly.

Sometimes an empty chair can be used with an inner circle group and anyone from the outer circle can move into the inner circle to participate by sitting in the chair. After a few comments, the chair is vacated and open to someone else.

On occasion you can rotate small groups through the inner circle. For instance, suppose that you are working with a group of 30 students. You might have six inside chairs. You could divide the students into five small groups or teams. After working with the first small group in the inside circle, you can call on another small group to enter and take the place of the first group. This can keep everyone involved, especially if listening and observing tasks are used with those seated in the outside circle. When you occasionally stop, stand up and speak to the outside circle members.

Discussion teams. Another approach that has proven useful is that of putting students into teams of about five or six each and then moving these discussion teams into different arrangements, depending upon tasks and activities. This concept was used with the fourth grade classroom guidance unit described earlier.

Generally, students are first assigned to one of five teams. These teams are positioned around the room, usually in semi-circles facing the front of the room. You have the advantage of working with the large group, as though they were seated in rows, or working with them in teams. In a sense, you could change your perspective by treating each of the five teams as a person or a unit. You can refer to a semi-circled small group as a team, "Okay, Team One, where can you find information about the jobs that are available in our state?" Then, "All right, Team Two, what would you add?" Next, "Team Three, what is a question that you might ask of Team Four about any of the information that has been shared?"

When leading a large group discussion by referring to teams, you increase student involvement and raise the excitement level. The term "Team One" alerts five or six students instead of singling out one member of a team. A sense of belonging and togetherness among the teams is created quickly and, although a few side remarks or comments are inevitable, they are usually task related. The noise level in the room may be a little higher, but attention also increases.

Discussion teams arranged in semi-circles can, sometimes, close their semi-circles to form circles. A few go-around tasks, while the teacher or counselor moves around the room as a supervisor, increases student involvement and participation. Working with discussion teams also reduces isolation, increases eye contact, and heightens cooperation among students. It is the most feasible approach to help everyone to take an active part in a group guidance lesson.

There are some other arrangements which can be useful. For example, one small group of students might be positioned in front of the other students to make a presentation. In this case, the group might appear as a panel. In addition, if you work with groups of six students (e.g. five groups of six in a class of 30 students), you can further divide these groups into triads or dyads for special tasks. This would increase student involvement and participation even more. It is possible then to reconvene the larger group by asking triads to get back into their teams or by having teams move back to a large circle.

The different group arrangements create different group dynamics. You can use all these arrangements in your repertoire for managing large groups of students. As you work with various groupings, you will learn how they can serve you best as a facilitator and how they can be used with some guidance units and activities.

Maximizing Student Participation

While the group arrangements can make a difference in whether students feel stimulated and encouraged to participate, increased use of the facilitative responses when leading group discussions is still essential. In addition, you will want to elicit those facilitative responses from students. For example, you might say, "Let's stop for a moment. What are you hearing from Andrew, pleasant or unpleasant feelings?" In this way you need not be the only one to respond to a student's feelings. Likewise, you could also say, "Okay, would someone in Team 3 please summarize briefly what you've heard Team 1 say so far?"

Naturally, it is much easier to make high facilitative responses if you know them and have had some practice in using them. It seems practical, therefore, to teach group members how to work together and how to listen and respond. This was also suggested for small group counseling. It simply makes good sense to teach people more about group dynamics and interactions.

Target populations can receive group guidance, and within large groups there can be some target students. You might give particular attention to them. You can use certain opportunities to increase the use of high facilitative responses with them, or you might steer the discussion in their direction when it is appropriate.

If you have small discussion groups working within a large group and the noise level is getting too high or perhaps distracting other classes, you may need to interrupt the groups and caution them. Generally, however, the increased noise level does not take away from the group members' ability to listen and participate. Participants in small groups quickly pull in and focus their attention on the proceedings in their groups. If one group is becoming disruptive or appears to be going off task, then you can move to that group, pull up a chair, and join it for a short time. Help the group get back on task and then leave quietly, moving to another group.

Giving time signals such as, "You have three minutes left," can also help groups stay on task and increase their participation. Students can learn to manage their time and work together in various group arrangements. Unfortunately, cooperative learning tasks and various group arrangements have not been general practices with most teachers. Therefore, you may need to teach students how you want them positioned and how to work in small groups.

A general "rule of thumb," which might be helpful, is that about 80% of a large group can hear and follow directions the first time they are given. They stay on task without assistance. The other 20% of the group will need directions clarified and will need more help in following the task. They may need to be remotivated. Therefore, it is assumed that if you have five small groups or teams of students working in a large group setting, one of the teams is likely to need assistance in getting started or staying focused and on task. Be watchful and move to that group as soon as possible. Even if it appears that all groups are on task, move quietly from one group to another, pulling up a chair or kneeling beside the small groups to listen as members participate in a task. You might say, "You've got the idea," or some similar reinforcing comment, as you stand up and move on to the next group.

Developing Guidance Units

There are many published books which have outlined various kinds of group activities that can be used with large groups. In addition, there are some published kits and materials which have organized units with different sessions and recommended activities. Some of these kits have discussion questions.

There are many large group guidance units which have been developed by school counselors for use in their schools. Many of these are passed from one counselor to another, as part of professional meetings and presentations. Some school systems have formed writing teams of counselors who take two or three weeks in the summer to develop and outline new units. Sometimes these can be purchased from school systems or picked up at a professional meeting through "swap shops."

Group guidance activities and units are like folk songs, being passed on from one generation of counselors to another, from one school system to another, usually through mimeographed handouts. Sometimes it is difficult to identify the original authors. Frequently, in the eagerness to find and use some practical approaches, credit for authorship is omitted.

You may find that a guidance unit as outlined or described by someone else has many outstanding features, but it may not be suited for your purposes. The most practical approach is to use what you like and which fits your style. If you think you would be uneasy using a recommended activity, then do not use it. Find a substitute or make some changes.

Do not let published materials or printed outlines dictate your use of them. Be flexible, be selective, be creative, and use your best professional judgment in putting together large group guidance sessions that you enjoy presenting to your students.

Being Accountable

Surprisingly, many school counselors who work with large groups do not take the time to evaluate outcomes or to assess the process. In one study, 98% of the counselors reported that they believed a career guidance unit was effective. However, they did not take the time to ask students what they thought about the unit, if they would recommend it for other students their age, or if the basic objectives were accomplished. A few favorable testimonials are not enough.

As you put together a large group guidance unit, think of ways in which you can get some feedback from students. You might ask teachers or parents what they have observed because of students experiencing the unit. Evaluations may come at the end of a session or at the end of a unit. You might also delay evaluation for one or two weeks and then ask students what they learned or valued from a large group guidance unit.

Evaluation should not be seen as a passing or failing grade for the counselor or teacher. It is a form of feedback in which you gather information needed to make decisions. Will you make changes? What worked well and should be repeated? What was most time consuming for the least amount of return? How could the procedures and process be improved? The answers to these and other questions can help give you some direction.

Try to avoid taking criticisms as a personal rebuke or censure. In large groups, it is more difficult to please everyone, as there are more generalizations and fewer opportunities to meet all participants' needs. The 80-20% rule is likely to be an appropriate one when considering final outcomes, with the assumption that if you are accomplishing your objectives with 8 out of 10 students, then you are being highly successful.

In one study, 10 middle school counselors agreed to work with two groups of 20 students each on communication skills. Approximately 400 students took part in a four-session, large group guidance unit. Post-test only results were obtained, with special attention to how students experienced the group and if it affected them in any way. About 4% of the students said that they really disliked being in the group and would not want to be in one again. Another 4% believed that the group had little or no affect on them, while

6% were uncertain. The other 88% indicated that they gained something from the group and almost 92% would recommend it to other students.

Ironically, when the counselors who participated in the study met to review the evaluation results, they quickly became concerned about the 16 students who were very critical and outspoken about their not liking the group. "What do you think we could do to improve the group in order to reach them?" said one counselor. "Why do you think they were so negative?" said another. Finally, someone said, "Hey, it's time to take our gains. It was a very successful unit. Those few students who were unsure or who did not find it very valuable may have some valid reasons. We simply missed them in this group. Maybe we can reach them another time around or through some other approach." Be practical. Nobody is perfect and certainly no large group experience will always be 100% successful.

Advantages, Limitations, and Conclusion

Advantages of Large Group Guidance

1. Large group is the most parsimonious approach to the counselor's work, as there are many students who can benefit from a large group experience and need not be seen through other kinds of counselor interventions.

2. More students can receive the direct services of a counselor when large group guidance is used as a counselor intervention.

3. Because large group guidance is usually less intense and less confidential than individual or small group counseling, other adults can also help deliver guidance units and participate in the large group sessions. It is also possible to bring in outside resource persons who can make a contribution (e.g. senior citizens, military personnel, law officers, specialists, and experts in a particular area).

4. Some students feel more secure in large groups and prefer to avoid being singled out for individual or small group counseling. They may be feel less self-conscious and participate more.

5. Large group management and arrangements provide a unique experience to students (e.g. discussion teams) in

which adult supervision is present but not necessarily directly involved in topic discussion.

6. Large group guidance can help create a positive and caring atmosphere in a school faster than other counselor interventions. Moreover, exploration of ideas, feelings, and behaviors is done in a context that is familiar to most students. Guidance lessons have a greater chance of being generalized to the day-to-day events in school.

Limitations of Large Group Guidance

1. Some students need more attention than they can receive in large groups, as there is a tendency to generalize more in group guidance.

2. Some topics or student needs are too personal to be explored in large group settings. There is a greater chance for miscommunication since the size of the group makes it difficult to read everyone's reactions.

3. Counselor behaviors may differ in large group guidance and can communicate a different role than what some counselors want to have with students. For example, large group experiences usually require the counselor to be more structured and to give more directions. Later, perhaps in individual or small group counseling, this same perception of active leadership may be limiting to a counselor who wants to have a free-flowing spontaneous discussion. Students may expect a "lesson plan" and depend upon some structured group activities to help them communicate.

Conclusion

In elementary schools, large group guidance is often referred to as classroom guidance. In the middle and high schools, it is sometimes seen as part of advisor-advisee meetings or TAP. Counselors can also pull together a target group of students for a particular group experience.

Large group guidance need not be a question and answer session. Students do not have to be an audience, listening to a presenter. Sometimes it is appropriate to divide the large group into some smaller units or discussion teams so student participation and involvement can be increased.

Large group guidance is a practical intervention. It is the most efficient use of a counselor's time.

Chapter 9

Peer Facilitator Projects as a Counselor Intervention

An exciting turn of events in education has been the systematic training and use of students as peer facilitators. Young people are being trained to be the helping hands of counselors and teachers and, consequently, many more students can receive and participate in guidance services.

The concept of students helping students is not new. The idea began years ago in one room school houses, when older students were given the responsibility of tutoring younger students in basic skills. The process was not as refined as it is today. However, the value of having students help other students was learned early in the history of education and has never been forgotten. In more recent times, the helping roles of students have been expanded and so has the preparation for those roles. Subsequently, various titles have emerged to describe different student helper functions and programs.

During the 1970s, "peer counseling" programs were started in several schools and universities (e.g. Gray and Tindall, 1978; Hamburg and Varenhorst, 1972; Samuels and Samuels, 1975). Students helped their peers talk about personal problems. However, the term has been met with skepticism by parents, teachers, administrators, and counselors who reserve its use for crisis interventions or intense situations when a person is in trouble. Some see counseling as synonymous with therapy and, therefore, inappropriate for unlicensed people.

Very few students can learn to counsel other students. Counseling is a special skill that takes extensive preparation and practice. It has a graduate education base for certification and requires a specific course of study in which training is supervised. In addition, it is a term that has been used synonymously with therapy or intensive personal assistance. Therefore, many parents and educators are resistant when it is used as a title to describe peer helper programs.

In the 1970s, for instance, many of the peer counselor programs encouraged young people to counsel their peers who were truant, disruptive in school, having family problems, or abusing drugs. While this was an admirable objective, some early programs faltered and were abandoned because students were asked to do too much and with too little training. Nevertheless, "peer counseling" is a term that continues to be used and accepted in many areas of the country.

Peer Facilitator Defined

What is a "peer facilitator?" This term refers to a student who uses helping skills and concepts to assist other students—and sometimes adults—to think about ideas and feelings, to explore alternatives to situations, and to make responsible decisions (Myrick and Bowman, 1981b). Peer facilitator has been used synonymously with peer helper, student facilitator, peer tutor, Big Brothers and Big Sisters, student counselor, peer-group leader, and peer counselor.

The term "peer facilitator" was introduced (e.g. Myrick and Erney, 1978 and 1979) because it seemed more accurate in describing the limited role and function of young people as helpers. It communicates best what students are asked to do when helping others. At the same time, it provides enough flexibility to incorporate several helping roles and functions. In addition, the term is easier to explain to parents and educators.

The first ASCA position statement on peer counseling, adopted by its Delegate Assembly, was published in 1978 when that term was commonly used to emphasize how peer helpers could augment a guidance program. The statement was changed in 1984, using the new term "peer facilitator," and emphasized peer facilitator roles, training, counselor responsibilities, and how peer facilitators could help professional counselors in their work.

Almost all students can learn to be facilitators. They can learn basic skills and concepts which can then be used to assist others in their academic and personal development. Some peer facilitators will be more effective than others, particularly those who have participated in an organized and comprehensive program.

The Power of Peer Relationships

It is about the age of three and four that children begin to interact in a purposeful way with other children, forming friendships in the neighborhood, the park, or wherever children congregate. From this point on, a young person's destiny seems to be determined in part by the power of peer relationships.

Although parents have a substantial influence on the development of their children, other children ultimately contribute as much or more than adults. It is in the presence of other children that a child is most often discovering, exploring, remembering, and coping with the real world. No matter how many efforts a conscientious parent might make, interactions with other children frequently determine a child's sense of self-worth and well-being. These same interactions also influence the enduring behaviors, personal style, and social skills that one uses to cope with school, society, and a changing world.

Some adults fear that young people can be led astray by their peers, especially deviant peer groups who delight in defying established norms. Parents worry that their children might be influenced by their classmates to enter into drugs, sexual promiscuity, delinquency, or other unwholesome activities. Those who enjoy growing up in a family with solid bonds and who experience a caring, sensitive family structure can usually resist being manipulated into antisocial or self-destructive behaviors. Yet, the need for peer acceptance is so strong with some young people that it can become a consuming interest, to the detriment of self-development and academic learning.

Peer relationships are powerful and they should be engineered to the extent that young people learn how to interact positively with one another. This is not a matchmaking process. School programs must recognize that students need to take an active part in building helping relationships and positive learning environments. They need opportunities to learn social skills, as well as those in math, science, English, and history. They need to learn life-management skills and how to encourage and support each other in the learning process.

Ideally, all students should learn how to be peer facilitators. They would be better listeners and facilitate better discussions among their peers. They would also know the value of helping relationships and how to foster them. They could take more responsibility for their situations and feel more support. Their efforts to develop their unique selves would be enhanced.

It is generally recognized that as students pass from elementary grades to high school, they rely more on their peers for help with their concerns, interests, and problems. When asked, "If you had a personal problem, to whom would you talk first?" Most teen-agers indicate that they would turn to a peer—a close friend their age— before turning to adults. Therefore, it makes sense to prepare students to facilitate their peers, younger students, and adults.

Four Basic Helping Roles

There are many things that peer facilitators might do. It can be helpful if you think in terms of four distinct helping roles.

Special Assistant

Peer facilitators who work as student assistants provide timely assistance to teachers and counselors, especially through such activities as working in an office, distributing and collecting materials, monitoring projects, constructing bulletin boards, and participating in the planning of educational activities. Safety patrols, for example, assist other students to adjust to school rules and procedures.

In general, this role tends to focus on indirect assistance to peers and interaction is usually limited. It is included here because it is a traditional helping role frequently given some students. In the past, this role has not emphasized personal interactions among students as much as routine tasks. Yet, it appears that with peer facilitator training, all student assistant roles could be improved.

For instance, safety patrol members might be be more sensitive in giving directions and be more responsive when students have problems. Office workers might be able to greet the public more cordially and answer telephone calls with more efficiency. If student assistants are engaged in a project that does not require contact or communication with other students, training may not be necessary. But, if they are asked to talk and work closely with others, then peer facilitator training can be valuable.

Tutor

Peer tutors are used in almost every subject area. Devin-Sheehan, Feldman, and Allen (1976) examined more than 100 studies and articles and concluded that tutoring programs can effectively improve academic performance of both tutors and students being tutored. Yet, an examination of these and other studies suggests that seldom is the tutor systematically prepared or trained to work with students. The primary criteria for selection as a tutor is academic achievement.

Not all those being tutored willingly participate in the tutoring process, especially when it is being done in a manner similar to a drill sergeant or lion tamer. Too many students who are asked to help others with their studies are unfamiliar with basic helping skills.

It is usually the students who have persistent problems in their studies who need extra assistance. They are often resistant to help and find studying an unpleasant experience. They might be embarrassed, feel guilty, and become defensive when help is offered. Some may decline any assistance because they worry that other students would think less of them and maybe tease them.

It is not enough to rely on natural instincts when tutoring other students. Without special preparation as peer facilitators, even the best academic students are frequently unable to help motivate their peers. They are unsure of what to do, experience frustration, and become discouraged themselves.

On the other hand, participation in a training program where they learn how to build helping relationships and how to encourage those they are helping can make a difference. It is a new type of tutor that results from peer facilitator training, one who is responsive to the tutee's feelings, and one who can help the individual explore problems associated with studying or getting along better in class.

Special Friend

As special friends, peer facilitators develop close helping relationships with selected peers. This enables the peer facilitators to provide timely encouragement and support regarding personal matters that detract from learning in school.

Students feel left-out when they do not have friends in school. Do you remember the friends you had in school? How important were they to you? Did you ever wish that you could have more friends? Or, did you ever need a special friend you could trust, someone with whom you could talk about your interests and concerns?

When high school students are asked the most common problem facing students their age, the problem of loneliness is singled out above all others. Many students feel isolated or even alienated. It is not easy to grow up in today's world. Positive peer relationships are sometimes difficult to form, especially when one lacks skill and experience in developing them.

To become a fully-functioning adult, a young person needs to experience friendships. It is through one friendship that a person learns to develop others. Experiences are shared, ideas are explored, feelings are heard, and there is a special trust or bond that is developed out of mutual respect and acceptance. Without this base, school is viewed as an unfriendly place where people are tested, rejected, and ignored. Consequently, some students never learn well.

There are many students who need the help of a special friend who can listen to them on occasion and show interest in their ideas and feelings. These special friends need not be people with whom to party, or "hang out with," in a social sense. They are people who are available at certain times to talk about personal feelings and ideas.

When peer facilitators work as special friends, they take time to initiate a conversation with others. Students may even be paired as "friends." Some counselors identify target students from their caseloads who need a special friend to talk with on occasion. Although the assignment may be contrived, the process of building a positive relationship has a way of bringing people closer together. The conversations are friendly and can benefit both parties.

New students to a school, for example, might be assigned to peer facilitators who orient them to the building and introduce them to other students. All new students for a grading period might meet with a few peer facilitators on Friday afternoons to ask questions, discuss common problems, and meet other new students. As students become more familiar with a school, and feel a part of it, they leave the group on their own accord. Besides creating a friendly atmosphere for new students, it also frees counselors and teachers to give more time to others who need their help.

The concepts associated with Big Brothers and Big Sisters programs are especially pertinent in the special friend role. Younger students tend to admire and imitate older students. Older students working as peer facilitators or special friends can serve as positive models and can be powerful influences on student behavior in school.

A fourth grader was assigned a "big brother" who was a member of a middle school peer facilitator group. The peer facilitator made appointments to see his "buddy" and talk with him about school. They sometimes played catch with a football or kicked a soccer ball, while talking about different matters. The facilitator encouraged the boy to talk about his behavior in class and they explored alternative ways to make school better for him.

In one high school, some peer facilitators became special friends to young people who were hospitalized for an extended time, taking time to visit and talk with them at the hospital. Other peer facilitators became special friends to elderly people in retirement homes. Still other peer facilitators befriended young students who were identified by teachers as being shy or withdrawn in their classes, perhaps preoccupied with special concerns or interests.

Peer facilitators learn to recognize their limits and are taught to refer students to counselors or teachers when it is appropriate. The facilitators are also supervised by their program coordinators and obtain guidance from them. One young boy talked with his peer facilitator about a lack of interest in school. After some discussion it was clear that the boy had a conflict with two of his teachers. He was becoming increasingly defiant despite efforts of the facilitator to help him explore the consequences of his behavior. The peer facilitator was unsure how to help and suggested that the boy talk with one of the school counselors about his situation. Together they went to see a counselor and a referral was initiated.

Secret pals, pen pals, playground buddies, and other experiences can be arranged so that peer facilitators can form special friendships with students. The reason for the first meeting together is not as important as what happens when they meet, when the basis for friendship is formed in the interaction that happens.

Small Group Leader

Peer facilitators can be trained to be effective small group leaders. This can give both counselors and teachers a valuable source of helpers who can help make learning experiences more personal and exciting. With the assistance of peer facilitators as small group leaders, more students can participate in learning activities, be more involved in the learning process, and experience the facilitative conditions of a relationship (understanding, acceptance, and so forth).

One common teacher complaint is there are too many students and too few teachers. The average classload is about 30 students and, in some schools, it can reach as high as 40. Most teachers would prefer to have about 20 to 25 students. Even then, they find it difficult to engage all students in a classroom discussion. The group dynamics associated with large groups often mean that more people are listening than talking. The listening that takes place is not as personal or focused as that which happens in small groups.

Similarly, counselors also experience the frustration of trying to personalize the discussion of a topic when they do classroom guidance activities. Sometimes counselors meet with large groups of 50 students or more, usually to pass out information and answer questions. But, this format can lead to little involvement and low energy from students. With the help of peer facilitators, large groups can be divided into smaller groups and more students can participate.

Peer facilitators can lead small groups (perhaps from four to six members). The groups are usually assembled as a team in a circle. For example, in a class of 30 with five peer facilitators as helpers, there might be five teams stationed around the room in circles, each with a peer facilitator as a leader. The peer facilitator introduces a topic or task. Go-around procedures might be used so that each group member in turn shares ideas. The leader facilitates the group by making or eliciting high facilitative responses.

Myrick and Bowman (1981b) described a classroom guidance project entitled "My Friends and Me," in which peer facilitators from the fourth and fifth grades were small group leaders. Second grade classes were divided into teams of five, with a peer facilitator assigned to each team. Teams met at their assigned stations and five small group experiences happened simultaneously, as the teacher and the counselor moved around the room supervising the different groups.

The unit focused on friendship. Its objectives for students were to listen to others and to practice listening skills, to have an opportunity to speak and be heard, and to talk about the qualities of friendship. The topics for the four sessions included: 1) Tell about when you did something with a friend; 2) Tell something about yourself that you think would make you a good friend; 3) Tell about something that would make you happier; and 4) Tell one way that a person can make new friends; and, then what did you learn about the persons in your group? Each session took about 15 minutes.

The facilitators were prepared to ask members a question after they responded to the topic and then to clarify the answer or respond to a feeling. They were also instructed to give simple acknowledgements and to look for opportunities to link ideas or feelings. It was something that they had experienced themselves and practiced, as part of their training.

Teachers were excited about the project since it gave each second grade child an opportunity to say something in a structured group experience which fostered acceptance, understanding, caring, and other facilitative conditions. It also gave the peer facilitators an opportunity to practice group leadership skills and to be recognized for their contributions.

Bowman (1982) constructed a project in which third grade students who were viewed as disruptive were paired with peer facilitators who served as special friends and small group leaders. They participated in small group sessions similar to the project discussed above. There were significant differences in terms of positive classroom behaviors and attitudes about school in favor of students who worked with peer facilitators, as compared to a group of students who did not receive such help.

Aside from small group discussions which involve guidance topics, peer facilitators can also be used to help students study various academic topics. Problem-solving groups, for example, can be facilitated in social studies and science classes. Learning centers, study circles, and demonstration groups might have peer facilitators as leaders, making it possible to have more working groups in a classroom and, consequently, more student participation and involvement.

Some high school peer facilitators experienced a set of structured small group experiences as part of their training. They analyzed the activities and group leader's behavior. Next, they practiced leading the activities among themselves before going to a junior high school where they used the same activities with small groups of eighth grade students. In this case, all the activities focused on the general objective of setting goals and making decisions. Some of the peer facilitators were paired as co-leaders for some of the groups.

Peer facilitators can also play an important part in a counselor-led large group guidance intervention. One high school counselor decided to disseminate test and career information in groups of 60 students. Peer facilitators were available to assist as small group leaders. The counselor first presented general information via overhead projectors to the large group. About 10 to 12 small groups were then formed, each with a peer facilitator as the group leader. The groups discussed various topics and did different tasks, as the counselor moved from one group to another answering questions and supervising. At the end of the time period, the large group was reassembled and a final question-answer session took place based on questions that arose in the small groups. Student involvement was increased and the general session was more personalized. More needs were addressed and the evaluation proved that it was an efficient way to use both student and counselor time.

Although peer facilitators can work in many places and do many functions, most of the things that they do can be categorized into one or more of the four basic roles. These roles provide a focus for training and for developing helping projects in which they can participate.

Peer Facilitator Training

There are many types of peer facilitator training programs. Some have developed with little planning, but they have been successful because of the caring, commitment, and energy that characterizes the trainers or people involved. Still other programs have been even more successful because they have developed well-organized and systematic procedures for teaching interpersonal skills and preparing facilitators for different roles. In addition, they have identified helping projects in which the peer facilitators can put their skills to use while being supervised. The latter approach is the current trend and these training programs have been described in detail elsewhere (e.g. Foster, 1983; Gray and Tindall, 1978; Myrick and Bowman, 1981a and 1981b; Myrick and Erney, 1978 and 1979). Most of these training programs are a minimum of 20 to 30 hours in duration, especially for secondary school students. However, these are comprehensive programs, ones in which students are prepared for all four roles.

Helping projects are those in which peer facilitators, under the supervision of teachers and/or counselors, work with other students. A project has general and specific objectives and helping roles for the facilitators are identified. Skills and strategies learned in training are applied. The peer facilitators meet with their trainer or project coordinator to talk about their work.

Peer facilitator programs and projects might be considered in the light of being a) beginning; b) intermediate; or c) advanced. Each of these levels is commensurate with the skills, self-confidence and experience that students have obtained in their training. Some beginning projects might be planned to give peer facilitators an initial experience in helping others. Beginning projects tend to be more limited in scope and are more structured. There is closer supervision and the skills are simple, usually focusing on listening and responding to feelings, clarifying ideas, and asking open-ended questions.

Intermediate and advanced projects require more flexibility and spontaneity. They involve a combination of helping skills and the use of some less structured problem-solving models. In advanced projects, peer facilitators work with a minimum of supervision and direction, using their past experiences and more practiced skills to do various tasks.

In elementary schools, training tends to consist of about 10 to 20 half-hour sessions, although the training could be less depending on the nature of a project. Most projects are specific and structured. High school training programs, on the other hand, are usually longer, perhaps a minimum of 30 hours. Some high school students receive even more hours of preparation and supervision, if enrolled in a course for peer facilitators. Students can be trained briefly, if a project is limited in scope and duration and is closely supervised.

Many high schools throughout the nation are moving toward offering courses for credit in which peer facilitators can be trained. The courses are part of the social studies department, feature an organized curriculum, are an elective for students who qualify, and are viewed as leadership classes.

For example, one high school course is based on two semesters of work, with four nine-week grading periods. During the first nine weeks, the students, usually about 20 to 25, study the helping relationship, the facilitative model, and some basic problem-solving and decision-making approaches. The class meets five days a week. During the second nine weeks, the peer facilitators work on different beginning projects three days a week during their facilitator class period. They receive supervision and more training the other two days for projects in an elementary school, where they are special friends or small group leaders. In addition, special projects are implemented within the high school. Training and supervision continue into the third nine weeks, where more group skills and activities are given attention. Related projects usually involve group experiences for middle or junior high school students. Some more high school projects are also developed, especially as related to orientation, working with new students, tutoring, and working with teachers in classes.

The state of Florida has approved high school social studies courses entitled Peer Counseling I, II (1st year) and III and IV (2nd year), each with a half credit for each semester (18 weeks) of work completed. There is a curriculum framework which consists of the purpose of the course, the content to be emphasized, the special learning conditions required, the teacher certification required, and the intended outcomes. Performance standards exist for each class which are designed to measure the outcomes. A list of the intended outcomes for the courses are provided in Appendix B.

Other states also have approved courses for credit. While credit is desirable for students, and while it can give more credibility to the program, credit itself never seems to be a critical issue. When such courses are offered, teachers and counselors have a regularly scheduled time when they can meet with peer facilitators for training and projects. Accessibility to students is probably the most important consideration for developing a program.

There are, of course, other factors that you will want to consider. As you will recall, it is recommended that a school counselor budget about one hour a day for peer facilitator work, either training students or working with them on projects. Sometimes the training might be done by a teacher, especially in the secondary schools. Nevertheless, as a counselor, you will want a peer facilitator program to be part of the total guidance program and part of the services that you provide.

Factors to Consider

There are several factors to consider before developing a peer facilitator program with training sessions and helping projects. Here are a few.

Who should be a peer facilitator?

Your first consideration is to work with students who are potential school leaders. They are easy to get along with and capable of helping others. They have a positive attitude about themselves, others, and school and they tend to be characterized as caring, sensitive, and friendly persons. Verbal skills are valued since most of the peer facilitator work involves talking with others. And, practically speaking, these students have enough "clout" or influence with their teachers to be released from class on occasion and to be trusted in various projects.

Some trainers consider selection to be the most important decision that they will make about a program. A high school trainer interviewed all those who applied the first year (about 35) and then used the first year's peer facilitators to help interview the next group·who applied (about 185). Depending upon the visibility of your program, you too may have the luxury of choosing from a large number of interested students.

The peer facilitator course has often become an elective for juniors and seniors who have recommendations from their teachers and parents. Counselors frequently select students who have personalities suited to form helping relationships and those who are available for training and projects. No one should ever be forced to be a peer facilitator.

The selection and number of students also depends upon your own commitment and involvement. An elementary school counselor had three small groups of peer facilitators (six in each group) for a total of 18 "Helping Hands" who were available for different projects in the school. Each group was given a basic set of communication skills based on the facilitative model. Then each group was given specific training for a particular project.

A high school course is best suited for about 18 to 24 students. Because so much supervised practice is required, a larger number usually means more extended training time before projects can be developed. In addition, it also means that more time is needed to coordinate helping projects.

However, if you are wondering where to begin, and there is no organized program in your school, you might start with about five or six of your favorite students. Ask for their help in working with you on some projects. After you have some experience, you can add other students to your groups.

Who should be the trainer or coordinator?

Many school counselors, especially at the secondary level, have been asked to train peer facilitators. Some resisted the idea of committing time to such a program, although it could save time and energy in other ways. Consequently, teachers from various subject areas have taken the lead. For example, in Texas some home economics teachers train peer facilitators. In Florida and Indiana there are many social studies teachers who are responsible for the program.

Peer facilitator programs are recommended as part of a school counselor's work load. Both the training program and organizing projects can be considered counselor interventions. You might teach a peer facilitator course or have a peer facilitator training club. If someone else in the school is assigned to do the training, perhaps a teacher, then you will want to work closely with that person. You may help coordinate some projects or design a guidance project in which peer facilitators are used.

Peer facilitator programs can provide you some positive visibility. Seize upon the opportunity, if you can. You will not be disappointed and it will provide an extra lift when you face less rewarding tasks.

What type of training should be given?

The training program is usually dependent upon the time available to work with students and projects. Almost all authors and experts in the field, however, agree that training should not be a replica of a counselor education program nor should it focus on advanced theories and strategies associated with counseling and therapy. There are a few basic facilitative concepts and skills that might need attention (e.g. See Chapter 5). An examination of Apppendix B will also give you an idea of the skills that could be intended outcomes.

More specifically, it appears that peer facilitators need to learn about the characteristics of a helping relationship and how they might become better listeners when someone is talking to them. Next, they need to learn how to facilitate individuals to talk more about their ideas and feelings. A simple problem-solving model can be useful, including a few ground rules and procedures for leading small group discussions. After that, training is usually related to specific projects or problem moments that result from helping people.

If you can arrange for about 10 - 12 hours of training, you can have a program. You can add skills later as they are required for different projects and experiences. These minimum hours of training might be started or completed in marathon-type sessions (e.g. one day). A few middle schools have trained their peer facilitators on teacher-work days when school is out for most students. This avoids taking students from their academic classes. Other schools have formed clubs and have used weekend retreats to provide the initial training.

Project P.R.O.M.I.S.E. (Peer Reach Out for Maryland Involving Students and Educators) was an ESEA, Title III, grant in Baltimore, Maryland. Its training manual was divided into four topics: Communications (9 lessons); Values (7 lessons); Decision-making (6 lessons); and Techniques (7 lessons). It was used to train students in a statewide program that was very successful. Maryland was one of the first states in the nation to sponsor state conferences for peer facilitators.

Likewise, outstanding curriculum guides for peer facilitator courses have been developed in the Broward and Orange counties of Florida. The purpose of the courses, the content to be emphasized, and the learning materials to be used were carefully outlined. These particular programs were designed to meet the performance standards recommended by the state department of education and adopted by the school boards.

What do peer facilitators do?

After peer facilitators have received some basic training, they are ready to participate in some helping projects. The four different roles might suggest different projects which could be done around a school. In addition, it is also possible to combine the roles when working with a target population.

Some examples of things that peer facilitators have done include:

> *Group leader with elementary school children:* drawing upon the *Developing Understanding of Self and Others (DUSO)* kit for structured lessons and activities.

> *Group leader with high school students:* helping students talk about their test results (*DAT, SAT*) in a series of meetings arranged and supervised by counselors.

> *Group leader with high school students:* exploring vocational interests, skills, and goals in a series of struc-

tured group experiences. In addition, each group member was assisted to plan a four year program around a tentative job goal.

Special friend with high school students: working with students who had been given in-school suspensions. Peer facilitators were assigned to a "time-out" room where they talked with students about problems they were having with teachers and other students.

Special friend and tutor: talking with students who had been retained in a juvenile shelter home and who disliked school. Counselors matched peer facilitators with students who needed extra attention in friendship and tutoring.

Tutor: meeting with a middle school student who had missed three weeks of school because of an extended illness.

Tutor: studying with a cooperative, willing middle school student who wanted to pass Algebra I but who was confused and worried about failing.

Special friend: visiting with an elderly retired person in a retirement center, who appreciated the extra time and attention received from a high school peer facilitator.

Tutor: leading students through a learning center in a classroom. Students in small groups came to the center to watch a peer facilitator demonstrate a skill and concept and then received some coaching as they tried it.

Student assistant: developing a project for promoting student morale and school spirit, which led to a pep assembly with fun and thought-provoking skits.

Once training is complete, peer facilitators themselves can identify projects around the school. They would then know more about their skills and roles, and have a better idea of the purpose of the program. Their enthusiasm for helping others often leads to some exciting and rewarding projects.

Teachers are also an excellent source of projects, once they understand the purpose of the program and the roles in which peer facilitators can function. In addition, teacher support has proven to be essential to successful programs. Help the teachers of your school to know more about your program, and help them see how it can assist them in their work.

Peer Facilitator Programs and Projects

The *Peer Facilitator Quarterly (PFQ)* was first published in 1983. It provides inspirational articles and pieces, including suggestions for developing programs. In every issue there are examples of what schools at different grade levels are doing with their peer facilitators. The following were included among some of the reports.

At Warren Central High School, Indianapolis, Indiana, peer facilitators are part of an Educational Intervention (I.V.) Program. The I.V. program provides help for students who are troubled with academic failures or personal setbacks and who are seeking companionship. It is not to be confused with an in-house suspension program. The I.V Center is located next to the school cafeteria and is available to students upon self-referral or upon referral by teachers. It is also supervised by a faculty member.

In addition, peer facilitators at Warren Central provide: before and after school tutoring; assistance with English as a second language; extended illness homework assistance; new student orientation programs; a lost and found area; a bus and school information center; a school visitor's center; and opportunities to experience someone who will listen to problems and concerns.

In Hillsborough County (Tampa), Florida, peer facilitators have assisted students in many ways, as the program there is one of the oldest and best established in the nation. Peer facilitator programs exist in all the elementary, middle, and high schools and training programs are aimed at all four helping roles. One of the many projects which drew attention was when peer facilitators provided special assistance in the area of careers by leading students through a *Vocational Exploration Group (VEG)*. Group members explored their job interests, skills, satisfiers, and tentative plans. The group members, no more than six at a time, were led through various procedures and tasks according to a leader's book. Peer facilitators were responsible for all tenth grade students participating in the small group on career exploration.

In addition, peer facilitators also learn about materials in the Career Resource Centers of their schools and assist students in using these materials. In one activity, copies of the *Occupational Outlook Handbook* were used with a class of students which was divided into five groups of six students each. Peer facilitators, working as co-leaders, led discussions based on questions and tasks related to the books. Sessions concluded with group members responding to such open-ended statements as: I learned..., I noticed..., I was surprised that... and I now realize that....

At Westside Elementary School, River Falls, Wisconsin, a comprehensive developmental guidance and counseling program consists of a "students assisting students" program. Peer facilitators there participate in various helping projects, including a student companionship program for students with low self-concepts. Peer facilitators have lead group discussions and assisted counselors and teachers in such projects as "Black History Awareness," "My Buddy and Me" (the value of friendship), "Test Buster Pep Rally" (test anxiety and achievement), and "Just Talk" (a program for teen-agers and their parents).

"Friends for Friends" is a special peer facilitator program at Dawkins Middle School, Spartanburg, South Carolina. Twelve students are trained each year in two groups. After four one-hour training sessions, peer facilitators begin working in helping projects that involve tutoring and working as a special friend for students who have school or home problems.

Eighteen seventh graders are selected each year by teacher recommendation and parental permission in Newton-Conover Middle School, Newton, North Carolina. They meet twice each week in 45-minute sessions for five weeks and then periodically throughout the school year. As co-leaders, the facilitators present 20-minute group guidance activities to sixth grade homerooms. They also help orient new students to the school, including visitations to elementary schools in the spring of the year.

The counselors in Selden Junior High School, Centereach, New York, organized a Peer Leadership Program. Since its beginning in 1980, the training of peer facilitators has usually taken place before school starts each morning. Peer facilitators in the program go to the school districts' elementary schools and talk with fourth, fifth, and sixth grade students, leading them in various group activities and exercises. In addition, the facilitators also take part in such activities as Volunteers for Special Olympics and Walk America for the March of Dimes. Each year there is an annual Alumni Peer Leaders Party, which is a family affair for peer leaders and their parents. Counselor and parent enthusiasm runs high in such successful programs.

Peer facilitators in Buchholz High School, Gainesville, Florida, helped create their own helping projects, including one in which they developed a puppet show for elementary school children. The topic was child abuse and teams of peer facilitators visited all 18 elementary schools in the county. Children and teachers praised the project.

Huey and Rank (1984) investigated the effects of group assertiveness training on 48 black adolescent boys who were selected because of their aggressive classroom behavior. Using pre- and post-test measures, and comparisons with control groups, their results suggested that professional counselors and peer facilitators were equally effective in teaching skills and in reducing aggressive classroom behavior. In addition, the subjects in the study were equally satisfied with peers or professionals as group leaders.

Canning (1985) described how children, trained as peer facilitators, can play an important role in a counselor intervention called *Play Times*. It is a project based on developmental play and involves the natural play of children. Objectives are to increase self-awareness, improve interpersonal relationships, build social skills, experience feelings of self-worth, increase language development, and enhance learning.

Play Times follows a format based on about 30 minutes of interaction, in which peer facilitators play with their assigned younger special friends. Each sessions opens with all participants in a beginning circle (about 5 to 10 minutes), as students get reacquainted. The paired "friends" have individual time in which they play together and share ideas in various play activities (about 10 to 15 minutes). Supervision is considered essential to the success of the program. Peer facilitators meet after each session with the counselor to talk about their experiences and to plan for the next session. Canning (1985) outlined 15 sessions and related supervision activities, which can be used effectively with primary grade children who work with fourth and fifth grade peer facilitators.

Peer facilitators are not going to replace school counselors. Working with counselors, they can provide some valuable assistance. Sometimes, when peers are equally effective as professional counselors, it may be more practical for counselors to invest their time training peer facilitators and coordinating peer projects to reach more students. A peer facilitator project can be a powerful counselor intervention.

Helpful Hints

When starting your peer facilitator program, examine some recognized references and articles to give you some direction. You also might consult with other counselors who have started programs in their schools. Here are a few more helpful hints.

Start Small and Learn With Students

Almost all successful peer facilitator trainers have started with groups with whom they thought they could be successful. There is no use making your work any harder than it already is. Therefore, identify a few students with whom you would like to work, perhaps some you have already met with in small group counseling or group guidance. Ask them if they would like to help you work with other students on some projects and find some times when you can work together.

Finding time for training is a critical factor in training peer facilitators, especially in elementary and middle schools where courses may not be offered. It may be easier to identify times when students are most available and then look for students during those times with whom you would most like to work. As your program develops, other students will want to know how they can become peer facilitators and you can establish more formal guidelines for selection.

One high school counselor noticed that a large group of students was scheduled for a study hall during the fourth period of the day. Looking over the group, it was obvious that some would make excellent peer facilitators because of their personalities, their academic success, and their willingness to be involved. The counselor worked with a few students and trained them three days a week for three weeks. Thereafter, they worked on their own time and during the fourth period as tutors and special friends.

Another counselor worked with a small group of students in a counseling situation. After the group was complete, the counselor asked the group members if they would be interested in helping in a similar project with other students. Everyone said yes and they were trained how to lead students through some of the same activities that they had experienced. With the assistance of the trained facilitators, more students were able to participate in the guidance activities while the counselor supervised.

As you work with your peer facilitators, you will learn a lot about helping others. The program forces you to review the basics of the helping process and facilitative responses. It helps you identify brief interventions that can make a positive difference with students. If you begin with a small group, you can learn from your experiences and note things to repeat or do differently when you expand the program. In addition, your first group may also be the nucleus for a second and larger group of peer facilitators.

Train for Special Projects

If your time is limited and you are unable to put a comprehensive peer training program in place, it might be best to train the facilitators for a particular project that you have in mind. Give the facilitators a few concepts and then focus specifically on skills as needed for the project.

One counselor trained students to meet and greet new students to school. An organized set of procedures were reviewed, including how a set of slide pictures would be shown and how a tour of the school might be conducted. Peer facilitators were prepared to ask open-ended questions at different points and to lead a student through a set of materials and activities.

Training Can Be Treatment

When you first get started, you will probably work with students who are among the top 25% academically. They have the support of teachers to miss, on occasion, some class time while participating in helping projects. In addition, top students are easy to work with and they make training go faster.

Yet, some less academically able students who need special attention can benefit from being peer facilitators. They may not be among the top students. Some may even have been referred to you for counseling or for special help because they are having adjustment problems. In this case, some may be candidates for the peer facilitator group because training could be the treatment that they need. Training might be more appealing to them than counseling or some other form of help.

Roger, a fifth grade boy, was having trouble adjusting in school and following school rules. The counselor talked with a group of students, including Roger, about being peer facilitators. The group talked about the causes of misbehavior in school, the problems that students have in adjusting to situations in school, and the consequences of inappropriate behavior. They talked about ways in which they could help students who had such problems and they learned how to facilitate problem-solving. Then, they were matched with younger students as part of a helping project. Roger willingly took part in the short training program (10 half hour sessions). He worked with his special friend for about three weeks. His classroom teacher soon became aware of how Roger was behaving better in class, although he still had moments when he regressed to old ways. Training was treatment for Roger. He benefited as much, or more, than the boy whom he was assigned to help.

In another instance, a trainer worked with adolescent boys who had been placed in a social adjustment center in Orlando, Florida. The boys were labeled by authorities as misfits and none were living with their families. All had been suspended from school. A counselor decided peer facilitator training would be treatment for them.

The boys participated in 12 one-hour training sessions. They were generally negative and uncooperative during training, enough to make the trainer wonder if the planned project should be undertaken. The project consisted of taking the boys to an elementary school where they were to lead fourth grade students through structured group activities for four sessions.

On the day the boys were picked up to go the school, some dramatic changes had taken place. They had cut their hair, put on their best clothes, and were asking pointed questions about how they could help. They wanted to know more about what they might do if the children acted as they had done during training. They obviously wanted to do a good job.

The result was an unqualified success. The young students enjoyed working with the boys from the Center and the boys felt appreciated, special, and needed. "When are you coming back, Frank?" asked one little girl. Upon Frank's return to the Center, he talked about his group, his kids, and how special they were to him. Supervisors at the Center reported that the boys were positively changed because of the experience, which reached its full effect only when the project was implemented (Myrick and Sanborn, 1983).

It appears that training is more palatable to some students who need help because it says, "We need your help" instead of "You need my help." Training alone may not be enough; rather, it is the implementation of training that apparently fosters change.

Link the Program to Learning

All guidance programs need to be linked to helping students learn more effectively and efficiently. Peer facilitator programs are no exception. There seems to be ample evidence that tutors gain as much or more than the students whom they are tutoring. Therefore, both the peer facilitator and the student receiving the facilitator's help benefit from the experience. In addition, peer facilitator programs may also be viewed as a study in social skills or perhaps an application of leadership training.

All programs need to be evaluated. When learning outcomes (e.g. Appendix B) are identified and performance standards are outlined, there can be little doubt that peer facilitator programs have their place in schools. Most important, as teachers and administrators see how learning is enhanced, more support for the program will be gained.

Participate in Networking

Networking is a popular term used to describe a means by which people communicate with one another about special interests. They do this through newsletters, professional seminars and conferences, computer terminals, personal letters, and telephone conversations. You can do some informal networking at the local level with other counselors who share similar interests in peer facilitator programs. Encourage them to share their ideas and explore some of your own thoughts and experiences.

The Hillsborough County Schools, Tampa, Florida, has a mimeographed newsletter which describes various programs, projects, activities, and experiences from peer facilitators, trainers, and counselors in the district. It also includes comments by students and peer facilitators themselves. The newsletter helps link all school programs together, giving them more visibility and appeal to a common interest group. While a similar newsletter might be formed for counselors about general news, the *Peer Facilitator Togetherness* has a special place. It has an editor who assembles news from the different schools across grade levels. It describes things that have happened and what to look for in the future.

Hillsborough County was also among the first to sponsor local conferences where peer facilitators and their trainers meet to participate in workshops, listen to featured speakers, and share experiences. For instance, about 400 peer facilitators from all three grade levels meet for a two-day conference each year. The annual event is covered by local television and newspapers and provides positive visibility for the programs and participants. It has enhanced the reputation of guidance services in the area.

School systems in Hillsborough, Orange, and Broward counties, Florida, formed the nucleus of a statewide convention which is open to peer facilitators and their trainers. Other states also have had state conventions related to peer facilitator programs and peer leadership.

The California Peer Counselor Association has about 100 members. The 1986 spring CPCA conference drew about 1,000 participants. Likewise, the North Carolina Association for Peer Helpers has grown to about 250 members and publishes a statewide newsletter entitled *The Peer Helper*. The association offers annual conferences, drawing between 300 and 500 students, peer program coordinators, and other interested professionals.

Other states which have reported statewide conferences promoting peer facilitator programs and peer leadership efforts include Maine, which publishes the *Peer Priority* newsletter and Pennsylvania, which features the *Peer Education News* for peer educators. It also has The Pennsylvania Peer Counseling/Peer Facilitating Network which was formed by 16 peer program leaders in the state. In addition, special statewide networking efforts have been made in such states as Missouri, Colorado, Massachusetts, Iowa, South Carolina, and Texas. A strong and expanding network of peer programs has also developed in Canada. The list grows rapidly as the interest seems to increase each year.

You can build your own network by identifying counselors and program coordinators in your area who have already started programs. You can also learn more by participating in the local and statewide conferences. You can subscribe to the *Peer Facilitator Quarterly*. The *PFQ* is published by Educational Media Corporation as the official newsletter of the National Peer Helpers Association, a new organization designed to network peer programs on a national level.

Evaluate Programs and Projects

One of the biggest regrets of those counselors who are in their first year of a program is that they did not take time to plan an evaluation of their projects. They under-estimated the impact that the program would have on young people, even a program that is just beginning or one where training did not meet expectations. A project may be new and untried but, given the power of peer facilitators, there is likely to be some gains. Look for them. Measure them. You can use the results to obtain more support for your efforts, to reinforce some things you found which worked well, and to chart some new directions.

Advantages, Limitations, and Conclusion

There are many advantages to having a peer facilitator program in your school. They far outnumber the disadvantages.

Advantages of Peer Facilitator Programs and Projects

1. The program is for all students and it helps students learn leadership skills that can be used throughout life.

2. It encourages more students to become actively involved in helping their schools to have better learning environments. Students communicate more effectively and are more positive with each other. They learn more about how to be sensitive to others and how to stand up for their own rights.

3. More students receive guidance services because there are more helpers in the school. Peer facilitators are the helping hands of teachers and counselors. They help deliver guidance services and, consequently, many more students are involved.

4. It is a highly visible program that brings positive public relations to a school's guidance program.

5. It mobilizes more resources in the school—the power of peer relationships.

6. Training can be treatment for some students, who are less likely to be resistant to learning something when they learn their help is valued and wanted.

7. It is a positive experience for the program coordinator and trainer. It is often reported as the highlight of a counselor's week.

8. It is one of the best staff development programs that counselors can experience. As they teach students how to be helpers, they become more effective school counselors. In their review and teaching of basic facilitative skills, they learn and relearn techniques and strategies which make them more effective in other areas of their jobs.

9. The program is developmental in nature, going beyond crisis interventions. Peer facilitator programs do not replace counselors. To the contrary, they tend to increase student referrals to counselors. Most important, many of these referrals come before events that result in a crisis.

10. Peer facilitators, acting as models for other students and implementing effective interpersonal skills as part of a school day, can help build positive environments which make schools better places to be for everyone, including teachers and counselors.

Limitations of Peer Facilitator Programs and Projects

Being a peer facilitator trainer or coordinator of peer facilitator projects takes time away from direct services that a counselor may give to students who need counseling.

Conclusion

Students at all school levels can be trained to be peer facilitators. They work in four helping roles: special assistant, special friend, tutor, and small group leader. Guidance projects can be organized so that peer facilitators can be used in these roles, helping deliver more services to all students.

Systematic training programs make a positive difference. Such programs center on leadership training, and students learn about themselves and others. The programs benefit the peer facilitators themselves, perhaps as much or more than the students with whom they work in helping projects. Peer facilitator programs and projects are professionally and personally rewarding interventions for counselors.

Chapter 10

Consultation as a Counselor Intervention

Young people are influenced by their environment, which includes many adults. Counseling a student, therefore, may be only partly effective unless attention is given to the adults who are an integral part of a student's life. In this case, consultation is a valuable counselor intervention.

Consultation has been considered a primary function of school counselors for many years, especially at the elementary level. Although some critics have worried that consultation takes time away from counseling, it also has been argued that the two are compatible and they both need to be included in a developmental guidance and counseling program. Consultation with parents, teachers, and administrators is an intervention which can enhance changes in learning environments, benefiting both students and those who are part of their lives.

The Need for Consultation

Dale was a high school science teacher who was concerned about his classes. Although the students appeared to like him at the beginning of the school year, they became less cooperative and more disruptive as the weeks passed. Some students made crude remarks in class which were barely audible, while others carried on distracting side conversations as he was leading class discussions. Sensing he was losing control, he made repeated threats and sent some students to the main office for discipline. He tried penalizing the unruly classes with lower grades and longer assignments, but nothing seemed to work. At mid-point, he began wondering if he would be able to finish the year. Discouraged and disillusioned, he was not sure what to do next.

Trish was a fourth grade teacher who had attended a workshop about learning styles. She wanted to try some ideas, but she was unsure about using grouping procedures. She was concerned that some activities might not work. She thought it would be helpful if she could talk with someone to clarify her thoughts and plans.

Aaron was having problems in school. His grades were below average, although it appeared he had the potential to do better. He complained about headaches and he frequently thought of excuses to stay home instead of attending school. The more school he missed, the farther he got behind his classmates in doing homework assignments. His performance in class was dropping rapidly. His parents decided that it was time to find out more about events at school and what part they played in Aaron's attitude and behavior.

In all three cases, school counselors became involved in consultation. In each situation, a counselor-consultant guided the helping process so that the individuals could resolve their problems to some degree.

While counseling has been an accepted function in most schools, this has not been true for consultation. It was debated as a role and, at one point, it was suggested that counselors not be trapped into losing valuable time with students by working with adults (Mayer and Munger, 1967). In addition, consultation seemed less difficult than counseling, and there was some concern that school counselors would be content to work with adults and ignore the counseling needs of students.

Consultation, however, quickly became an accepted role in elementary schools where developmental guidance was first emphasized. With only one counselor per school in most places, and in some districts counselors working in more than one school, consultation with teachers became a primary intervention because counselor time was limited. It was not possible for elementary counselors to see all the students who needed their services; therefore, counselors consulted with teachers regarding how they might help children.

Some people have claimed that changes in student's behavior are more likely to be accomplished through behavior changes in significant adults in a student's life, perhaps more so than through direct services to the student. Most, however, believe that consultation and counseling are compatible services. They are often integrated into a helping approach (Fullmer and Bernard, 1972).

Consultation with teachers and parents is based on the assumption that these people see their children or students more often than does a counselor. Improving teacher-student or parent-child relationships through consultation may have a more pervasive effect than counseling in a one-to-one relationship. Teachers and parents are in the best position to implement and support helping techniques and strategies.

Consultation Defined

The counselor's consultant role, then, includes working with teachers, parents, administrators, and other educational specialists on matters that involve student understanding and management. It seems evident that consultation is something that happens when significant adults in a student's life get together and talk about ways of helping the student. However, it has not always been clear what happens in those meetings or how to approach them systematically.

The American School Counselor Association described consultation as:

> "...a process of sharing with another person or group of persons information and ideas, of combining knowledge into patterns and making mutually agreed upon decisions about the next step needed" (ACES-ASCA, 1966).

Dinkmeyer (1968) attempted to provide a more comprehensive definition:

> "Consultation involves sharing information, ideas, coordinating, comparing observations, providing a sounding board, and developing tentative hypotheses for action. In contrast to the superior-inferior relationship involved in some consultation, emphasis is placed on joint planning and collaboration. The purpose is to develop tentative recommendations which influence the uniqueness of the children, the teacher, and the setting" (p.187).

There are still some unanswered questions in these definitions. Who is the client? Who is the consultee? What is the focus of consultation? And, how is consultation different from other helping approaches and interventions?

Caplan's work (1970) is considered a major reference point for defining consultation, especially in terms of mental health counselors. His definition is also appropriate for community-industrial type settings and models. He said,

> "Consultation is a process of interaction between two professional persons—the consultant who is a specialist, and the consultee, who invokes the consultant's help regarding a current work problem with which he is having some difficulty and which he has decided is within the other's area of specialized competence. The work problem involves the management or treatment of one or more clients of the consultee, or the planning or implementation of a program to cater to such clients" (p.9).

Caplan emphasizes that the problem is a work-related one and uses the term "client" to denote the external unit or third party who is the primary concern of the "consultee." His definition is further restricted to those professional interactions in which the consultant has no responsibility for the client. The responsibility for implementing a plan developed through the course of consultation remains with the consultee. This approach is not only aimed at helping a consultee with the particular problem that has been presented, but also at increasing the consultee's general level of competence so that the consultee may be more effective later when similar problems arise.

The Consultation Process

Generally speaking, the external unit or third party causes some uneasiness or discomfort in the consultee, enough to make the person want to seek out a consultant for help. The consultant and consultee talk about matters and, through the process of consultation, a plan of action is identified which is then implemented by the consultee.

Using Figure 10.1, the process can be illustrated. Let's assume a student has become increasingly disruptive in a teacher's classroom and causes the teacher some concern (No. 1). Eventually the teacher experiences enough discomfort to seek some help from a school counselor (No. 2). The counselor-consultant and teacher share information, explore ideas, and arrive at a plan of action (No. 3). The teacher, or consultee, then puts the plan into action with the student (No. 4).

Developmental Guidance and Counseling

Figure 10.1

The Consultation Process

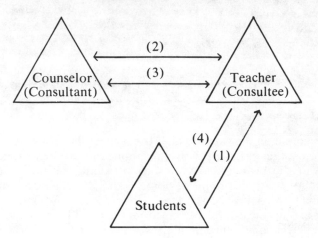

Faust (1968) argued convincingly that the consulting and counseling relationships are distinctive and differ in several ways. He noted that

> "...the primary differences can be found in (a) focus and (b) the kinds of relationships that are developed.... The consultant focuses on some unit external to the consultee. In the case of a consultant to a teacher, the external unit my be a child, instructional method, course content, etc.... A second major difference... is found in the kinds of relationships established outside the consultation and counseling settings. Since in consultation the chief focus is on a unit external to the self of the consultee, the personal risk is not as great as it is in counseling, where internal units (the person of the counselee) receive a majority of attention" (p.33).

The relationship to the consultee is more objective and exterior to self, while that of the counselor is more personal and subjective. Although counseling and consultation relationships both involve self-disclosure and the other facilitative processes, the nature of the relationship is different.

Some of the differences between counseling and consultation are shown in Figure 10.2. In the counseling relationship, the counselor focuses primarily on the counselee (No. 1) who is the client. The third party or outside unit (students) receives only secondary emphasis (No. 2). In counseling, the students are viewed only in terms of how they come into the life space of the teacher, their roles, their impact, their meaning, and their influence on the teacher.

In the consultation relationship, however, the counselor-consultant assists the teacher (No. 2) to talk about feelings, self-perceptions, and personal problems, but only as related to the external unit—the students (No. 1).

For example, in the case of Dale, the teacher described above, the school counselor talked with him about the problems that were happening in his classes. As he began to talk, he interjected the idea that he was still living at home with his parents and that this complicated his life. He wondered aloud if he should find different living arrangements and perhaps then he would feel better about himself. His unhappiness made it difficult for him to prepare his lesson plans.

In a counseling situation, the counselor might think, "What are the underlying sources of conflict between the client and his parents, and what has prevented the client from doing something about this conflict and his unhappiness?" Dale might be asked to talk more about his relationship with his parents. In consultation, however, this information is only useful as it is related to the external unit and the counselor might be thinking, "How is what is happening at home related to his classroom effectiveness? What are some things that can be done to resolve some of the problems that are confronting him here at school?"

When troubled teachers have an opportunity to work with a consultant, they sometimes try, at either a conscious or unconscious level, to manipulate the counselor-consultant into a counseling relationship. If successful, then the primary focus and greatest amount of time in the session would be given to discussion of personal insecurities or problems instead of how those experiences are related to school work and what can be done in the work situation.

Three Types of Consultation

Consultation may be viewed as crisis, remedial, or developmental. During *crisis consultation*, the counselor-consultant works with a consultee who is experiencing an urgent problem. For instance,

Figure 10.2

Counseling and Consultation Relationships

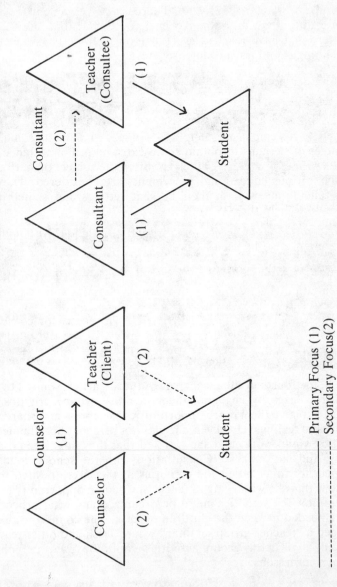

Primary Focus (1)
--------- Secondary Focus(2)

two girls were teasing each other in class and suddenly a fight between them erupted. The teacher asked the counselor for help in how to work with the girls. This type of case usually involves emergency first aid approaches. There is a "hurry up and fix it" attitude during consultation. When people wait to consult about matters that have reached a critical stage, there is always more psychological stress and defensiveness.

In *remedial consultation*, the consultee may not be experiencing a crisis, but senses that one could develop unless some action is taken. Particular behaviors or events may signal a teacher that a student is headed toward a problem and that some intervention is needed. This emphasizes helping a student to make up some deficiencies or perhaps to obtain some extra help. For instance, students with learning disabilities are often the subject of staffings in which various educational placements are considered. They are not functioning well in their current settings and something is planned to help them.

The third type is called *developmental consultation*. Although this type might also be seen as preventive, the emphasis is more on helping to create facilitative conditions and to improve the learning environment as part of the growth process. Developmental consultation is concerned with learning climates and educational processes. It focuses on the needs and interests of all children, instead of only those who have problems. The counselor-consultant works as a behavior and relationship specialist, helping consultees (teachers and parents) to explore their attitudes, behaviors, and interactions which influence student growth.

Trish, the fourth grade teacher introduced earlier, wanted to help children learn by engaging them in more group activities. She wanted to give them more opportunities to express and share their ideas and feelings. However, she was not sure that her planned activities would work, and she worried that they might be no more than "fun and games." Consultation with the school counselor helped her think about the activities as they were related to the lessons that she was trying to teach. She had an opportunity to talk about how the activities might be organized and what procedures were needed to keep the children on task. The counselor also arranged a "teacher group seminar" where Trish and other teachers talked about how group activities could be used to enhance classroom lessons.

Parent effectiveness training and child study groups (e.g. Dinkmeyer and McKay, 1976) might be viewed as developmental approaches to consultation. The meetings feature discussions about typical concerns and general ways to improve family relationships and living conditions. If parents come to a counselor and ask for help because they are worried that their child is abusing drugs, the problem is more specific. Therefore, the other types of consultation would be indicated.

Consultation also may be classified as individual or group. It may be viewed in terms of who is present when it happens. For example, one might use such terms as parent consultation, teacher consultation, in-service teacher training, case conference, staffing, guidance committee meeting, child study group, teacher seminars, and so forth. Still another means of classifying consultation is by methods or theories used (e.g. behavioral consultation). All these, however, can be related to the three types described above and to the four different approaches described below.

Four Approaches to Consultation

There are four basic approaches to consultation. These might be described as general modes or perspectives. They each have a special focus and they give direction to the consultation process.

Diagnostic-Prescriptive Approach

This approach is the oldest and most established of all approaches to consultation, regardless of field or setting. The counselor-consultant is asked to help analyze a situation or problem and then to arrive at a recommendation or prescription.

The diagnostic-prescriptive approach is used most often during child study meetings or staffings. Teachers, counselors, school psychologists, social workers, and administrators may be present to discuss a case. Information is presented and analyzed. Alternatives are considered and, finally, a recommendation is made regarding the educational placement of the child.

In the case of Aaron, mentioned earlier, the boy had some learning problems. Could these have been related to some learning disabilities? Was he lacking in some basic skills that needed attention? Were there physical problems that prevented him from learning? What was his tested academic aptitude and was he in the best class for him? These and other questions might be answered in a staffing or child study meeting, at which time some decisions could be made based upon the pooled judgment and recommendations of those at the meeting.

Staff Development and Training Approach

Sometimes people lack certain skills in their work which prevent them from being successful or from doing more. On occasion they need to review their skills and attitudes or to be stimulated to think about new ideas and techniques which could be used in their work. This might be done through staff development and training approaches to consultation.

Consultants from outside a school are often asked to lead teachers through skill development activities. Typically, this is done as part of staff development meetings and happens as part of preparation for a school year. It sometimes happens on special days during the year that have been set aside for staff development. However, the training approach need not be limited to these occasions.

One counselor-consultant listened to a teacher describe how frustrated she was in working with a child who seemed unresponsive and who refused to participate in class. After some discussion, the consultant concluded that this teacher lacked some classroom management skills and might benefit from talking with other experienced teachers. Three "rap sessions" with four teachers were arranged on Wednesday afternoons, following the time when students were dismissed from school. The informal sessions lasted about 30 minutes, but the counselor-consultant focused the brief discussions on teacher concerns. Later, it was decided to add two more meetings to which the counselor invited a specialist in the school district to talk about a few specific classroom management skills. The teachers then applied the techniques and talked about their results.

Caplan (1970) suggested there are typically four questions to consider when a consultee presents a problem: Lack of knowledge? Lack of skill? Lack of self-confidence? Lack of objectivity? He described in detail some strategies for working with consultees who have a lack of objectivity, suggesting that the consultant not use counseling or therapy as a means of helping the person become more objective about a case. Others believe that sometimes brief counseling may be appropriate for some consultees whose personal styles or problems prevent them from working well.

Staff development and training can directly address the lack of knowledge and skill. It can also give people more self-confidence and occasionally help them gain a different perspective so they can be more objective.

Case Management Approach

The case management approach to consultation focuses on a particular case that is of concern to a teacher or consultee. The third party, usually a student or group of students, has a problem which is affecting the consultee in some way.

When the consultant talks with the consultee about a case, there are some typical steps that are part of the consultation process: 1) Identify the problem; 2) Identify a desirable outcome in operational terms, so that one will know if the outcome has been achieved; 3) Observe the situation for relevant information; 4) Identify the events or behaviors that affect students; 5) Develop a plan around these behaviors and events; 6) Try out the plan; and 7) Observe the results and compare what happened with what was desired (Lauver, 1974).

There are, of course, other ways to describe these basic stages. Different terms can be used. Perhaps the most important factor is: Can the consultee be facilitated to talk about the case in a systematic way so that some plan of action can be obtained and that a plan can be implemented by the consultee?

Process Approach

Sometimes the problem rests not in the outside unit but in the system where the outside unit resides. More specifically, the problem may not be the student as much as the environment in which the student lives or works.

When the system or environment is a dysfunctioning one, attempts at resolving problems can be frustrating and unproductive. If the problem, for example, is the classroom environment or teaching style of a teacher, then attention to a student's disruptive behavior alone may prove futile. The student may be behaving appropriately to a set of events or conditions which evoke disruptive behavior. Most teachers and parents do not see themselves as part of the problem, and they prefer to keep the focus on the outside unit or third party.

This is a difficult approach to use. It recognizes that decision-making processes, values, interpersonal relationships, traditions, rules, and regulations often influence the way in which people solve their problems with a third party. More specifically, a teacher may feel locked in to some school rules and procedures which prevent some creative solutions to a problem. Or, the same teacher may have a conflict of values with a student, or perhaps classroom procedures may be arbitrary, one-sided, and lack objectivity.

In this approach, the consultant attempts to help consultees increase their awareness of the system in which they are working and the personal system that they tend to use when making decisions, solving problems, and setting goals. A person's strengths and weaknesses in the system are considered, and particular attention is given to the way in which the consultee communicates with others within that system. This is preferably a joint effort when it comes to analyzing the situation. Often certain cases stimulate consultees to examine the system more carefully. Some consultation cases are catalysts for effecting changes in ineffective systems.

System is different from structure. Structure refers to such things as school buildings, number of faculty and staff, classroom space, school curricula, books, materials, and time schedules. System refers to the interpersonal relationships that are within that structure and the process by which decisions are made. If part of the problem is the system itself, then some efforts can be made to help change the system. Most consultants do not focus on structure unless they are experts in that area and have been requested to help restructure the organization or system.

A combination of all four consultation approaches also is possible, but such a comprehensive approach takes careful planning and experience. It demands skill in the facilitative model and a thorough understanding of the objectives of everyone involved.

Collaboration and Consultation

Some authors have suggested that collaboration and consultation are essentially the same (e.g. Dinkmeyer and Carlson, 1973; Brown and Pate, 1983) and that collaboration may even be a preferred term (Keat, 1974). However, the two are distinct in terms of the degree of responsibility.

In consultation, the consultant assumes no responsibility for helping implement a plan of action, although the consultant will have played an important role in helping the consultee arrive at that plan. That is what the consultation process is about. It is the consultee who must initiate the plan, make decisions about its direction and progress, and evaluate the outcomes. Helping the consultee think through a plan is not collaboration.

Collaboration happens when the consultant agrees to be a part of a plan. In doing so, the consultant loses some objectivity and increases one's ego investment in seeing that the plan works. In collaboration, planning and implementing are a joint effort.

Suppose that a teacher talks with a counselor-consultant about a particular class that is causing a problem. If the consultant offers to talk with the class, or to lead the class through a few self-appraisal activities, as part of preparing them for a new set of rules and procedures that the teacher wants to use, then the consultant has become part of the solution to the problem and must share success or failure of the plan of action. If, at any point during consultation, the consultant assumes responsibility for intervening with the outside unit or third party, then the consultation becomes a collaboration.

This is an important distinction you need to recall when making professional judgments about entering brief counseling, consultation, or collaboration with a person who has asked you for help. Each role gives you a different perspective and suggests different directions that you might proceed, perhaps even different techniques and strategies. The decision is yours, of course, but know what role you are playing and the possible consequences. It is not enough to be a universal helper and to assume all your helping skills will always apply, no matter the situation.

Factors to Consider

Consultation is a helping process that has been ignored for study and research for many years. While the process is going on in work settings almost every day, the level of awareness at which it is happening is usually very low. Subsequently, people do not always follow the best procedures when consulting with others. Here are some factors that you can consider when consultation is a possible intervention.

Who is the client?

As already suggested, the client in consultation is the outside unit or third party. In most cases in schools, it is usually a student or group of students. It is only during process consultation that the client question becomes an issue, since it is then that a consultee's self-confidence, objectivity, and personal style come into play, and may need attention as related to working with students.

This is also true when you consult with parents. Occasionally you may be aware in talking with parents that a student's problem rests within the family structure and system. It is assumed that if the family could resolve some issues at home and become more fully-functioning, then some of the problems that the student is having at school might lessen or disappear. Family counseling might be appropriate and recommended. However, sometimes, as a consultant, you are limited to helping the family think of what can be done for their child. The focus of consultation continues to remain on the child. While some family therapists are discouraged at the thought of working on only part of the problem, and probably not the source of the problem, it is possible that a plan of action aimed at the child and arrived at through the consultation process can ultimately benefit all the family.

You can only do so much in your job. There will be times when you want to do more, especially when you recognize the severe conditions with which a young person is coping while trying to learn in school. Take your gains where you can and use those interventions which give the most payoff for the time invested.

Which consultation approach should be used?

Staffings or child study teams are commonplace in most schools and you will want to perfect your skills in those areas. While the facilitative model will be useful, most of the specific skills and relevant procedures are learned in the context of your job, with each school system providing its own unique structure and set of procedures.

Consultation with groups of teachers (Teacher Seminar) might be a regular part of your weekly schedule. It is in these sessions, perhaps a series of about four or five meetings of 30 minutes each, that a training and staff development consultation approach can be used. While outside consultants can be drawn upon for their expertise, teachers can be excellent resources to one another. They often need only a facilitative consultant to bring them together and to provide a little direction so that they might share their ideas and develop their skills.

Your own professional judgment will determine which consultation approach to use. On occasion, a combination of approaches may be appropriate.

Where and when does consultation happen?

You may consult with teachers individually or in small groups in your office; however, many counselor-consultants in the schools find it helpful to go to areas where teachers work. Because their responsibilities, duties, interests, and commitments often confine them to their work areas, teachers sometimes find it difficult to go to the guidance office unless it is conveniently close to them. While you might arrange a small group meeting of teachers for a teacher seminar in the guidance office, you can also identify times when teaching-teams meet during planning periods and make arrangements to meet with the teams in their rooms.

On some occasions privacy will be essential, as the information shared may be sensitive or confidential. Finding a place without interruptions may not be easy and, for that reason alone, it might be appropriate to meet in your office. Look for opportunities to meet teachers where it is most convenient for them.

Who initiates consultation?

Self-initiated consultation suggests that the consultee is highly motivated and willing to give some time to an issue or problem. However, not all teachers, parents, and administrators are eager to talk about their problems. Sometimes, the counselor-consultant must present the problem.

Other-initiated or invited consultation usually comes because of a person being perceived by someone else as in need of help. In these cases, the consultation process can be more difficult because consultants must prepare consultees for consultation and introduce them to the idea. No matter how much you may want to help, the ultimate responsibility rests with the consultee, including the desire to participate in the consultation process.

It is the consultee who must experience a readiness to work on an issue or problem. It is the consultee who must want to change matters. For some people, to admit that a change is needed is also to admit defeat. To admit defeat is to acknowledge oneself as a failure. This tarnished perception can be a painful one and can make a consultee defensive and uncooperative.

Therefore, if you are asked, for instance, by a building principal to initiate consultation with a teacher or a parent because it appears that the person needs to consider some changes, you will have to plan how to introduce the consultation process and how to extend an invitation to work with you. A referral to you might be clearly justified, but your first task is to help the consultee become a willing participant in consultation.

Sometimes confrontation can be effective, but preferably you will already have had some "chips in the bank"—a positive relationship built on high facilitative responses. A straight-forward and candid approach may have merit, but it is also risky. If you tell teachers, for example, that their principal was concerned about their classroom management and it was suggested that you work together on the problem, you could get even more resistance to change than normal. Perhaps it would be more effective to get a teacher to first talk generally about some classroom experiences, with the intent of learning how the teacher views the situation.

Imagine that a counselor says to you, "I was told that you are having some problems with some students in your class and one of our assistant principals asked me if I could help you. Where would you like to start?" Such a statement might ruffle your feelings and you might say to yourself, if not aloud, "Who do you think you are?" On the other hand, if you were asked to talk about your work and experienced a genuine interest, then you might be willing to share more about some of your concerns.

Contrast the former question with these questions: "At this time of the year, what would you say has been one of the most satisfying aspects of your work... and then, what about one of the most dissatisfying?" Or perhaps, "How do you think the students see the class at this point?" These open-ended questions might help a teacher develop the right frame of mind for entering into consultation.

If you need to call in parents for "consultation," you might consider doing those things that help the parents talk first, giving you a chance to be a facilitator and to let them see how understanding, caring, and accepting you can be. After they have opened with some of their ideas, you might then share your thoughts.

When a consultee is confronted or approached because of a referral, it is an uncomfortable feeling to be singled out as someone in need of help, even when the person senses that need. There is an initial feeling of being evaluated, judged, and labeled as inadequate. Ironically, even when a person has initiated consultation and has helped identify the problem, these same unpleasant feelings can come rushing in to create defensiveness. You may experience a person pulling away, perhaps saying, "Well, I guess it really isn't that much of a problem, and I'm sorry if I bothered you. Your time is too important to talk about such matters."

Is consultation confidential?

Generally, the same ethical standards that apply to counseling are also true for consultation, including the right to privacy or confidentiality. Likewise, it is your duty to report to authorities those situations which are regulated by law (e.g. child abuse, threat of suicide, or bodily harm to others).

If you receive information that you believe needs to be reported to other professionals or authorities, you can encourage the person to make a report or you can go with that person to assist in making a report. You are legally bound by professional ethics and have no choice in some matters.

A consultant must be perceived as a trustworthy person before a consultee will explore matters in detail and be open to looking at changes. Trust is a critical factor in consultation relationships. It should not be violated, except in the most troublesome cases.

Individual or group consultation?

The consultation process can be used with a group or an individual. The group approach may be the most effective and efficient use of a counselor-consultant's time and energy.

The group might work toward a common goal, with each member contributing some part to a joint effort. For instance, a high school social studies department may consult with a school counselor regarding the high number of students who are failing. Or, maybe the teachers want to talk about what can be done with seniors whose graduations are in jeopardy because of classroom performance. While each teacher might devise an approach to help improve the situation, the group might decide upon a more comprehensive plan where teachers work together toward a desired outcome.

Teacher seminars and department meetings are, therefore, a favored approach to consultation. Besides obtaining a joint effort, the consultation process is usually enhanced because there are more people facilitating each other to think about the problem and offering support, understanding, and experience. The group has more potential to be resourceful than one-to-one consultation.

Yet, some individuals may prefer to work alone with a consultant. Sometimes individual consultation helps expedite the helping process since there are less people and fewer dynamics to address. Often it is a matter of personal preference for both the consultant and consultee; but, more often than not, individual consultation is easier to arrange and provides a quicker response.

What are some pitfalls?

Eliciting excessive guilt or defensiveness. Although anxiety can motivate a consultee, overwhelming guilt gets in the way of working through problems. For example, in desperation one group of teachers was using some strict and rigid rules as a means of controlling students. They were using corporal punishment and harsh talk. When they participated in a workshop which focused on new ways of discipline, their methods were unknowingly ridiculed by the outside consultant, who also labeled such teachers as insensitive and incompetent. During the workshop some of the participants became argumentative and later almost uncommunicative. The group was defensive and dismissed the consultant as not knowing much about the real world of education.

If teachers or parents feel too much guilt over what they have been doing in the classroom or at home, it may be difficult for them to be open to new ideas. Guilt forces people to rationalize and to justify their behaviors. It can make them less likely to consider or try new ideas.

An elementary school faculty almost unanimously agreed that their school was different from all the others in the school system because of its student body. The students were from low socioeconomic families and were disadvantaged in many ways. "Nothing works with them," complained a group of teachers as they listened to a consultant who was proposing some new ideas. And, as part of their self-fulfilling prophecy, all new strategies and procedures met with failure. To accept any new ideas and to make them work was the same as admitting that they had been wrong about the children and had failed them because of ineffective methods. It was easier to blame the children for failing to achieve than point to themselves and the system in which they worked.

Being an expert. When teachers and parents have problems with students, they tend to look for simple answers. They hope that an expert will quickly analyze the situation and give them some easy solutions. They do not want to give too much time or to suffer through too many hassles. After all, an expert is supposed to know immediately what to do.

In reality, most counselor-consultants feel uneasy in giving quick advice. Being viewed as a knowledgeable, resourceful, experienced, and willing helper is different from being the "resident expert." The latter perception tends to create distance between counselor-consultants and teachers or parents. The same low facilitative responses (advice, evaluation, interpretation, and reassurance) that limit self-disclosure in counseling also hold true in consultation. Likewise, the high facilitative responses seem to be the most effective in helping consultees think through a problem and assume responsibility for resolving it.

There will be times when you have some expert advice to give, perhaps based on something you have studied or experienced. Timely advice or suggestions are always appropriate, but knowing when to offer them is a mark of an effective consultant.

Talking down to the consultee. Talking down to the consultee often happens when a consultant theorizes too much, using jargon which is presumed to be known by the consultee. It also involves talking too long and too intensely "at" the consultee. Do not get trapped into telling stories about what you once did or what you heard that someone else did, as this can be both boring and inappropriate. Consultees frequently see these stories as irrelevant to their own situations and listen for little clues to show why their situations are different or unique.

Sometimes it is helpful to teach a consultee some new procedures, perhaps even a new theory and vocabulary. But, this is best done within the context of the problem or situation presented by a consultee. The more personal it can be to the consultee, the more likely it will be learned and the better the chance of it being put into practice. This is one reason so many consultants who work as trainers in staff development workshops fail to reach consultees. Instead of personalizing and giving relevant examples, consultants too often use textbook cases or hypothetical incidents. It puts a consultee in an inferior position and one conclusion typically reached is: "This consultant really doesn't understand me or what's happening here."

Results at any cost. Someday you will be asked for help in managing a student, but it will appear that the problem rests more with the consultee than with the student. The consultee will ask for your assistance in getting a student to adjust, to stay on task, to keep in line, to shape up, to be cooperative, or to do what is told. The consultee may not have talked with the student or even considered the student's point of view. You, in turn, may be in an untenable position of helping develop a plan of action which meets the needs of the teacher but not the student.

Some consultants have relied on behavior modification strategies, for instance, to help teachers manage their classes. In behavior consultation, teachers are encouraged to manipulate the contingencies in their classes through reinforcers, discrimination procedures, and behavior consequences. There is nothing wrong with this, unless a teacher favors obedience more than achievement or, perhaps, control more than participation in the exploration of ideas.

What if a teacher prefers "in-seat behavior" and "on-task behavior" at the expense of group discussion and spontaneous discovery methods? What if the teacher's lesson plans are dull and unimaginative, and students find it difficult to sustain interest? A plan to reinforce control or obedience might ignore the issue of creating a positive and effective learning environment. As a consultant, you should be wary of helping a consultee devise a plan which reduces the consultee's anxiety to the detriment of student learning and well-being.

Failing to follow up. A common mistake is to limit the consultation process to the point of talking about a plan and then not finding out what actual steps the consultee took. Talking with a consultee is only the first part. A plan still needs to be implemented.

A consultant can, on occasion, provide timely support and encouragement by following up a consultation meeting, especially when a new method or technique is being used by the consultee. Away from the eyes of others, including the consultant, the consultee may feel inadequate in putting a plan into action. Self-doubt may creep in and commitment may dissipate. Too frequently, the lament of a teacher after consultation is, "I plan to get started right way, but I just haven't had time to get around to it yet."

It is also important for those consultees who have been successful with a plan of action to have an opportunity to talk about their experiences. A follow-up meeting in which consultees tell what was accomplished can be enjoyable, and it can help reinforce those behaviors which contributed to success.

While these pitfalls have been discussed in terms of teachers, they can also be applied to parents and others. Avoiding the pitfalls means emphasizing the positive aspects of consultation and being systematic about the process.

A Systematic Approach to Case Consultation

Myrick (1977) proposed a seven-step model for consultation that provided a systematic approach to facilitating a case. A case is viewed as a situation in which a consultee is having a problem with a third party or client (student). These steps have been extended and modified and are reviewed below. An outline of the model is shown in Figure 10.3.

Step 1: Identify the Problem.

Identifying the problem tends to be the most difficult part of consultation and requires the consultant to concentrate on being a listener and facilitator, especially at the beginning. Regardless of the problem presented, which may not be the one that eventually receives special attention, the consultee needs to talk out or "get out" the feelings, impressions, and reactions about the situation or case. As the consultee vents feelings and focuses on important issues, the consultant is establishing the conditions of a helping relationship. Generally, the more intense the crisis, the more important it is to listen and establish that relationship. The amount of time given to this step is often in proportion to the nature of the problem and the intensity of emotions.

Audrey was a high school teacher who taught typing and business education courses. She was an experienced teacher, but her reserved personality made it difficult for her to establish order in her classes. Some students were disrespectful and defied her directions. Several students chose to get in small groups and talk, instead of working on their assignments. A few left the classroom and walked the hallways. Two girls said such things as, "Oh, you don't know what you're talking about," and "Why don't you just leave us alone?" It appeared that less than half of her classes were doing their assignments and trying to stay on task. Audrey was discouraged. The central administration was concerned. Some of the more cooperative students were becoming irritated and angry.

Audrey's situation can be used to illustrate the systematic approach to case consultation. She was desperate and eager to work with a counselor-consultant. A few excerpts are presented here.

The Case of the Desperate Teacher

Consultant:
What can you tell me, Audrey, about your situation? Help me get some idea of what is happening.

Figure 10.3

The Systematic Facilitative Approach to Consultation

Step 1: Identify the Problem

Be a listener. Help the consultee to tell about the situation.

Step 2: Clarify the Consultee's Situation

Be a selective listener, giving attention to the following:

a) Feelings—consultee's and client's
b) Specific behaviors—consultee's and client's
c) Consultee expectations in the situation
d) What the consultee has done up to this point
e) Positive consultee attitudes and and behaviors

Step 3: Identify the Goal or Outcomes

Specify the outcome in observable behaviors.

Step 4: Observe and Record Behaviors.

Obtain some baseline data on desireable or undesireable behaviors.

Step 5: Develop a Plan of Action—The Consultee's Intervention

This is usually something that can be done within the next two weeks.

a) What are some possible interventions that the consultee might do? Of these, which one is most appealing as a first step?

b) How might the intervention work? (i.e. Role-play, discuss consequences, practice skills, and think about procedures).

c) When will the first step be taken?

Step 6: Consultee Initiates the Plan

Step 7: Follow-up

This provides an opportunity for evaluation and discussion of next steps.

Audrey:
The kids are driving me crazy. Nothing is going right. I know that I'm a good teacher, but they just won't behave. How can I teach them anything if they won't listen. It's just awful.

Consultant:
You're really frustrated... at your wit's end.

Audrey:
Ooohh! ...It can be so terrible. (Audrey gets tears in her eyes).

Consultant:
It's so discouraging... and you're feeling really down right now.

Audrey:
I really am. I just don't know what to do. I've tried, believe me, I've tried. But nothing works. I know that Mr. Helstrom (the vice principal) *is getting tired of me sending kids to his office, but they* (the administration) *don't help. They just send them back and nothing is changed. The kids cause problems but I'm the one that is getting in trouble. I know it doesn't look good on my record.*

Consultant:
It doesn't seem fair to you.... You're not feeling much support right now.

Audrey:
You just can't believe what goes on. Those kids are crazy and they don't care who they hurt.

Consultant:
Which one of your classes concerns you the most?

Audrey:
It's the third period class. Joanna and Valerie are there. And, Cynthia, too. They are so weird... and mean to me.

Consultant:
What are some examples of the things that the girls do.

Audrey:
Well, I'll ask Joanna to do something and she will just stare at me, not saying a word. She doesn't move and she doesn't do what I say—just stares at me. Then Valerie will start giggling. When I ask her to stop and get back to work, she says crude things like, "Oh, up yours," or she might say, "Yes, ma'am," but in a sarcastic way. Then, others in the class get to laughing and things fall apart. It happens every day. They are the ringleaders... and....

Consultant:
So they start something and then soon everybody is involved... and you feel out of control.

Audrey:
Yes, that's it, exactly. I can't spend all my time talking with those girls and at the same time try to teach the rest of the class. I'm not sure what to do.

Consultant:
Okay, what else do they do?

Audrey:
The other day Joanna was working on her nails and talking with Valerie. When I told them to take their seats and get to work, they said that they had already done their work (a typing lesson). *I asked them where it was and they gave me the run-around. I knew they were lying and told them so. Then they said that I was unfair and the worst teacher that they had. They left, saying they were going down to Mr. Helstrom's office and file a complaint about me. Can you imagine that?*

(The consultant was taking notes during this part, responding to the consultee's feelings, asking questions, and clarifying matters. Audrey needed an opportunity to tell her story and she also needed someone who would help her identify specific behaviors which contributed to the problem, instead of generalizations and labels which characterized it.)

Consultant:
(After some more questions) *All right, let me see if I understand what you've said. The class that upsets you the most is third period and, more specifically, there are two girls who tend to disrupt the class. They refuse to do their work, clown around in the room and sometimes walk out. They talk back to you and embarrass you when you give them instructions, and others stop work and laugh when you and the girls get going at each other.*

Audrey:
Yeah, that's about it.

Step 2: Clarify the Consultee's Situation

Most people talk rapidly about a lot of ideas. They have a tendency to jump from one topic to another and several pieces of information may be introduced in a rambling way. It is common for people to string several ideas together and to digress from one point to another, sometimes presenting irrelevant information. A consultant can become lost when a consultee tries to explain a problem. For the same reason, the consultee is probably experiencing some confusion.

In this second step the consultant is a selective listener. Using high facilitative responses, the consultant encourages the consultee to talk and to be more precise in thinking about the problem. More specifically, the consultant listens for: a) the pleasant and unpleasant feelings of the consultee; b) specific behaviors of the third party which have influenced the consultee's conclusions and generalizations; c) what the consultee seems to expect of the third party; d) what the consultee has already done to the current point in time; and e) any positive attitudes and behaviors that are in the situation, especially those experienced by the consultee.

Each of these considerations tend to flow sequentially in Step 2. High facilitative responses are the glue and catalytic action for each part. For example, facilitative feedback as a compliment seems appropriate because consultees need to hear something positive about themselves, after discussing at length the unpleasantness of the case. A compliment about something heard or noticed can provide consultees extra incentives. It encourages them to go beyond venting feelings and ideas, and wondering if they are talking too much or appearing inadequate.

In the case of our typing and business education teacher, Audrey, the counselor-consultant noted a list of seven specific problem behaviors mentioned in the first session. These behaviors provided a focus and, when placed on a five point Likert—type rating scale, they also made up a baseline from where the consultee was starting in consultation (See Figure 10.4).

1. Starts assignments when assigned
2. Completes assignments
3. Follows directions
4. Stays in seat or at work station
5. Argues with teacher
6. Distracts other students through loud talk
7. Makes crude remarks (e.g. "Crap," "Shove it")

The following excerpts are taken from the second meeting between the counselor-consultant and Audrey, as they attempt to identify some target behaviors.

Consultant:
These are some of the things that we talked about last time (Shows Audrey the list, repeated on three sheets of paper). *We can take a closer look at them this time. Please rate each of these girls, Joanna, Valerie, and Cynthia, and then rate the class generally.*

Audrey:
I don't know. That's so hard to do. This is only part of what they do. For example, yesterday the whole class was just sitting around talking. When I asked them to get busy, Joanna said, "Hey, it's party-time. Wanna party?" and started a little dance. I told her to sit down and she did. But, when I turned around, she went to talk with Julie. If I could just get her out of my class, things would be so much better.

The consultant realized that Audrey was defensive. She may have been worrying about who would see such a rating or what purpose it served. Or, upon seeing the items, her frustration may have been heightened and it stimulated her to vent more of her feelings and wishful thinking. The consultant took time to again respond to her feelings, clarify what was said, and present the list.

Consultant:
So, it seems that many things are happening and this list has only a few things that concern you. What others would you add, then? (Audrey looks over the list and, using a number from the rating scale, rates each girl.)

Consultant (later):
All right, it seems from what you've said that numbers 4 and 5 concern you the most. I'm wondering if it might be best to pick one or two items from this list to work on, then perhaps some others will also start to improve. All of them, of course, will get some attention.

Audrey:
Okay, let's say we pick the last one, number 7. What are you going to do about that? What should I do?

Step 3: Identify the goal or outcomes

Goals can be general or specific. In consultation, specific goals usually focus on observable behaviors or outcomes. It is more effective to state such goals in the positive, suggesting what you want to accomplish, instead of want you do not want to have happen (e.g "Don't interrupt" can become "Each person gets a turn" or "Raise your hand when you want to participate."

In the case of Audrey, it may seem as though she is now looking for advice. Generally, it is best to avoid rushing in with advice or a quick recipe for change. First, consultees are somewhat suspicious of specialists and frequently report, "Their advice never works." Or, "They don't understand the situation." And, "They have great ideas, but they are not practical."

Since most people tend to resist advice, it is not given hastily, even when a person asks for it. The consultant also wants to avoid early interpretations of behaviors, either of the consultee or the third party (e.g. "Joanna defies you because she is striving for attention and believes that others in the class look up to her when she talks back to you"). Interpretations can be helpful when they are viewed as part of a rationale for a plan of action; but, like advice, they are too often seen as easy textbook answers and insignificant to the problem.

Instead of premature advice or classic interpretations (e.g. Joanna needs understanding because she comes from a broken family and she's angry with the world for giving her a raw deal), the counselor-consultant might first respond to feelings and clarify ideas so that the consultee will share all aspects of the problem. This includes a focus on the feelings and behaviors of both the consultee and the third party.

In our illustration, Audrey has requested the counselor to tell her what to do. The consultant resists the urge to give advice at this point and helps her focus on what has already been done. Why make suggestions if the teacher has already tried them? Or, if she has tried something, it is important to know how she went about it and what resulted.

Consultant:
Well, let me ask you. What kinds of things have you done so far?

Audrey:
Hmmmmmmmmmm! Let me see.... I've told Joanna that she was going to fail the class, if she didn't change her ways, but that didn't seem to make any difference. I've written up several discipline reports and sent them to Mr. Helstrom, who never does anything. And, I've tried to ignore her rude behavior, but that only seems to encourage Valerie and the others to join in. I know I'm not supposed to reinforce Joanna by giving her attention when she does those stupid things, but it's hard not to. Sometimes I get so mad I just walk away so that I don't slap her face.... Well, (embarrassed), *that's what I'd like to do.*

The consultant facilitated some discussion about what had been done, how it was done, and the results. A summary was attempted, emphasizing events that contributed to the problem, the teacher's and students' feelings, and how these feelings were related to teacher and student behaviors.

Consultant:
All right, what else could you do?

Audrey:
I'm not sure, everything seems so impossible.

Consultant:
It's not easy to think about other possibilities. Things look a little bleak right now.

Audrey:
Yes, but maybe I could call the girls' parents in and talk with them. That might work for Valerie, but I understand Joanna isn't even living with her parents any more. That girl has problems and, you know, she's smart enough to do the work too.

Consultant:
Although you're discouraged and wondering what to do next, you can see how Joanna has the potential for doing more work, even though she's not getting much support at home.

Audrey:
That's right. Sometimes she surprises me. She might come in and sit right down, do her work, and say nothing. The next day; Whammo! ...and it starts all over. She goes berserk.

Consultant:
So, there are some days when things go better and Joanna is not so disruptive. You appreciate those times.

Audrey:
Yeah, but they are too far apart. If Joanna could be transferred out, most of my problems would disappear. Then, again, Valerie and Cynthia can also be little devils. They can get things going just as much as Joanna.

Step 4: Observe and record behaviors

Baseline data can be helpful in the consultation process, such as the general ratings that Audrey provided the consultant. They were based on a list of behaviors generated from their first meeting. If you do not know your starting point, progress is difficult to assess.

The counselor-consultant listened to Audrey and made a chart of behaviors, as baseline data and so she could get a picture of how often the behaviors were happening. Perceived frequency is acceptable baseline data and it also heightens teacher awareness regarding the extent of a problem. A checklist often takes little time and it can highlight target behaviors that need attention.

Audrey rated all seven behaviors. They were then rated periodically after a plan of action was introduced. A pre-post rating is shown in Figure 10.4 for the three girls.

Step 5: Develop a plan of action

Many writers have suggested that the consultant and the consultee analyze the situation together and jointly develop a plan of action. Although it is the responsibility of the consultee to take the major role in implementing a plan, it is possible that the counselor-consultant could collaborate and play a part in it.

The consultant usually begins this step by asking, "What is something that you want to accomplish or see happen immediately (usually with a week or two weeks)?" Then, this is followed by: "Okay, what are some things that you might do to bring this about?" At this point, the consultant might also add to the list of possible things to do (e.g. "One thing you might consider is..." Or, "What about the possibility of...?"

As a list of possible things to do is studied, an appropriate question for each one might be, "And, how would this be done? Or, "How would that work?"

Finally, the consultee selects a next step from the list. Then, the consultee answers the last question from the consultant, "And, when do you see yourself doing this?" Selecting an immediate next step and identifying a starting time are all essential parts of the consultation process.

Consultant:
All right, Audrey, we've narrowed down some of the things that you might try: 1) Compliment the class when they are on task; 2) Call Joanna aside after class and compliment her when you notice her

Figure 10.4

Teacher Ratings:
Pre-Post Consultation

(Case example)

Behaviors	Joanna Pre	Joanna Post	Valerie Pre	Valerie Post	Cynthia Pre	Cynthia Post
1. Starts assignments when assigned.	1	(3)	1	(3)	2	(3)
2. Completes assignments	3	(3)	3	(3)	3	(4)
3. Follows directions	1	(3)	1	(3)	2	(4)
4. Stays in seat or at work station	1	(3)	1	(4)	3	(4)
5. Argues with teacher	5	(3)	4	(2)	3	(1)
6. Distracts students through loud talk	5	(2)	5	(3)	3	(1)
7. Makes crude remarks ("Crap" Shove it")	5	(2)	4	(1)	1	(1)

★ ★

The 5-point Rating Scale

5	4	3	2	1
Very Often	Often	Some-times	Seldom	Very Seldom

being on task and starting assignments on time; 3) Set up some situations in which assignments are fun, short, and perhaps require cooperation from class members to complete—so that you compliment the girls and the class for their behavior; 4) Change seat assignments so that everyone is at a new station, separating some of those who prefer to talk instead of work; and 5) Announce to the class some of the changes that you plan for them, including some new typing skills games.

Audrey:
That's a lot. Did we talk about all that?

Consultant:
It seems like a lot to do now. Where can you start? Pick one that you can work on first.

Audrey:
Will you be talking with the girls? I need some help in explaining some of the consequences to them. I'll try to change, but they will have to change too.

Consultant:
Would you like me to be present when you talk with them?

Audrey:
Yes, I'm not sure they'd listen to me. I know they'd listen to you.

Consultant:
All right (agreeing to collaborate), let's bring a group of students from your class into my office, including Joanna, and let's talk about everyone's concerns. After listening to them, you can share your feelings and talk about some of the changes you want to make. We can get their reactions and work toward getting a commitment on everyone's part to change the class into something better.

Audrey:
That sound's good. How about next Monday? That would be the best time for me.

Consultant:
Audrey, it hasn't been easy for you and you've been discouraged... enough to make you want to quit. But, you've hung in there and you've been open to exploring some changes that might be made, by you and by some of your students. You are trying to see the positive side of things. I'm proud of you for taking the time and having the courage to explore the situation with me. It makes me want to work some more with you until things are better for you and your students.

Audrey needed support, but more than support she needed understanding, caring, acceptance, and a relationship with someone she could trust while exploring a difficult problem. She needed time to think through the problem and she needed an opportunity to identify those factors which contributed to it. She also needed to be facilitated toward a plan of action, something that could be implemented in a short time and that could be evaluated. She needed a next step, not an elaborate scheme with which to change everything and everybody. The systematic approach to case consultation gave her what she needed.

A Training Approach with Teachers

When teachers think of consultants who provide training and staff development, they often think of external consultants who work out of the central office or who have been hired from outside the school district. This training might be part of pre-service or in-service agreements with teachers, who dutifully sit through various seminars, workshops, and conferences, hoping to learn something that might apply to their work. Some workshops are better than others, but in general, teachers do not evaluate them highly.

Teachers want training that is relevant to their concerns and interests. Therefore, counselor-consultants in a school can provide a valuable service by organizing teacher seminars. Sometimes, a small group will meet to examine some new methods or materials.

In one case, a group of teachers were inspired by the counselor to examine a teacher effectiveness training program. The teachers agreed to meet twice a week for ten 30-minute sessions. The counselor, as consultant, was to have the materials ready, start the group on time, and facilitate the teachers in the structured activities.

After the word spread that the experience was an interesting one and that it gave teachers an opportunity to share ideas and to practice some interpersonal skills which could be used in the classroom and around school, a second group was formed. One group met in the morning before classes started and the other met at the end of the day after classes ended.

An interpersonal and communication skills workshop can be designed for teachers to learn the facilitative model, as outlined in this book. One advantage would be that more people in the same school would have a common professional language in which to communicate about cases and to plan interventions. Support is not enough. Support needs to be accompanied by knowledge and understanding.

After a few brief presentations about the facilitative model, and after studying a few brief handouts, a school faculty could practice the high facilitative responses in groups of three (triads). In this procedure, one teacher talks about a topic, while a second teacher is the facilitator and practices using the high facilitative responses in different combinations. The third teacher observes the process and tells the facilitator what was heard and observed. After three rounds, the three teachers eventually will have experienced each role.

The topics are personalized and they are based on things of general interest to teachers. Teachers are asked to tell something about themselves: 1) When you felt successful as a teacher; 2) When you felt unsuccessful; 3) A child who is of concern to you right now; 4) A child to whom you would like to give a special award; 5) Something you like to do when you are not at school or when you are not thinking about teaching; 6) A special vacation you would like to take, if you had all the time and money you needed; 7) A favorite teacher who had a big influence on your own teaching style; 8) What or who influenced you to become a teacher; 9) A teacher whom you disliked and would not want to work with again; and, 10) A job outside education that you would like to have, if you did not have to worry about training.

These ten topics, and similar ones, are thought-provoking and interesting to teachers, especially when they have some time (approximately four minutes) to share their ideas before listening to the others share their thoughts and feelings in same amount of time. It takes about 15 or 20 minutes to complete a round when triads are used.

When teachers participate in training activities in which they are given an opportunity to put theory into practice and they can get to know one another better through some fun and stimulating topics, there is a tendency for more cohesiveness to develop among a faculty. Faculty members are more cordial and friendly to one another. They feel they can take more risks and break away from old ineffective habits, especially as they learn more about their colleagues and see them open to trying new ideas and skills.

The triad training experience was incorporated into some faculty meetings at one school. The principal decided that such an activity would be an appropriate way to end some faculty meetings, after announcements were made and discussed. By accident, the principal learned that having beginning and experienced teachers in triads together, sharing times when they felt successful and unsuccessful, was encouraging to new staff. Some thought they were the only ones who experienced problems. The more experienced faculty members learned more about their new colleagues and this contributed to a friendly working climate in the school. New friends and more support groups resulted.

Consulting in Child Study Teams

School districts may have different terms for child study, staffings, or educational placement teams, but most have meetings in which different students are presented for study and educational placement.

For example, some child study teams involve the school counselor, school psychologist, classroom teachers, building principal, and social worker. Others who have special information about the child, including parents, can be invited. During a meeting, a "case" is studied, relevant records are examined, test scores interpreted, and concerns are identified. After hearing from various specialists and after some discussion, recommendations are made about the case.

The *1975 Education for All Handicapped Children Act (PL 94-142)* had a profound impact on all education, including the work of school counselors. The national law requires that handicapped children be identified and given an appropriate educational placement, including an Individual Educational Plan (IEP) which outlines ways to help the child. Consequently, a large number of meetings of educational specialists and teams of educators have taken place within the past decade, all for making placement decisions and developing educational plans.

In most schools, the counselor-consultant is part of such teams or staffings. Sometimes counselors are given full responsibility for coordinating a team's meetings and the follow-up procedures. Such staffings can take as much as 30% of a counselor's time, depending upon the student body and the paperwork that must be completed to prepare for a staffing and follow-up. In some schools, the school psychologist takes the lead. In others, it might be an assistant principal or a member of the special education staff.

In almost every staffing related to *PL 94-142*, the diagnostic-prescriptive approach to consultation is used. Emphasis is given to assembling information, analyzing it, and making recommendations. Typically, such case conferences average about 30 minutes each and are often arranged on one day a week in a school.

It is not easy to assemble several teachers, administrators, and specialists. The more organized the meeting, the more time that can be given to other duties. Be cautioned that this type of work can become consuming, especially at certain times of the year. Look for assistance. For example, an aide can assemble and organize a lot of information, materials, and forms. Avoid being a secretary for a group and making appointments for others. If this becomes a problem, talk with the group about it and discuss how the responsibility can be shared among group members.

Unfortunately, there are far too many counselors who do not have a planned work week and who have failed to develop a comprehensive guidance and counseling program. Their programs are frequently out of balance, many times because of staffings and other meetings related to educational placement.

A Process Approach to Rebuilding a Guidance Program

A group of high school counselors decided that they wanted to make some changes in their program. They realized that they had become administrative assistants over the years and that far too much time was spent in scheduling students for classes, making schedule changes, and completing paper work. After a study of their weekly schedules, it was obvious they did not have a developmental guidance program and that some counselor interventions (e.g small group counseling, large group guidance, peer facilitator projects) were seldom used. As criticism of their work and lack of support among teachers increased, they met together to discuss what might be done.

An outside consultant was asked to help. The consultant could easily have been one or two counselors from another school in the district who would agree to facilitate the process, especially if the following plan was used to help the group members process their situation.

The counselors needed to look at the system in which they were working, since the school board had already determined the structure by deciding how many counselors would be employed in the school. Therefore, the consultant began by asking the group to list all the things that an effective guidance and counseling program might accomplish if it were in place.

After the list was compiled on newsprint by using magic markers, it was posted. The consultant facilitated a discussion to help clarify the items. Examples were given. Other factors were added and items were linked. The group was then asked to rank order the top five or six items, things that would be given the highest priority in an effective program. This ranking was done quickly by group consensus.

Next, the group examined each of the highly ranked items in terms of what was currently being accomplished at the school. Each item was rated by the group, using a scale of 0 to 5, according to how well it was being done at the school from the counselors' point of view. Again, discussion was facilitated, with an emphasis on feelings, clarifications and perspectives that others might have (teachers, administrators, students, and parents).

This process required the use of high facilitative responses by the consultant, although the tasks were simple enough. Counselors waxed and waned from becoming defensive and justifying what was happening to admitting that certain things were not going well or were being ignored. They confronted themselves with their own information.

The consultant asked the group to list what they were doing to accomplish those things on the first list. This emphasized the kinds of interventions that were being used. Discussion followed, with additional clarification of how interventions were alike and different. At one point, the consultant introduced the six basic counselor interventions (See Figure 4.1 in Chapter 4) and those items on the second list were categorized according to this format. This was done to conceptualize their work into a manageable plan. Then, it was possible to consider what a typical counselor work week might look like in a balanced comprehensive program.

Having listed what they wanted to accomplish, the group evaluated themselves on how skilled they were in each of the interventions. By this time, the group was becoming more open to looking at possibilities, and defensiveness was dropping since the facilitative responses avoided judging, labeling, or excusing the counselors. Again, a rating (1 to 5) was used to determine perceived effectiveness.

It followed that the group wanted to get more skill training in each of the counselor-intervention areas, except coordination. They reviewed the facilitative model and concentrated on how the problem solving model might be used with various target students. In subsequent training sessions, they focused on identifying target groups of students for small group counseling and discussed how some large group procedures could be used to make scheduling and educational placement more effective and efficient. The counselors also took some time to list and examine the barriers in their work and ways to reduce or work around them.

In this case, process consultation led to training consultation. As training took place and as the counselors tried new techniques with different students, there was a need for case consultation. As some students received counselor attention, more information was also available for staffings, when educational placement was an issue and the diagnostic-prescriptive consultation process was being used.

This same model, with some modifications, might be used with teams of teachers as they consider their teaching methods and materials. It might also be modified for use with parents, who could examine the type of interaction that happens at home and the manner in which the family makes decisions.

Helpful Hints

What is the problem?

The presenting problem may not be the real problem, but it is the best that the consultee can do at the time. As much as 90% of the time, the presenting problem is only a surface problem, perhaps a symptom, and the source of the consultee's frustration and discouragement may be in another area.

Identifying the problem is the most difficult part of consultation. Some consultants prefer to work with whatever is presented to them by the consultee, assuming working with one problem at a time and achieving success will enable a consultee to take a look at the next problem with more confidence. Still others believe that a consultant should take extra time at the beginning, asking questions and clarifying issues to pinpoint the critical problem.

What you see as the major problem, as an objective observer, may not be what the consultee sees. Only the consultee has full knowledge of the events, personalities of the people involved, working conditions, and a host of other factors. It may take a lifetime for a consultant to fully understand or comprehend all the circumstances and details of a problem. It is impossible for the consultant to enter the life-space of the consultee. Therefore, the consultee is in the best position to identify the problem or the parts of the problem that need attention. It may not be productive to second guess consultees, especially if you take time to coach them through a thinking process and facilitate them in exploring their situations.

Resistance to Change

Although a consultee may be sincere in wanting to find a solution to a problem with a third party, there may be some resistance to implementing a plan of action. Putting the plan into action constitutes a change for the consultee.

Sometimes a consultee will feel better having talked about a problem or issue and, subsequently, may not feel the need to develop a plan or to take a next step. Consultation may provide a catharsis experience in which anxiety is reduced and some balance is restored. The problem remains, perhaps to be encountered again.

Of the three types of consultation mentioned earlier, crisis consultation is likely to produce the most anxiety and to result in some action begin taken. There is more discomfort and motivation to change, although defensiveness and tunnel vision can happen when a person is overwhelmed with stress.

Likewise, a remedial approach to consultation usually has more energy behind a desire for change than a developmental approach. Although developmental consultation makes the most sense logically, there is often too little discomfort to generate a commitment to change.

For example, a workshop on interpersonal skills could improve classes and create better learning environments. It is logical and sensible to work on relationships in advance of a crisis. Then, when a crisis happens, positive relationships can be used to hasten the resolution of any problems that have developed. But, that is often too logical, too intellectual, and too far removed from the immediate concerns of teachers. They are concerned about survival, meeting the day-to-day crises and resolving the day-to-day problems. Those are the problems that are on their minds and the ones that they want to talk about.

Consequently, if you are working from a developmental approach, you may want to look for ways to create a little discomfort, perhaps a gentle confrontation. Without some anxiety, there is no motivation for change.

Making Time for Consultation

Finding time for consultation can be a problem for counselors, especially if it is not built into their weekly schedules. One of the best times to consult with teachers is during planning periods and immediately before and after school. Sometimes the first half-hour of the day can be productive, as some teachers arrive early and sometimes they are willing to talk with a counselor-consultant about a case.

Setting aside time for teacher seminars is also important, although the time may not be used each week. The title of a seminar can attract people. Expert consultants or materials may play a minor role, as teachers can become their own resources by sharing ideas and practicing techniques together.

Parent conferences are always difficult to schedule. Some schools have parent nights. But, this is seldom satisfactory since there are often too many parents to be seen in a short time. The parents that need to be seen by school personnel are not often present. A teacher seminar about parent conferences usually is well received by teachers. If teachers, as advisors, met with their advisee's parents on teacher workdays and special occasions, there would be more parent involvement in their children's education.

Key to Multiple Intervention

Consultation is only one intervention that might be used by a counselor to help a student. A multiple intervention suggests that a counselor is using several means to help a student. However, consultation is probably the key to any plan using more than one intervention, since it involves helping people support and cooperate with each other.

For example, as a counselor you might meet with a student individually for a few counseling sessions. Then, based upon what you have learned, you might consult with a student's teachers to see what might be done to help in the classroom. Parents also might be consulted. Perhaps the student could also participate in some group experiences. Multiple interventions involve some form of consultation and are most effective when they are systematically planned.

Share the Challenge

On occasion, teachers or parents will want you to counsel a student. The student may be a problem to them and they want you to make things right through some magical interpersonal process. They want you to find out what makes students do what they do and to correct them. In far too many referrals, teachers do not see themselves as being part of the helping process.

Share the responsibility of helping students change. Share the involvement and the energy that it takes to confront students and to help them become better. Although individual and small group counseling might be effective, it is through consultation that you can obtain teacher assistance and get others to share in the challenges and responsibilities.

Advantages, Limitations, and Conclusion

Advantages of Consultation

1. Consultation mobilizes more resources in the school to help students.

2. Consultation can be a learning experience for a consultee which can be applied in similar situations at later times. In this sense, consultation might reduce the number or change the nature of problems that reach a counselor, especially as teachers and parents learn how to be more effective with students.

3. Helping make one teacher more effective through consultation enables a counselor-consultant to affect the wellbeing and personal development of many students who would otherwise not be seen by a counselor. Counseling for one hour with one student, for example, enables the counselor to reach only one student. Consulting with a teacher who has 30 students in the classroom enables the counselor-consultant to reach 30 students.

4. Some teachers already have positive relationships with troubled students. Through consultation they can be assisted to provide help to these students, perhaps in a more planned and systematic way. Consultation as an intervention is particularly appropriate with these teachers because they may be the best persons in the school to approach the troubled students.

Limitations of Consultation

1. Consultation often happens when people are having a crisis and they may not be ready to examine their own behaviors as part of the cases they present.
2. Consultation is an indirect service which takes time away from more direct counseling interventions.
3. Consultation is often too brief in the schools.

Conclusion

Consultation is different from counseling. It has its own unique place as a counselor intervention. When effective, consultation can help more students receive guidance services. Teachers, especially, can benefit from consulting with a school counselor about students and classroom management. The school counselor, as a counselor-consultant, can also be of help to other school personnel.

The four basic approaches to consultation focus on diagnosis and prescribing a treatment, discussing a case, providing a training workshop, and examining the process of a system (e.g. school or classroom). These approaches may be applied to teachers, administrators, or parents. The facilitative model and problem-solving techniques are integral parts of the consultation process.

Developmental Guidance and Counseling

Chapter 11

The Counselor
as Guidance Coordinator

Since developmental guidance and counseling is an organized effort to personalize education for all students, it requires a cooperative endeavor by all school personnel. Sometimes resource programs and people outside the school should be involved. Everyone works together to share information, exchange ideas, set goals, and identify and implement interventions. The school counselor is often the coordinator of such efforts.

The counselor as guidance coordinator is a common role in most schools. It is the sixth and final intervention around which our comprehensive developmental guidance and counseling program has been organized. While not always a highly visible function, it is a routine part of a counselor's work. Like consultation, coordination is an indirect service to students. It must be approached cautiously, because, without some restraint, it can almost totally consume a counselor's time. In those schools where direct services to students by counselors are valued and protected, many of the guidance coordinating activities are assumed by or shared with others.

Coordination Defined

Coordination as a counselor intervention is the process of managing different indirect guidance services to students, including special events and general procedures. It usually involves collecting data and information, allocating materials and resources, arranging and organizing meetings, developing and operating special programs, supervising and monitoring others, and providing leadership.

Coordination involves organizing and participating in activities related to peer facilitator training and projects, teacher advisor programs, child study teams, student appraisal, staffings, educational placement, paraprofessionals, and student records. It is organizing cooperative efforts to assist students, and it is being an advocate of developmental guidance.

The coordinating function or intervention is influenced by several factors. First, school organizations and grade levels can determine a counselor's coordinating activities. In most elementary schools, for example, there is only one full-time counselor. This counselor must coordinate guidance services to a greater degree than counselors at other school levels. There are not as many school personnel with whom to share the responsibility. There are usually more counselors in a school building at other grade levels, and they can divide some of the coordinating duties. In addition, as students move through different school levels, their needs and interests change.

Tradition also has a way of influencing the coordinating function. "It's always been done that way," is a strong statement and a powerful source of resistance for change. New counselors are indoctrinated quickly by experienced ones regarding the way things work. The "old guard" counselors know what has worked in the past and have established a set of working procedures, which they understand and accept as part of their routine. Any effort to change that routine can be upsetting and threatening. Therefore, some coordinating activities and procedures have lingered far beyond their usefulness because "that's the way it's always been done."

Most administrators do not have a full understanding of developmental guidance and counseling programs. Very few have had courses in guidance. Subsequently, building principals and administrative assistants are most familiar with traditional roles, ones which many of them helped create. Many administrators remember when counselors were first employed to help primarily with career guidance, personal testing, and planning. In far too many high schools, both tradition and a lack of leadership have resulted in counselors becoming administrative assistants. Counselors are frequently asked to collect admission information, make schedule changes, and complete district forms. Some have assumed a host of responsibilities that are unrelated to guidance and counseling, partly because they have been willing to perform such duties and because they seem to have the flexible time to take on an extra task or job.

When school counselors are minimally prepared to function in a comprehensive guidance and counseling program, the coordinating function typically becomes a preferred role for counselors. Some counselors, for instance, are unsure of themselves in leading groups and rarely, if ever, do they use small or large group procedures in working with students. These counselors are shuffled off to some unrelated duties which are convenient to administrators. There are some counselors who are afraid to work with disruptive students, perhaps because they are uncertain of what to do or they are convinced that nothing can be done with such students except to give them warnings. Lack of skill and self-confidence is the breeding ground for counselors who spend all their time providing indirect, rather than direct, services to students.

Finally, new demands and trends can influence the coordinating activities of counselors. When a primary education bill was passed in the state of Florida in 1979, it was welcomed by many administrators and counselors because it emphasized early identification of learning problems in grades K-3 and it helped fund more school counselor positions. While it added a degree of job security for elementary school counselors, it also added more coordinating duties. Child study and placement are typically part of a counselor's coordinating function. However, the new legislation required more information and more child study meetings, all of which took counselor time away from direct services to children.

A common complaint among school counselors has to do with the many requests they receive for information about students. These requests are often given to them when time is limited. Apparently, there are many people who perceive counselors as having enough time to gather information. In one case, an urgent request came from a superintendent, who suddenly had thought that it would be a good idea to write a note of personal congratulations to each graduating senior who had earned some type of award or recognition at school. Since graduation ceremonies were near, the task of collecting the special information was passed on to the counselors, who always seems to be available to respond to such requests on the spur of the moment.

Coordination as a Counselor Intervention

Coordination has not received much attention as a counselor intervention since it was identified some years ago as one of three major counselor roles: counseling, consultation, and coordination (ACES-ASCA, 1966). Apparently, there are many activities which might fall under the term "coordination."

In a survey of 193 elementary and middle school counselors (Kameen, Robinson, and Rotter, 1985), more than 20 different functions were listed and ranked. Some of the functions were not considered part of the guidance program or given a high ranking by counselors; however, counselors felt obligated to do them.

What follows are some representative samples of activities which might be included in the work of a counselor as a coordinator. It is not an all inclusive list. No doubt, some school districts use a different nomenclature and have their own variations when describing these activities. Also, each school system adopts its own rules, regulations, and procedures around which coordination occurs.

Coordinating the Total Guidance Program

Perhaps the most important coordinating function is assuming responsibility for the overall guidance and counseling program. Its success and continued improvement is dependent on professional leadership and effective management, which often rests with the school counselors.

Some writers (e.g. Gibson, Mitchell, and Higgins, 1983) have attempted to identify the characteristics of a program leader. They concluded that the person should have a record of past professional accomplishments, which inspires confidence and support from others. A favorable record usually demonstrates that one has an ability for getting things done. Naturally, it helps if the person is a respected member of the profession and has knowledge of the history and latest information about it. More credibility is added if the person has also proven to be an expert practitioner in both individual and group work.

Strong leadership can be demonstrated in a program through convincing presentations and written statements. You could, for example, outline a model program and present it to the administration or faculty, enlisting their cooperation and support. Such a plan might detail goals and expected outcomes, various roles for school personnel, possible interventions, and guidance activities. This leadership position relies on your ability to inspire and influence people. It also suggests that you have carefully thought out a plan, including your own position and how your role complements the helping roles of others. Your comprehensive program should have a rationale based upon an accepted philosophy of developmental guidance and this has to be communicated to others.

A strong leadership approach is welcomed by busy administrators and teachers who want someone to assume control and direction of a program that is closely identified with your position, preparation, and skill. They want you and your colleagues to take charge of the guidance program. However, you must also demonstrate that you are sensitive to the needs and interests of those with whom you work. They will not be responsive to someone who ram-rods a program which ignores their own priorities and the demands on their time.

While strong leadership may call forth an image of a dynamic, forceful, and commanding personality, one's objectives can be accomplished without playing "General Patton." There may be occasions when such a role is needed and called for, but one should be cautioned about blustery or flamboyant styles, no matter how brilliant the idea.

An effective leader is adept at articulating the program. Being creative and innovative is appreciated, if the person is also open and receptive to the ideas of others. "Telling and selling are two skills you need, if you are going to develop an effective guidance program," reported one administrator. You don't need all the answers, but you have to be able to talk about a program that addresses the needs of faculty, parents, and students.

A bold approach to leadership need not be the only avenue. To the contrary, effective leadership can be more subtle, occurring within a system where others are the directors or administrators. In this sense, the facilitative model plays a significant part. Skilled professionals know how to lead and accomplish things, regardless of their titles or positions.

More specifically, leadership might be asserted through committee meetings, where you listen carefully to ideas that are expressed, clarify and summarize key points, and then make timely suggestions. It is not too different, at times, from some helping strategies that are used in counseling and consultation. Being an effective facilitator has all the components of being an effective leader.

Leadership results from being familiar with the roles and interventions that school personnel can play in a guidance and counseling program. It also means looking for opportunities when you can communicate your role, reinforce the basic philosophy of developmental guidance, introduce your ideas, and take the initiative to implement appropriate interventions.

Effective leaders in developmental guidance and counseling, at this point in history, recognize that most people have only minimal knowledge and understanding of a comprehensive program and what roles are encompassed. There are not enough exemplary programs to make the concept commonplace in today's education. Therefore, the coordinating and leadership function must consider the education and re-education of school personnel, parents, and students.

Coordinating the Guidance Committee

Regardless of grade level, an organized guidance committee or guidance council can be useful. It is usually composed of a small number of representatives from the faculty. It may also include support personnel, such as the school psychologist, media specialist, and administrators. It may even include students.

The primary purpose of such a group is to discuss the guidance and counseling needs which exist in a school and the various ways in which these needs can be met. The group is a sounding board for counselors, who can test their ideas and receive some assistance before involving the entire faculty. One counselor, for example, needed assistance in planning for the introduction of classroom guidance units in some classes and asked for suggestions about ways to present the idea to teachers and to coordinate schedules.

A common activity in many guidance committees is to develop or review a needs assessment instrument which can be administered to students and teachers in the school. The survey can then be used to increase faculty or public awareness, gain more support, identify goals, and set priorities. Specific target students or target populations can be identified with more confidence and, subsequently, a counselor might receive more support for the use of an intervention. The committee can discuss management problems that are related to guidance programs and work on resolving them. Committee members can talk with others outside the group in a networking scheme to aid communication within a school regarding guidance.

District-wide committees or councils can also be organized. This networking group might consist of different school levels and representatives who review guidance and counseling programs.

Coordinating Student Appraisal

Standardized testing is still considered within the realm of guidance services. Consequently, school counselors frequently coordinate school testing programs. This may consist of organizing test materials and school rules, administering tests, and distributing and interpreting test results to students, teachers, and parents. This is a traditional role for counselors, first emphasized when high school counselors in the 1960s were looking for ways to identify gifted and talented students.

Most school systems now have someone at the central administration office who is primarily responsible for the school district's testing program. This includes standardized intelligence and achievement tests. Testing programs have such high visibility in contemporary education that procedures must be systematic and well-organized. School psychologists in many school districts work out of a central office and accept referrals for individual assessments from schools to which they are assigned. However, the contact or resource person for testing programs within a school is typically the school counselor.

The actual administration of standardized tests by counselors is limited to a few intellectual or aptitude assessments. This kind of testing is usually done when a school psychologist or psychometrist is not available and the counselor is qualified to administer the tests.

Even when all teachers are involved in administering county or district-wide achievement tests, or when school psychometrists or school psychologists are available to administer specialized tests, the counselor is usually the coordinator of such events. In some cases, an assistant administrator, a curriculum specialist, or a resource teacher might assume the largest share of the responsibility. But, usually counselors are involved to some degree in coordinating testing programs in their schools.

Coordinating Child Study Teams

Child study teams are used in most schools. They are organized differently and may have different names, but their general purpose is to assemble a group of professionals together to review the status of a student. Some child study teams focus on helping teachers work with students in their classes. Others look specifically at learning disorders and educational placements. School counselors are a member of these teams and help coordinate them.

There seem to be more child study meetings and staffings at the elementary level. When students reach the secondary schools, most placements have been resolved. However, some students may still need special attention. New students to a high school may need to be studied by teams and then staffed for placement. Some students may begin to show more signs of emotional disturbance and may be candidates for placement in emotionally handicapped classes. Previous placements must be periodically reviewed for current appropriateness.

In general, a teacher first identifies a child who is having problems and who needs special attention. Alternative education may be a possibility. The teacher refers the child to a school counselor by filling out some referral forms developed by the school district. The counselor consults with the referring teacher and follows a screening process to determine whether the child is a candidate for staffing and placement.

Sometimes the case is taken before a child study team within the school (e.g. Educational Planning Team), as a preliminary intervention before staffing. Some interventions and additional observations are planned. In one school district, at least two interventions of at least six weeks in length are required before a "staffing" can happen. If a child, for example, does not respond to the interventions, the counselor refers the child for more testing by a school psychologist or psychometrist. Then, after all information is assembled, the "Student Services Committee" meets to review the case in terms of educational placement and individual educational plans (IEPs).

Public Law 94-142 increased the number of staffings that counselors coordinate, especially at the elementary level (Humes, 1978). In every school system, the law forced school counselors, school psychologists, exceptional child education teachers, administrators, and parents to work closer together, as they form the nucleus of a team responsible for making placement decisions and developing individual education plans for handicapped students.

School counselors are typically the coordinators of such staffings, although others (e.g. a school psychologist or a resource teacher) might just as easily be chairpersons. Counselors have to know and understand the law, district procedures, and appraisal measures in order to be effective members of the group. They may be either consultants on the teams or work as coordinators for the groups. They may decide to follow up with some students and to include them as part of their counseling caseload, or to coordinate some guidance efforts which might be implemented by others (e.g. teachers, parents, social services workers, school aides, or volunteers).

Unfortunately, many counselors are inadequately trained to work with exceptional children. One study suggested that 57% felt unprepared for the task (Lebsock and DeBlassie, 1975) and another study reported that as many as 66% (Huber and Westling, 1978) felt inadequate. However, the experience of being a member of a child study team and participating in staffings may be the only way in which counselors can learn about this special area. It is usually not a part of counselor education preparation in most colleges and universities.

Coordinating Multiple Interventions

Multiple interventions in guidance involve several people who are working with a student or a group of students. These may be certified personnel (e.g. teachers, social workers) or uncertified aides (e.g parent volunteers, auxiliary workers from community agencies).

Students may be referred to you because someone is concerned about their well-being. A student may or may not be a candidate for staffing under the *P.L. 94-142* provisions. Still, there is a problem. As a counselor, you might call together a group of people who might be able to help. As coordinator, you could encourage the group to explore the situation and then to develop a plan which could involve a multiple intervention.

The counselor as coordinator of multiple interventions is a role that cannot be ignored. Otherwise, a fragmented approach to helping students results, which is usually less effective and an inefficient use of time. Initiating and coordinating multiple interventions is the responsibility of the counselor.

Coordinating Referrals

Sometimes students' problems exceed the resources that are available in a school. The situation may be too complex or beyond the scope of the regular guidance and counseling services. Sometimes, young people need more intensive help, perhaps therapy or more extended remedial treatment, to help them cope with problems in their lives.

The counselor works as a coordinator in referring students and their families to professionals in the community who have the time, experience, and resources to help. This requires a knowledge of available referral sources and an open communication system with them.

Practical counselors have a referral source notebook nearby, which includes the names and addresses of agencies, contact persons and their titles, and telephone numbers. They have taken the time to learn how a receiving agency typically works with referrals and they know what to expect when a case is referred. With frequently used agencies, they usually have a first-name working relationship with someone with whom there can be a candid exchange of information and ideas.

If you find yourself working with a particular agency several times, it would be valuable to visit that agency and talk with its personnel at a time when a crisis is not at hand. An informal gathering at the school or the agency can help build positive working relationships and clarify the practical procedures that are considered most effective and efficient. For example, a breakfast meeting of agency and school personnel might provide an opportunity to become better acquainted and to share information. Advanced preparation is part of the developmental model and can make referrals easier.

Referring young people to outside agencies requires some carefully planned procedures. First, there must be some recorded observations of behaviors by responsible people who are concerned about the student. The behavior is usually chronic and disruptive. It interferes with the learning process of both the troubled individual and others. Parents are contacted and consulted. Sometimes they need to be encouraged to work with an agency.

While it might be helpful to do a complete diagnostic work-up within the school, it is usually not done as a practical matter. Most agencies have their own diagnostic procedures and may repeat many of the things that might be done at the school. However, accurate behavioral observations, specific relevant data taken from existing school records, and a summary of the student's work habits and progress in school can be useful. It is unnecessary to identify the underlying dynamics of the problem before a referral is made. Referral procedures should be streamlined.

Referral does not mean that the responsibility for the case is ended. It implies that some follow-up procedures will result. Many community agencies are so overwhelmed with their own caseloads that they may not provide progress reports, in which case the counselor might have to make a periodic check on those young people who have been referred. Recommendations for in-school treatment or assistance should be sought from the agency. There might be valuable leads for consulting with teachers.

A classroom teacher suspected that a child, Tyrone, was being neglected at home and a referral was made to the school counselor. The teacher noticed that Tyrone often wore the same clothes, complained of being hungry, and stayed around the school building after school hours. The counselor suspected child neglect and was obligated by law to refer the case to professionals in community health and rehabilitation services. The coordination of the case was jointly assumed by a social worker and the counselor.

The social worker investigated the situation and learned that the mother was divorced, unemployed most of the time, and seldom home. Tyrone and his younger siblings were often left on their own. The community agency made some provisions for assisting the mother, who was eventually confronted by legal authorities. Help from other adults who were related to the mother and children was also elicited. Meanwhile, Tyrone attended school regularly. His school was the cleanest and most positive environment in which he lived. The counselor further coordinated special efforts at the school, including some consultation with the referring teacher and providing some brief counseling to the child.

Systematic referral procedures coordinated by a counselor can ensure that significant problems do not go unnoticed or ignored. In addition, the referral process is improved when inservice or staff development workshops assist a faculty to become aware of potential problems and to know how to make appropriate referrals.

Coordinating Staff Development and Inservice

A counselor is sometimes asked to help assess the professional needs and interests of a school faculty and to help plan some appropriate staff development or inservice workshops. Sometimes, a counselor studies the situation, perhaps with the help of the Guidance Committee, and then makes recommendations to the principal. The principal may give the counselor the task of coordinating a workshop, particularly if it is closely associated with guidance and counseling. Administrators often see counselors, as experts in human relationships and group development, to be the best ones to organize and coordinate staff development programs in their schools.

The most effective staff development programs are those that are continuous or are carried out over time. They usually involve a presentation of ideas, demonstrations, practice, and an assignment in which the techniques are implemented. In addition, teachers like the opportunity to meet and talk about successes and problems related to something that was learned in an in-service workshop. Follow-up meetings can reinforce the concepts that were discussed in a workshop, and they encourage more people to try them in their work.

Coordinating Paraprofessionals and Volunteers

Every school relies upon the assistance of people who work as aides, special helpers or volunteer staff. The term paraprofessional has been used to describe people who are not certified as professionals in a school. They need both training and supervision to be most effective, regardless of assignment or duties.

Coordinating a training program for paraprofessionals can fall to counselors. The training is like an abbreviated peer facilitator training program, with special attention given to school rules and procedures, facilitative skills in working with students and teachers, and related skills for a specific job function.

Coordinating Student Records

Formerly, most school counselors were in charge of organizing and coordinating school records. With the advent of test scoring services, computers, and other assistance, this responsibility has diminished considerably. Many schools now have a registrar or a secretary, who, with the help of clerical aides, is responsible for maintaining school records, their storage and retrieval. However, some schools still assign school counselors to coordinate the collection of information for students' cumulative files and the management of records.

Parents have the right to inspect and review their child's school records and they may consult with a school counselor about them. The "Buckley Amendment" to the *1974 Family Educational Rights and Privacy Act* gives parents the opportunity to challenge the content of those records in terms of accuracy and misleading or inappropriate data. Consequently, record keeping in the schools is now under close scrutiny.

A school counselor is encouraged to work with parents who want to review and discuss their children's records. Sometimes a counselor will consult with a teacher about something that has been placed in a student's cumulative file. One teacher was very angry when she wrote a blistering note reprimanding a student. Later, upon reflection with the help of a school counselor, the teacher decided to retrieve the note and to use more professional language to express her concerns. Instead of labeling the child as "obscene and mentally sick," the teacher reported what she actually observed and heard. Inferences were withheld, but recommendations were unchanged.

This brings to mind the issue of confidentiality, at one time the sacrosanct of the counselor's role and image. School counselors do not have privileged communication and their records can be reviewed by court order. The general rule is that counselors will do whatever they can to safeguard the confidential relationships that they have with their students before releasing any information. If subpoenaed, counselors will try to exhaust all arguments (short of being held in contempt of court and jailed) before testifying in court. A case is often made that such testimony is only hearsay, lacks proof, and not legally valid (Swanson, 1983).

When a counselor acts in "good faith" and breaches a confidential relationship, it should be in the best interests of the student. Apparently, there are some procedural differences among counselors at different grade levels. Many elementary school counselors feel obligated to share information with parents about their children (Wagner, 1981).

Counselors must recognize the limitations of their skills and, when appropriate, refer to others who are more competent or in a better position to provide the specific assistance needed. Counselors are also obligated by law, in most states, to report such cases as child abuse, suicide, or instances when a student intends to do bodily harm to another person.

It might be remembered that rights guaranteed by the *U.S. Constitution* (e.g. 1st, 4th, 5th, and 14th Amendments) have been extended to students. Students have the right to be heard, to due process, and to be safeguarded against unreasonable search and seizure. One court held that the privacy rights of public school students must give way to the "overriding governmental interest in investigating a reasonable suspicion of illegal drug use" by students. Student lockers can be searched and illegal contraband can be seized. Yet, an accused student has constitutional rights, protected more than ever before, and these should not be violated.

In addition, legally speaking, students have a right to counseling services within a school. Teachers or administrators cannot prevent a student from seeking those services.

As ethical standards of the counseling profession, student and adult rights, and the influence of legal statutes come into play with each other, it behooves counselors to become more familiar with the national and state laws which affect their work. It is essential that counselors know their limitations, obligations, and potential liabilities. Systematic procedures, based on professional guidelines and careful record keeping, can strengthen a guidance and counseling program and provide more confidence to counselors in their work.

School records can provide a resource from which to identify meaningful trends, potential problems, and students who might be targeted for assistance. A review of summary reports and certain data gleaned from records might help identify patterns or trends in a school. Such information can be used to build a case for developmental guidance or perhaps to emphasize a need that should be addressed.

Regarding your own records, even handwritten notes can be subpoenaed by courts and are open for inspection as part of school records. All notes or recorded conversations are subject to being part of litigation proceedings, if found essential to a case by legal authorities. Record keeping among counselors varies considerably, although counselors in the elementary schools tend to keep more notes and to have more systematic procedures for keeping records on their interventions and work with others than do counselors at other grade levels.

A few school systems require counselors to use code systems and to record the number of individual or small group counseling sessions that they provided. Other activities are also coded. Then, a summary report might be written at the end of a grading period or at the end of the year. However, such coding is not the same as writing details about a case.

Coordinating the Teacher-As-Advisor Program (TAP)

A school counselor might be appointed coordinator for TAP. Such programs need a person who can help organize the curriculum, make arrangements for materials and resources, and be a trouble-shooter when problems develop. In middle and high schools, this could involve one counselor employed in a school. Other counselors might help coordinate part of the program.

Some schools have elected to have a teacher serve as the full-time or part-time coordinator of TAP. However, counselors work closely with the TAP Coordinator and help coordinate the guidance services delivered through TAP.

Coordinating Peer Facilitator Programs and Projects

As a counselor, you might be a peer facilitator trainer and project coordinator. If someone else in the school is the trainer, then you will want to work closely with that person to identify, develop, and coordinate some helping projects for the facilitators.

One group of high school peer facilitators decided to be special friends to a group of elementary students identified by their teachers as needing extra attention. The peer facilitator trainer (a teacher) and a school counselor worked together to coordinate the project. An elementary school counselor was also involved. Together they explored the project with several teachers who agreed to refer some students to the peer facilitators and to provide some time during the day for them to meet. The counselors from both schools coordinated the project procedures, and they jointly coordinated an evaluation of the project.

Coordinating Special Guidance Events

Each school has special guidance activities or events which are coordinated by school counselors. For example, in most high schools throughout the nation, there is a College Night when parents can talk with counselors and other resource people about their childrens' educational future. They learn how to apply to different colleges and to meet the entrance requirements. They hear about financial loans and scholarships. Although most of the information is available in college bulletins, mimeographed handouts, and other places, such an event is considered a traditional service in most high schools. If it is well planned and coordinated, it is creates a favorable perception with the public.

Career Nights or Career Fairs are frequently organized and coordinated by school counselors. Students might visit different booths where business people have been stationed to talk with them about various job opportunities. Similarly, recruiters from the military service might be brought into a school to talk with students who are especially interested in military services.

A group of parents were concerned about the sex education curriculum which was going to be introduced to their children as part of a planned school program. The elementary school counselors organized and coordinated meetings in which parents and concerned citizens were given a preview of the program and an opportunity to ask questions. Counselors reported that coordinating such a meeting was important and so was the use of the facilitative model in leading the discussions with parents.

A community group had raised enough funds to purchase the services of a group of professional actors who were doing dramatic plays about alcohol and drug abuse. A school counselor met with group representatives and talked with them about their goals and presentations. After some consultation, it appeared that the plays were related to several objectives in the school's guidance program. The counselor agreed to work as liaison and coordinator so that students could see the plays and share reactions in their classes.

Participating on the Curriculum Committee

A school counselor will often be a member of a school planning committee, such as the curriculum committee. This committee examines the curricula of a school in terms of objectives and desired outcomes. The counselor listens attentively to discussions, offering suggestions when appropriate, and takes the position of being the advocate for developmental guidance. Therefore, the committee has at least one member who is "listening with a third ear" for those things which involve the guidance of young people within the regular school curricula.

Factors to Consider

Time waster or saver?

Although as much as 50% of a counselor's time might be used for coordinating guidance events and activities, some counselors report that this is still not enough time to do all that is expected of them. They feel overwhelmed with what might be done and with what is assigned to them as duties.

One way to protect the other five counselor interventions from being encroached upon by the coordinating one is to have a weekly calendar which shows time blocs where certain interventions are regularly scheduled. Some events that demand extra attention at a particular time of year must be scheduled on a counselor's yearly calendar, showing events by the different grading periods. Then, the coordinating function can be managed through the year, with some activities or events being spread out over more than one grading period and others receiving concentrated effort for a particular time.

If the coordinating function is managed effectively within counselors' schedules, then it can be a time saving feature, since the coordination of guidance activities gains the help of others. If too many events or activities which are unrelated to guidance creep into the counselor's workload, then coordinating may be a waste of time.

A group of counselors were asked to patrol the hallways between classes and to coordinate a meeting between the sheriff's office and school representatives regarding student parking problems. Another group of counselors spent considerable time obtaining information for a community group that was thinking of sending a girl to the Miss Teen-Age America Contest. None of these requests seem to merit counselor time. They took away time that could have been spent delivering counseling services to students.

Some counselors, in their eagerness to be helpers and to receive appreciation from others, rush to assume the coordination of some unrelated responsibilities. This may give them a feeling of importance or a sense that they are needed. A few counselors see their positions as a stepping-stone to administration and they welcome the opportunity to coordinate almost anything to demonstrate their administrative skills.

Who else can help?

Perhaps the most important question for a counselor who wants to deliver a balanced program with more direct guidance and counseling services to students is: Who else can do this job? Who else can help?

You might, for example, be able to identify certain tasks that could be coordinated by one of the administrators in your school or perhaps an aide under that administrator's supervision. A teacher might be willing to chair or coordinate a school activity, especially if it is of special interest to the person.

What is on the calendar?

Taking note of the days when standardized tests are administered in a school or when special events are scheduled can help a counselor plan for certain interventions. Counselors in one middle school worked closely with teachers in a TAP program to help all eighth graders to develop four-year high school plans. This unit was scheduled in the spring of the year before registration for classes at the high school. Each academic department was asked to review some of the terminology and language which students needed to make class selections.

Is this the only way?

Some high school counselors continue to see students individually in order to schedule classes, when this could just as easily be done in small or large groups. Schedules could be checked for accuracy by peer facilitators who are working with a counselor in a large group. Likewise, "arena scheduling" might be appropriate to reduce the number of days that it takes students out of their classes. In this case, students move around in a large area, signing up for classes. Computers and monitors are also helpful, particularly when a large student body is being scheduled.

Some counselors continue to call individual students to their offices to talk about low grades or the possibility of their not graduating because of a lack of credits. This might just as easily be done in small or large groups, or perhaps as part of TAP.

A group of high school counselors assumed that they were the best people to schedule students for classes because they had the cumulative folders in their office, they were responsible for tallying credits, and they "knew the students best." These were erroneous assumptions. Classroom teachers not only had more opportunity to know students better, but they were probably in the best position to determine their educational placements. For instance, math teachers who were familiar with the math curriculum and the way in which the math department was organized were probably in a better position to schedule students for math classes than were the counselors. This also was true for English, social studies, science, and physical education.

The same group of counselors assumed that students preferred individual counseling to small group counseling, believing that confidentiality was the key to providing counseling and that confidentiality was best protected through individual counseling. Yet, the counselors had not evaluated other counseling approaches or asked students about their ideas. They continued to operate from a "therapy" model which seemed inappropriate considering the large number of counselees who had been assigned to them.

A coordinating effort may be an effective trade-off for another intervention. For example, coordinating a child study team or staffing might enable you to work as a consultant with the teachers involved and to build a working relationship which you could draw upon later when constructing a multiple intervention for an individual.

Case Studies

The Case of Shellie

Shellie was a second grade girl who drew the attention of her classroom teacher because she appeared tired and withdrawn. She sometimes cried for no apparent reason. On occasion she complained of stomach aches. The teacher wondered if there might be child abuse when she heard Shellie say to another little girl, "I hate Uncle Fred, cuz he's always putting his hands under my dress where they shouldn't be."

The teacher was afraid to pursue the matter for fear that she might cause a problem if there wasn't any. She consulted with a school counselor, who agreed to talk with Shellie. During an individual counseling session, the girl told the counselor about "Uncle Fred" and how he sexually abused her.

The counselor was obligated by law to report the situation and explained that to Shellie, although she pleaded that the secret be kept. If the secret wasn't kept, she said she would surely be in "big trouble." The counselor continued to work with Shellie, talking about what she might do in the presence of Fred and about some matters related to the girl's school work.

Meanwhile, the counselor also called the community health and rehabilitation services agency, where suspected cases of child abuse were reported. A case worker at the agency went to the child's home and talked with the mother. It was revealed that Fred was not a relative. He lived in the same trailer court and he talked and played with the children in the court, during the interim when school was out and parents arrived home from work. There was nobody to supervise Shellie. Her mother was trying to save money on child care. As a result of the caseworker's visit, she showed the girl how to take a key they had hidden together and let herself into the trailer. She was to watch television until her mother arrived home. A neighbor woman agreed to be watchful of Shellie, although she was not paid to tend to her.

Nothing could be proved about Fred. There was no evidence of physical or sexual abuse that could be taken to court. However, the investigator warned the mother that Shellie was being neglected and not receiving proper supervision after school. The mother agreed that the girl should not be with Fred without supervision.

The investigator did not continue with the case beyond the initial visit with people at the trailer court and a conference with the mother. Unfortunately, the deposition of the case and its outcome were not reported to the counselor until the counselor took the initiative to call the agency and ask to speak with the person to whom the case was assigned. After some discussion, it was agreed that Shellie needed to work more with the counselor to learn how to take care of herself.

The counselor talked with the classroom teacher, reporting some of the findings. The teacher was still worried and consulted more with the counselor. Together they planned a few things that might help Shellie: a classroom guidance unit on sexual abuse; a few more opportunities for Shellie to meet with the counselor to talk more about her after-school hours; and a lesson in both small group counseling and classroom guidance about assertiveness and saying "No" to people who were "pushy."

It was later observed that Shellie's attitude about school seemed to improve. It was difficult to assess her after-school care, but it was reported that she no longer spent time alone with "Uncle Fred." Shellie said to her counselor, "He's real nice to me now, but my

Mommy said I can't go to his trailer anymore. I can only talk with him when other children are there... and on the porch (an outside patio)."

Other Cases

In another case, a classroom teacher noted that a kindergarten boy had burns on his hands and arms. He complained about the "whippings" he received from his grandmother, with whom he and his sister lived. "She really hurts me bad when she gets mad." The teacher wondered if the burns were from a cigarette and consulted with the school counselor. The counselor, in turn, talked with the boy, looked at the sores and suspected that they were burns, perhaps from child abuse.

The community health services were called to help with the case. The agency reported that an investigator talked with the grand-mother and the boy's arms apparently had some natural skin discoloring. The case was dropped. A few weeks later, however, the teacher and counselor noticed that the "discoloring" had disappeared and that they boy no longer complained about being beaten at home. The counselor, working as a consultant and a coordinator, may have started an intervention which positively affected the boy's well-being.

Still another example of a counselor working as a coordinator and consultant took place with a boy who was experiencing severe depression. His therapist had called the school counselor and said that the boy was not responding well to treatment. The boy had threatened suicide and talked of life as meaningless. His mother had been committed to the psychiatric ward of a local hospital for attempted suicide on three different occasions.

The school counselor consulted with the boy's teacher and learned that he once or twice had said, "I can't do this, what's the use...? I should just die (or kill myself)." The matter was not dismissed as idle talk or as a histrionic gesture to gain attention, especially because of the boy's family history.

The therapist and the counselor talked about the kinds of guidance interventions at the school which could be helpful and how the counselor's work might supplement the work of the therapist. The counselor and teacher were more alert to the boy's moods and tried to establish positive relationships with him. Coordinating a multiple intervention can be a valuable guidance service.

Coordinating a Child Study Team

Child study meetings have been an important part of guidance for many years. However, since 1975, with the passage of *Education for all Handicapped Children (P.L. 94-142)*, these meetings and staffings have taken a more prominent place in the work of school counselors.

P.L. 94-142 has several major provisions which affect the work of most counselors. First, it emphasizes that free, appropriate public education was to be made available for all children and that handicapped children were to be identified and mainstreamed in the least restrictive environment possible. Individual education plans (IEPs) were to be developed for each handicapped child and reviewed annually. In addition, parents were also given the right to participate in the placement process and to challenge decisions made by school teams.

Most educators agree that school counselors should participate in the decision-making process and meet with members of the staffing team. They can also help develop IEPs, consult with parents, provide some supportive counseling interventions, and help monitor student progress. In addition, coordinating the team's meetings often rests with counselors because they are on-site and familiar with school records, procedures, and personnel. Many administrators assign their counselors to chair the meetings.

Child study teams are generally composed of participants representing several aspects of education: principal, vice-principal, administrative assistants, social workers, visiting teachers, counselors, school and public health nurse, school psychologist, and classroom teachers. When appropriate, parents or students will be present, along with specialists in exceptional child education. In addition, reading specialists, speech therapists, representatives of community health or welfare agencies, and others who have a special expertise might attend. It is a challenge to organize and lead team meetings.

Team members, especially those who meet regularly and are the core of the team, learn to work together as a cohesive unit. They become more sensitive to the needs of students and the people who are trying to assist them. They learn to share their feelings and ideas openly and to recognize the contributions that various people have to make as team members, working individually and collectively. It is also an excellent opportunity to learn more about how team members' roles complement each other and how a comprehensive developmental guidance and counseling program can help all children.

If the best procedures are to be followed, time used wisely, and the most desirable outcomes achieved, effective communication among team members is essential. For the most part, much of the work of a team can be accomplished before teams meet. Data about a student, for example, are assembled and summarized in a familiar format and presented by various team members. Team members then explore a case. They use all their skills and knowledge to facilitate each other in considering the merits of the case, alternative solutions, placement, and IEPs. Perhaps no single prescribed outline or pattern can be ascribed to such meetings, because of the different variables found in cases and school systems. However, a few suggested procedures may be helpful as guidelines.

The Case of Charles

Rhonda was an elementary school counselor whose building principal assigned her to organize, coordinate, and chair the child study teams and staffings, especially as related to *P.L. 94-142* cases. She recognized the importance of preparing for team meetings, screening and selecting students for review, and facilitating the discussion of the cases.

Charles was a fourth grade boy whose teacher thought he was an "E.H. child" (emotionally handicapped). She described Charles as inattentive, disruptive in class, and lax in his school assignments. It appeared that he had little interest in school. The teacher wondered if he had a learning disability which went with his emotional problems, recognizing that he had a slight speech defect.

Because of her work with the child study team, Charles came to Rhonda's attention. He was one of several cases that would receive the team's attention and, subsequently, benefit from her efforts as a coordinator, which are described briefly below.

Preparation for the team meeting. Rhonda encouraged each team member to be familiar with how the team would work together and some of the general procedures that might be used at each meeting. A general philosophy, a statement of district policies related to such meetings, and a summary statement of related state and national laws were typed, mimeographed, and placed in notebooks for team members.

Rhonda knew some of the things for which the chair was responsible included:

1. Establishing a regular meeting time for the team and noting meeting times on the guidance calendar. It is often easier to cancel a regularly scheduled meeting than to assemble the group each time a case is to be reviewed. Therefore, Wednesday afternoons from 12:30 until 3:30 were scheduled for team meetings. This allowed Rhonda an opportunity to notify people on Monday if no cases or business needed attention.

2. Coordinating the selection of students to be discussed at the meeting and reviewing past cases when appropriate. It was Charles' first time before the team and his records were carefully assembled.

3. Preparing an agenda, preferably a written one that might be distributed in advance of the meetings.

4. Arranging for teachers or parents who do not regularly attend the meetings to be present when their presence is desired. For example, Rhonda decided that it would be helpful to have the speech therapist present when Charles' case was discussed, since she had extra information that would be helpful to the team's deliberations.

5. Reminding or requesting team members to bring certain information that might be useful in a particular case. Rhonda developed a form letter that allowed her to check certain items to remind members of materials or information they were to bring to the meeting.

6. Appointing a recorder, someone who would keep a brief record of the proceedings and any specific recommendations. Rhonda had the assistance of an aide who was familiar with various district forms that needed to be completed. The aide confirmed that specific information was obtained where appropriate.

Select the cases to be presented.

1. Rhonda checked her faculty mail box each day, looking for referrals made by teachers. The general procedures were: 1) A teacher referral on a student was received, which included

name, observations, general academic information, and reason for referral; 2) The referral form was attached to a checklist which Rhonda had developed regarding information that was needed before a team meeting. More specifically, this included: standardized group and individual IQ score; standardized achievement test scores that were administered in the school district; pertinent health records; school attendance records; and special notes from the student's cumulative file.

2. Rhonda studied the list of students who met the criteria for review. If there were more students than the team might review in one day, she prioritized the list and made an agenda with students' names listed in the order that they would be discussed. Charles's case did not seem to be a difficult one and Rhonda estimated that it would take the usual 30 minutes.

3. Sometimes pre-screening procedures eliminate cases that might otherwise be brought before the team. They might be given attention by the team later or in other study teams. *P.L. 94-142* cases were given highest priority to both comply with the law and to achieve the best educational placement when possible.

Facilitating the meeting. Ysseldyke, Algozzine, and Mitchell (1982) analyzed the process used by child study teams (special education teams) in 16 different schools, especially for *P.L. 94-142*. A summary of items used to analyze the meetings served as a general checklist for Rhonda.

A. Discussion Regarding Procedures.

1. The purpose of the meeting is clearly stated.

2. Additional goals for improving or evaluating team functioning or productivity are stated.

3. The roles of the team members are defined.

4. A statement is made about the desirability of participation by all team members.

5. The decision(s) to be made during the meeting is (are) clearly identified.

6. The reason for referral is stated.

B. Data Presentation and Use.

7. Data are explained in terms of how they are related to the case or problem (i.e. what they tell you, not just the scores).

8. The student's strengths and weaknesses are discussed.

Charles was reportedly well-liked and respected among his peers, he was considered well coordinated, and he took an active part in the athletic activities on the playground. However, he also resented being criticized, displayed a temper on occasion, and was self-conscious about his habit of stammering when he talked. Instead of talking during a conflict, Charles' style was to shove, grab, pull, hit, and bully.

9. Comparisons occur across different sources of data with implications.

10. Everyday school behavior and academic data about the student are presented.

11. The provisions and changes which have been made in the regular classroom in an attempt to deal with the problem are presented.

12. Systematic behavioral observation data, as well as formal testing data, are presented.

C. Evaluating Alternatives.

13. The team states the criteria for evaluating the alternatives.

14. A team member verbalizes the need to reach a placement decision offering the least restrictive alternative.

15. Each alternative is evaluated in terms of the child's educational needs or the selected criteria.

D. Making the Final Decision.

16. Members attempt through discussion to reach a decision that all are willing to support.

17. A decision(s) is (are) made.

18. The final decision is clearly stated.

The team listened to members tell about their knowledge of Charles' behavior, with particular attention to what could be observed in his classroom and playground behavior. Teacher's comments, test scores, and the school psychologist's report about

Charles' negative behavior and attitude in the testing situation were considered. The psychologist also reported on a series of tests that attempted to appraise Charles' emotional maturity and stability. It was difficult to conclude whether the boy's speech disability had predisposed him toward a negative attitude about school and people in general or the boy was emotionally handicapped. Therefore, a decision was made to first address his speech problem through participation in a program of speech therapy which was available at the school. It was also agreed that the counselor would continue to consult with the boy's teachers and to provide him with individual counseling.

E. Implementing the Decision.

19. The method for evaluation is specified.

20. A timetable for the program is specified.

21. The role of each member in implementing the decision is described.

22. The team evaluates its meeting as having attained or not attained its goals.

F. Meetings with Parents Present.

23. In the beginning of the meeting, parents are asked about their expectations for the meeting.

Following the meetings, Rhonda and her aide summarized the recommendations and action taken for each case, including Charles'. All cases were categorized by number and the date when reviewed by the team. This allowed for some follow-up discussions and progress reports related to team decisions.

Maybe the most difficult part of Rhonda's coordinating efforts was the time that it took to implement placement actions which were recommended by the team. In Charles's case, it was necessary to consult with two different teachers, give information to the central office staff regarding class changes, and to make appropriate notes on the boy's cumulative records. His parents were notified of the decision to change his class schedule. They agreed that the change was in his best interest and signed the parental approval form. It was returned to Rhonda, who then made all final arrangements.

If you are not assigned to coordinate or chair a child study team or child staffings, the guidelines presented above can still be useful as you participate in team discussions. You can use them to make suggestions or to draw attention to productive procedures.

Helpful Hints

Work Within a Schedule

The need for a weekly schedule built around a guidance calendar and grading periods of the school year becomes increasingly clear as you try to manage the coordinating function. Many counselors give as much as 50% of their time to coordinating guidance activities. When preparing your weekly schedule, try to schedule some coordinating efforts at specific times, although flexible time periods will likely be used for coordination activities. For example, team meetings might be scheduled one afternoon a week.

Scheduling a minimum number of hours for each intervention, except coordinating, can provide balance to your program. Except regularly scheduled meetings or special events that occur during the year, coordinating functions are not usually recorded on the weekly schedule. If coordinating functions begin to take too much time from direct services to students, then negotiate with those who can help you protect time for other interventions. Once you have developed a schedule, try to work within it.

Keep a Record of Interventions

Develop a system by which you can record the number of coordinating activities in which you are involved. Preferably, the amount of time should also be noted. This can provide you with information that might be useful in building a case for more counseling time.

Recruit Helpers and Delegate

Peer facilitators, volunteer workers, auxiliary aides, and other paraprofessionals might be trained and supervised to do some guidance activities which take counselor time away from students. Counselor aides can be trained to record student information, make preparations for meetings, return calls to people who request general information, and provide basic information to students.

Prioritize Activities

Identify those activities that you do well, that you enjoy doing, and that provide an important service to students and faculty. Concentrate on delivering those services or activities. Decide which activities give you and the school the least pay-off for the energy and time expended. Eliminate or revise them.

Tell Your Story

Let others know the kinds of things that you are doing. If you have numerous cases that need attention from the child study team, announce the number of cases to teachers as part of keeping them informed. If you find there is not enough time to meet with students individually or in groups for counseling, talk with the guidance committee about how you might find more time. Then, talk with the faculty members.

Advantages, Limitations, and Conclusion

Advantages of the Coordinating Intervention

1. Some coordinating activities, although indirect, help many students obtain the help they might not otherwise receive.

2. Because of their flexible schedules and access to student information, counselors might be in the best position to coordinate some guidance activities and events in the most effective and efficient manner.

3. Many of the coordinating functions involve opportunities to consult with teachers, administrators, and parents that might not otherwise be initiated. Sometimes coordinating a guidance event or activity can foster positive working relationships with other professionals.

4. Coordinating some specific guidance events can provide counselors visibility among parents, teachers, and students.

Limitations of the Coordinating Intervention

1. Many coordinating functions assigned to or assumed by school counselors are not related to guidance and counseling, which can discredit counselors and create an unfavorable image.

2. Coordinating activities is time consuming. It frequently takes more time than a counselor might use to counsel students individually or in small groups.

3. The coordinating intervention tends to foster "burnout" among many dedicated counselors because it takes time away from direct services to students. Time-consuming efforts with very little reward are fatiguing, boring, and depressing.

4. Some counselors deceive themselves by doing busy work through coordinating various school activities. Because they work hard at coordinating, they believe that they are making a significant contribution. This often leads to an unbalanced program. Eventually, they feel that their work is unappreciated despite long working hours and dedication.

5. Coordinating activities appear to many teachers to be soft administrative jobs without much pressure or reward. They think many of the coordinating tasks could be done by someone with less training.

Conclusion

Coordinating guidance activities is one of the six counselor interventions around which to build a comprehensive program. When used appropriately, coordinating efforts can help students in many ways. Particularly, coordination of multiple interventions and child study teams are productive ways to use a counselor's time. Consultation and coordination often work well together.

The problem facing most counselors is that many activities and events around a school are not necessarily related to guidance or counseling. Sometimes they become the responsibility of a counselor, who then begins to have an image of an administrative or clerical assistant. Because counselors have more flexible time than most other personnel in a school, they are often the first persons to whom others turn when they need assistance in a project. Gleaning out those projects which are unrelated to guidance and counseling, protecting time for other counselor interventions, and providing a balanced program are challenges that face all school counselors. The coordinating function can be a millstone around a counselor's neck, or it can lead to some productive outcomes in guidance. It depends upon the ability of a counselor to use the intervention appropriately.

Chapter 12

The Counselor and Accountability

In recent years, there has been a demand for educators to be more accountable. People want to know what services they are getting for their tax dollars and if those services are making positive differences. They are interested in cost efficiency and good investments. Superintendents, principals, teachers, counselors, and other educational specialists can use accountability studies to boost their school programs.

Guidance and counseling services once had so much general appeal that counselors were accepted on "faith" and "goodness of intent." One person said, "I'm really not sure what you do, or if you're successful, but I like the idea of it." But, times have changed and blind support is no longer enough. More questions are being posed, "What do you do in your job?" "Who do you help?" "Are you getting any results?" More than ever before, counselors, like other educators, are being challenged to be accountable.

Accountability Defined

To be accountable means to be responsible for one's actions, particularly for the objectives, procedures, and outcomes of one's work or program. It involves an explanation of what has been done, including information and data to support any claims that are made. The basic principles of accountability suggest there is some evidence on which to make a decision or judgment.

Accountability can be a matter of being responsible to one's self or to someone else. Both aspects are relevant to guidance and counseling programs. Each counselor needs to ask the basic questions: "What are my objectives? Am I effective? Are there better ways of getting the same thing done?" Accountability systems are built by responsible individuals who are accountable to themselves and to others.

Krumboltz (1974) identified seven criteria for an effective accountability system. As applied to school guidance and counseling programs, they are:

1. The general goals of counseling must be agreed to by all concerned parties.

2. Gains must be stated in observable behavioral changes by students.

3. Counselor interventions and activities are viewed as costs, not accomplishments.

4. The accountability system must be positive and not designed to cast blame or to punish poor performance. It is a constructive approach to working toward professional effectiveness.

5. To promote more accurate reporting, reports of failures or unknown outcomes must be permitted without reprimands.

6. Those participating in the accountability system must be involved in designing it.

7. The accountability system itself must be subject to evaluation and modification.

A well-designed accountability system enables administrators and counselors to obtain feedback on their work and, subsequently, to make modifications where necessary or to maintain present procedures. While helping to identify student needs and ways to meet them, accountability studies can cause some discomfort and may result in some confrontations when related goals are not achieved or counselor interventions do not seem to be working. But, these studies can also be a source of comfort, especially when there is evidence that the goals are being achieved. They can be personally satisfying, professionally rewarding, and spark a sense of pride in one's work.

The term "evaluation" is related to accountability. It refers to a judgment of something's worth or significance. For many people, an accountability system is a set of procedures for bringing together pieces of information which can be evaluated. There is also an attempt to look for some meaningful patterns.

Evaluation and research are not new topics to counselors. They are included in most graduate training programs and in certification requirements. Yet, far too many counselors dislike the idea of researching and evaluating their work. Part of this resistance may stem from a lack of faith in the interventions they use, a lack of planning so that interventions can be evaluated systematically and objectively, a lack of knowledge about brief assessment instruments which can be used within the context of their jobs, or a lack of self-confidence (Myrick, 1984). They may also lack a familiarity with or appreciation for the positive uses of evaluation.

In addition, in the past counselors have not necessarily been encouraged by administrators or their colleagues to be accountable. While teachers have been judged by the scores their students receive on achievement tests and coaches by their win-loss records, counselors have withstood efforts to reveal what they are doing and accomplishing, except the most visible part of their work—coordinating.

Some of the immunity that counselors seem to have had rested in the "counselor mystique," which is cloaked in confidentiality. A counselor's work, by its nature, has been safeguarded from being evaluated by others, because to share information with others would seem to violate a trust relationship.

It would certainly be inappropriate to point to a young man and say, "He has parents who are abusive and I helped him learn how to cope with them so that he would not run away from home and school, which is what he was planning to do until he received counseling." There is something about this type of reporting that is clearly unacceptable; yet, the issue of counselor accountability can no longer be assumed to be too private for evaluation.

Resistance to accountability studies can also be traced to some defensiveness, such as: a) "Studies without positive results can cost counselors their jobs;" b) "I have a good relationship with my principal, who knows what I'm doing;" c) "My job isn't in jeopardy, so I don't have to do any studies;" and d) "I don't have time to do research."

Some counselors claim that the sophisticated research designs described in graduate school are too rigorous to be used in school settings and too time-consuming for what they produce. Others add that if they did a thorough job and evaluated all their interventions, there would not be enough time left to work with many students. It has also been argued that most surveys and tests take too long to administer, are too expensive, and are not related to a counselor's work.

There may be some truth behind these objections. Yet, they all ignore the fact that accountability studies can make a counselor's work more effective and efficient and that counselors can personally benefit from them. Actually, it is unprofessional and irresponsible to dismiss accountability as not needed or undesirable.

Types of Accountability Studies

There are at least three basic ways to look at accountability studies, regardless of grade level. The first focuses on knowing people's needs and interests which could receive attention from counselors. The second is concerned with the guidance and counseling services or interventions that addresses those needs. Finally, the outcomes of the services or interventions must be examined.

Sometimes one approach is used at the expense of the other two. Yet, all three are useful in a comprehensive accountability system, one in which counselors look at all aspects of their work. An unbalanced effort tends to produce a distorted picture or one in which something is missing. Let's take a closer look at these three approaches, particularly through the questions they attempt to answer.

What are the needs to be met?

Who will receive guidance and counseling and what are their problems? What special interests and needs do they have? Such basic questions might be directed to students, teachers, parents, or administrators.

Student needs, for example, may appear obvious. "Walk-in traffic," plus referrals, can easily dictate who receives counselor services. In such cases, counselors are very busy. Or, they may have nothing to do. Regardless, it is not a very efficient system and counselors experience burnout quickly.

After working in a school for a few years, many counselors believe they know what students are thinking and feeling at certain stages in life and that the students' problems, issues, and needs can be anticipated. However, times change and it might be a serious mistake to assume all students at a certain age are alike. There is a need to know the guidance and counseling needs of a student body. In addition, there is a need to know the specific needs of certain target populations within a student body (e.g. college-prep, emotionally handicapped, test-anxious, potential dropouts, and so forth).

To depend on "whatever comes through the door" may be acceptable to some counselors, but it is too fragmented and unsystematic. It also puts a counselor in a crisis and reactive position, instead of a developmental and proactive one. Without knowing the needs and interests of students, counselors may have trouble developing an organized approach to their work and time.

Needs Assessment. Needs assessments come in many forms and, when well organized, they can provide valuable information. Generally, a needs assessment is a formal or informal survey in which respondents indicate their concerns, needs, and interests.

One first year counselor was unsure of what might be needed in her school, although graduate studies and talks with experienced counselors had given her some ideas. In her first month on the job, she developed a brief job description for herself and attached it to a checklist which she sent to teachers in the school. They helped identify student and teacher interests and needs. Teachers were encouraged to add other items to the list and to make comments. The counselor then tallied the responses from the returned forms and made a report to the faculty. From this needs assessment, it was possible to pinpoint some high priority items for teachers, such as helping students learn study habits, school rules and regulations, and communication skills.

Another counselor also used teachers as a resource to identify student needs but chose to work through the school's Guidance Committee. The teachers on the committee talked with other teachers about some of their concerns and student needs. Through committee discussions, the counselor identified a few priorities that needed attention at the beginning of the school year when students were settling into routines.

It is also possible to survey parents, using newsletters, task forces, and Parent-Teacher Organizations. Community agencies can provide some insights. A community crisis intervention center reported there had been a sudden increase in the use of "crack" among young people in the school district. Cocaine in this form was being sold in $5-pieces to make it more affordable. School counselors received more information and training in a county-wide workshop, based on the assumption that every school needed to address the problem immediately.

Perhaps the most important source for learning more about student needs and interests is the students themselves. Surprisingly, students are seldom asked. "It only confirms what we already know," said one experienced counselor who believed that needs assessments were a waste of time. Closer examination, however, suggests that some needs are not identified without systematic procedures.

A brief needs assessment can give counselors more reason for organizing and providing a particular intervention. For instance, in one middle school, students were surveyed during their advisor-advisee periods (TAP). It was learned that many students wanted to talk more about how to get along better with their parents and how to have an organized plan of study. Others felt the need to talk more about making friends, being assertive, and coping with teachers. Some issues and concerns were related to objectives that already were built into the guidance curriculum for TAP, but the survey alerted teachers and counselors to the value of some particular guidance units.

Three counselors in a high school surveyed students in the sophomore class and asked them to indicate their plans upon graduation: 1) Get a job; 2) Go into military service; 3) Go to a technical or community college; 4) Go to a four-year college or university; or 5) Undecided. After reviewing the results of this brief survey, the sophomore class was divided into five career guidance groups. Special large and small group guidance units were designed particularly for the undecided group, assuming they needed to have tentative job goals to make school more meaningful.

An effective needs assessment can be put together quickly and is usually no more than one page in length. The length of time to administer a survey and the time it takes to tally the results are always considered. Instead of putting together a lengthy instrument, it might be better to focus on a particular area and direct a few specific questions to students. This can provide a quick picture and some possible leads for counselor interventions.

Problem check-lists, administered anonymously in TAP homebase rooms and with the option of signing names or checking a box requesting a meeting with a counselor, have also been effective. There are students who want to talk with a counselor but who are unsure of the procedures. They may be too shy to walk into the guidance office to request help.

Conducting an annual or periodic needs assessment is not as common as it once was among counselors. Part of the reason is that the instruments used were often impractical and the results took too long to tally. Perhaps most important, they emphasized things that needed attention but were often ignored. One group of counselors at a middle school pointed to a tall stack of papers (a needs survey) and said, "Now what do we do with them?" It was easier to put together the instrument and to administer it than it was to tally the results and to decide upon a next step. Consequently, the survey responses sat in a corner of the guidance office and they were never used effectively.

A practical approach suggests that counselors should use simple procedures and brief instruments which can be tallied quickly. They should have an idea of how the results can be interpreted and used. Finally, needs assessments are much easier to compile when there is TAP. Teacher-advisors might administer different surveys developed in the guidance office. They can then tally the results for their groups. The reports from each group could be summed for a final school report. TAP also makes it easier to administer more than one needs assessment instrument, related to a particular areas (alcohol and drug abuse, personal safety, study habits, and so forth). TAP makes it practical to do needs assessments in small pieces instead of one extended survey.

What is being done to meet those needs?

A brief and precise answer to this question alludes many counselors. They have trouble telling others what they do in their jobs. A written job description often seems inadequate.

If this question were asked of you, as a counselor, what response would you give? Suppose you were asked by a school board member to give a concise description of what you do, in about three minutes, could you do it? Without some forethought and practice, most counselors could not. They would leave out important ideas and concepts or fumble for words. They could regret their choice of words or that they spent too long describing one aspect of the job.

It may be helpful to picture in your mind the Chart of Counselor Interventions (Figure 4.1). Then, beginning with some typical student needs or problems, you can cite the six basic interventions that counselors use in a developmental guidance and counseling program. Each of the interventions might then be described briefly, perhaps with an example.

This organized presentation has proven to be effective with students, teachers, parents, and administrators. For some people who want more specific information, this is still not enough. They want facts and figures.

Tallying Interventions. Some school districts require their counselors to keep a record book in which different counselor interventions are logged. Counselors can note the type of intervention that took place with a student, perhaps the amount of time that it took (perhaps recorded in 15-minute intervals), and the general focus of an intervention. A few schools have developed cards which can be keypunched and analyzed by computer.

Microcomputers are making keypunch operations outdated and many counselors are now recording their daily operations in coded files on a computer disk. Computer programs are already available which enable counselors to see within seconds the sums of their daily, weekly, monthly, and yearly interventions (e.g. Lee and Pulvino, 1984). This information can be used as part of a final report to a central administration.

At one time record keeping of this kind was laborious, tedious, and questionable. Counselors complained that such recording and tallying by hand took too much time and there were so many things happening in their job that could not be recorded accurately. One school system listened to the counselors and decided to take a random sampling of counselors' work weeks, but this also had its problems. Some counselors could not resist arranging their schedules to accommodate the sampling procedures. Some said that the sample was skewed because of the dominance of some activities at the times when the samples were taken.

A district director of guidance asked counselors to tally and report the kinds of interventions that they were using. First, it was assumed that all professionals need some type of record of the services they are providing. This is especially true of people in business or professions in which they are charging for services; and, time is money. It seemed logical to expect the same from counselors. Therefore, counselors recorded their interventions weekly and this led to a summative report for all counselors at different grade levels.

The district director examined the data and used it to make a general report to the superintendent, highlighting the kinds of services that students, teachers, and parents received from school counselors. Budget requests were based on some of the findings. At one point it was suggested that more counselors were needed and the data supported the need. Staff development needs were also identified, such as when it appeared that junior high school counselors seldom used small group counseling as an intervention.

It was also possible for the guidance director to consult with counselors regarding balanced programs and with administrators in terms of counselor needs. The data that was collected systematically had more power than a few general statements. Some counselors who had problems organizing a comprehensive program were targeted for assistance. Previously, administrators might have questioned their counselors' contributions or value to the school, but they could not pinpoint problems with confidence and supportive information. Some marginally performing counselors began to take a more active interest in their work when they knew that their efforts were being monitored.

Shaw (1973) provided a detailed example of how counselors in one school district used time study cards to report information about counselor interventions. Seven major time categories were derived and various subcategories were listed on the cards. Results of the study with 20 high school counselors showed that counselors spent significant amounts of time in nonprofessional and nonrelevant activities in every month of the year. The average was over three hours per day per counselor for every day of the school year. It was also obvious from the data that major fluctuations occurred in the use of counselor time, depending upon events at the school. There was a clear need to help counselors manage their time and to learn more skills.

Is the counselor intervention making a difference?

The state of Texas has shown leadership in the area of accountability for many years. As early as 1973, the Texas Education Agency released a guide for the development of a competency-based outcome-stated guidance plan, which also included some descriptive statements about the process to be used by counselors. This plan identified three major domains (educational, vocational, and social) and specified objectives in observable and behavioral terms. It was among the first management-by-objectives plans (Texas Education Agency, 1973) and has since been expanded as the state moves in the direction of having a state-wide guidance curriculum.

For the first time there was a precise statement about counselor competencies and measureable outcomes of student achievement.

Because it specified and outlined five sequential phases, many counselors found it helpful in developing and planning their guidance programs (assessing needs, setting priorities, developing objectives, developing activities to achieve objectives, and evaluating the program). It was a guide for a complete study of a program.

Currently, most school districts in the United States are content to build accountability systems for guidance programs around answers to the first two questions: What are the student needs and what is being done to meet them? These questions, of course, can just as easily be asked of teacher or parent needs. However, the answers to these questions are still not adequate for those who want to know if counselors are making a positive difference in their work.

The very idea of inquiry being a base for counselor work makes sense for the professional. But, it is an alien thought for some educators who do not embrace the scientific method as a part of their work. They may never have been exposed to its practical application when they were going through school and learning to be an educator. For some, the scientific method is something that is learned and applied in science classes or laboratories. Systematic inquiry is a practical approach to the work of a counselor. It is the essence of accountability.

Scientific inquiry can be done in many ways. It is acceptable to use a case study approach, as is done in such areas as sociology, anthropology, and history. Or, inquiry may be done through a careful manipulation of different variables and specific observations. A research design which attempts to control for sources of invalidity might be used so that results of a study could be statistically analyzed and more confidence given to inferences. You may already recognize this language as that of an experimental researcher.

The counselor, as a researcher-practitioner, looks at problems and wants to know how they can be solved effectively and efficiently. It involves careful observations, a collection of reliable data, a means for analyzing the data and, finally, a report of the results, conclusions, implications, limitations, and recommendations.

In addition to the three questions on accountability, perhaps a fourth question might be: What can be concluded about the guidance program? Some writers (e.g. Lewis, 1983; Lombana, 1985) have suggested some ways to think about evaluating a guidance program, emphasizing that counselee and program objectives need careful planning and need to be systematic.

Finally, when it comes to accountability, it is always advisable to ask the consumers of guidance and counseling services—students, parents, and teachers—what they think. How do they see the process? The outcomes? The program? The data collected from them will have its limitations too. Nevertheless, if the recipients of the services are not satisfied, then the rest of the conclusions may be meaningless. Let's look at some factors you will want to consider in planning accountability studies.

Factors to Consider

What are the basic steps?

The basic steps should include defining the goals or objectives to be studied, identifying the intervention to be used, if any, and then using a measuring device to collect data for evaluation. There are also practical procedures that you might consider.

First, it is important to identify the goals and objectives of an accountability study in observable behaviors, although some internal variables (e.g self-esteem, attitude, or values) may be of particular interest. The question to ask is: How can you tell if a person has a positive self-concept? It is usually easier to find or develop some valid measurements when goals are stated in behavioral terminology. In addition, goals stated in behavior terms can clarify the intervention process.

Selecting one goal or objective for study is another practical consideration for accountability studies. But most counselors assume, if they are going to the trouble of organizing a study, they should look at several variables. Therefore, a compromise is to identify some primary and secondary objectives.

Select practical and valid assessment instruments which are directly related to desired outcomes. Some instruments used to measure a goal may be time-consuming to administer, difficult to score or interpret, expensive to purchase, or may be only indirectly related to goals. If a goal for eighth grade students is that they all have four-year high school plans before entering high school, then the desired outcome is clear. It is easy enough for counselors to count the number of students who have a plan on file. If the goal is to improve eighth grade students' self-concepts, a score on a standardized test may suggest some improvement. In addition, perhaps behaviors related to a positive self-concept could be rated.

Selecting a target group of students can narrow the focus of an accountability study and make it easier to manage. Studying the effects of group counseling on students who are not completing their homework assignments might be one example. In addition, two or three different approaches to group counseling might also be examined, as one looks for the most effective and efficient method. Studying both the process and the outcome is desirable in accountability systems.

It makes practical sense to carefully plan and organize accountability studies. All the services that a counselor delivers do not necessarily have to be evaluated. Every student a counselor meets does not have to complete a set of evaluation instruments for an accountability study.

Select something of value and interest to study, one that represents the things you do in your work. If a study can be arranged so that the effects of a structured small group counseling approach can be investigated, the results might be considered a sample of times when you have used the same group procedures or approach. If your study is planned and organized, you can generalize from the sample you have taken.

Finally, it is practical to write a brief report of any findings that result from an accountability study. The report can highlight the effort and outcomes. It can be used to make decisions about a counselee, an intervention, or the program.

How do you design an accountability study?

You might first think about answering the questions: "From where are we starting?" "What's the baseline?" Next, ask yourself, "What do I want to do in this situation?" "What intervention can be used?" "How long will it last and how often will it occur?" Keep some records to show what was done, perhaps a description of the intervention by activities or techniques used. If the intervention you planned to use at the beginning gets changed along the way, make note of it. This is a practical consideration for a counselor so that the intervention can be modified or repeated in the future and described in a report. Although most final reports require only a general explanation of the intervention, the trend among counselors is to outline it in detail so that it might be used easily again or replicated by other counselors.

After the intervention has been completed, you ask: "Where are we now and how can we tell?" This involves an examination of any information that has been collected along the way or another administration of the instrument that was used to obtain some baseline data. The data are then compared, looking for any gains that might have been made.

This simple "before and after" design can be improved by comparing results with a classical control group, one that did not receive the intervention at the time of the study. Some refer to it as the "delayed treatment group," assuming, if the intervention is proven effective, it will be given to participants in the control group at a later time. If the experimental or treatment group and the control group are similar in nature before the intervention and different afterwards, it might be concluded that the intervention had an effect. Was it a favorable one?

The "before and after" design is one of the most practical research designs that a counselor can use and is favored over an "after only" design where baseline data were not collected. It is preferred, though it has limitations, when it is not possible to have an equivalent or matched control group.

In addition to experimental type designs which look for effects, it is also possible to collect data to describe a population or a situation. A group of students might be described in terms of test scores or by a survey which they completed. In this case, the accountability study focuses on providing a composite picture of a group.

It is also possible to collect data as you move through the process of counseling, perhaps following the procedures of single case research (e.g. Tracey, 1983). Single case research designs are intense, provide more depth of information, and are not difficult to be incorporated into the everyday work of a counselor. Single case designs emphasize measuring variables repeatedly over time.

How do you measure the outcomes?

Although testimonials and subjective reports have their place, objective data is preferred in accountability studies. Any instrument that helps you collect objective data on which to make evaluations deserves special consideration. Standardized instruments have credibility because they have reported validity and reliability data which help determine their value and use. Knowledge of the instrument itself plays an important part when examining results and interpreting them.

Standardized instruments are particularly useful when you are trying to study some complex variables (e.g. personality, abilities, aptitudes), and you do not have time or resources to build a valid measure of your own. They are also valuable when you are looking for a total score or a few categorical scores that result from several items on the instrument. However, many of the best standardized instruments are not readily available, machine scored only by the company that distributes them, time consuming to administer, and difficult to work into most accountability studies. They can also be expensive.

You can build a survey instrument by asking open and closed questions of students. The data can be summarized using descriptive statistics such as means, medians, modes, percentages, and percentiles to report your findings. Knowing how to construct a useful instrument that has face validity is an important skill for counselors. Test-retest reliability can be obtained with your own students.

Again, an instrument which identifies the specific behaviors you want to focus on may be the most practical approach. In one study, a group of counselors were asked what they wanted to accomplish with students. After some discussion about such terms as "classroom adjustment," "positive self-concepts," "better attitudes," "cooperation with teachers," and "stop fooling around," the group was asked: "What are the things that students must do to be perceived as cooperative, having a positive attitude, and so forth?" "What do students need to do to achieve well?"

Subsequently, a list of classroom behaviors related to achievement was developed (See Figure 12.1). A Likert-type scale (five points) was placed beside each item so that behaviors could be rated in terms of how often they occurred (Very Often to Very Seldom). The rating scale could be changed, on occasion, to give respondents an opportunity to report the degree to which they agreed with an item (i.e. Strongly Agree to Strongly Disagree). It was also possible to select out a few items for study, to add some others, perhaps those specific to a teacher's concern (e.g. Turns in current event from newspaper each Friday), or include those behaviors to be eliminated or reduced (e.g. "Pushes and hits in cafeteria line," "Spits on children").

Figure 12.1

Learning Behaviors Related to School Achievement

Student _____ Teacher _____ Date _____

Please check the frequency of each behavior listed.
Add other items or make addition comments, if you wish.

	Very Often	Often	Some-times	Seldom	Very Seldom
Attends class					
Is punctual to class					
Brings study materials					
Takes part in discussions					
Pays attention in class					
Follows directions					
Starts assignments					
Attends to a given task					
Completes assignments					
Talks at appropriate times					
Works independently					
Follows school rules					

When drawn from a general list, behavior-focused instruments are easy to put together. They give attention to specific outcomes related to school and can be administered to respondents in a brief time. Items can be rated easily by students or their teachers. Peers and parents can also be asked to respond to the items about a student. The versatility and ease of interpretation of such instruments make them a practical consideration for use by counselors.

How do you analyze data and report results?

A report was once made to a school board which was composed of some highly educated members, including a university professor, two medical doctors, and an accountant. All board members were college graduates. When the report focused on sophisticated testing of hypotheses, significance levels, and statistical procedures, the board lost interest. When graphs were used to illustrate progress from baseline data to when the study was completed, their interest perked. When gains were presented in percentages, the comparisons were easy to see and board members were impressed. Keep reports simple and avoid detailed statistical reports. They might be kept as backup or supplemental reports for those who are particularly interested in pursuing the data. Most people want to know the general results and simple pictures are preferred over complex ones.

Accountability studies are important because they give you feedback on your work. They help you evaluate the interventions that you are using. They can provide some hints regarding whether new directions are needed or whether you want to continue what you are doing. In addition, some reports lend themselves to gaining more support for your work, perhaps for a new project that you want to try. Those findings which prove particularly satisfying in terms of achieving desired outcomes make excellent news for the public. They can be used to promote positive relations with teachers, administrators, school boards, and the general public.

This chapter is limited. It is a brief discussion of research concepts and procedures which might be applied in an accountability system for counselors. Other books might be consulted regarding statistical procedures which can be used in your work. You might also consult with someone in the school district who enjoys designing studies and analyzing data. Let's look more specifically at two methods which can be used to study the effectiveness of your interventions: 1) Systematic Case Studies and 2) Comparative Group Studies.

The Systematic Case Study

The following is an example of a systematic case study. It is a practical approach, one that can be used with a group of students or an individual. The general outline guides you through five basic steps. It can become more sophisticated if you add more steps or procedures. However, that is rarely necessary for most accountability studies.

The five steps include: 1) Identify the target student or a group of students for study; 2) Collect baseline data; 3) Provide the intervention; 4) Collect post-baseline data; and 5) Analyze the findings and write a report. The case of Kevin illustrates how the study might be implemented.

The Case of Kevin

Kevin was a seventh grade student who was a problem to most of his teachers. He was referred by one teacher, Mrs. Crowell, who wanted Kevin removed from her class. She said, "He's rude and inconsiderate of others. He hates school and wants to be kicked out of class, probably so that his tough guy image can be reinforced. I don't want to do that, but that's what it may come to. In plain English, the kid's a real bozo... and, I know, you're going to tell me that he comes from a family that doesn't care about him. But, that doesn't change things. He's a problem."

The counselor listened patiently and facilitated the teacher to talk about Kevin. The consultation model (Chapter 11) was applied, as the teacher explored the situation. Then, it came time to focus specifically on what the teacher wanted to see from Kevin, if he were to remain in class. The counselor encouraged Mrs. Crowell to put her ideas into behavioral terms, asking such questions as, "And, what are some specific ways in which he is disruptive?" or, "Okay, what does he do that makes you say that he doesn't care?" The counselor showed Mrs. Crowell the list of behaviors related to achievement (Figure 12.1) and said, "Let's see if we can get an idea of some things that we want him to do and figure out where we might be starting."

The teacher rated Kevin on all of the behaviors. The counselor proceeded to consult with Mrs. Crowell about what she might do in class. The counselor, as part of a collaboration and multiple intervention, counseled with Kevin individually for a few sessions. Later, Kevin participated with five other students in small group counseling, which focused on school attitudes and coping with teachers. At the time, it seemed to be the ingredient which helped Kevin's behavior improve. He received recognition from the group and they were all trying to improve their image in school.

Every Friday afternoon, Mrs. Crowell rated Kevin on his classroom behaviors for that week. There was not much change the first two weeks, but in the third week, when Kevin started working with the group, there was a marked change. She said, "Well, there may have been some little changes earlier, enough to give me a little hope, but nothing much to report.... However, this week he was much better, especially on items 4, 7, and 8." Such a checklist helped the teacher identify the progress that was being made. It reinforced her and the counselor for their efforts. It had heightened the teacher's awareness of specific classroom behaviors that were desired from Kevin. The study and the interventions were concluded after a period of seven weeks, the end of a grading period. The final ratings of Kevin by Mrs. Crowell are shown in Figure 12.2 and the final report is shown in Figure 12.3.

Figure 12.2

Behavior Checklist—Kevin
(Teacher Ratings—Pre and Post)

	Very Often	Often	Some-times	Seldom	Very Seldom
Attends class	1/2				
Is punctual to class		2		1	
Brings study materials		2			1
Takes part in discussions					1/2
Pays attention in class			1/2		
Follows directions			2	1	
Starts assignments		2			1
Attends a given task			1/2		
Completes assignments			2	1	
Talks at appropriate times			1/2		
Works independently		2	1		
Follows school rules			1/2		

Pre-ratings = 1 Post-ratings = 2

Developmental Guidance and Counseling

Figure 12.3

Final Written Report on K.J

K.J. (initials for Kevin) is a seventh grade student attending South Marion Junior High School. He has a Wechsler IQ of 105 (Full Scale) and was once referred for the emotionally handicapped program in elementary school. However, special placement was not recommended. In October he was referred for counseling by one of his teachers, who rated him on a classroom behavior checklist (See Figure 12.2). K.J. also rated himself on the same items during the first stage of counseling.

The counselor first consulted with the referring teacher regarding the boy's classroom behavior and about some possible techniques the teacher might use in the classroom to improve K.J.'s behavior. In addition, the school counselor intervened by providing the boy four individual counseling sessions, once a week for four weeks, and four sessions of small group counseling, which started at the beginning of the third week of assistance. K.J. was the target child in a group of five students. The counselor also tried to talk with the parents via phone, but the phone had been recently disconnected.

At the end of the grading period, the referring teacher rated the boy again, as she had done each Friday afternoon from the time the interventions started. Her final rating is shown in the attached graph. It can be seen that on six of the ten items K.J. showed some improvement. Regarding a specific disruptive behavior, "Starts assignments," there was considerable positive change, moving from "very seldom" to "often."

K.J.'s teacher reported that he is continuing to do much better in class and that their working relationship has improved.

This case focused only on the use of a behavior checklist by the teacher, but it could have included other data from school records (attendance, and so forth) and other teachers. More information could have been included about the individual counseling approach (e.g. "During this time Kevin was asked to talk about what he liked and disliked about school, what he hoped to get from school, and how he might get along with his teachers better.") Or, perhaps an outline of the group objectives and titles of the group meetings might have been included, to suggest the kind of approach that was used.

Single case studies in counseling have an important place and may be the most appropriate way to study the effects of counseling with a student. This approach has received special attention (Frey, 1978) as more people recognize that studying counseling effects through group research designs can be limiting. Single case studies, when approached systematically, are interesting. They can also be pooled to help make a point.

A group of counselors, representing all grade levels, agreed to provide their district guidance coordinator with at least four systematic case studies. All counselors agreed to follow the same outline when writing a final report on each case, using the same appropriate headings. Reports were limited to two and three pages in length. The guidance coordinator took the cases and sorted them according to type of problem, grade level, and kind of interventions used. Approximately 72 cases were included in an Accountability Book, which was available to parents and the general public for examination. The book was divided into sections which provided cases on disruptive behavior, shyness, excessive absences, and other problems. The cases were considered to be representative of things that counselors were doing to help students.

The Collaborative Study

The collaborative study follows the same basic outline as the systematic case study, except that there is an effort to work with more students as a target group and counselors pool data before it is analyzed. The pooling of data, providing that certain assumptions are met, allows counselors to analyze data based on a larger number of subjects and to use different statistical procedures.

A group of 16 elementary school counselors met together for staff development meetings and expressed their concern about underachieving students. Since it was a common problem in all the schools and of interest to the public, the group decided to work together in a collaborative study.

Defining and Identifying the Population

First, the counselors agreed upon common criteria for defining and identifying underachieving children. All participants in the study were to have a minimum Slosson IQ of 90, and they were to have been cited by their teachers as having a marked discrepancy between IQ and achievement scores on standardized tests or school grades. It was further agreed to concentrate on students from grades 3, 4, and 5.

Selecting the Sample or Participants

Using the common criteria, the counselors each identified 20 underachieving students in their respective schools. Then, using a table of random numbers, 10 of the students were assigned to an experimental group and the other 10 served as controls, receiving no counselor assistance until the study was completed. Thus, the 16 counselors identified 320 students for assignment. At the end of the study, data were complete on 155 experimental and 146 control students.

Collecting Data

A teacher evaluation rating form and a student self-rating form were devised for the study. They were administered before and after counselor interventions took place. The teacher form consisted of nine behaviors associated with academic performance in the classroom and included items similar to those in Figure 12.1. Frequency of behavior was reported using a five-point Likert-type scale. The student self-rating consisted of the same behavioral items as those that appeared on the teacher form, but they were placed on separate 3 x 5 cards. The cards were read aloud to students by their counselors in an individual session and sorted by students into the different ratings. The two instruments provided a comparison of teacher and student pre- and post-ratings by both experimental and control groups.

Implementing Counselor Interventions

The counselors, as a staff development group, discussed possible methods and procedures for working with underachieving students. Several arguments were made for everyone using the same approach and evaluating only one kind of intervention. It was finally decided, however, to investigate the overall effectiveness of counselors working with underachieving children, rather than a particular method or approach. Some counselors said they were more effective in using some approaches than others and that individual counselors should use their best skills and resources to bring about change.

The counselors brainstormed together and developed a list of possible procedures or specific interventions that might be used with the experimental group. The list was mimeographed and distributed to all counselors. It was agreed that each counselor would be responsible for carefully recording the specific interventions that were used with each student. Thus, the counselors were free to do whatever they wanted to do to help students, as long as they recorded the number and nature of student contacts. Although this approach lacked the precision of generalization that might come when only one intervention is investigated, it was practical and reduced the need to have more staff development meetings.

Limiting the Duration of the Study

The study was limited to a school grading period of nine weeks. Baseline data was collected in the first week. Counselor interventions then took place for seven weeks. Post-data was collected in the last week.

Analyzing the Findings

The findings or results were analyzed in terms of: 1) Type and number of interventions used by counselors; 2) Teacher pre- and post-ratings; 3) Student pre- and post-ratings; and 4) Comparison of experimental and control groups.

Five categories of counselor interventions were used to record what counselors did with students. A summary of the total interventions used with students in the experimental group are shown in Figure 12.4. The data showed that 95% of the experimental group were involved with group counseling and 93% received the benefits of a counselor consulting with teachers. The data showed that case conferences, consultation with administrators, group consultation with teachers and parents, as well as referral to other professional personnel, were less preferred approaches but were used on occasion.

Most students received more than one kind of counselor help. Approximately 64% of the children in the experimental group received from three to five types of intervention. The general pattern consisted of teacher consultation, followed by one or two individual counseling sessions and some form of small group counseling. Only 2% of the children received one type of intervention alone. About 25% received two types and only 9% received more than five types of intervention.

Table 12.4

Collaborative Study:
The Counselor Interventions

Type of Intervention	Number
1. Consultation	
a. Case Conferences	8
b. Teacher Consultation	98
c. Parent Consultation	39
d. Administrator Consultation	11
TOTAL	156
2. Groups	
a. Problem-centered (Students)	117
b. Growth-centered (Students)	65
c. Teacher Group (Seminar)	6
d. Parent Group (Seminar)	2
TOTAL	188
3. Individual Counseling	
a. With structured activities	67
b. Unstructured	41
TOTAL	108
4. Referral	8
5. Other	63

Percentage differences for pre- and post-ratings on the nine items for the experimental group were reported in Table 12.5. An examination of the data revealed that after counselors intervened, teachers and students reported an increase in behaviors related to achievement.

Analysis of variance procedures were used to statistically compare the experimental and control group students on both student and teacher ratings. Significant differences were found between the experimental and control groups for teacher ratings (.01 level of confidence) and students (.05 level of confidence). Analysis of pre-data also indicated that there were no significant differences between the experimental and control groups at the beginning of the study. Thus, it was concluded that counselors had made a positive difference with underachieving students.

Figure 12.5

Percentage Gains for Experimental Group (Pre and Post Comparison)

| Behaviors | Percentage Difference | |
	Student Ratings	Teacher Ratings
1. Contributes to discussion	+ 15	+ 6
2. Does not start assignments	- 6	-13
3. Completes assignments (homework)	+ 13	+ 15
4. Does not work without individual teacher attention	-16	-15
5. Attends to assigned task	+ 2	+ 14
6. Does not follow directions	- 4	-18
7. Attempts new activities	+ 2	+ 9
8. Does not do work correctly	- 5	-12
9. Demonstrates a readiness to work	+ 11	+ 16

Making a Final Report

Data were summarized and put into tables and figures. A four-page report was compiled and sent to the superintendent of schools and each building principal. A brief report was also made to the school board by the guidance coordinator for the district, with some representative counselors present to discuss the study and answer questions. The local newspaper and television station also received copies of the report and they, subsequently, interviewed the guidance coordinator for news stories.

Myrick, Merhill, and Swanson (1986) reported a study describing a collaborative study by counselors in two different states, yet using the same intervention. One study in a Florida school district involved 72 elementary school counselors who followed the steps outlined above and pooled their data for analysis. In Indiana, 30 school counselors from different schools and districts followed the same guidelines and used the same procedures, thus pooling their data. The final report of the two collaborative studies demonstrated the effectiveness of classroom guidance with student attitudes about school.

Helpful Hints

Work With Someone Else

Accountability studies can bring professionals together as a team. They provide a focus for everyone's work and they stimulate thinking. People can pool their ideas about interventions as well as data collected. Because everyone is working on a project together, there is more support and enthusiasm. The *esprit d' corps* that develops among counselors who work on an accountability study is a prime benefit.

Work with Models or Examples

Look for a few simple models that you can use as guidelines. They might be drawn from this book or from professional journal articles. For instance, with the systematic case outline in front of you, insert the relevant information for one of your own cases. Use the same common language to provide a description of the study. This can save you time in planning and reporting.

Recognize Limitations

There are many reasons why research is difficult to do in the schools and why people do not try. An accountability study may not be perfect. It may not control for all sources of invalidity or be rigorous enough to be published in a professional journal. Yet, it is better to recognize the limitations and then do what you can, rather than do nothing at all.

A few counselors, who have perhaps studied with some excellent researchers, may be quick to point out flaws in a study. They may say, "But, there are too many problems with the research design. You can't control for some factors." Listen carefully to what they say and try to address the issues in some way. Then, do the study, citing the limitations that need to be considered when one examines the data and the conclusions that were reached.

Living with limitations is part of doing accountability studies in a school. Accepting limitations when nothing can be done about them is the only practical thing to do. Telling others that there are limitations to a study and citing them is a professional and responsible way to respond to critics. Almost any effort toward more research will encounter limitations. In fact, few researchers can control for all the variables and sources of invalidity. They all live with limitations.

Develop Relevant Measures

Do not be afraid to develop your own measurement devices. With a little extra effort, you can establish some validity and reliability for them. You might, for instance, do a test-retest on an instrument with a group and use the data to determine the consistency of the instrument. Face validity might do for a start, although construct validity might be improved by asking other professionals to review the items on the instruments and to critique them. When a group of reviewers agree, you can probably proceed with confidence.

When items are stated in observable behaviors, then it is usually easy to obtain both validity and reliability for an instrument. Each item on an instrument can also be analyzed. When items are pooled for a total score, some additional problems are introduced and you will need to recognize some statistical limitations.

Invite Researchers to Help

Most school districts have someone who is interested in accountability and knows something about research methodology. This may be a teacher in a school building or it may be someone at the district's central office who is familiar with research procedures and who could serve as a consultant.

Counselor educators at colleges and universities might be invited to help construct an accountability study with you. Professors from other disciplines might also be asked for help. The Minnesota Department of Education (Miller, Gum, and Bender, 1972), for example, provided an excellent example of how various researchers and school districts in a state can work together to demonstrate counselor effectiveness.

Accountability studies should not be boring, laborious tasks. While there are special issues to be resolved, the studies can be stimulating and professionally rewarding. Sometimes, all that is needed is a little extra encouragement and timely assistance.

Use Studies to Tell About Your Work

A case has already been made for collecting data to give you some feedback about your work. If something is working, continue using it. If it is not working, based on a study that you have made, then consider some modifications or a different approach altogether. At the same time, when favorable results are found, then they might also be used to tell about your job and the work you do (Wiggins, 1977).

You will not be breaking confidentiality by presenting a brief report that focuses primarily on the interventions used and statistical data. You need not reveal names, cite particular events, or provide indiscreet details in a final report. The welfare of counselees is always honored. If in doubt, ask students and parents for their permission to use data collected from them in a study. The AACD code of ethics provides guidelines for doing research with counselees.

There are many teachers who do not understand the work of a counselor. It can help when you show them how you have organized your week and how you are trying to achieve a comprehensive program through the six different interventions. But, it is also impressive when you provide them with a few examples of how you have worked with a particular student or group. It is even more impressive when you have some data to support your claims.

School board members want to know more about what is happening in the schools they serve. They want to hear success stories. Superintendents and building administrators need examples they can use when speaking at various public meetings or when answering questions by the public media. District guidance coordinators need accountability studies to justify budget requests, including ones for the addition of more counselors and staff development training.

In the past, counselors have not done a good job of telling their story with accountability studies. They have relied on a few positive statements from students who have benefited from their services. But now, more difficult questions (See Figure 12.6) are being asked which demand more supportive information and data.

Avoid Being on the Defensive

Some counselors assume that every service is valuable. This may not be the case. Only by systematically collecting feedback from students and other reliable sources can outcomes be evaluated ac-

Figure 12.6

Questions for School Counselors

1. Goals and objectives—
   What are you trying to accomplish as a counselor? What are your goals? Which ones are for all students? For target populations? For selected students? Which goals are given highest priority?

2. Roles and functions—
   What are you doing to accomplish your goals? How is your contribution unique? What is missing or needed in order to have a more comprehensive approach?

3. Schedules and calendars—
   How are you managing your time? What minimum number of counselor interventions can be scheduled for the week? How is the weekly calendar of events related to the yearly one? What special topics are getting attention and when?

4. Skills and tasks—
   What skills are needed to be successful in your roles and interventions? How do you rate yourself on them? In which roles or interventions do you need additional training or retraining?

5. Activities and procedures—
   How have you organized and arranged activities? Have some been arranged in a sequential series or as a set of structured experiences? What kind of guidance or counseling units have you developed and implemented?

6. Evaluation and accountability—
   What kind of results are you getting? How are you accountable? Are you making a difference? What are you doing to let others know about your work?

7. Professionalism and personal growth—
   What are you doing to keep alive professionally? What contributions are you making to your profession and what are you getting in return? What does your profession mean to you? What are you getting out of being a counselor?

----

curately. Still, there are many counselors who are not inclined to take part in accountability studies for fear that they might be discovered as being ineffective. To them, studies might draw unwanted attention and create a problem that was not there before. When pushed for more explanation, they reply that, unless requested by the district office or unless they are about to lose their jobs, accountability studies are a waste of time.

Counselors in a developmental guidance and counseling program usually have lots of positive evidence at hand to help tell their story. Rather than waiting until they are someday forced on the defensive, they want to make their achievements known to others. How can others speak favorably about counselors if they do not know how effective they are in their work? Avoid waiting until you are challenged. Have some accountability studies at hand to show what you are doing to school board members, parents, and the general public.

Be Selective

It is not practical to study all aspects of your work at the same time. You cannot conduct systematic case studies with all your students. There will be times when you cannot collect baseline data or reports from teachers. Therefore, select a few places where you want to concentrate your efforts. Set some priorities, just as you have done with other parts of your program.

If you and your colleagues as a group have not agreed to an accountability project in which you are all going to participate and teaming is not possible at the time, then identify one or two areas in which you want to be especially accountable in a given period of time. Select a few target students for study. This selection might be influenced by circumstances, convenience, availability of data, or some special interest. The reason may not matter as much as the commitment to be accountable.

Advantages, Limitations, and Conclusion

Advantages of Accountable Studies

1. There is more feedback on which counselors can make decisions about their work or an intervention. It gives them more confidence in making decisions.

2. Studies can be used for more public recognition for counselor accomplishments.

3. Accountability studies almost always improve a counselor's professional standing. It demonstrates to a considerable degree how counselors see themselves as professionals.

4. Through networking it is possible to share studies, and some are suitable for publication in a professional journal. Many can be discussed at professional meetings, workshops, and conferences.

5. There is much to be gained personally from knowing what is being accomplished or that your work is improving.

6. Accountability studies can help identify students who require special help, perhaps from outside resources.

7. They can also be used to highlight staff development needs. Staff development training can precede an accountability study or be the result of one in which the need for more competencies was demonstrated.

Limitations to Accountable Studies

1. Accountability studies take time that could be given to other services and responsibilities.

2. Almost all data has limitations. Some counselors have to be cautioned, when interpreting data and discussing conclusions, not to go beyond the data in their enthusiasm and to recognize the limitations of a study.

3. Most accountability studies are little pieces of the big picture of guidance and counseling. Rarely are there funds or resources to do a comprehensive accountability study of guidance and counseling programs.

Conclusion

While many people exhort counselors to be accountable and to provide data which can be used to tell about their work, accountability studies are only occasionally carried out in most school districts. The fact that counselors are extremely busy with a myriad of responsibilities is no longer acceptable as a justification for not evaluating their work. Accountability is an essential part of a developmental guidance and counseling program.

There are many ways to be accountable. Following some fundamental steps based on research methodology can be useful. However, it is important to acknowledge that accountability studies are not the equivalent of doctoral or master theses, where rigorous attempts are made to control many variables. Rather, accountability studies by counselors have their recognized limits. Nevertheless, these limited studies provide some important data which can be useful to counselors and their public.

Being accountable involves a systematic approach to research and evaluation. It means taking time to plan, perhaps with some other counselor colleagues who are also interested in evaluating their work. Perhaps most important, it involves counselors seeing themselves as professionals, having positive attitudes about themselves and their work, and wanting to know more about their interventions with students.

Challenges and Changes for Guidance and Counseling

With the pursuit of excellence in education a primary concern of the nation, proposed changes for schools are coming in flurries. The central issue is always the same: programs to help young people learn more and which help secure the nation's future. School counselors can play important parts in shaping the nature of their work and the future of their profession. But, this requires a sound rationale for guidance and counseling programs, a clear understanding of their job potential and roles, and a willingness to accept the challenges and changes which will affect them.

Replicating and Revising

There are many useful ideas, techniques, strategies, and activities which have been published and described over the years. Some of them need to be replicated or revised. They need to be recycled, with a modern twist. You may have heard the expression, "Everything goes in cycles...." The work of the counselor is no exception.

One counselor who had several years of experience was reminded of a favorite group counseling activity which she used quite successfully. She remarked, "You know, I'd forgotten about that activity. It was popular with the kids.... I guess I just got tired of using it." Another counselor had a similar experience when he attended a state conference and listened to a program presenter. "That's nothing new. We did that years ago. They just made a few changes to update the language and procedures." But, the presenter was also reporting some data which showed how the counseling experience, with a few modifications from what had been done in the past, had a positive impact on students.

Many effective procedures that were popular ten or more years ago have been discarded by experienced counselors because they grew tired of them. As one counselor said, "If I have to talk to that little puppet one more time and read the story of how he learned to make friends, I'll go crazy." Yet, each year a new group of children love to hear the story and watch her work magically with the puppet. Monotony, boredom, waning enthusiasm, and fatigue have contributed to the disuse of many effective techniques and strategies.

In addition, some published programs and strategies are not read by a lot of practitioners. Professional journals in counseling are not commonplace in many school offices and there have been complaints that such publications are not practical. Experimental studies may show that a counselor intervention was effective, but the final report or article often lacks specifics regarding how the intervention was implemented, the procedures that were used, and practical suggestions to help counselors replicate the idea.

Recycling some "oldie goldie" activities and procedures, with a contemporary emphasis, may be just what is needed to revitalize a once successful counselor activity or strategy. Some old familiar ideas are often welcomed when repackaged, especially if they are practical. The challenge is to find out what works and what doesn't, and to keep both students and counselors interested.

The Changing of the Guard

Some counselors are finding the new programs and challenges to be stimulating and they welcome the change. They approach their work with new enthusiasm and provide valuable leadership, especially when they are given opportunities to be professionally renewed or retrained. Other counselors, however, are feeling the pressure of having more expectations put on them and having to learn new approaches and skills. Some find the new developments to be so stressful that they are asking to be reassigned or taking early retirement, thus creating more job openings.

Moreover, the average age of most high school counselors in the United States is over 55 years. Thus, it appears that in short time, the nation will face a dramatic need for more counselors at the secondary level, especially with early retirement plans coming into vogue. There has been a shortage of elementary school counselors for many years in several states and, based on the number of graduate students who are currently enrolled in school counseling, it appears that the shortage will continue for several years. There is a need for new counselors and this need is going to reach dramatic proportions in the future.

As new people enter the field of counseling and guidance, it is important they not drift into old traditions and habits that are no longer relevant or be tutored by people who lack the interest and energy to try new ideas. It is not easy to make changes in a system, but counselors who want to implement a comprehensive developmental guidance and counseling program will generally find support among administrators and teachers of all ages.

As new leadership emerges, it is likely that developmental guidance and counseling programs will become the accepted standard for all schools (K-Adult). The "changing of the guard" need not be a traumatic one, as there are many productive procedures that have been developed over the years which are still relevant and there are many accomplishments of which counselors who pioneered early programs can be proud. Perhaps it is time to blend the best of the old and the best of the new, as you are challenged to build your own program and create your own role and image.

Change is inevitable, and as society changes its institutions also change. In many respects, educational systems may be among the slowest to respond to new trends and issues. They are like solid rocks, resisting the waves of change until little pieces are chipped away.

School guidance and counseling is such a young profession that its image has never been solidified. Perhaps that is because many of the first counselors did not have a clear vision of school guidance and counseling programs and what they could mean to students and their teachers. The result is that many counselors have felt tossed about without direction and have wondered if they can survive the current waves of change in education.

Yet, more realistically, school guidance and counseling programs have always been in a state of evolution since the time they were first introduced. To outline the approach proposed in this book, for example, was not possible 30 years ago, although certainly some of the fundamental concerns and program ideas were there. It took experience, trial and error, new insights to how people learn and relearn, more knowledge of fundamental counseling theories and skills, and a breaking away from some traditions before a practical comprehensive program could be designed. Make no mistake, the evolution of school guidance and counseling programs is still not over.

The first guidance programs focused on vocational placement. The next ones gave attention to students who were gifted and talented, the hope of the future, and, finally, some programs were developed for those who were less talented and motivated. Testing and diagnostic procedures, crisis-interventions, and therapy models dominated the early thinking of counselors and counselor educators. Such a restricted and reactive approach simply was not practical. There were too many student needs that were ignored, needs that influenced the learning environment and educational outcomes.

The next wave of change introduced the idea of developmental guidance and encouraged organized efforts in the elementary school years. It was evident that all students had conflicts in their lives and that all struggled with problems as part of moving through life stages. The manner in which students resolved their problems and made decisions had a powerful influence on their personal and academic growth, and it also affected the educational experience of their peers. Therefore, developmental guidance and counseling programs emerged as the most logical and practical approach for all schools.

This approach quickly gathered many supporters. It was common-sense to have a guidance program which mobilized the positive growth resources in a school, rather than wait and react to problems. A few people continued to hang on to the thought that counselors were primarily problem-solvers who worked with troubled youth. Or, counseling consisted of helping students pick a career and telling them what courses to take and what adjustments to make.

Although the philosophy was sound and theories were clear in the early years, there were no prototypes or exemplary models for counselors to follow as they set about building their programs and creating their jobs. Counselors amounted to the "new kids on the block" in the schools and nobody knew much about them or what to expect. Unsure of their roles and competencies, a lot of counselors floundered and became discouraged. They wondered if it were possible to do everything that was expected of them, and they doubted their impact. Others, thinking that the job of counseling was overwhelming, retreated to the few areas in guidance where they felt comfortable and where there appeared to be some job security.

Fortunately, some counselors had a vision. They pictured more comprehensive programs. They took the opportunity to experiment, to try new ideas, to find effective ways of helping students, parents, and teachers. They were innovative. These counselors led the way for the rest of us. They demonstrated what could be done. From their experiences, we learned how to be more realistic, practical, and open to change.

Now, a new wave of change is taking place. It goes beyond a revised list of general objectives and roles of a counselor, which were identified some years ago. Rather, this new wave advances developmental guidance for all schools (K-12). It challenges counselors to manage a basic set of counselor interventions and provide a balanced and comprehensive program, based on practical strategies and procedures. These are welcomed changes because more students will benefit and counselors will find their work more productive and enjoyable.

Appendix A

The Florida Classroom Guidance Project
(Fourth Grade—Six Sessions)

The Guidance Unit

The guidance unit will consist of six 30-minute sessions. Each session will be divided into four parts: Introduction (3-5 minutes); Activity I (8-10 minutes); Activity II (8-10 minutes); and Closure (5-10 minutes).

In general, the introduction will be used to: 1) gain the class' attention; 2) prepare the students for the session; 3) provide transition from the previous session; and 4) introduce the session's topic or focus. Activity I will be counselor/teacher led with the total class. Activity II will feature small group interaction with specific tasks. Closure will be counselor/teacher led again with the total class and also include both summary and assignment.

Time management is important. Follow the time allocations listed above. If additional time is available, not to exceed 45 minutes, further discussion is possible.

Room arrangements also need special attention. The following organization is recommended. In the first session, students will be shown how to participate in class and small group discussions through five teams of about six students each. These teams will be positioned around the room in semi-circles during the Introduction period. During Activity I, the counselor speaks to the class via the semi-circled groups. During Activity II, the teams close their small groups for discussion. Groups can then reposition themselves quickly in semi-circles for closure. This organization reduces disruptive movements and saves time while maximizing opportunities for student participation.

Each session will have a topic, an idea or focus related to the purpose and goals of the guidance unit. Activities are structured procedures that are followed in order to stimulate thinking and elicit discussion. Tasks are specific questions or assignments in the activities.

Counselors and teachers work together to implement the guidance sessions. They present general information, introduce topics, use high facilitative responses to lead discussions, structure the session through the activities and related tasks, move about the room and supervise the small groups, elicit student ideas and feelings, and make summary statements and outside assignments. They model behaviors and help make the sessions positive experiences.

Student and Teacher Inventories may be used as a pre and post assessment to determine gains or outcomes.

Session One: "Understanding Feelings and Behaviors"

Purpose:
To help the class get organized for this and future sessions and to help students recognize how feelings and behaviors are related. Pleasant and unpleasant feelings are explored.

Materials:
Chalkboard or newsprint to recording feeling word lists.

Introduction:
Begin by saying, *"Have you ever wondered why people do the things they do? Have you ever thought about what makes some people successful, while others have so many problems? What do people do if they want to change something about themselves? What are some things we can do to make our lives better? Well, we are going to think about these and other questions during our time together. We are going to meet six times and our sessions will last about 30 minutes. That's not much time and we want to use it wisely. You are going to form some working teams so that we can have some interesting class discussions and everyone will get an opportunity to participate."*

Divide the class into five groups of about five or six students each. You may want to assign target students to different groups. Each group should have both boys and girls. Groups are positioned around the room in semi-circles for ease of discussion. Take time to position the groups, identifying them by number, so they will be familiar with this arrangement. It can be used each session. Encourage students to move quickly and quietly. Have them practice moving to and from their groups once or twice, or until they have an understanding of the process and can move efficiently.

As soon as the teams are positioned in semi-circles, say: *"We will have our class discussions while you are seated with your team. Sometimes we will also do some small group activities so that you can work together and everyone will get a chance to share."* Show them how one person can move a chair to form a closer group for discussion. While the students are in this closed position, give the following task.

"Now, introduce yourself to your team members by telling two things about yourself. Since you will be working closely together in the

future, it will help if you know each other better. First, give your name and then tell what you like to do when you are not in school. Then, tell what you would do with $1,000 if you had it to spend any way you wanted to spend it."

In a go-around, students take turns introducing themselves. Move about the groups, helping to clarify the task if needed. As soon as the team members have introduced themselves, ask for the one person to move back so that the semi-circle is again formed.

Activity I:
Say, *"Everyone has feelings. Some feelings are pleasant and others are unpleasant. Let's think of some words that describe our pleasant feelings and I'll list them here."* Develop a list, making sure that each team has contributed some words to the list. Add a few of your own, as a way of stimulating their thinking. Then, make a second list—unpleasant feeling words. Now say, *"We have two lists—one for unpleasant and one for pleasant feelings. There are other words, too, and we can add them later."*

"How we feel can affect what we do. Let's look at one of our words (select one) *and think of how people might behave if they felt that way."* Elicit some behaviors from the class. Then, give a second illustration, again eliciting behaviors from the class and adding examples of your own.

Activity II:
"We know that feelings and behaviors are closely related. When persons feel something, they might also act in certain ways. Let's continue to think of how people behave when they feel pleasant or unpleasant feelings by working in our teams. I will give you two tasks. First, I am going to give each team two words, one from the pleasant feeling list and the other from the unpleasant feeling list." Give each team two words.

"Think of something that you might do if you felt the unpleasant feeling your team was assigned. Take turns by going around. If you are having trouble thinking of something, you can 'pass' and the group will come back to you later."

"Now, using any word from either of the two lists, each person pick a feeling word and tell about a time when you saw someone who might have felt that way. What was the person doing?" Again, have the students go around the circle.

Closure:
Move the teams into their semi-circles for class discussion. *"Each team has been talking about feelings and behaviors. Let's hear about*

some of your ideas." Call on each team to share one of their words and how people might behave. If time permits, repeat.

"People have all kinds of feelings. Everyone has had, at different times, pleasant and unpleasant feelings. Do you think that is also true for students who attend school? Do students have both pleasant and unpleasant feelings about school? What are some examples? How do feelings affect the way people behave at school? Is it possible for the way a person behaves at school to also affect that person's feelings?"

Summary:
"There are lots of words to describe our pleasant and unpleasant feelings. Sometimes people have more than just one feeling. They might even have mixed feelings about something. But, feelings do affect our actions. They do affect what we do at home, with our friends, at school, and in class. How are you feeling right now? Pleasant or unpleasant?"

"Well, I am feeling some pleasant feelings because of our class discussion today and the way in which you all cooperated in moving to your teams and working together. Those feelings make me want to thank you for your contributions and to say that I am looking forward to our next session which will be _____ ."

Assignment:
"In the meantime, I want you all to do one thing. Pay attention to your classmates and see if you can tell how they might be feeling by the way they behave. And then, pick one person and tell that person the kind of feelings that you think that person is having. See how close you can come to being accurate about feelings."

"Until next time, have a nice day and have many pleasant feelings."

Session Two: "Attitude Glasses"

Purpose:
To help students recognize how attitudes affect their lives and that attitudes can be changed.

Materials:
Glasses can be imaginary or inexpensive eye glass frames might be used to dramatize the session. Chalkboard or newsprint.

Introduction:
Begin by saying, *"First, do you remember how we formed teams the last time we met? Let me see the hands of the first team. Do you remember where and how you sat for our class discussion? Okay. Now, let me see the hands of the second team... (and so on)."* Assign the teams to their positions in semi-circles.

"Who remembers what we talked about last time? That's right, we talked about pleasant and unpleasant feelings. And, we also talked about how our feelings and the way we act are closely related. Let me see the hands of those who did the assignment—who took time to tell someone in the class about some feelings they noticed. What feelings did you notice?"

Activity I:
Say, *"Today I have some special glasses. They are called attitude glasses* (write the word 'attitude' on the board). *When you wear attitude glasses, you also put on the same attitude as the glasses. In other words, you see things in that particular way."*

Hold up a pair of glasses or pretend to take out a pair of glasses. *"These attitude glasses are called 'Suspicious Glasses.' What do you suppose a suspicious attitude is?"* After a few responses, put the glasses on and look over the class in a suspicious manner. Then say something like this: *"Oh, just look at them sitting there. They are just waiting for me to make a mistake. They don't want to do things with me. They probably don't even want me to be here. I'll bet we don't have a very good discussion either. I wonder if they even like me? They probably say mean things about me after I leave, too!"*

Have the teacher put on the same glasses and then tell the teacher that the principal has asked for a meeting after school. The teacher might respond with, *"Oh, no. Why does she want to see me? I haven't done anything wrong. She's probably going to give me some extra things to do. Or, maybe she's going to tell me that I don't have a job here any more. I wonder what the problem is?"*

Next, pull out another set of glasses and call these "Gloomy Glasses." Ask the class what gloomy means. Then, have two volunteers respond in a gloomy way to all questions posed to them from the rest of the class and the teacher.

After a brief time, introduce a third set of glasses, the "Rosy Glasses." The counselor and teacher go through the same situations—remarks about the class and about the meeting with the school principal—to illustrate the difference. Again, two volunteers might be used for more examples, perhaps asking the same questions, but this time giving rosy responses.

Now, ask the class to help you make a list of other kinds of attitudes they know about (e.g. scared, curious, nobody likes me, you can't make me, sneaky, I'm mad, nothing ever works right, complainers, I'm great, bored, woe is me, everything is okay). Write them on the board or show them a list to which they can add a few of their own.

Activity II:
Next, tell the class that here is a situation that could be affected by attitudes: You have been told that before you can play with your friends this weekend or do what you want to do, you must first complete a list of household chores.

They say, *"Now, look over the list of attitudes. Each team can pick one that they would like to act out for that situation."* Each team pantomimes (no talking) the situation. The rest try to guess the kind of attitude glasses the team members have on.

Give each team about one minute to pick an attitude and to talk about related behaviors. Give each team about 15-20 seconds to pantomime the situation before guesses are taken from the other teams.

Closure:
The remainder of the time might include the following questions: *"What kind of world would it be if everyone wore the same kind of attitude? Okay, then it can be helpful to have a lot of different attitudes. But, what about attitudes that keep us from doing our best? From even trying? Have there been days when you thought you had a particular set of attitude glasses on most of the day? Situations? Do you know people who seem to wear only one kind of glasses most of the time? Is it possible to change attitudes—like you would change glasses?"*

Summary:
"How we go about our work and play is often determined by the attitudes we have. We can change our attitudes, if we want. Some attitudes are more helpful than others and they also influence the way others react to us."

Assignment:
"For the rest of the day, put on your "Rosy Attitude Glasses." Approach everything here at school and at home with your rosy attitude. If your glasses start to slip a little, remind yourself that today you are going to wear your rosy attitude. If you see others letting their glasses slip, gently remind them that today everyone is going to wear rosy glasses."

Session Three: "Someone New"

Purpose:
To help students identify behaviors that contribute to success at school and with friends.

Materials:
Newsprint or chalkboard, small slips of paper

Introduction:
Using the same procedures as in the previous two sessions, position the class into their teams and semi-circles. Then say something like this: *"We have been talking about feelings that people have and how people behave. And, we have also talked about how attitudes can affect the way we do things. Today, I want you to put on your "I Can Help" Attitude Glasses. I need your help, especially with new students who come to our school."*

"Every year we have new students and they are never quite sure if they are going to like it here, if they will have friends here, or if they can be successful in class. So, I need your help in thinking about what it takes to be successful and to enjoy school here."

Activity I:
Begin by saying, *"Let's imagine that you were asked to talk with some new students about our school and how they might get along here. First, let's think of some things that they might like about our school."* After a few responses, and perhaps a few by the teacher and counselor, continue by saying, *"Okay, now let's talk about some things that students must do if they are going to learn some things in class and get good grades."* Make a list of learning behaviors. It should eventually include, in one form or another, the following:

have materials ready to work
follow directions
start work as soon as assigned
work hard and don't quit
finish assignments on time
turn in assignments
take part in class discussions
be open to suggestions and help

Add whatever else seems appropriate, especially those routine behaviors that a particular teacher expects in class. Summarize the learning behaviors at this point, perhaps in the order listed above so that students see some continuity and relationship.

Next, *"All right, now what are some things new students can do to make friends at this school?"* Make another list of suggestions.

Activity II:
Begin with something like this: *"How many of you have heard of E.T.? Some of you may have seen the movie about him. That right, E.T. was the stumpy little extra-terrestrial from another planet who came to earth. He received some help from children. He needed help*

in order to survive on earth and to phone home. It is a fun story and very popular now. Well, I have a surprise for you. E.T.'s little friend, 'E.T.2' was left behind and he wants to go to our school. But, he has some problems. He doesn't think positive thoughts about himself."

"I am going to give each team a concern or problem that he has. Working as a team, you are to: 1) identify how he might be feeling when he talks that way; 2) think of how he might behave around the school, if he felt that way; and 3) give him some suggestions."

Distribute the following problems, written on slips of paper. Give each team a different problem. Then, move about the room and encourage students to think of feelings, behaviors, and one or two suggestions. Tell them that they can share their ideas with the total class later.

1. Things never go right for me.
2. Nobody wants to hear what I have to say.
3. Teachers don't like me.
4. I'm nobody special.
5. I'm so different from everybody else.

Closure:
Teams take turns, first reading the problem statement and then reporting related feelings, behaviors, and one or two suggestions.

Later, *"Do you think that what we talked about today can also apply to students in our school right now? Can these ideas be used to get a fresh start? You might ask yourself, how are my problems like E.T.2, a new student? How are they different?"*

Summary:
"In other words, if new students are to be successful at this school and enjoy it, they should find things they like about the school, pay attention to what needs to be done in class, and try to make new friends."

Assignment:
"Pick two things, one thing from each of our two lists (learning in class and making friends), *that you want to improve upon during the rest of the week. Does everybody have one in mind? Now, think about what you have to do. Try it and see what happens."*

Session Four: "Making Changes"

Purpose:
To help students identify some steps in the process of change and to set some goals in school.

Materials:
Newsprint or chalkboard upon which to write sentence stems, pencils and paper for each student.

Introduction:
Use the same procedure as before and move the students into their teams and semi-circles. Then say, *"We are changing all the time. Change is a part of living. Changes, of course, can be for better or for worse. However, if we know the kind of changes that we want to make, set some goals, and work hard toward those goals, then changes can be for the best."*

Activity I:
"Think of some things you used to be or do but now are different." Point to this sentence stem on the board: *"I used to be..., but now I am...."* Elicit some examples from the class. Some possible ones include:

I used to be shorter, but now I am taller.
I used to be in the first grade, but now I am in the fourth grade.
I used to be scared of the water, but now I can swim.
I used to be afraid of the dark, but now I can sleep without a light.
I used to write sloppy letters, but now my writing is neater.

After some responses, say, *"Who was Martin Luther King? Okay, he was famous for many things. But one thing we remember him for is because he had a dream—a goal. He helped us think about the importance of having a dream or goal to achieve in life. Who was Thomas Edison? Alright, he was a famous inventor who sometimes lived in Fort Meyers, Florida. He once said, 'Genius is 1% inspiration and 99% perspiration.' What did he mean? That's right, he believed that working hard was the biggest part of being smart and developing ideas."*

"Using your pencil and paper, draw two little pictures or symbols for two goals that you hope to accomplish someday—your dreams of what you would like to have happen to you." Give the class about two minutes to draw their pictures, with one minute time signals for each goal.

Activity II:

Encourage team members to share individually one of their two pictures with the other team members. If time permits, they can share their second goal. Then, move them back to their semi-circles for further class discussion.

Say, *"To obtain our goals, we also need to have positive attitudes about ourselves. We also need to say positive things. Have you ever heard anybody say, 'I can't do that?' Almost everyone has said it at one time or another.'"* Point to the phrase written on the board in large letters: *"I can't...."* Ask the students to complete this sentence stem five times, drawing upon their experiences at school and home.

Next, have the students in their teams read aloud the statements that they have written. There is no discussion or reaction from the team members. After all of the students have read their statements, ask them to substitute the words, "I won't" in place of "I can't." Have them read the same sentences aloud again. Explain that the words may not feel right at first, but to say them anyway as an experiment.

Lead the class in a discussion of the differences they experienced. Take and give examples. Some possible responses or questions might be: Which one made you feel:

> more powerful?
> in control?
> an attempt at making excuses?
> a crybaby?
> that you could do something?
> in charge?
> that it was possible?

Then, say something like this: *"How we talk about and to ourselves—our inner talk—can influence the way we try things and the direction in which we change. Is there a difference between these ideas?"* Point to the following phrases written on the board or newsprint.)

(Negative)		(Positive)
I can't	vs.	I won't
I should	vs.	I want to
I might	vs.	I will
I could	vs.	I am

"Which ones show the most responsibility? The most power? The most control? The most positive? The greatest strength? The most likely to produce results? To obtain goals?"

Closure:
"Everyone has goals. When you have clear goals in mind, they are easier to obtain. When you have clear goals, you can also find some

little steps that lead to those goals. Remember, the journey of 1,000 miles begins with the first step."

Summary:
"Setting goals and finding some first steps are important if we are to bring about positive changes in our lives. How we think and talk about our first steps and the things we want to do can affect how things turn out. Being positive is a valuable part of having a happier life."

Assignment:
"What is one goal in school that you would like to achieve this year? Can you think of some first steps—not giant steps but little ones that lead to your goal? Use the positive statements to think about your next step and take that step this week.

Session Five: "IALAC"

Purpose:
To help students understand how positive and negative actions can affect their self-pictures and attitudes and to identify ways in which they can be positive with others.

Materials:
The IALAC story, a paper sign, five drawn pictures of a person's figure or head, pencils, and scotch tape.

Introduction:
Make a paper sign with the letters IALAC (pronounced I-uh-lack) in bold print. Hold or pin it to your chest so that it can be easily seen by the class. Move the class into their teams and semi-circles.

Then say, *"All people carry an invisible IALAC sign around with them, no matter where they go. IALAC stands for 'I Am Lovable And Capable.' It is how we feel about ourselves. But, it is often affected by how others interact with us. If somebody is nasty or mean to us, teases or makes fun of us, calls us names or puts us down in some way, then a piece of our IALAC sign is torn away."* (Illustrate this by tearing a corner piece off the sign.)

Activity I:
"I am going to tel you a story to illustrate how this can happen in everyday life." Tell the IALAC story. Following the story, some discussion questions might be: *"How does an IALAC sign get destroyed? How do you think people feel when their IALAC sign is torn up? What are some things that happen in school to destroy IALAC signs? Is it possible to rebuild or build-up an IALAC sign?"*

Have the students think of times in school when they felt put down or rejected and their IALAC signs were torn.

The Florida Classroom Guidance Project   449

Activity II:
Give each team a picture. It is torn into five places or one for each member of a team, thus making a puzzle. Members individually write at least two ideas to help build up a student in school. Members read what they have written on their own pieces of paper. After all have read their statements, the picture is pieced together with transparent tape.

Teams then tell of things they suggested to build-up the imaginary student (picture).

Closure:
Discussion continues on ways to build up individual IALAC signs and times when students felt built-up or put down.

Summary:
"Although we all start out in life being positive about ourselves and others, sometimes people are negative to us and tear us down. There are, however, some ways we can be built-up."

Assignment:
"Notice times in school when people's IALAC signs are torn away and times when they are built up. Do something with someone to help build up that person's IALAC sign. Do something for yourself to build up your own sign."

The IALAC Story

Danny was sleeping soundly when suddenly he was awakened by his brother pounding on his blanket and shaking him. "Danny, you lazy jerk, get out of bed and get downstairs before Dad has to come up here." (rip!) Danny gets out of bed, rubs his eyes, and gets dressed. His mother sees him and tells him to go back and get another shirt. It's all wrinkled and has a tear. "You just don't care how you look, do you?" (rip!)

When he goes to brush his teeth, his older sister has locked the bathroom door. He asks how much longer she is going to be and she yells back, "Drop dead, Danny, who do you think you are, the King around here?" (rip!) He goes to breakfast, but there is no toast and very little milk left to put on his cereal. Everyone else has left the table (rip!)

As Danny leaves for school, his mother calls out to him, "Danny, you've forgotten your lunch again. I don't know what I'm going to do with you. (rip!) You'd forget your head if it weren't tied on!" (rip!) As he gets to the corner, he sees his bus pull away. He has to walk to school and is late. He has to get a pass from the office where he gets a lecture about not being responsible enough (rip!).

He walks into class late and remembers he forgot to do his homework. He thinks, "Oh well, she doesn't expect me to hand it in anyway. (rip!) She doesn't like me and didn't want me to be in her class in the first place. (rip!) His teacher asks him to stay in at recess to finish his work while the others go outside to play baseball. (rip!) He rushes through his lesson and hurries outside, but they have already chosen sides. He stands around for awhile and nobody seems to notice. (rip!) Then, the P.E. teacher tells him to join a team. One of the boys yells, "Hey, Danny, join the other team; we got stuck with you last time." (rip!)

Later that day, Danny gets his homework back and it has a low grade on it. The teacher put a sad face on the paper and wrote, "Danny, your work is sloppy and careless." (rip!)

When he gets home, he learns that he will not get the dog he wanted for his birthday. "You're just not responsible enough to take care of a dog, Danny! There is no way you can have a dog as long as you act the way you do around here." (rip!) Later that night, Danny goes to bed. He gets tears in his eyes and thinks, "Nobody likes me. I might as well give up!" (rip!) Yet, he secretly hopes that tomorrow will be better. Will it?

Session Six: "Looking for Strengths"

Purpose:
To help students identify personal strengths and relate these to achievement and success.

Materials:
Chalkboard or newsprint, pencils and paper for each student.

Introduction:
Move the class into teams and semi-circles. Start by summarizing the previous sessions. Say something like this: *"We have been talking about attitudes, feelings, and behaviors. What we say and do can make a lot of difference in our lives at school and at home. For example, the more positive we are about ourselves and others, the better things will go for us and those around us. Being positive also helps us obtain our goals."*

"But, being positive is a problem for some people. It is not always easy. It becomes easier, however, if we are aware of our strengths. Today, we are going to think about strengths that people have.

Activity I:

"There are many words that name strengths—good things about people that you like or that you think help make them successful. Let's begin by making a list of words or ideas."

Brainstorm words or phrases and list them on the chalkboard or newsprint. (optional: Have some words and phrases already written out to expedite the process.) If it helps, have the students think of personal strengths in terms of relationships (friendships, family), skills (competencies that enable a person to do something), school (successful habits and behaviors), attitudes, and experiences.

Here are some examples:

> listens to me
> tries to understand
> accepts me as a person
> is tolerant of others
> can be trusted
> has a nice smile
> is friendly
> has a sense of humor
> catches a ball well
> is a good reader
> adds numbers fast
> says kind things to people
> respects the rights of others
> shows interest in others' ideas
> works hard at things
> finishes what is started
> knows a lot about space travel
> is a powerful hitter in baseball

Help broaden their concepts and ideas about strengths that people have. Then say, *"Sometimes we learn about and gain more strengths by observing others. Taking notes of other people's strengths and telling them what you notice can be a compliment, and fun, too."*

Activity II:

Distribute a piece of paper to each student. Instruct the students to draw a circle in the middle of the paper and to write their names on it. Next, ask them to make six or seven lines running out from the circle, as if spokes in a wheel or rays from the sun. *"These lines are our sunrays. They can provide us with strength and energy, especially if we use them to identify personal strengths."*

Identify a recorder in each team (a student who can write well and fast). Recorders collect all the papers into one pile. Then, a team recorder reads the name on the first paper. Others, in turn and in a go-around, tell one strength that they believe this person has. Encourage them to use the list made earlier or tell whatever else comes to mind. As each person responds, the recorder writes, on the sunray lines, a few words or phrases of the main idea that was said. Thus, each person receives one comment from every person in the group. After all names have been read, including the recorder's, and all have heard their strengths as seen by other team members, the papers are passed back to their owners. Two extra lines remain on each paper.

Now say, *"You will notice that therv are two more lines from the sun. While it helps to have others tell you about your strengths as they have noticed them, it is also important for you to be aware of your own strengths and to tell yourself that you have some strengths. Therefore, use the other two lines and write in two more strengths about yourself of which you are proud or happy. Do that now."*

Closure:
Lead a discussion about the value of knowing your own strengths, hearing them from others, and assessing yourself. *"Can others sometimes see strengths in^J s that we don't see? Do we have strengths that can't be seen by other people? Of all the strengths that are written on your paper, which one pleases you the most? Surprises you? Is it possible to develop new strengths? How would you go about gaining some new strengths? How do your strengths help you at school? With your friends/ In planning for the future? Does a person have to be strong in everything? Is it possible for people to lose sight of their strengths? To abuse or misuse a strength? How does one's attitude affect a strength?"*

Summary;
"We have been studying about people and ourselves. If the principal were to ask you what you have been learning in our sessions, what would you say?" (Elicit a final summary from the students and add what you need to conclude the unit.)

Assignment:
"We can make our school a better place to be if all of us are kind to each other and try to understand one another. Having a positive attitude can be one of your most important strengths. Your final assignment is: Say something kind to someone in our school, in our class..., and don't forget... the teacher. Be positive and keep smiling!"

Developmental Guidance and Counseling

Appendix B

Peer Facilitator Curriculum (High School)

Course Title: Peer Counseling I

INTENDED OUTCOME:

After successfully completing this course, the student will be able to:

1. Demonstrate an understanding of the fundamental characteristics for all counseling/facilitative relationships.
   PERFORMANCE STANDARDS:

   1.01 Identify the role of a peer facilitator.
   1.02 Establish and adhere to designed ground rules.
   1.03 Maintain an ongoing journal of personal responses to class and related activities.
   1.04 Identify the aspects of trust in a helping relationship.
   1.05 Identify the aspects of confidentiality in a helping relationship.
   1.06 Identify the aspects of positive human regard in a helping relationship.

2. Demonstrate an understanding of self, others, and community.
   PERFORMANCE STANDARDS:

   2.01 Develop an increased awareness of self.
   2.02 Develop an increased awareness of self in relation to one's environment.
   2.03 Identify interpersonal skills necessary to maintain positive peer relationships.
   2.04 Assess the concepts of prejudice and discrimination and their impact on peer relationships.

3. Demonstrate an understanding of facilitative communication skills.
   PERFORMANCE STANDARDS:

   3.01 Identify and apply skills used in the art of listening.
   3.02 Identify a variety of verbal and nonverbal communication behavior.
   3.03 Identify and apply the six facilitative responses (highs and lows).

3.04 Develop ability to use the feedback model to facilitate communications.

3.05 Identify various blocks to communication and how they affect behavior.

4. Demonstrate an understanding of problem-solving techniques.
PERFORMANCE STANDARDS:

4.01 Describe the 5-step decision-making process.

4.02 Demonstrate the use of the 5-step decision-making process.

4.03 Identify resources for appropriate referrals.

4.04 Identify methods for conflict resolution.

5. Demonstrate an understanding of basic leadership skills.
PERFORMANCE STANDARDS:

5.01 Describe the functions and characteristics of a leader.

5.02 Identify the effects of the individual's self-concept on behavior and interpersonal relationships.

5.03 Demonstrate leadership functions and characteristics through selected group process.

6. Demonstrate an understanding of group dynamics and be able to perform group-oriented tasks.
PERFORMANCE STANDARDS:

6.01 Identify elements of group interaction.

6.02 Identify various group-oriented tasks.

6.03 Utilize elements of successful group interaction by participating in a variety of roles within group settings.

6.04 Participate in assigned targeted groups within the school and community.

Course Title: Peer Counseling II

INTENDED OUTCOME:

After successfully completing this course, the student will be able to:

1. Demonstrate an understanding of the effects of peer pressure on the individual and society.
   PERFORMANCE STANDARDS:
   1.01 Define positive and negative aspects of peer pressure.
   1.02 Give examples of how peer pressure affects behavior.
   1.03 Identify "subcultures" or groups within the school.
   1.04 Demonstrate ways of saying no to negative peer pressure.
   1.05 Indicate a variety of alternatives to negative peer pressure.
   1.06 Describe and evaluate the role of peer pressure as it pertains to teenage social issues.

2. Demonstrate an understanding of the impact of interpersonal skills on all aspects of life.
   PERFORMANCE STANDARDS:
   2.01 Identify the characteristics of healthy relationships.
   2.02 Identify the effects of being socially dysfunctional.
   2.03 Identify methods of establishing and maintaining positive personal relationships.

3. Demonstrate an understanding of personal behavior as it relates to long and short range life and career goals.
   PERFORMANCE STANDARDS:
   3.01 Identify the need for setting goals.
   3.02 Identify and apply decision-making and problem-solving models for setting goals.
   3.03 Exhibit personal responsibility in setting goals.
   3.04 Exhibit how self-awareness relates to career life choices.
   3.05 Identify personal strengths, weaknesses, skills, and abilities.
   3.06 Explore various careers appropriate to individual needs, interests, and skills.
   3.07 Develop a career-life plan (including career/educational planning).

4. Demonstrate an understanding of academic motivational skills.
   PERFORMANCE STANDARDS:

   4.01 Identify the aspects of motivation.
   4.02 Assess personal study habits.
   4.03 Develop and organize effective study habits.
   4.04 Develop and utilize effective test-taking skills.
   4.05 develop and implement educational contracts.

5. Demonstrate an understanding of the aspects of assertiveness.
   PERFORMANCE STANDARDS:

   5.01 Discriminate between passive, assertive, and aggressive behavior.
   5.02 Identify areas in personal lives where assertive responses could be made.
   5.03 Identify the thoughts, feelings, and behaviors that support non-assertiveness, assertiveness, and aggressiveness.

6. Demonstrate an understanding of the effects of stress and related coping skills.
   PERFORMANCE STANDARDS:

   6.01 Identify the factors leading to stress.
   6.02 Identify the impact of stress on human behavior.
   6.03 Assess various coping strategies in relation to self and others.

Course Title: Peer Counseling III

INTENDED OUTCOME:

After successfully completing this course, the student will be able to:

1. Identify the needs and concerns of the student population.
   PERFORMANCE STANDARDS:

   1.01 Identify techniques for conducting needs assessment.
   1.02 Conduct a needs assessment.

2. Demonstrate a knowledge of school resources and community youth servicing agencies.
   PERFORMANCE STANDARDS:

   2.01 Demonstrate familiarity with school and community resources.
   2.02 Demonstrate knowledge of the referral processes.

3. Demonstrate a knowledge of program planning and implementation.
   PERFORMANCE STANDARDS:

   3.01 Utilize research skills in program planning.
   3.02 Devise and coordinate program delivery with school personnel and community agencies.
   3.03 Analyze and evaluate program effectiveness.

Course Title: Peer Counseling IV

INTENDED OUTCOME:

The purpose of this course is to provide students with varied experiences in program continuity and development. After successfully completing this course, the student will be able to:

1. Utilize a variety of facilitative strategies applicable to given situations.
   PERFORMANCE STANDARDS:

   1.01 Identify appropriate facilitative strategies applicable to given situations.
   1.02 Demonstrate knowledge and skills of peer counseling intervention strategies in a variety of settings.

2. Utilize knowledge and understanding gained through individual and group research projects.
   PERFORMANCE STANDARDS:

   2.01 Conduct individual and/or group research projects to explore personal/social, academic/career goals.

References

ACES-ASCA (1966). *Report of the ACES-ASCA joint committee on the elementary school counselor.* Washington, DC: APGA Press.

Alexander, W.M. & George, P.S. (1981). *The exemplary middle school.* New York, NY: Holt, Rinehart, & Winston.

Amidon, E.J. & Flanders, N.A. (1967). *The role of the teacher in the classroom.* Minneapolis, MN: Association for Productive Teaching.

Arbuckle, D.S. (1950). *Teacher counseling.* Cambridge, MA: Addison-Wesley Press.

Atkinson, D.R., Skipworth, D., & Stevens, F. (1983). Inundating the school board with support for counselors: An eleventh hour strategy for saving an endangered species. *Personnel and Guidance Journal, 61,* 387-393.

Aubrey, R.F. (1977). Historical development of guidance and counseling and implications for the future. *Personnel and Guidance Journal, 55,* 288-295.

Aubrey, R. (1979). Relationship of guidance and counseling to the established and emerging school curriculum. *School Counselor, 26,* 150-162.

Aubrey, R.F. (1982). A house divided: Guidance and counseling in 20th century America. *Personnel and Guidance Journal, 61,* 198-204.

Aubrey, R.F. & Lewis, J. (1983). Social issues and the counseling profession in the 1980s and 1990s. *Counseling and Human Development, 15,* 1-15.

Aubrey, R.F. (1984). Reform in schooling: Four proposals on educational quest. *Journal of Counseling and Development, 63,* 204-213.

Aubrey, R.F. (1986). The professionalization of counseling. In M.D. Lewis, R.L. Hayes, & J.A. Lewis, *The counseling profession.* Itasca, IL: F.E. Peacock.

Axline, V. (1947). *Play therapy.* Boston, MA: Houghton Mifflin.

Bandura, A. (1969). *Principles of behavior modification.* New York, NY: Holt, Rinehart, & Winston.

Benjamin, A. (1969). *The helping interview.* Boston, MA: Houghton Mifflin.

Bentley, J.C. (1968). *The counselor's role.* Boston, MA: Houghton Mifflin.

Berne. E. (1961). *Transactional analysis in psychotherapy.* New York, NY: Grove Press.

Bierman, R. (1969). Dimensions for interpersonal facilitation in psychotherapy and child development. *Psychological Bulletin, 72,* 338-352.

Blackham, G.J. & Silberman, A. (1971). *Modification of child behavior.* Belmont, CA: Wadsworth.

Blocher, D. (1974 2nd ed.). *Developmental counseling.* New York, NY: Ronald Press.

Bloom, B.S. (1956). *Taxonomy of educational objectives handbook I: Cognitive domain.* New York, NY: David McKay.

Bloom, B.S. (1964). *Stability and change in human characteristics.* New York, NY: John Wiley.

Bonebrake, C.R. & Borgers, S.B. (1984). Counselor role as perceived by middle school counselors and principals. *Elementary School Guidance and Counseling, 18,* 194-199.

Bowman, R. (1982). A student facilitator program: 5th graders helping primary grade problem behavior students. Unpublished dissertation. University of Florida, Gainesville, FL.

Boy, A.V. (1962). The school counselor's role dilemma. *School Counselor, 9,* 129-133.

Boy, A.V. (1972). The elementary school counselor's role dilemma. *School Counselor, 19,* 167-172.

Boy, A.V. & Pine, G.J. (1963). *Client-centered counseling in the secondary School.* Boston, MA: Houghton Mifflin.

Boyer, E. (1983). *High school: A report on secondary education in America.* New York, NY: Harper & Row.

Brammer, L.M. (1973). *The helping relationship.* Englewood Cliffs, NJ: Prentice-Hall.

Brown, J. & Pate, R. (1963). *Being a counselor: Directions and challenges.* Monterey, CA: Brooks/Cole.

Canfield, J. & Wells, H.C. (1976). *100 ways to enhance self-concept in the classroom.* Englewood Cliffs, NJ: Prentice-Hall.

Canning, J. (1985). *Play times: A structured developmental play program utilizing trained peer facilitators.* Minneapolis, MN: Educational Media Corporation.

Caplan, G. (1970). *The theory and practice of mental health consultation.* New York, NY: Basic Books.

Carkhuff, R.R. (1969) *Helping and human relationships, Volume II: Practice and research.* New York, NY: Holt, Rinehart, & Winston.

Carkhuff, R.R. (1983). *Interpersonal skills (IPS).* Amherst, MA: Human Resource Development Press.

Carkhuff, R.R. & Berenson, B. (1967). *Beyond counseling and therapy.* New York, NY: Holt, Rinehart, & Winston.

Chase, L. (1975). *The other side of the report card.* Santa Monica, CA: Goodyear Publishing.

Clark, R. & Frith, G.N. (1983). Writing a developmental counseling curriculum: The Vestavia Hills experience. *School Counselor, 30,* 292-298.

Corey, G. & Corey, M. (1983). *Groups: Process and practice.* (2nd ed.) Monterey, CA.: Brooks/Cole.

Daresh, J.C. & Pautsch, T.R. (1981). A successful teacher-advisor program. *Middle School Journal, 14,* 3.

Devin-Sheehan, L., Feldman, R.S., & Allen, V.L. (1976). Theory and research on cross-age and peer interaction: A review of the literature. *Review of Educational Research, 46,* 365-385.

Dinkmeyer, D.C. (1968). The counselor as consultant: Rationale and procedures. *Elementary School Guidance and Counseling, 3,* 187-194.

Dinkmeyer, D.C. (1970). *Developing understanding of self and others (DUSO), kit D-1.* Circle Pines, MN: American Guidance Service.

Dinkmeyer, D.C. (1973). *Developing understanding of self and others (DUSO), kit D-2,* Circle Pines, MN: American Guidance Service.

Dinkmeyer, D.C. & Caldwell, E. (1970). *Developmental counseling and guidance: A comprehensive school approach.* New York, NY: McGraw-Hill.

Dinkmeyer, D.C. & Carlson, J. (1973). *Consulting: Facilitating human potential and change processes.* Columbus, OH: Charles Merrill.

Dinkmeyer, D.C. & Dinkmeyer, D., Jr. (1982). *Developing understanding of self and others (DUSO), Kits 1 and 2,* Revised ed. Circle Pines, MN: American Guidance Service.

Dinkmeyer, D.C. & McKay, G. (1976). *Systematic training for effective parenting (STEP).* Circle Pines, MN: American Guidance Service.

Dinkmeyer, D.C., McKay, G., & Dinkmeyer, D., Jr. (1980). *Systematic training for effective teaching (STET).* Circle Pines: MN: American Guidance Service.

Drury, S.S. (1984). Counselor survival in the 1980s. *School Counselor, 31,* 234-240.

Duncan, J.A. & Gumaer, J. (1980). *Developmental groups for children.* Springfield, IL: Charles C. Thomas.

Eckerson, L. & Smith, H. (1966). *Scope of pupil personnel services.* Washington, D.C: Office of Education, U.S. Department of Health, Education, and Welfare.

Egan, G. (1975). *The skilled helper.* Monterey, CA: Brooks/Cole.

Ellis, A. (1973). *Humanistic psychotherapy: The rational-emotive approach.* Jullian Press: McGraw Hill Paperbacks.

Erickson, E.H. (1963). *Childhood and society.* New York, NY: W.W. Norton.

Faust, V. (1968). *The counselor-consultant in the elementary school.* Boston, MA: Houghton Mifflin.

Flanders, N. (1965). *Teacher influence, pupil attitudes, and achievement.* Washington, D.C: U.S. Dept. of Health, Education, and Welfare.

Foster, E.S. (1983). *Tutoring: Learning by helping.* Minneapolis, MN: Educational Media Corporation.

Fullmer, D., & Bernard, H. (1972). *The school counselor-consultant.* Boston, MA: Houghton Mifflin.

Frey, D. (Editor) (1978). Special issue: Single case study in counseling. *Personnel and Guidance Journal, 56,* 263-304.

Gallup, G. (1979, 1983). The 11th and 15th annual Gallup poll of the public's attitudes toward the public schools. *Phi Delta Kappan, 66,* 23-28.

Gardner, D. (1983). *A nation at risk: The imperative for educational reform.* Washington, DC: U.S. Department of Education.

Garfield, N.A. (Editor) (1985). Special issue: AACD and its divisions. *Journal of Counseling and Development, 63,* 394-454.

Gazda G.M. (1977). *Human relations development: A manual for educators.* Boston, MA: Allyn & Bacon.

Gazda. G.M. (1978). *Group counseling: A developmental approach.* (2nd ed.) Boston, MA: Allyn & Bacon.

Gesell, R. & Ames, L. (1956). *Youth: The years from ten to sixteen.* New York, NY: Harper & Row.

Gesell, R. & Illg, F. (1946). *The child from five to ten.* New York, NY: Harper & Row.

Gibson, R.L, Mitchell, M.H., & Higgins, R.E. (1983). *Development and management of counseling programs and guidance services.* New York, NY: Macmillan.

Ginott, H.G. (1972) *Teacher and child.* New York, NY: Macmillan.

Glasser, W. (1965). *Reality therapy.* New York, NY: Harper & Row.

Glasser, W. (1969). *Schools without failure.* New York, NY: Harper & Row.

Goodlad, J. (1983). *A place called school: Prospects for the future.* New York, NY: McGraw-Hill.

Gordon, I. (1956). *The teacher as a guidance worker.* New York, NY: Harper & Row.

Gordon, T. (1970). *Parent effectiveness training.* New York, NY: Wyden.

Gordon, T. (1974). *Teacher effectiveness training.* New York, NY: Wyden.

Gray, H.D. & Tindall, J. (1978). *Peer counseling.* Muncie, IL: Accelerated Development.

Gribbin, A. (1973). Teen-age students' counselors: No-help helpers, *The National Observer*, January 20, 1.

Hamburg, B.A. & Varenhorst, B.B. (1972). Peer counseling in the secondary schools: A community health project for youth. *American Journal of Orthopsychiatry*, 42, 566-581.

Harris. T.A. (1969). *I'm O.K.—You're O.K..* New York, NY: Harper & Row.

Hart, J.T. & Tomlinson. T.M. (Eds). (1970). *New directions in client-centered therapy.* Boston, MA: Houghton Mifflin.

Havighurst, R.J. (1953). *Human development and education.* New York, NY: Longmans.

Havighurst, R.J. (1972). *Developmental tasks and education.* (3rd ed.) New York, NY: McKay, 1972.

Hays, D.G. & Johnson, C.S. (1984). 21st century counseling. *School Counselor*, 31, 205-214.

Herr, E.L. (1981). Comprehensive career guidance: A look to the future. *Vocational Guidance Quarterly*, 30, 367-376.

Herr, E.L. (1986). Life-style and career development. In M.D. Lewis, R.L. Hayes, & J.A. Lewis, *The counseling profession.* Itasca, IL: F.E. Peacock.

Hollis, J.W. (1980). Guidance and counseling in school: An historical approach. In *The status of guidance and counseling in the nation's schools.* Washington, D.C., APGA Press.

Huber, C.H. & Westling, D.L. (1978). School guidance counselors and the mildly retarded: Roles and preparation. *Mental Retardation, 16*, 174-177.

Huey, W.C. & Rank, R.C. (1984). Effects of counselor and peer-led group assertive training on black adolescent aggression. *Journal of Counseling Psychology, 31*, 95-98.

Humes, C.W. (1978). School counselors and P.L. 94-142. *School Counselor, 25*, 3.

Hutchins, D.E. (1979). Systematic counseling: The T-F-A model for counselor intervention. *Personnel and Guidance Journal, 57,* 529-531.

Ivey, A.E. & Alschuler, A.S. (1973). Psychological education: A prime function of the counselor. *Personnel & Guidance Journal, 51,* 586-691.

Ivey, A.E. & Simek-Downing, L. (1980). *Counseling and psychotherapy: Skills, theories, and practice.* Englewood Cliffs, N.J: Prentice-Hall.

Jenkins, J.M. (1977). The teacher-advisor: An old solution looking for a problem. *National Association of Secondary School Principals, 61,* 29-34.

Johnson, D.W. (1972). *Reaching out: Interpersonal effectiveness and self-actualization.* Englewood Cliffs, N.J: Prentice-Hall.

Johnson, D.W. & Matross, R. (1977). Interpersonal influence in psychotherapy: A social psychological view. In A.S. Gorman & A.M. Razin (Eds.). *Effective psychotherapy.* New York, NY: Pergamon Press.

Johnson, R.L. & Salmon, S.J. (1979). Caring and counseling: Shared tasks in advisement schools. *Personnel and Guidance Journal, 57,* 474-477.

Kagen, J. & Moss, H.A. (1962). *Birth to maturity.* New York, NY: Wiley.

Kameen, M.C., Robinson, E.H., & Rotter, J.C. (1985). Coordination activities: A study of perceptions of elementary and middle school counselors. *Elementary School Guidance and Counseling, 20,* 97-104.

Keat, D.B. (1974). *Fundamentals of child counseling.* Boston, MA: Houghton Mifflin.

Kehas, C.D. (1980). Theoretical and conceptual foundations of guidance and counseling in school. In *The status of guidance and counseling in the nation's schools.* Washington, D.C.: APGA Press.

Kohlberg, L. & Turiel, E. (1971). Moral development and moral education. In G.S. Lesser, *Psychology and educational practice.* Glenview, IL: Scott, Foresman.

Kornick, J. (1984). Counselor-specialist and teacher-counselor: A plan for the future. *School Counselor, 31,* 241-248.

Krasner, L. & Ullman, L.P. (1965). *Research in behavior modification.* New York, NY: Holt, Rinehart, & Winston.

Krathwohl, D.R., Bloom, B.S., & Masia, B.B. (1964). *Taxonomy of educational objectives, handbook II: Affective domain.* New York, NY: David McKay.

Krumboltz, J.D. (1966). *Revolution in counseling.* Boston, MA: Houghton Mifflin.

Krumboltz, J.D. (1974). An accountability model for counselors. *Personnel and Guidance Journal, 52*, 639-46.

Krumboltz, J.D. & Krumboltz, H.B. (1972). *Changing children's behavior*. Englewood Cliffs, N.J: Prentice-Hall.

Krumboltz, J.D. & Thoresen, C.E. (1969). *Behavioral counseling*. New York, NY: Holt, Rinehart, & Winston.

Krumboltz, J.D. & Thoresen, C.E. (1976). *Counseling methods*. New York, NY: Holt, Rinehart, & Winston.

Kurpius, D.J. (1985). Consultation interventions: Successes, failures, and proposals. *The Counseling Psychologist, 3*, 368-389.

Kurpius, D.J. (1986). The helping relationship. In M.D. Lewis, R.L. Hayes, & J.A. Lewis, *The counseling profession*. Itasca, IL: F.E. Peacock.

Lampe, R.E. (1985). Principals' training in counseling and development: A national survey. *Counselor Education and Supervision, 25*, 44-55.

Lauver, P.J. (1974). Consulting with teachers: A systematic approach. *Personnel and Guidance Journal, 52*, 535-540.

Lazarus, A.A. (1971). *Behavior therapy and beyond*. New York, NY: McGraw-Hill.

Lebsock, M.S. & DeBlassie, R.R. (1975). The school counselor's role in special education. *Counselor Education and Supervision, 15*, 128-134.

Lee, J.L. & Pulvino, C.J. (1984). *Counselor accountability system*. Minneapolis, MN: Educational Media Corporation.

Lewis, J.D. (1983). Guidance program evaluation: How to do it. *School Counselor, 30*, 111-119.

Leviton, H.S. (1977). Consumer feedback on a secondary school guidance program. *Personnel and Guidance Journal, 55*, 242-244.

Lombana, J.H. (1985). Guidance accountability: A new look at an old problem. *School Counselor, 32*, 340-346.

Lounsbury, J. (1984). Survey of national association of secondary principals, 1904 Association Drive, Reston, VA 22091.

Luft, J. (1984). *Group processes: An introduction to group dynamics* (3rd ed.). Palo Alto, CA: Mayfield.

Mahler, C. (1969). *Group counseling in the schools*. Boston, MA: Houghton Mifflin.

Macnow, G. (1982). School counselors face layoffs, need for services grow. *Education Week*, March 31, 7.

References   467

Mayer, G.R. & Munger, P.F. (1967). A plea for letting the elementary school counselor counsel. *Counselor Education and Supervision, 6,* 341-346.

Meeks, A. (1968). *Guidance in elementary education.* New York, NY: Ronald Press.

Michael, J. (1986). *Adviser-advisee programs.* Columbus, OH: National Middle School Association.

Miller, G.D., Gum, M.F., & Bender, D. (1972). *Elementary school guidance: Demonstration and evaluation.* St. Paul, MN: Minnesota Department of Education.

Mitchell, A. & Gysbers, N.C. (1980). Comprehensive school guidance and counseling programs: Planning, design, implementation, and evaluation. In *The status of guidance and counseling in the nation's schools.* Washington, D.C: APGA.

Mosher, R.L. & Sprinthall, N.A. (1971). Psychological education: A means to promote personal development during adolescence. *Counseling Psychologist, 2,* 3-82.

Muro, J. (1970). *Counselor's work in the elementary school.* Scranton, PA: International Textbook.

Muro, J. & Dinkmeyer, D.C. (1977). *Counseling in the elementary and middle schools.* Dubuque, IA: Wm.C. Brown.

Myrick, R.D. (1977) *Consultation as a counselor intervention.* Ann Arbor, MI: ASCA/ERIC.

Myrick, R.D. (1980). The practice of counseling in the elementary schools. In *The status of guidance in the nation's schools,* Washington, D.C: APGA Press.

Myrick, R.D. (1984). Beyond the issues of accountability. *Measurement and Evaluation in Guidance, 6,* 214-222.

Myrick, R.D. (1986). Challenger 10 and our school children: Reflections on the catastrophe. *Death Studies, 2,* 111-118.

Myrick, R.D. & Bowman, R.P. (1981a). *Becoming a friendly helper.* Minneapolis, MN: Educational Media Corporation.

Myrick, R.D. & Bowman, R.P. (1981b). *Children helping children.* Minneapolis, MN: Educational Media Corporation.

Myrick, R.D. & Dixon, W. (1985). Changing negative attitudes through group counseling. *School Counselor, 32,* 325-330.

Myrick, R.D. & Erney, T. (1978). *Caring and sharing.* Minneapolis, MN: Educational Media Corporation.

Myrick, R.D. & Erney, T. (1979). *Youth helping youth: A handbook for training peer facilitators.* Minneapolis, MN: Educational Media Corporation.

Myrick, R.D. & Haldin, W. (1971). The use of play process in counseling a first-grade boy. *Elementary School Guidance and Counseling, 5,* 256-265.

Myrick, R.D., Highland, M., & Highland, W. (1986). Preparing teachers to be advisors. *Middle School Journal, 17,* 15-16.

Myrick, R.D., Merhill, H., & Swanson, L. (1986). Changing student attitudes through classroom guidance. *School Counselor,* 1986, *33,* 244-252.

Myrick, R.D. & Sanborn, J. (1983). Peer facilitator programs for troubled youth. *American Mental Health Counselor Association Journal, 5,* 12-21.

Myrick, R.D. & Wittmer, J. (1972). *School counseling: Problems and methods.* Pacific Palisades, CA: Goodyear Publishing.

Orlando, M. (1981). Survival for counselors is possible. *The ASCA Counselor, 19,* 1.

Parsons, F. (1909). *Choosing a vocation.* Boston, MA: Houghton Mifflin.

Paterson, C.H. (1959). *Counseling and psychotherapy.* New York, NY: Harper & Row.

Peer, G.G. (1985). The status of secondary school guidance: A national survey. *School Counselor, 32,* 181-189.

Perls, F.S. (1969). *Gestalt therapy verbatim.* Lafayette, CA: Real People Press.

Peters, H.J. (1962). The school counselor's emerging responsibilities. *School Counselor, 9,* 129-133.

Peters, D. (1980). The practice of counseling in the secondary schools. In *The status of guidance and counseling in the nation's schools.* Washington,D.C.: APGA Press.

Piaget, J. (1970). *Science of education and the psychology of the child.* New York, NY: Onion Press.

Pilkington, R.A. & Jarmin, H.R. (1977). Is there a difference? Teacher-advisor or teacher-counselor. *National Association of Secondary School Principals, 61,* 80-83.

Pine, G. (1976). Troubled times for school counseling. *Focus on Guidance, 8,* 1-16.

Powell, A.J. (1985). Being unspecial in the shopping mall high school. *Phi Delta Kappan, 67,* 255-261.

Prout, H.T. & Brown, D.T. (1983). *Counseling and psychotherapy.* Tampa, FL: Mariner Publishing Co.

Purkey, W. (1970). *Self-concept and school achievement.* Englewood Cliffs, NJ: Prentice-Hall.

Ranbom, S. (1983). School counseling: New demands on a diverse profession. *Education Week,* March, 11-14.

Randolph, N. & Howe, W. (1963). *Self-enhancing education.* Palo Alto, CA: Sanford Press.

Raths, L., Harmin, M., & Simon, S. (1966). *Values and teaching.* Columbus, OH: Charles E. Merrill.

Ritchie, M.H. (1986). Counseling the involuntary client. *Personnel and Guidance Journal, 64,* 516-518.

Rogers, C.R. (1951). *Client-centered therapy.* Boston, MA: Houghton Mifflin.

Rogers, C.R. (1957). The necessary and sufficient conditions of therapeutic personality change. *Journal of Consulting Psychology, 21,* 95-103.

Rogers, C.R. (1961). *On becoming a person.* Boston, MA: Houghton Mifflin.

Rogers, C.R. (1962). The interpersonal relationship; The core of guidance. *Harvard Educational Review, 32,* 416-429.

Roush, D.W. (1984). Rational-emotive therapy and youth: Some new techniques for counselors. *Personnel and Guidance Journal, 62,* 414-417.

Safran, J.S. & Safran, S.P. (1985). Teaching behavior awareness in groups. *Elementary School Guidance and Counseling, 20,* 91-96.

Samuels, D. & Samuels, M. (1975). *The complete handbook of peer counseling.* Miami, FL: Fiesta Publishing.

Sermat, V. & Smyth M. (1973). Content analysis of verbal communication in the development of a relationship: Conditions influencing self-disclosure. *Journal of Personality and Social Psychology, 26,* 332-346.

Shaw. M.C. (1973). *School guidance systems.* New York, NY: Houghton Mifflin.

Shertzer, B., & Stone, S.C. (1968). *Fundamentals of counseling.* Boston, MA: Houghton Mifflin.

Shertzer, B. & Stone, S.C. (1981). *Fundamentals of guidance* (4th ed.). Boston, MA: Houghton Mifflin.

Simon, S., Howe, L., & Kirschenbaum, H. (1972). *Values clarification.* New York, NY: Hart.

Simonson, N. & Bahr, S. (1974). Self-disclosure by the professional and paraprofessional therapist. *Journal of Counseling and Clinical Psychology, 42*, 359-363.

Sprinthall, N.A. (1971). *Guidance for human growth.* New York, NY: Van Nostrand Reinhold.

Sprinthall N.A. & Erickson, V.L. (1974). Learning psychology by doing psychology: Guidance through the curriculum. *Personnel and Guidance Journal, 52*, 396-405.

Stanford, G. (1972). Psychological education in the classroom. *Personnel and Guidance Journal, 50*, 585-592.

Stefflre, B. (1965). *Theories of counseling.* New York, NY: McGraw-Hill.

Strong, J.H. & Turner, J.H. (1983). Computer scheduling: Is it worth the effort? *Electronic Education, 3*, 56-57.

Super, D.E. & Bohn, M.J. (1970). *Occupational psychology.* Belmont, CA: Wadsworth.

Swanson, C.D. (1983). The law and the counselor. In J.A. Brown and R.H. Pate, *Being a counselor.* Monterey, CA: Brooks Cole.

Taber, G. (1984). The affective domain and a nation at risk. *National Association of Secondary School Principals, 68*, 49-52.

Texas Education Agency (1973). *Accountability in guidance services.* Austin, TX: Division of Guidance Services, Texas Education Agency.

Tracey, T.J. (1983). Single case research: An added tool for counselors and supervisors. *Counselor Education and Supervision, 22*, 178-184.

Truax, C.B. & Carkhuff, R.R. (1967). *Toward effective counseling and psychotherapy.* Chicago, IL: Aldine.

Trump, J.L. (1977). Are counselors meeting student and teacher needs? *National Association of Secondary School Principals, 61*, 26-28.

Tugend, A. (1984). *Education Week*, August 29, 7.

Van Ripper, B.W. (1971). Student perceptions: The counselor is what he does. *School Counselor, 19*, 53-56.

Wagner, C.A. (1981). Confidentiality and the school counselor. *Personnel and Guidance Journal, 59*, 305-310.

Ward, D.E. (1984). Termination of individual counseling: Concepts and strategies. *Journal of Counseling and Development, 63*, 21-25.

Weinstein, G., & Fantini, M.D. (1970). *Toward humanistic education.* New York, NY: Praeger.

Wells, C.E. & Ritter, J.Y. (1979) Paperwork, pressure, and discouragement: Student attitudes toward guidance services and implications for the profession. *Personnel and Guidance Journal, 58*, 170-175.

References   471

Wells, B. (1983). Dropouts are not always failures: the schools often share the blame. *Education Week*, April 6, 18.

Wiggins, J.D. (1974). One counseling program for all students: An idea whose time has come—again. *School Counselor, 22*, 44-45.

Wiggins, J.D. (1977). Some counseling does help: Some evidence. *School Counselor, 25*, 48-51.

Wiggins, J.D. & Mickle-Askin, K. (1980). Reported work emphasis on effective and ineffective counselors. *School Counselor, 27*, 294-299.

Wiley, R. (1960). *Guidance in elementary education.* New York, NY: Harper & Brothers.

Williamson. E.G. (1950). *Counseling adolescents.* New York, NY: McGraw Hill.

Wilson, N.H. & Rotter, J.C. (1982). School counseling: A look into the future. *Personnel and Guidance Journal, 60*, 353-357.

Wittmer, J.P. & Loesch, L.C. (1986) In M.D. Lewis, R.L. Hayes, & J.A. Lewis, *The counseling profession.* Itasca, IL: F.E. Peacock.

Wittmer, J.P. & Myrick, R.D. (1980). *Facilitative teaching: Theory and practice* (2nd ed.). Minneapolis, MN: Educational Media Corporation.

Wrenn, C.G. (1957). Status and role of the school counselor. *Personnel and Guidance Journal, 36*, 175-183.

Wrenn, C.G. (1962). *The counselor in a changing world.* Washington, D.C: APGA Press.

Wrenn, C.G. (1973). *The world of the contemporary counselor.* Boston, MA: Houghton Mifflin.

Yesseldyke, J., Algozzine, B., & Mitchell, J. (1982). *Personnel and Guidance Journal, 60*, 308-313.